New Perspectives on
Corel®
WordPerfect® 7
for Windows® 95

INTRODUCTORY

The New Perspectives Series

The New Perspectives Series consists of texts and technology that teach computer concepts and the programs listed below. Both Windows 3.1 and Windows 95 versions of these programs are available. You can order these New Perspectives texts in many different lengths, software releases, custom-bound combinations, CourseKits™ and Custom Editions®. Contact your CTI sales representative or customer service representative for the most up-to-date details.

The New Perspectives Series

Computer Concepts

dBASE®

Internet Using Netscape Navigator™ Software

Lotus® 1-2-3®

Microsoft® Access

Microsoft® Excel

Microsoft® Office Professional

Microsoft® PowerPoint®

Microsoft® Windows® 3.1

Microsoft® Windows® 95

Microsoft® Word

Microsoft® Works

Paradox®

Corel® Presentations™

Corel® Quattro Pro®

Corel® WordPerfect®

New Perspectives on Corel® WordPerfect® 7 for Windows® 95

INTRODUCTORY

Beverly B. Zimmerman
Brigham Young University

S. Scott Zimmerman
Brigham Young University

COURSE TECHNOLOGY

ONE MAIN STREET, CAMBRIDGE, MA 02142

an International Thomson Publishing company I(T)P®

Cambridge • Albany • Bonn • Boston • Cincinnati • London • Madrid • Melbourne • Mexico City
New York • Paris • San Francisco • Singapore • Tokyo • Toronto • Washington

New Perspectives on Corel WordPerfect 7 for Windows 95—Introductory is published by CTI.

Managing Editor	Mac Mendelsohn
Series Consulting Editor	Susan Solomon
Senior Editor	Kristen Duerr
Senior Product Manager	Barbara Clemens
Product Manager/Developmental Editor	Robin Geller
Production Editor	Daphne Barbas
Text and Cover Designer	Ella Hannah
Cover Illustrator	Nancy Nash

© 1997 by CTI.
A Division of Course Technology – I(T)P®

For more information contact:

Course Technology
One Main Street
Cambridge, MA 02142

International Thomson Editores
Campos Eliseos 385, Piso 7
Col. Polanco
11560 Mexico D.F. Mexico

International Thomson Publishing Europe
Berkshire House 168-173
High Holborn
London WCIV 7AA
England

International Thomson Publishing GmbH
Königswinterer Strasse 418
53227 Bonn
Germany

Thomas Nelson Australia
102 Dodds Street
South Melbourne, 3205
Victoria, Australia

International Thomson Publishing Asia
211 Henderson Road
#05-10 Henderson Building
Singapore 0315

Nelson Canada
1120 Birchmount Road
Scarborough, Ontario
Canada M1K 5G4

International Thomson Publishing Japan
Hirakawacho Kyowa Building, 3F
2-2-1 Hirakawacho
Chiyoda-ku, Tokyo 102
Japan

All rights reserved. This publication is protected by federal copyright law. No part of this publication may be reproduced, stored in a retrieval system, or transmitted in any form or by any means, electronic, mechanical, photocopying, recording, or otherwise, or be used to make a derivative work (such as translation or adaptation), without prior permission in writing from Course Technology.

Trademarks
Course Technology and the open book logo are registered trademarks and CourseKits is a trademark of Course Technology. Custom Editions and the ITP logo are registered trademarks of International Thomson Publishing.

Windows 95 is a registered trademark of Microsoft Corporation.

Corel and WordPerfect are registered trademarks of Corel Corporation and its subsidiaries.

Some of the product names and company names used in this book have been used for identification purposes only and may be trademarks or registered trademarks of their respective manufacturers and sellers.

Disclaimer
CTI reserves the right to revise this publication and make changes from time to time in its content without notice.

ISBN 0-7600-3539-3

Printed in the United States of America

10 9 8 7 6 5 4 3 2

From the New Perspectives Series Team

At **Course Technology** we have one foot in education and the other in technology. We believe that technology is transforming the way people teach and learn, and we are excited about providing instructors and students with materials that use technology to teach about technology.

Our development process is unparalleled in the higher education publishing industry. Every product we create goes through an exacting process of design, development, review, and testing.

Reviewers give us direction and insight that shape our manuscripts and bring them up to the latest standards. Every manuscript is quality tested. Students whose backgrounds match the intended audience work through every keystroke, carefully checking for clarity and pointing out errors in logic and sequence. Together with our own technical reviewers, these testers help us ensure that everything that carries our name is error-free and easy to use.

We show both how and why technology is critical to solving problems in college and in whatever field you choose to teach or pursue. Our time-tested, step-by-step instructions provide unparalleled clarity. Examples and applications are chosen and crafted to motivate students.

As the New Perspectives Series team at Course Technology, our goal is to produce the most timely, accurate, creative, and technologically sound product in the entire college publishing industry. We strive for consistent high quality. This takes a lot of communication, coordination, and hard work. But we love what we do. We are determined to be the best. Write to us and let us know what you think. You can also e-mail us at NewPerspectives@course.com.

The New Perspectives Series Team

Joseph J. Adamski	Kathy Finnegan	Dan Oja
Judy Adamski	Robin Geller	June Parsons
Roy Ageloff	Roger Hayen	Sandra Poindexter
David Auer	Charles Hommel	Mark Reimold
Rachel Bunin	Chris Kelly	Ann Shaffer
Joan Carey	Mary Kemper	Susan Solomon
Patrick Carey	Terry Ann Kremer	Christine Spillett
Barbara Clemens	Melissa Lima	Susanne Walker
Kim Crowley	Nancy Ludlow	John Zeanchock
Kristen Duerr	Mac Mendelsohn	Beverly Zimmerman
Jessica Evans	Jennifer Normandin	Scott Zimmerman

Preface — The New Perspectives Series

What is the New Perspectives Series?

CTI's **New Perspectives Series** is an integrated system of instruction that combines text and technology products to teach computer concepts and microcomputer applications. Users consistently praise this series for innovative pedagogy, creativity, supportive and engaging style, accuracy, and use of interactive technology. The first New Perspectives text was published in January of 1993. Since then, the series has grown to more than 40 titles and has become the best-selling series on computer concepts and microcomputer applications. Others have imitated the New Perspectives features, design, and technologies, but none have replicated its quality and its ability to consistently anticipate and meet the needs of instructors and students.

What is the Integrated System of Instruction?

You hold in your hands a textbook that is one component of an Integrated System of Instruction: text, graphics, video, sound, animation, and simulations that are linked and that provide a flexible, unified, and interactive system to help you teach and help your students learn. Specifically, the *New Perspectives Integrated System of Instruction* consists of five components: a CTI textbook, Course Labs, Course Online, Course Presenter, and Course Test Manager. These components—shown in the graphic on the back cover of this book—have been developed to work together to provide a complete, integrative teaching and learning experience.

How is the New Perspectives Series different from other microcomputer concepts and applications series?

The **New Perspectives Series** distinguishes itself from other series in at least four substantial ways: sound instructional design, consistent quality, innovative technology, and proven pedagogy. The applications texts in this series consist of two or more tutorials, which are based on sound instructional design. Each tutorial is motivated by a realistic case that is meaningful to students. Rather than learn a laundry list of features, students learn the features in the context of solving a problem. This process motivates all concepts and skills by demonstrating to students *why* they would want to know them.

Instructors and students have come to rely on the high quality of the **New Perspectives Series** and to consistently praise its accuracy. This accuracy is a result of CTI's unique multi-step quality assurance process that incorporates student testing at three stages of development, using hardware and software configurations appropriate to the product. All solutions, test questions, and other CourseTools (discussed later in this preface) are tested using similar procedures. Instructors who adopt this series report that students can work through the tutorials independently with minimum intervention or "damage control" by instructors or staff. This consistent quality has meant that if instructors are pleased with one product from the series, they can rely on the same quality with any other New Perspectives product.

The **New Perspectives Series** also distinguishes itself by its innovative technology. This series innovated Course Labs, truly *interactive* learning applications. These have set the standard for interactive learning.

How do I know that the New Perspectives Series will work?

Some instructors who use this series report a significant difference between how much their students learn and retain with this series as compared to other series. With other series, instructors often find that students can work through the book and do well on homework and tests, but still not demonstrate competency when asked to perform particular tasks outside the context of the text's sample case or project. With the **New Perspectives Series**, however, instructors report that students have a complete, integrative learning experience that stays with them. They credit this high retention and competency to the fact that this series incorporates critical thinking and problem solving with computer skills mastery.

How does this book I'm holding fit into the New Perspectives Series?

New Perspectives microcomputer concepts and applications books are available in the following categories:

Brief books are about 100 pages long and are intended to teach only the essentials. They contain 2 to 4 chapters or tutorials.

Introductory books are about 300 pages long and consist of 6 or 7 chapters or tutorials. An Introductory book is designed for a short course or for a one-term course, used in combination with other Introductory books. The book you are holding is an Introductory book.

Comprehensive books are about 600 pages long and consist of all of the chapters or tutorials in the Introductory book, plus 3 or 4 more Intermediate chapters or tutorials covering higher-level topics. Comprehensive applications texts include Brief Windows tutorials, Introductory and Intermediate tutorials, 3 or 4 Additional Cases, and a Reference Section.

Advanced applications books cover topics similar to those in the Comprehensive books, but in more depth. Advanced books present the most high-level coverage in the series.

Custom Books The New Perspectives Series offers you two ways to customize a New Perspectives text to fit your course exactly: *CourseKits*™, two or more texts packaged together in a box, and *Custom Editions*®, your choice of books bound together. Custom Editions offer you unparalleled flexibility in designing your concepts and applications courses. You can build your own book by ordering a combination of titles bound together to cover only the topics you want. Your students save because they buy only the materials they need. There is no minimum order, and books are spiral bound. Both CourseKits and Custom Editions offer significant price discounts. Contact your CTI sales representative for more information.

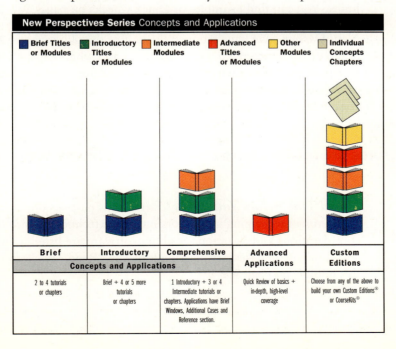

In what kind of course could I use this book?

This book can be used in any course in which you want students to learn all the most important topics of Corel WordPerfect 7 for Windows 95, including creating, editing, and formatting documents, mail merge, desktop publishing, and integration. Students create realistic business documents, including letters, reports, business plans, proposals, and newsletters. This book assumes that students have learned basic Windows 95 navigation and file management skills from Course Technology's *New Perspectives on Microsoft Windows 95 Brief* or an *equivalent* book.

How do the Windows 95 editions differ from the Windows 3.1 editions?

Larger Page Size If you've used a New Perspectives text before, you'll immediately notice that the book you're holding is larger than the Windows 3.1 series books. We've responded to user requests for a larger page with larger screen shots and associated labels. Look on page WP 8 for an example of how we've made the screen shots easier to read.

Sessions We've divided the tutorials into sessions. Each session is designed to be completed in about 45 minutes to an hour (depending, of course, upon student needs and the speed of your lab equipment). With sessions, learning is broken up into more easily-assimilated chunks. You can more accurately allocate time in your syllabus. Students can better manage the available lab time. Each session begins with a "session box," which quickly describes the skills students will learn in the session. Furthermore, each session is numbered, which makes it easier for you and your students to navigate and communicate about the tutorial. Look on page WP 22 for the session box that opens Session 1.2.

Quick Checks Each session concludes with meaningful, conceptual Quick Check questions that test students' understanding of what they learned in the session. Answers to all of the Quick Check questions are at the back of the book preceding the Index. You can find examples of Quick Checks on pages WP 21 and WP 41.

New Design We have retained the best of the old design to help students differentiate between what they are to *do* and what they are to *read*. The steps are clearly identified by their shaded background and numbered steps. Furthermore, this new design presents steps and screen shots in a larger, easier to read format. Some good examples of our new design are pages WP 11, WP 12, and WP 13.

What features are retained in the Windows 95 editions of the New Perspectives Series?

"Read This Before You Begin" Page This page is consistent with CTI's unequaled commitment to helping instructors introduce technology into the classroom. Technical considerations and assumptions about software are listed to help instructors save time and eliminate unnecessary aggravation. The "Read This Before You Begin" page for this book is on page WP 2.

Tutorial Case Each tutorial begins with a problem presented in a case that is meaningful to students. The problem turns the task of learning how to use an application into a problem-solving process. The problems increase in complexity with each tutorial. These cases touch on multicultural, international, and ethical issues—so important to today's business curriculum. See page WP 3 for the case that begins Tutorial 1.

Step-by-Step Methodology This unique CTI methodology keeps students on track. They enter data, click buttons, or press keys always within the context of solving the problem posed in the tutorial case. The text constantly guides students, letting them know where they are in the course of solving the problem. In addition, the numerous screen shots include labels that direct students' attention to what they should look at on the screen. On almost every page in this book, you can find an example of how steps, screen shots, and labels work together.

TROUBLE? Paragraphs These paragraphs anticipate the mistakes or problems that students are likely to have and help them recover and continue with the tutorial. By putting these paragraphs in the book, rather than in the Instructor's Manual, we facilitate independent learning and free the instructor to focus on substantive conceptual issues rather than on common procedural errors. Two representative examples of TROUBLE? are on pages WP 14 and WP 23.

Reference Windows Reference Windows appear throughout the text. They are succinct summaries of the most important tasks covered in the tutorials. Reference Windows are specially designed and written so students can refer to them when doing the Tutorial Assignments and Case Problems, and after completing the course. Page WP 24 contains the Reference Window for Saving a Document for the First Time.

Task Reference The Task Reference contains a summary of how to perform common tasks using the most efficient method, as well as references to pages where the task is discussed in more detail. It appears as a table at the end of the book. In this book the Task Reference is on pages WP 283 to WP 288.

Tutorial Assignments, Case Problems, and Lab Assignments Each tutorial concludes with Tutorial Assignments, which provide students with additional hands-on practice of the skills they learned in the tutorial. The Tutorial Assignments are followed by four Case Problems that have approximately the same scope as the tutorial case. In the Windows 95 applications texts, there is always one Case Problem in the book and one in the Instructor's Manual that require students to solve the problem independently, either "from scratch" or with minimum guidance. Finally, if a Course Lab (see next page) accompanies the tutorial, Lab Assignments are included. Look on page WP 41 for the Tutorial Assignments for Tutorial 1. See page WP 42 for examples of Case Problems. The Lab Assignment for Tutorial 1 is on page WP 44.

Exploration Exercises The Windows environment allows students to learn by exploring and discovering what they can do. Exploration Exercises can be Tutorial Assignments or Case Problems that challenge students, encourage them to explore the capabilities of the program they are using, and extend their knowledge using the Help facility and other reference materials. Page WP 42 contains Exploration Exercises for Tutorial 1.

The New Perspectives Series is known for using technology to help instructors teach and administer, and to help students learn. All of the technology-based teaching and learning materials available with the New Perspectives Series are known as CourseTools. What CourseTools are available with New Perspectives textbooks?

Course Labs: Now, Concepts Come to Life   Computer skills and concepts come to life with the New Perspectives Course Labs—highly interactive tutorials that combine illustrations, animation, digital images, and simulations. The Labs guide students step-by-step, present them with Quick Check questions, let them explore on their own, test their comprehension, and provide printed feedback. Lab Assignments are included at the end of each relevant chapter or tutorial in the text book. The Lab available with this book and the tutorial in which it appears is:

Word Processing
Tutorial 1

Course Online: A Website Dedicated to Keeping You and Your Students Up-To-Date   When you use a New Perspectives product, you can access CTI's faculty and student sites on the World Wide Web. You can browse the password-protected Faculty Online Companion to obtain online Instructor's Manuals, Solution Files, Student Files, and more. Please see your Instructor's Manual or call your CTI customer service representative for more information. Students may access their Online Companion in the Student Center using the URL **http://coursetools.com**.

Course Presenter: Ready-Made or Customized Dynamic Presentations
Course Presenter is a CD-ROM-based presentation tool that provides instructors with a wealth of resources for use in the classroom, replacing traditional overhead transparencies with computer-generated screenshows. Course Presenter includes a structured presentation for each tutorial or chapter of the book, and also gives instructors the flexibility to create custom presentations, complete with matching student notes and lecture notes pages. Instructors can also use Course Presenter to create traditional overhead transparencies.

Course Test Manager: Testing and Practice at the Computer or on Paper
Course Test Manager is cutting-edge Windows-based testing software that helps instructors design and administer practice tests and actual examinations. This full-featured program allows students to randomly generate practice tests that provide immediate on-screen feedback and detailed study guides for questions incorrectly answered. Instructors can also use Course Test Manager to produce printed tests. Course Test Manager can automatically grade the tests students take at the computer and can generate statistical information on individual as well as group performance.

What additional supplements are available with CTI textbooks?

Instructor's Manual New Perspectives Series Instructor's Manuals contain Instructor's Notes and printed solutions for each tutorial. Instructor's Notes provide tutorial overviews and outlines, technical notes, lecture notes, and extra case problems. Printed solutions include solutions to the Tutorial Assignments, Case Problems, and Lab Assignments.

Solution Files Solution Files contain every file students are asked to create or modify in the tutorials, Tutorial Assignments, and Case Problems.

Student Files Student Files contain all of the data that students will use to complete the tutorials, Tutorial Assignments, and Case Problems. A Readme file includes technical tips for lab management. See the inside covers of this book and the "Read This Before You Begin" page before Tutorial 1 for more information on Student Files.

The following supplements are included in the Instructor's Resource Kit that accompanies this textbook:

- Instructor's Manual
- Solution Files
- Student Files
- Word Processing Course Lab
- Course Test Manager Test Bank
- Course Test Manager Engine

Several of the supplements listed above are also available over the World Wide Web through CTI's password-protected Faculty Online Companions. Please see your Instructor's Manual or call your CTI customer service representative for more information.

Acknowledgments

Our appreciation goes to our reviewers, whose comments and suggestions helped shape this book: Jerry Plummer, Tennessee State University, and Prasad Kilari, University of Nevada at Reno. We would like to thank all the members of the New Perspectives team who helped in the development and production of this book. Special thanks to the unequaled quality assurance and technical support from Jeff Goding, Greg Bigelow, and U Jin Wong, and QA testers Chris Hall, Bob Keaveney, and Claire Martinez; to the excellent production work of Daphne Barbas and the staff at Gex; and the editorial support of Mac Mendelsohn, Susan Solomon, and Barbara Clemens. Finally, we would like to thank our developmental editor, Robin Geller, for her dedication and hard work, for her numerous suggestions and additions, and for her constant encouragement.

Beverly B. Zimmerman
S. Scott Zimmerman

Table of Contents

Preface	vi
Corel WordPerfect 7 for Windows 95 Introductory Tutorials	WP 1
Read This Before You Begin	WP 2

INTRODUCTORY TUTORIAL 1
Creating Documents

Writing a Business Letter for Crossroads	WP 3
Using the Tutorials Effectively	WP 4
Session 1.1	**WP 5**
Producing Documents with WordPerfect	WP 5
Planning and Creating a Document	WP 5
Editing a Document	WP 6
Formatting a Document	WP 6
Printing a Document	WP 6
Starting WordPerfect	WP 7
The WordPerfect Screen	WP 8
Common Windows 95 Features	WP 8
The Toolbar, Power Bar, and Ruler Bar	WP 9
Status Bar and Insertion Point	WP 10
Margin Guidelines	WP 10
Choosing Commands	WP 11
Using the Menu Bar	WP 11
Using the Power Bar	WP 12
Using Shortcut Keys	WP 13
Using Shortcut Menus	WP 14
Checking the Screen Before You Begin Each Tutorial	WP 15
Sizing the Document and WordPerfect Windows	WP 15
Setting the Document View to Page View	WP 16
Displaying the Toolbars	WP 16
Setting the Font and Point Size	WP 16
Displaying Nonprinting Symbols	WP 18
Correcting Errors	WP 19
Using the Backspace Key	WP 19
Using Spell-As-You-Go	WP 19
Using QuickCorrect	WP 20
Closing the Document Window	WP 21
Quick Check	WP 21
Session 1.2	**WP 22**
Typing a Letter	WP 22
Entering Text	WP 23
Saving a Document	WP 24
Observing Word Wrap	WP 26
Scrolling	WP 27
Saving the Completed Letter	WP 29
Previewing and Printing a Document	WP 29
Printing an Envelope	WP 31
Exiting WordPerfect	WP 32
Quick Check	WP 32
Session 1.3	**WP 33**
Opening an Existing Document	WP 33
Moving the Insertion Point	WP 35
Inserting Text	WP 35
Deleting Text	WP 36
Using Typeover Mode	WP 37
Saving a Document with a New Filename	WP 38
Getting Help	WP 38
Using Context-Sensitive Help	WP 39
Using the Help Topics Window	WP 39
Quick Check	WP 41
Tutorial Assignments	WP 41
Case Problems	WP 42
Lab Assignment	WP 44

INTRODUCTORY TUTORIAL 2
Editing and Formatting a Document

Investment Plan Description by Right-Hand Solutions	WP 45
Session 2.1	**WP 46**
Planning the Document	WP 46
Content	WP 46
Organization	WP 46
Style	WP 46
Presentation	WP 46
Opening the Document	WP 46
Renaming the Document	WP 48
Moving the Insertion Point	WP 49
Selecting and Modifying Text	WP 50
Selecting and then Deleting Text	WP 51
Undoing an Edit	WP 53
Moving Text Within a Document	WP 54
Dragging and Dropping Text	WP 54
Cutting and Pasting Text	WP 56
Copying and Pasting Text	WP 57
Quick Check	WP 59

Session 2.2	WP 60
Formatting the Document	WP 60
Specifying the Page Size and Orientation	WP 60
Changing the Margins	WP 61
Justifying Text	WP 62
Formatting Lines and Paragraphs	WP 64
Centering a Line of Text	WP 64
Indenting Paragraphs	WP 65
Setting Tabs	WP 67
Aligning Vertical Columns	WP 68
Moving Tab Stops	WP 70
Keeping Lines of Text Together	WP 70
Setting Widow/Orphan Protection	WP 72
Quick Check	WP 73

Session 2.3	WP 74
Changing the Font	WP 74
Adding Bullets and Numbers	WP 76
Changing the Font Appearance	WP 78
Bolding Text	WP 79
Underlining Text	WP 80
Italicizing Text	WP 80
Using QuickFormat	WP 81
Revealing Format Codes	WP 82
Deleting Format Codes	WP 84
Getting Document Properties	WP 85
Switching Between Documents	WP 86
Printing the Document	WP 87
Quick Check	WP 88
Tutorial Assignments	WP 89
Case Problems	WP 90

INTRODUCTORY TUTORIAL 3
Creating a Multiple-Page Report

Writing a Recommendation Report for AgriTechnology	WP 93

Session 3.1	WP 94
Planning the Document	WP 94
Content	WP 94
Organization	WP 94
Style	WP 94
Presentation	WP 94
Opening the Draft of the Report	WP 94
Finding Text	WP 96
Finding and Replacing Text	WP 98
Running the Spell Checker	WP 101
Using the Thesaurus	WP 103
Using Grammatik	WP 104
Quick Check	WP 107

Session 3.2	WP 107
Centering a Page Vertically	WP 107
Adding Headers and Footers	WP 109
Creating a Header with Automatic Page Numbering	WP 109
Changing the Page Numbering	WP 111
Inserting a Footer	WP 112
Adding Footnotes and Endnotes	WP 112
Deleting or Moving a Footnote or Endnote	WP 114
Quick Check	WP 114

Session 3.3	WP 114
Formatting with Styles	WP 114
Applying Styles	WP 116
Modifying Styles	WP 117
Modifying a Style by Example	WP 117
Modifying a Style with the Styles Editor	WP 119
Creating Styles	WP 120
Saving the Styles in a Separate File	WP 122
Retrieving a Styles File	WP 123
Editing the Header	WP 124
Quick Check	WP 125
Tutorial Assignments	WP 126
Case Problems	WP 127

INTRODUCTORY TUTORIAL 4
Creating Outlines, Tables, and Tables of Contents

Writing a Business Plan for EstimaTech	WP 131

Session 4.1	WP 132
Planning the Document	WP 132
Content	WP 132
Organization	WP 132
Style	WP 132
Presentation	WP 132
Creating an Outline	WP 132
Modifying an Outline	WP 136
Moving Outline Paragraphs Up and Down	WP 136
Opening the Business Plan	WP 137
Suppressing Headers	WP 138

Inserting Tables	**WP 139**
Creating a Table Using the Table Button	WP 139
Entering Text in a Table	WP 141
Editing a Table	**WP 142**
Selecting Text in a Table	WP 142
Sorting Rows in a Table	WP 142
Modifying an Existing Table Structure	**WP 145**
Inserting Additional Rows in a Table	WP 145
Deleting Existing Rows in a Table	WP 145
Performing Mathematical Calculations in Tables	**WP 146**
Quick Check	**WP 147**
Session 4.2	**WP 147**
Creating a Table with the Table Create Command	**WP 147**
Transferring Data Between Documents	**WP 148**
Copying and Pasting Between Documents	WP 149
Viewing Two Document Windows	WP 150
Dragging and Dropping Between Documents	WP 151
Formatting Tables	**WP 153**
Changing Column Width	WP 153
Justifying Text Within Cells	WP 153
Adding Borders, Rules, and Shading to Paragraphs	**WP 155**
Quick Check	**WP 156**
Session 4.3	**WP 157**
Formatting Tables Automatically	**WP 157**
Centering a Table	**WP 158**
Modifying a Table Format	**WP 159**
Adding Captions	**WP 159**
Generating a Table of Contents	**WP 160**
Quick Check	**WP 163**
Tutorial Assignments	**WP 163**
Case Problems	**WP 164**

INTRODUCTORY TUTORIAL 5

Creating Form Letters and Mailing Labels

Writing a Sales Letter for The Pet Shoppe	**WP 169**
Session 5.1	**WP 170**
Planning the Document	**WP 170**
Content	WP 170
Organization	WP 170
Style	WP 170
Presentation	WP 170
The Merge Process	**WP 170**
Merge Codes	WP 172
Data Files and Records	WP 173
Creating a Data File	**WP 173**
Entering Data into a Data File	**WP 176**
Quick Check	**WP 180**
Session 5.2	**WP 180**
Creating a Form File	**WP 180**
Editing a Form File	**WP 181**
Inserting Merge Codes	WP 181
Merging the Form File and Data File	**WP 185**
Sorting Records	**WP 186**
Selecting Records to Merge	**WP 188**
Quick Check	**WP 191**
Session 5.3	**WP 191**
Creating Mailing Labels	**WP 191**
Creating a Telephone List	**WP 194**
Quick Check	**WP 197**
Tutorial Assignments	**WP 197**
Case Problems	**WP 199**

INTRODUCTORY TUTORIAL 6

Desktop Publishing

Creating a Newsletter for FastFad Manufacturing Company	**WP 203**
Session 6.1	**WP 204**
Planning the Document	**WP 204**
Content	WP 204
Organization	WP 204
Style	WP 204
Presentation	WP 204
Characteristics of Desktop Publishing	**WP 204**
Elements of a Newsletter	WP 205
Using TextArt to Create a Title	**WP 206**
Changing the Text Shape	WP 208
Editing the TextArt Image	WP 209

Adjusting the Space Between Lines	WP 210
Inserting Rules and Fills	WP 212
Quick Check	WP 213

Session 6.2 — WP 214

Formatting Text into Newspaper-Style Columns	WP 214
Inserting WordPerfect Clipart	WP 215
Inserting an Existing Image	WP 216
Sizing an Image	WP 217
Inserting Drop Caps	WP 218
Inserting a Pull Quote	WP 219
Formatting the Text in a Text Box	WP 220
Editing a Text Box	WP 221
Quick Check	WP 222

Session 6.3 — WP 222

Inserting Symbols and Special Characters	WP 222
Hyphenating a Document	WP 226
Adding a Border Around the Page	WP 229
Inserting a Vertical Line Between Columns	WP 230
Quick Check	WP 231
Tutorial Assignments	WP 231
Case Problems	WP 232

INTRODUCTORY TUTORIAL 7
Integrating WordPerfect with Other Windows Programs
Writing a Proposal to Open a New Branch of Family Style, Inc. — WP 237

Session 7.1 — WP 238

Planning the Document	WP 238
Content	WP 238
Organization	WP 239
Style	WP 239
Presentation	WP 239
Integrating Files from Other Programs	WP 239
Importing	WP 240
Embedding	WP 240
Linking	WP 241
Choosing Among Importing, Embedding, and Linking	WP 241
Importing Files into WordPerfect	WP 242
Importing a Microsoft Word Document	WP 242
Formatting the Imported Text	WP 243
Importing One WordPerfect Document into Another	WP 244
Importing a Picture into WordPerfect	WP 245
Moving the Picture	WP 246
Quick Check	WP 247

Session 7.2 — WP 248

Embedding a Quattro Pro Spreadsheet	WP 248
Centering the Embedded Spreadsheet	WP 249
Modifying an Embedded Quattro Pro Spreadsheet	WP 250
Embedding a Graph Created with Chart	WP 251
Modifying the Chart	WP 253
Quick Check	WP 254

Session 7.3 — WP 255

Linking and Modifying an Object	WP 255
Linking a Paint File	WP 255
Modifying the Linked File in Paint	WP 257
Updating a Link	WP 259
Modifying the Linked File in WordPerfect	WP 260
Quick Check	WP 262
Tutorial Assignments	WP 262
Case Problems	WP 263

Answers to Quick Check Questions — WP 266

Index — WP 273

Task Reference — WP 283

Reference Windows

Closing a Document Without Saving Changes	WP 21
Saving a Document for the First Time	WP 24
Exiting WordPerfect	WP 32
Opening an Existing Document	WP 34
Reversing Edits with Undo, Redo, or Undelete	WP 54
Dragging and Dropping (Moving) Text	WP 55
Cutting and Pasting (Moving) Text	WP 57
Copying and Pasting (Copying) Text	WP 58
Changing the Page Size or Orientation of the Document	WP 61

Changing Margins	WP 61	Inserting a Table with the Table Create Command	WP 148
Justifying Text	WP 63	Transferring Data Between Documents	WP 149
Centering a Line of Text	WP 65	Formatting Tables Automatically	WP 157
Indenting Paragraphs	WP 66	Generating a Table of Contents	WP 160
Setting a Conditional End of Page	WP 71	Creating a Data File	WP 174
Setting Widow/Orphan Protection	WP 73	Creating a Form File	WP 180
Changing the Font	WP 75	Merging a Form File and Data File	WP 185
Creating a List with Bullets or Numbers	WP 76	Sorting a Data File	WP 187
Typing Text in Bold, Underline, or Italic	WP 79	Creating Mailing Labels	WP 192
Switching Between Open Documents	WP 86	Creating Text with Special Effects Using TextArt	WP 207
Finding Text	WP 96	Formatting Text Into Newspaper-Style Columns	WP 214
Finding and Replacing Text	WP 98	Inserting Graphics	WP 216
Correcting Spelling	WP 101	Resizing a Graphic	WP 217
Using the Thesaurus	WP 103	Inserting Drop Caps	WP 218
Checking Grammar in a Document	WP 105	Inserting Symbols and Special Characters	WP 223
Centering a Page Vertically	WP 107	Importing a File into WordPerfect	WP 242
Inserting a Header or Footer	WP 109	Embedding an Existing File	WP 248
Inserting Footnotes or Endnotes	WP 113	Modifying an Embedded Object	WP 253
Applying a Style	WP 116	Linking an Object	WP 255
Modifying a Paired-Auto Style by Example	WP 118	Modifying a Linked File	WP 258
Creating a New Style with the Styles Editor	WP 121	Updating a Linked File	WP 259
Saving Styles in a Separate File	WP 123		
Retrieving a Styles File	WP 123		
Creating and Editing Outlines	WP 133		

New Perspectives on

Corel® WordPerfect® 7 for Windows® 95

INTRODUCTORY

TUTORIALS

TUTORIAL 1
Creating Documents
Writing a Business Letter for Crossroads — WP 3

TUTORIAL 2
Editing and Formatting a Document
Investment Plan Description by Right-Hand Solutions — WP 45

TUTORIAL 3
Creating a Multiple-Page Report
Writing a Recommendation Report for AgriTechnology — WP 93

TUTORIAL 4
Creating Outlines, Tables, and Tables of Contents
Writing a Business Plan for EstimaTech — WP 131

TUTORIAL 5
Creating Form Letters and Mailing Labels
Writing a Sales Letter for the Pet Shoppe — WP 169

TUTORIAL 6
Desktop Publishing
Creating a Newsletter for FastFad Manufacturing Company — WP 203

TUTORIAL 7
Integrating WordPerfect with Other Windows Programs
Writing a Proposal to Open a New Branch of Family Style, Inc. — WP 237

Read This Before You Begin

TO THE STUDENT

STUDENT DISKS

To complete the Introductory tutorials, Tutorial Assignments, and Case Problems in this book, you need Student Disks. Your instructor will either provide you with Student Disks or ask you to make your own.

If you are supposed to make your own Student Disks, you will need 5 blank, formatted high-density disks. You will need to copy a set of folders from a file server or standalone computer onto your disks. Your instructor will tell you which computer, drive letter, and folders contain the files you need. The following table shows you which folders go on each of your disks, so that you will have enough disk space to complete all the tutorials, Tutorial Assignments, and Case Problems:

Student Disk	Write this on the disk label	Put these folders on the disk
1	Student Disk 1: Introductory Tutorials 1–5, Introductory Tutorial 6, Tutorial & Tutorial Assignments	Tutorial.01, Tutorial.02, Tutorial.03, Tutorial.04, Tutorial.05, Tutorial.06
2	Student Disk 2: Introductory Tutorial 6, Case Problems	Tutorial.06
3	Student Disk 3: Introductory Tutorial 7, Tutorial & Tutorial Assignments	Tutorial.07
4	Student Disk 4: Introductory Tutorial 7, Case Problems 1 & 2	Tutorial.07
5	Student Disk 5: Introductory Tutorial 7, Case Problems 3 & 4	Tutorial.07

When you begin each tutorial, be sure you are using the correct Student Disk. See the inside front or inside back cover of this book for more information on Student Disk files, or ask your instructor or technical support person for assistance.

Word Processing

COURSE LAB

The Introductory tutorials in this book feature an interactive Course Lab to help you understand word processing concepts. There are Lab Assignments at the end of Tutorial 1 that relate to this Lab. To start a Lab, click the **Start** button on the Windows 95 taskbar, point to **Programs**, point to **Course Labs**, point to **New Perspectives Applications**, and click **Word Processing**.

USING YOUR OWN COMPUTER

If you are going to work through this book using your own computer, you need:

- **Computer System** Microsoft Windows 95 and Corel WordPerfect Suite 7 for Windows 95 or Corel Office Professional 7 for Windows 95 must be installed on your computer. This book assumes a standard installation of WordPerfect 7.

- **Student Disks** Ask your instructor or technical support person for details on how to get the Student Disks. You will not be able to complete the tutorials or exercises in this book using your own computer until you have Student Disks. The student files may also be obtained electronically over the Internet. See the inside front or inside back cover of this book for more details.

- **Course Lab** See your instructor or technical support person to obtain the Course Lab software for use on your own computer.

VISIT OUR WORLD WIDE WEB SITE

Additional materials designed especially for you are available on the World Wide Web. Go to **http://coursetools.com**.

TO THE INSTRUCTOR

To complete the Introductory tutorials in this book, your students must use a set of files on Student Disks. These files are included in the Instructor's Resource Kit and they may also be obtained electronically over the Internet. See the inside front or inside back cover of this book for more details. Follow the instructions in the Readme file to copy them to your server or standalone computer. You can view the Readme file using WordPad.

Once the files are copied, you can make Student Disks for the students yourself, or tell students where to find the files so they can make their own Student Disks. Make sure the files get correctly copied onto the Student Disks by following the instructions in the Student Disks section above, which will ensure that students have enough disk space to complete all the tutorials, Tutorial Assignments, and Case Problems.

COURSE LAB SOFTWARE

Introductory Tutorial 1 features an online, interactive Course Lab that introduces basic word processing concepts. The Course Lab software is distributed on a CD-ROM included in the Instructor's Resource Kit. To install the Course Lab software, follow the setup instructions in the Readme file on the CD-ROM. Refer also to the Readme file for essential technical notes related to running the Labs in a multiuser environment. Once you have installed the Course Lab software, your students can start the Lab from the Windows 95 desktop by clicking the **Start** button, pointing to **Programs**/pointing to **Course Labs**/pointing to **New Perspectives Applications**, and clicking **Word Processing**.

CTI COURSE LAB SOFTWARE AND STUDENT FILES

You are granted a license to copy the Student Files and Course Lab to any computer or computer network used by students who have purchased this book.

TUTORIAL 1

Creating Documents

Writing a Business Letter for Crossroads

OBJECTIVES

In this tutorial you will:

- Start and exit WordPerfect 7 for Windows 95

- Identify the main elements of the WordPerfect window

- Choose commands using the Toolbar, Power Bar, and menus

- Correct spelling errors with Spell-As-You-Go and QuickCorrect

- Scroll through the document and move the insertion point

- Open, edit, save, and print a document and print an envelope

- Insert and delete text

- Get Help on WordPerfect's features

 Crossroads

Karen Liu is executive director of Crossroads, a small, non-profit organization in Tacoma, Washington. Crossroads distributes business clothing to low-income clients who are returning to the job market or starting new careers. Karen wants to make potential clients in the community more aware of the organization's services. She asks you to write a letter to the Tacoma Chamber of Commerce requesting information about their local job fair.

In this tutorial you'll create Karen's letter and accompanying envelope using WordPerfect 7 for Windows 95, a word-processing program in which you produce documents. A **document** is any written item, such as a letter, memo, or report.

Tutorial 1 is divided into three sessions. In Session 1.1, you'll start and exit WordPerfect, identify and use the parts of the WordPerfect screen, and insert text. In Session 1.2, you'll create a document and then name, save, preview, and print it. You'll also set up and print an envelope. In Session 1.3, you'll open an existing document, rename it, then edit it by inserting and deleting text.

Using the Tutorials Effectively

These tutorials, designed to be used at a computer, will help you learn about WordPerfect 7. Each tutorial is divided into sessions. Watch for the session headings, such as Session 1.1 and Session 1.2. It's a good idea to take a break between sessions. Each session is designed to be completed in about 45 minutes, but take as much time as you need. Before you begin, read the following questions and answers, which are designed to help you use the tutorials effectively.

Where do I start?

Each tutorial begins with a case that sets the scene for the tutorial and gives background information that helps you understand what you do in the tutorial. You can read the case before you go to the lab and then begin with the first session in the lab.

How do I know what to do on the computer?

Each session contains steps that you do on the computer to learn how to use WordPerfect. Read the text that introduces each series of steps. The steps you need to do at a computer are numbered and have a colored background. Read each step carefully and completely before you try it.

How do I know if I did the step correctly?

As you work, compare your computer screen with the figures in the tutorial. Don't worry if your screen display is somewhat different from the figures. The important parts of the screen display are labeled in each figure. Just be sure these parts are on your screen.

What if I make a mistake?

Don't worry about making mistakes—that's part of the learning process. Paragraphs labeled "TROUBLE?" identify common problems and explain how to get back on track. Do the steps in the TROUBLE? paragraph *only* if you're having the problem described. If you run into other problems, carefully consider the current state of your computer system, the position of the mouse pointer, and any messages on the screen. Plan from there what you want to do, determine how to do it using this book or online Help, then put your plan into action.

How do I use the Reference Windows?

Reference Windows summarize the procedures you learn in the tutorial steps. Don't do the steps in the Reference Window when you're working through the tutorial. Instead, use the Reference Windows when you work on the assignments at the end of the tutorial.

How can I test my understanding of what I learned in the tutorial?

At the end of each session, you can answer the Quick Check questions. The answers for the Quick Checks are at the end of the tutorials.

After you have completed the entire tutorial, you can do the Tutorial Assignments and Case Problems. They are carefully structured so you will review what you have learned and then apply your knowledge to new situations.

What if I can't remember how to do something?

You can use the Task Reference at the end of the tutorials; it summarizes how to accomplish tasks using the mouse, menus, and keyboard.

What are the Interactive Labs and how should I use them?

The Interactive Labs will help you review concepts and practice skills that you learn in the tutorial. The Lab icon at the beginning of Tutorial 1 indicates the topic that has a corresponding Lab. The "Lab Assignments" section includes instructions on how to use the Lab.

Now that you've seen how to use the tutorials effectively, you are ready to begin.

SESSION 1.1

In this session you will start and exit WordPerfect, identify and use the parts of the WordPerfect screen, and insert text. With the skills you learn in this session, you'll be prepared to use WordPerfect to create a document.

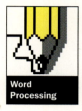

Producing Documents with WordPerfect

WordPerfect helps you produce quality work in minimal time. Not only can you type a document, you quickly can make editing changes and corrections, adjust margins and spacing, create columns and tables, and add graphics to your documents. You also can save interim versions of your document on the computer's hard disk or on a 3.5-inch disk. The document file contains all the text and formatting information about your document. Figure 1-1 shows the flow of producing documents with WordPerfect.

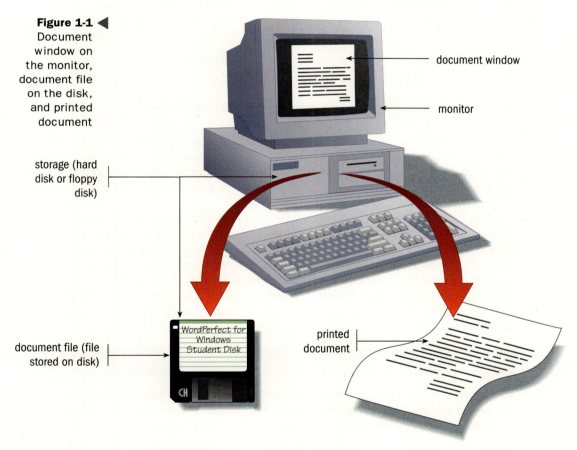

Figure 1-1 ◀
Document window on the monitor, document file on the disk, and printed document

Using WordPerfect, you can efficiently produce a document following a four-step process that consists of planning and creating, editing, formatting, and printing a document.

Planning and Creating a Document

Planning a document before you create it helps to improve the effectiveness and quality of your writing, reduce your editing time, and make your document more attractive and readable. In the long run, planning saves time and effort. First, you should determine the **content**, or what you want to say in the document. You should clearly state your purpose for writing and include enough information to achieve that purpose without overwhelming or boring your reader.

Karen has given you a handwritten note with all her questions for the Tacoma Chamber of Commerce, as shown in Figure 1-2. The note listing Karen's questions about the job fair will be the primary content of your letter.

Figure 1-2
Karen's questions about the job fair

> Please write the Tacoma Chamber of Commerce and find out the following:
>
> What are the location and dates for this year's job fair?
>
> Is a map of the exhibit area available? What size booths are available and how can we reserve a booth?
>
> Who do we contact about what physical facilities are available at each booth?
>
> Send the letter to the Chamber's president. The address is 210 Shoreline Vista, Suite 1103, Tacoma, WA 98402.

After determining the content of your document, you should decide its **organization** so you logically can order your ideas. You'll use the organization of a standard business letter, which consists of the date, inside address, and salutation; the body, or text, of the letter; and a complimentary closing with the writer's name and title, for the letter to the Tacoma Chamber of Commerce.

After deciding the content and organization of your document, you should determine how to say what you want to say—the **style** of your document—and the way you want your document to look—its **presentation**. Because this is a business letter, you'll use a direct style: simple words, clear sentences, and short paragraphs so your reader can easily grasp the meaning of the text while reading at a brisk pace. You'll present your letter to the Tacoma Chamber of Commerce in the form of a standard business letter.

After you've planned your document, you'll use WordPerfect's features to create it quickly and easily.

Editing a Document

Editing consists of reading through the document you've created, then correcting your errors and adding or deleting text to make the document more readable. After you create the letter, you'll read through it and make necessary corrections.

Formatting a Document

WordPerfect allows you to make your document visually appealing and readable by implementing your planned presentation. Formatting features, such as white space (blank areas of a page), line spacing, and headings, help to make your document more readable. Usually, a longer and more complex document, such as a report, requires more attention to formatting. A shorter and less complex document, such as a letter, requires less attention to formatting.

Printing a Document

Printing is the final phase in creating an effective document. As you'll do with this letter, you always should preview your document before you spend the time and resources to print it.

Starting WordPerfect

Before you can apply these four phases to produce the letter using WordPerfect, you need to start WordPerfect and know something about the general organization of the WordPerfect screen.

To start WordPerfect:

1. Make sure you have your WordPerfect Student Disk ready.

   TROUBLE? If you don't have a Student Disk, you need to get one. Your instructor or technical support person will either give you one or ask you to make your own by following the instructions on the "Read This Before You Begin" page before this tutorial. See your instructor or technical support person for more information.

2. If necessary, turn on your computer and get to the Windows 95 desktop.

3. Click the WordPerfect icon on the Corel DAD on the Windows 95 taskbar. See Figure 1.3.

   The Corel DAD (Desktop Application Director) is a set of icons you can click to start Corel programs.

Figure 1-3 ◀
Windows 95 Start menu and Corel DAD

WordPerfect program item on Start menu

Corel DAD (Desktop Applications Director)

taskbar

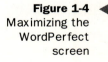

   TROUBLE? If your system doesn't have the Corel DAD, click the Start button on the Windows 95 taskbar, then move the mouse pointer over Corel Office 7. After a short pause, the menu of Corel Office programs opens. Move the mouse pointer over Corel WordPerfect 7 in the menu. Then click Corel WordPerfect 7.

   TROUBLE? If your Start menu doesn't list Corel Office 7, then after clicking the Start button, move the mouse pointer over Programs, then click Corel WordPerfect 7. If none of these methods for starting WordPerfect works, consult your instructor or technical support person.

   The WordPerfect window opens onto your screen.

4. If WordPerfect doesn't fill the entire monitor display, click the **Maximize** button in the upper-right corner of the WordPerfect window. See Figure 1-4.

Figure 1-4 ◀
Maximizing the WordPerfect screen

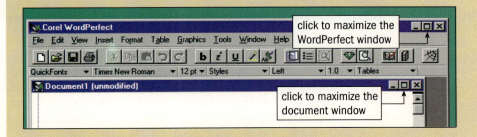

> **5.** If the document window isn't maximized, click the **Maximize** button in the upper-right corner of the document window, as shown in Figure 1-4.
>
> **TROUBLE?** If you see the paragraph mark character (¶) on your screen, just continue with the steps. The previous user left nonprinting characters displayed; you'll learn how to show and hide nonprinting characters shortly.

WordPerfect is running and ready to use.

The WordPerfect Screen

The WordPerfect screen is made up of both an application window and a document window. The **application window**, also called the WordPerfect window, opens automatically when you start WordPerfect and contains all your toolbars and menus. The **document window**, which opens within the WordPerfect window, is where you type and edit documents.

When both windows are maximized, they share the same title bar and borders and look like one window. You generally should maximize both the WordPerfect window and the document window when you start WordPerfect. Figure 1-5 shows the WordPerfect screen with both the application and document windows maximized.

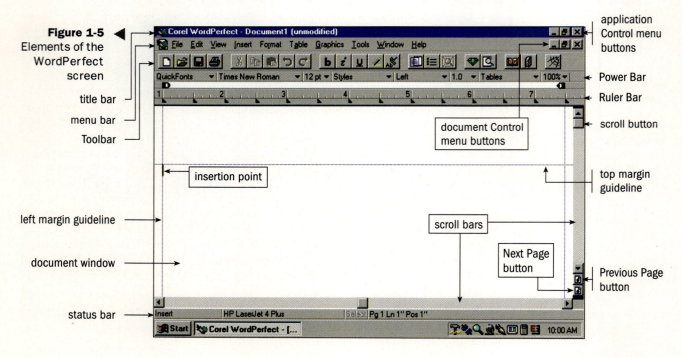

Figure 1-5 Elements of the WordPerfect screen

If your screen doesn't look exactly like Figure 1-5, just continue for now. During the rest of this session, you will learn how to change your screen to match those shown in the tutorial.

Common Windows 95 Features

Some features in the WordPerfect screen are common to all Windows 95 applications; these include the title bar, menu bar, Control menu buttons on both the application window and the document window, workspace, scroll bars, mouse pointer, and Windows 95 taskbar.

The **title bar** identifies the active program, in this case WordPerfect, and the name of the current document. If you haven't saved the current document, the document name is listed as Document1, and if you haven't modified the document window since the last save, the title bar also includes the word "(unmodified)."

The **menu bar**, located below the title bar, provides access to all the features of WordPerfect. You can click each menu title to display a group of WordPerfect commands. For example, the File menu contains commands that relate to document files, such as opening a file, saving a file, closing a file, and printing a file.

You use the **Control menu buttons** to shrink, enlarge, and close the WordPerfect screen. Two sets of Control menu buttons appear in the upper-right corner of your screen. The top set controls the WordPerfect window; the bottom set controls the document window. Whenever you start a new WordPerfect session, maximize both the application and document windows, as you did in the section "Starting WordPerfect."

The **document window**, or workspace, is the area where you enter the text and graphics that make up your document and where you view your document. The **scroll bars** allow you to quickly move any portion of your open document to the document window. The vertical scroll bar is on the right side of your screen and the horizontal scroll bar is just below the document window.

The **mouse pointer** is the indicator that moves on your screen as you move your mouse. The mouse pointer changes shape to indicate the type of task you can perform at a specific region of the screen. For example, in the Toolbar region it appears as ▹; in the left margin of a line of text, it appears as ◁.

The **Windows 95 taskbar**, always visible at the base of your screen, contains the Start button, buttons that show which windows are open, and the Corel DAD. You easily can start a new program or switch between open programs by clicking the appropriate button.

The Toolbar, Power Bar, and Ruler Bar

Like many Windows 95 applications, WordPerfect has several toolbars, as shown previously in Figure 1-5. You can display or hide any or all of these toolbars.

The **WordPerfect 7 Toolbar** (also simply called the Toolbar), located immediately below the menu bar, is a ribbon of buttons that provide command shortcuts. When you move the mouse pointer over each Toolbar button, WordPerfect displays a **QuickTip**, which is a yellow rectangle containing a description of the button.

The Toolbar contains the most important and commonly executed commands in WordPerfect. For example, you use the first four buttons on the Toolbar to create a new document, open an existing document, save the current document, and print a document.

The **Power Bar**, directly beneath the Toolbar, contains the most frequently used font and paragraph formatting commands, and displays important information about the appearance of your document, such as the name and size of the font. A **font** is a set of characters (letters, digits, and other characters such as ! @ and *) that has a certain design, shape, and appearance. Each font has a name, such as Courier, Times New Roman, or Arial (see Figure 1-6). The font size is measured in **points**, where one point equals ½ of an inch in height. In Figure 1-5, the left side of the Power Bar lists the font as Times New Roman and the font size as 12 point. Your Power Bar might show a different font or size, depending on how your copy of WordPerfect was installed.

Figure 1-6 ◂
Three sample fonts

```
This is Courier
```
This is Times New Roman

This is Arial

Directly below the Power Bar is the **Ruler Bar** (often simply called the Ruler). Using the Ruler, you easily can adjust margins, set tabs, and change column widths. The Ruler displays grid marks every ⅛ inch and tab stops every ½ inch.

You'll make sure that the Toolbar, Power Bar, and Ruler appear on your WordPerfect screen.

To display the Toolbar, Power Bar, and Ruler:

1. Position the mouse pointer over **View** on the menu bar, then press and release the mouse button to open the View menu.

2. Click **Toolbars/Ruler** to open the Toolbars dialog box. See Figure 1-7.

Figure 1-7 ◄
Toolbars dialog box

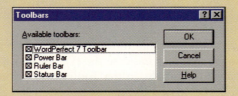

3. Make sure every check box is selected (checked). If any check box is not selected, click that check box.

4. Click the **OK** button in the Toolbars dialog box to close it. All four Toolbars appear on the screen.

The Toolbar, Power Bar, and Ruler help to make creating, editing, and formatting your document simple.

Status Bar and Insertion Point

The **status bar**, located below the document window, provides information about your document, including the name of the current printer, the date and time, and the location of the insertion point in the document. The **insertion point** is a blinking vertical bar that marks the location where the next character you type will appear in the document window. The status bar gives specific information about the insertion point. For example, in Figure 1-8, the status bar shows the location of the insertion point as *Pg 1 Ln 1" Pos 1"*. *Pg 1* means that the insertion point is currently on page 1—the first printed page—of your document. *Ln 1"* indicates that the insertion point is located on a line one inch from the top of the page. *Pos 1"* indicates that the insertion point is located at a position one inch from the left edge of the page.

Figure 1-8 ◄
Status bar
text input mode
printer

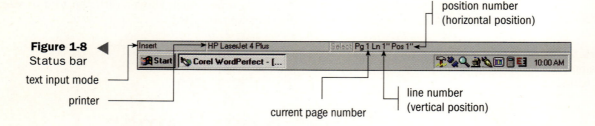

The status bar helps you keep track of where you are working in a document.

Margin Guidelines

The blue dashed lines in the document window shown in Figure 1-5 are called the **margin guidelines**. They mark the location of the left, right, top, and bottom margins. They currently are located one inch from each edge of the page.

To display the margin guidelines:

1. Position the mouse pointer over **View** on the menu bar, click the mouse button, then click **Guidelines** to open the Guidelines dialog box.

2. If any check box is not checked, click it. After all the check boxes are selected, click the **OK** button. The margin guidelines appear on the screen.

   TROUBLE? If you don't see the blue guidelines on your screen but all the check boxes in the Guidelines dialog box are selected, don't worry. You just need to change the view of your document window so you can see the guidelines. You'll do that shortly.

Now that you have seen how the WordPerfect screen is set up, you need to know how to choose commands.

Choosing Commands

In WordPerfect, as with other Windows 95 applications, you can choose commands by using the menu bar, the buttons on the Toolbar or Power Bar, or shortcut menus and keys. In some cases, you can perform a particular command by any one of these methods.

Using the Menu Bar

First you will choose commands using the menu bar. As you saw earlier, you use the menu bar in WordPerfect the same way you use any Windows 95 menu bar: position the mouse pointer over the appropriate command, then click the mouse button. The **menu**, a list of commands from which you can choose, opens on the screen.

You'll use the menu bar to insert today's date in your document so you have less to type and the date will be accurate.

To insert today's date using the menu bar:

1. Position the mouse pointer over **Insert** on the menu bar, then click the mouse button. The Insert menu opens and stays on the screen.

2. Move the mouse pointer over the **Date** command. The Date menu opens and contains three date commands. See Figure 1-9.

Figure 1-9
Date menu on Insert menu

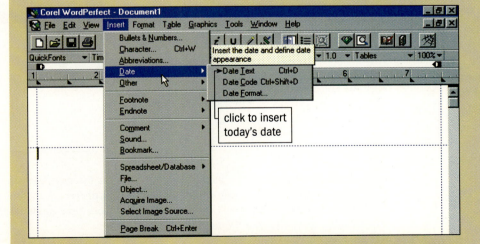

3. Click the **Date Text** command. WordPerfect inserts the current date into the document window at the location of the insertion point. See Figure 1-10.

Figure 1-10 ◀
Date inserted into the document

top margin (1 inch)

today's date

insertion point

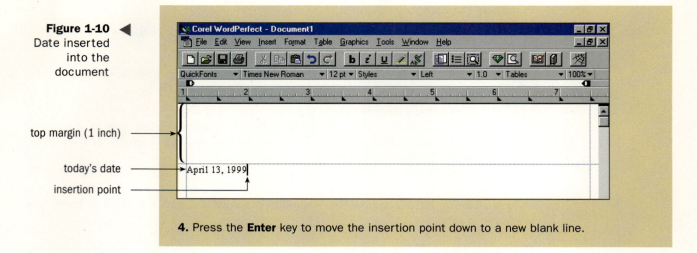

4. Press the **Enter** key to move the insertion point down to a new blank line.

The Date Text command—located on the Date menu, which in turn is located on the Insert menu—inserts the date of your computer's internal clock/calendar. If your computer's clock/calendar is not set to the current date and time, WordPerfect won't insert today's date when you use the Date Text command.

Using the Power Bar

Now you will choose a command from the Power Bar to change the date to a larger font size.

To change the font size using the Power Bar:

1. With the insertion point on the blank line below the date, move the mouse pointer to the **Font Size** button on the Power Bar. WordPerfect displays the QuickTip, "Change the font size."

2. Click the **Font Size** button. WordPerfect displays a list of font sizes. See Figure 1-11.

Figure 1-11 ◀
Font Size list

today's date in 12-point type

click to select 18-point type

3. Click **18**. WordPerfect closes the list and shows the new font size in the Font Size button on the Power Bar. Any text you type or any characters you insert into the document window will appear in 18-point type. Now you'll insert the date again, this time with the larger font size.

4. Click the **Insert** menu, move the insertion point over **Date**, then click **Date Text** to insert the date again. This time, the date appears in 18-point type rather than the original 12-point type. See Figure 1-12.

Figure 1-12
Date inserted in 18-point font size

font size on Power Bar

enlarged insertion point

date in 18-point font

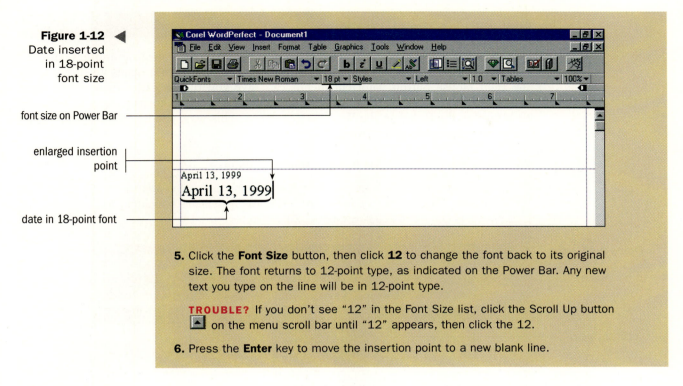

5. Click the **Font Size** button, then click **12** to change the font back to its original size. The font returns to 12-point type, as indicated on the Power Bar. Any new text you type on the line will be in 12-point type.

   TROUBLE? If you don't see "12" in the Font Size list, click the Scroll Up button on the menu scroll bar until "12" appears, then click the 12.

6. Press the **Enter** key to move the insertion point to a new blank line.

You have used a command on the Power Bar. As you'll see later, the Toolbar buttons work much the same way.

Using Shortcut Keys

Shortcut keys are another way you can choose many WordPerfect commands. A **shortcut key** is a keystroke or combination of keystrokes that provides quick access to a WordPerfect command. Shortcut keys save time because you don't have to lift your hands from the keyboard while you work.

To use a shortcut key, you press one of the lettered keys (A through Z), function keys (F1 through F12), or other keys, alone or in combination with one or more modifier keys. The **modifier keys** are Shift, Ctrl, and Alt. For example, WordPerfect provides a shortcut key for inserting the date. The command is a combination of the modifier key Ctrl and the letter D. You'll press this key combination to insert the date again into the document window.

To insert the current date using a shortcut key:

1. With the insertion point on the blank line below the other two dates, press and hold down the **Ctrl** key while you press **D**. (From now on, key combinations like these will be shown as, "Press **Ctrl** + **D**.")

2. Release both keys. Today's date again appears in the document window.

Whereas all commands are available from the menus, most but not all commands are available with shortcut keys.

Using Shortcut Menus

Besides shortcut keys, WordPerfect also provides shortcut menus, another efficient method for choosing commands. A **shortcut menu** is a menu that opens when you click the *right* mouse button. Shortcut menus can save you time because they appear right where you're working in the document window. You'll use a shortcut menu to hide and then display the Ruler on the WordPerfect screen. This way, you can see a quick way to make more space on your screen.

To hide/show the Ruler Bar using a shortcut menu:

1. Position the mouse pointer anywhere along the top part of the Ruler (where the numbers and grid marks appear), then click the right mouse button to open a menu of commands dealing with the Ruler. See Figure 1-13.

Figure 1-13 ◀
Ruler shortcut menu

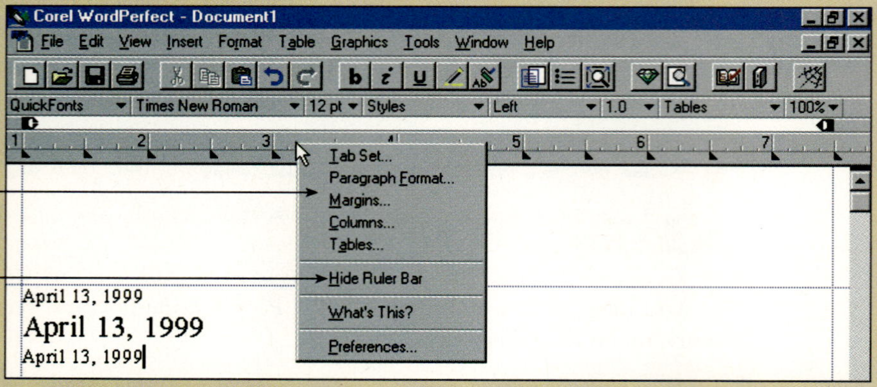

shortcut menu

click to hide Ruler

TROUBLE? If the Ruler shortcut menu doesn't appear, repeat Step 1, making sure you click the *right* mouse button with the pointer in the upper part of the Ruler.

2. Click **Hide Ruler Bar** on the Ruler shortcut menu. The ruler disappears. Notice that more of the document window is now visible. If you ever want more space in the document window and don't need the Ruler, you can use this procedure to hide the Ruler Bar.

3. Click **View** on the menu bar, then click the **Toolbars/Ruler** command to open the Toolbars dialog box.

4. Click the **Ruler Bar** check box, then click the **OK** button. The Ruler reappears and less of your document window is visible.

You've used four methods for choosing commands in WordPerfect. Which method is best? The answer depends on your level of experience and personal preference. These tutorials use the simplest method available, which in Tutorial 1 is usually the menu bar. As you become more experienced, you'll probably find it easier to use the Toolbar and Power Bar. Shortcut keys are very quick; however, the menu bar, Toolbar, and Power Bar are easier to use because you can simply select a command or click a button instead of memorizing a shortcut key. Shortcut menus save time because they appear at the location you're working, but they aren't available for all commands.

Checking the Screen Before You Begin Each Tutorial

WordPerfect provides a set of standard format settings, called **default settings**, that are appropriate for most documents. It is easy to change the appearance of a document by changing the default settings. Figure 1-14 lists some common WordPerfect default settings. The setup of your WordPerfect document might have different default settings from those in Figure 1-14. This often happens when you share a computer and another person changes the appearance of the WordPerfect screen.

Figure 1-14 ◀
Common WordPerfect default settings

Default Settings	
Left margin	1"
Right margin	1"
Top margin	1"
Bottom margin	1"
Justification	Aligned at the left margin only
Line spacing	Single
Paper size	8½" × 11"
Orientation	Portrait
Tabs	Every 0.5"
Page numbering	Off
Font	Times New Roman
Font size	12 point

These tutorials assume that your screen is set up the same way as the screens in this tutorial. The rest of this section discusses what your screen should look like and how to make it match those in the tutorials.

Sizing the Document and WordPerfect Windows

Whenever you start a new session in the tutorials in this book, make sure to maximize both the WordPerfect and document windows, just as you did when you started WordPerfect for this session.

Setting the Document View to Page View

You can view the WordPerfect document window in three ways while you edit a document:

- **Draft view**. Shows only the main text of your document and not other special features, like margin guidelines or page numbers.
- **Page view**. Shows the document as it will appear when you print it, complete with page numbers and other features. In Page view, WordPerfect displays the margin guidelines.
- **Two Page view**. Same as Page view, except shows two pages at once.

Although, generally, you can work in any of these three views, you should use Page view when completing these tutorials. The document view selected by the last person who used WordPerfect will remain in place, so you might need to change the document back to Page view when you start WordPerfect.

To change the document view:

1. Click **View** on the menu bar, then click **Draft** to switch to Draft view. See Figure 1-15.

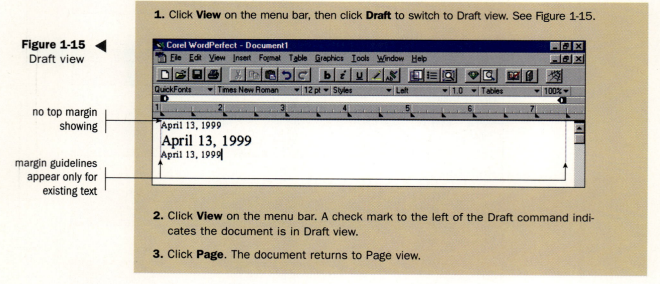

Figure 1-15 ◀ Draft view

no top margin showing

margin guidelines appear only for existing text

2. Click **View** on the menu bar. A check mark to the left of the Draft command indicates the document is in Draft view.
3. Click **Page**. The document returns to Page view.

As you can see, it is easy to switch between different views.

Displaying the Toolbars

These tutorials frequently use the Toolbar, the Power Bar, and the Ruler to help you work more efficiently. Each time you start WordPerfect, make sure all three appear on your screen, unless you're told to do something different. If one is missing, use the Toolbar/Ruler command on the View menu to display them, as you did in the section "The Toolbar, Power Bar, and Ruler Bar."

Setting the Font and Point Size

The documents you'll create in these tutorials will use the Times New Roman font in a font size of 12 points. This font size is attractive and easy to read. If your font setting is not 12-point Times New Roman, you should change the default setting to complete these tutorials.

To change the default font and font size:

1. Click **Format** then click **Font** to open the Font dialog box. See Figure 1-16.

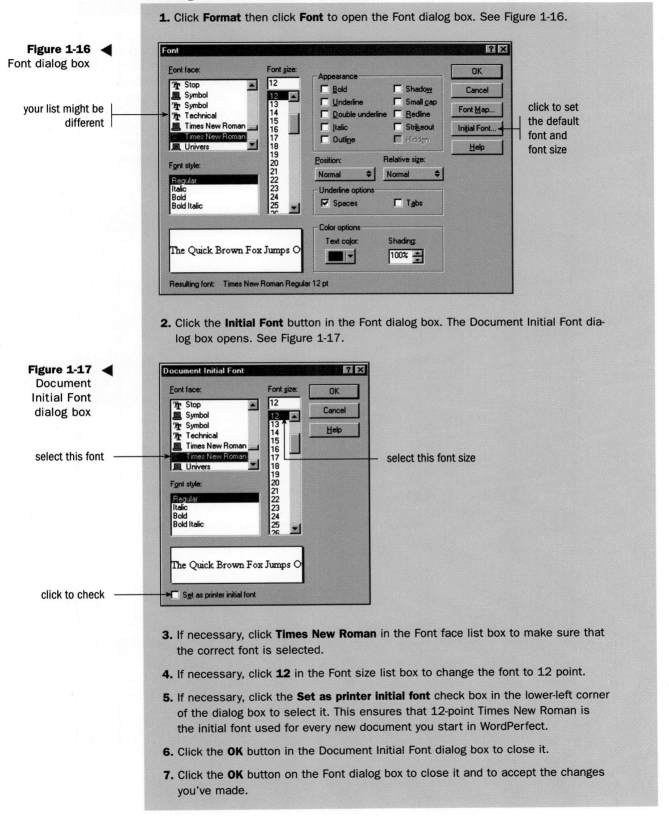

Figure 1-16 Font dialog box

your list might be different

click to set the default font and font size

2. Click the **Initial Font** button in the Font dialog box. The Document Initial Font dialog box opens. See Figure 1-17.

Figure 1-17 Document Initial Font dialog box

select this font

select this font size

click to check

3. If necessary, click **Times New Roman** in the Font face list box to make sure that the correct font is selected.

4. If necessary, click **12** in the Font size list box to change the font to 12 point.

5. If necessary, click the **Set as printer initial font** check box in the lower-left corner of the dialog box to select it. This ensures that 12-point Times New Roman is the initial font used for every new document you start in WordPerfect.

6. Click the **OK** button in the Document Initial Font dialog box to close it.

7. Click the **OK** button on the Font dialog box to close it and to accept the changes you've made.

From now on, all WordPerfect documents will have the default font set to 12-point Times New Roman.

Displaying Nonprinting Symbols

Sometimes you might find it difficult to determine if two words have a space between them or if two sentences are in different paragraphs or in the same paragraph. Fortunately, WordPerfect provides a way for you to see the spaces between words, the ends of paragraphs, and the locations of tabs and indents. **Nonprinting symbols** are characters that appear on the screen but do not show up when you print your document. For example, the nonprinting symbol to mark the end of a paragraph is ¶; the symbol to mark the space between words is •; and the symbol to mark the location of tabs is →. You can use these symbols to see whether you've typed an extra space, ended a paragraph, typed spaces instead of tabs, and so on. You'll display the nonprinting symbols now.

To display nonprinting symbols:

1. Click **View** then click **Show ¶**. This is the Show Symbols command. A dot indicating a space appears between each word, and a paragraph mark appears at the end of each paragraph in the document window.

   TROUBLE? If the Show ¶ command already was active before you clicked it, you have hidden nonprinting symbols. Repeat Step 1 to show the symbols.

2. Make sure the insertion point is positioned at the end of the third line, then press the **Enter** key to add a blank line. Notice the ¶ appears at the end of the third line.

3. Press the **Tab** key. The nonprinting symbol → marks the location of the tab in your document.

4. Type **This feature marks the location of the spaces and tabs in my document.**, then press the **Enter** key. See Figure 1-18.

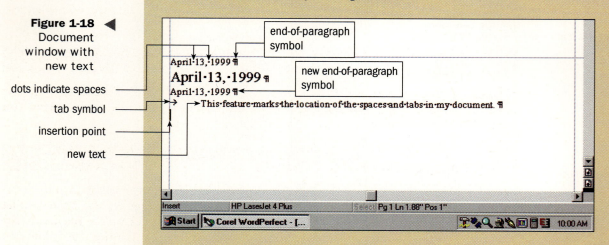

Figure 1-18 ◄
Document window with new text

dots indicate spaces

tab symbol

insertion point

new text

   TROUBLE? If you made a typing mistake in Step 4, don't worry. You'll learn how to correct errors in the next section. For now, just continue with Step 5.

5. Click **View** then click **Show ¶**. The nonprinting symbols disappear from the document window.

In these tutorials, you normally will hide the nonprinting symbols as you type and format your document.

To make the tutorials in this book as easy to follow as possible, check your screen every time you begin a new WordPerfect session as you did in this section. Complete the checklist in Figure 1-19 each time you sit down at the computer to begin a new session to ensure that your screen matches the screens in the tutorials.

Figure 1-19
Screen checklist

Screen Element	Setting	Check
Document view	Page	
Application and document windows	Maximized	
Toolbar, Power Bar, Ruler	Displayed	
Nonprinting symbols	Hidden	
Font	Times New Roman	
Font size	12 point	
Spell-As-You-Go	Active	
QuickCorrect	Replace text as you type	
Typing mode	Insert mode	

Correcting Errors

Both beginning and experienced WordPerfect users make typing mistakes. One advantage of using a word processor is that you can correct mistakes quickly and cleanly. WordPerfect provides several ways to correct errors when you're entering text or choosing a command.

Using the Backspace Key

If you discover a typing error as soon as you make it, you can press the Backspace key to erase the characters and spaces to the left of the insertion point one at a time. After you erase the error, you can type the correct characters.

Using Spell-As-You-Go

WordPerfect provides a feature, called **Spell-As-You-Go**, to check the spelling in your document as you type and to help you quickly correct potential spelling errors. If the spelling of a particular word doesn't appear as it would in the dictionary or isn't in the dictionary (for example, a person's name), a hatched red line appears beneath the word. You can accept your original spelling or use Spell-As-You-Go to help you find another spelling. You'll see how Spell-As-You-Go works by intentionally making some typographical errors.

To correct spelling with Spell-As-You-Go:

1. Carefully type the following sentence with the misspelled words "automaticaly" and "mispelled" as indicated: **WordPerfect automaticaly marks mispelled words**. Notice that as you press the spacebar after the misspelled words, a hatched red line appears beneath these words, indicating that the word might be misspelled.

   TROUBLE? If hatched red lines do not appear beneath incorrectly spelled words, the Spell-As-You-Go feature is not active. Click Tools, click Spell-As-You-Go, then continue with Step 2.

2. Move the mouse pointer over the word "automaticaly." Notice that as you move the mouse pointer within text, a vertical gray line, called a shadow pointer, also moves through the text. The **shadow pointer** marks the exact location that the insertion point would appear if you clicked the mouse.

   TROUBLE? When you move the mouse pointer through the text, you might notice a small gray icon in the left margin. This button is called the Paragraph Edit QuickSpot button. Just ignore it for now. You will see how to use it in a later tutorial.

3. Make sure the shadow pointer appears within the first misspelled word "automaticaly," then press the right mouse button. A shortcut menu opens with suggested spellings. See Figure 1-20.

Figure 1-20 ◀
Spell-As-You-Go shortcut menu

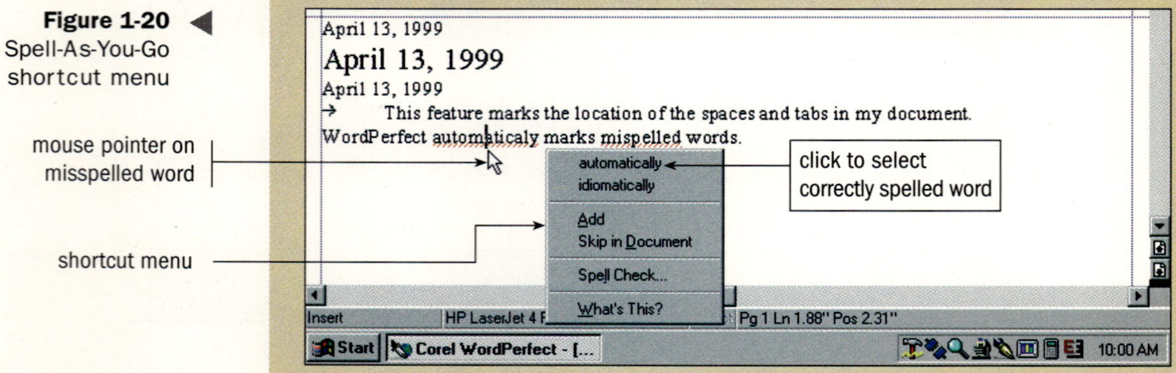

mouse pointer on misspelled word

shortcut menu

click to select correctly spelled word

4. Click **automatically** on the shortcut menu. WordPerfect replaces the misspelled word with the correctly spelled one.

5. Move the pointer to the next typing error, "mispelled," click the right mouse button, then click **misspelled** on the shortcut menu.

You have corrected both misspelled words. As you can see, the Spell-As-You-Go feature immediately identifies misspelled words and allows you to correct them quickly and accurately. WordPerfect also has a feature that automatically corrects common typing errors.

Using QuickCorrect

QuickCorrect automatically replaces commonly misspelled or mistyped words with the correct spelling as you type them, for example, "adn" for "and." You'll intentionally make some common typographical errors so you can see how QuickCorrect works.

To see QuickCorrect replace mistyped words with correct spellings:

1. If necessary, move the insertion point to the end of the last line in your document window, after the phrase "marks misspelled words," then press the **Enter** key to move the insertion point to a new blank line.

2. Carefully and slowly type the following sentence exactly as it is shown, including the errors, while watching your document window: **Mistakes ocur here adn everywhere.** Notice that when you pressed the spacebar after the word "ocur," QuickCorrect automatically corrected the spelling to "occur." As you pressed the spacebar after the word "adn," QuickCorrect automatically corrected the spelling to "and."

   TROUBLE? If the words aren't automatically corrected as you type, QuickCorrect is not active. Click Tools, then click QuickCorrect. In the QuickCorrect dialog box, click the Replace words as you type check box, then click the Close button. Press the Backspace key to delete the phrase you typed in Step 2, then repeat Step 2.

You can see how the Spell-As-You-Go and QuickCorrect features can help you quickly and easily produce error-free documents.

Closing the Document Window

Now that you are familiar with the WordPerfect screen and some basic WordPerfect skills, you're ready to begin typing Karen's letter to the Tacoma Chamber of Commerce. Before you create the letter, you must make sure the document window is empty. If it isn't, any text that appears in the window will be part of the document when you print it.

REFERENCE window

CLOSING A DOCUMENT WITHOUT SAVING CHANGES

- Click the document Close button (or click File then click Close).
- Click the No button to indicate that you don't want to save the changes to the document.

You'll clear the screen by closing the document window.

To close the document window without saving changes:

1. Click **File** then click **Close**. A dialog box with the prompt "Save changes to Document1?" opens. In this instance, you want to close the document window without saving the document.

2. Click the **No** button to close the current document window without saving it.

You have closed the current document window without saving its contents. The WordPerfect window remains open with a new, blank document window.

Quick Check

1. In your own words, list and describe the steps for planning a document.

2. Define each of the following in your own words:
   a. Toolbar
   b. Ruler
   c. status bar
   d. shortcut key
   e. default setting

3. What does the status bar message *Ln 3.3"* mean?

4. How do you automatically insert today's date into a WordPerfect document? Give two methods.

5. What is a font? How do you change the font size?

6. How do you display or hide the Ruler Bar?

7. What is Spell-As-You-Go, how does it indicate a potential spelling error, and how do you correct a spelling error?

8. What is QuickCorrect?

You have completed Session 1.1. If you aren't going to work through Session 1.2 now, you should exit WordPerfect by clicking the Close button on the WordPerfect window. When you're ready to begin Session 1.2, start WordPerfect, go through the screen checklist in Figure 1-19, then continue with the session.

SESSION 1.2

In this session you will create a document using WordPerfect. You'll scroll through your document, as well as name, save, preview, and print the document. You'll also set up and print an envelope.

Typing a Letter

You're ready to type Karen's letter to the Tacoma Chamber of Commerce. Figure 1-21 shows the complete letter printed on the company letterhead.

Figure 1-21 ◀
Job fair letter

You'll begin by inserting the date, then typing the inside address and the salutation of the letter. You need to start the date about 2½ inches from the top margin of the paper to allow space for the Crossroads letterhead.

To open a new document and insert the date:

1. Make sure a blank document window appears on the screen, then press the Enter key eight times. The insertion point moves down about 1½ inches from the top margin, allowing space for the letterhead. The Ln value on the status bar

should read about 2.57", indicating that the insertion point is about 2½ inches from the top of the page. See Figure 1-22.

Figure 1-22 ◄
Document window after inserting blank lines

top margin

inserted blank lines

insertion point at about 2.57 inches from top of page

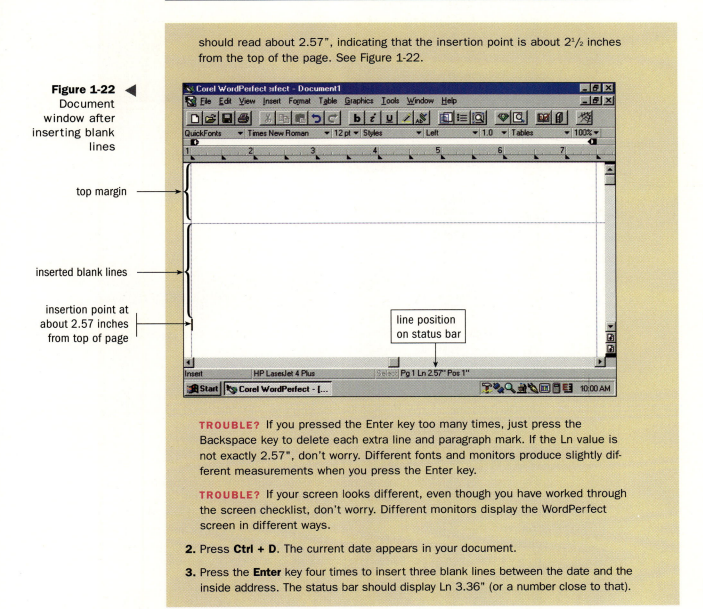

line position on status bar

TROUBLE? If you pressed the Enter key too many times, just press the Backspace key to delete each extra line and paragraph mark. If the Ln value is not exactly 2.57", don't worry. Different fonts and monitors produce slightly different measurements when you press the Enter key.

TROUBLE? If your screen looks different, even though you have worked through the screen checklist, don't worry. Different monitors display the WordPerfect screen in different ways.

2. Press **Ctrl + D**. The current date appears in your document.

3. Press the **Enter** key four times to insert three blank lines between the date and the inside address. The status bar should display Ln 3.36" (or a number close to that).

Next, you'll enter the inside address shown on Karen's note.

Entering Text

You'll enter the inside address by typing it. If you type a wrong character, simply press the Backspace key to delete the character and then retype it.

To type the inside address:

1. Type **Deborah Brown, President** then press the **Enter** key.

   TROUBLE? If a hatched red line appears beneath a word, check to make sure you typed the word correctly. If you did not, either press the Backspace key and retype it correctly, or use the Spell-As-You-Go shortcut menu.

2. Type the following text, pressing the **Enter** key after each line to enter the inside address.

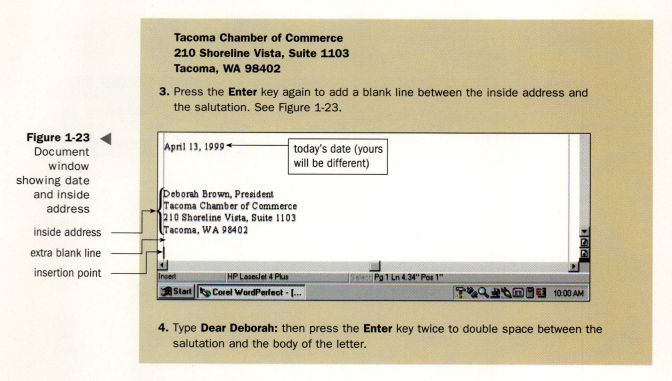

Figure 1-23
Document window showing date and inside address

inside address
extra blank line
insertion point

4. Type **Dear Deborah:** then press the **Enter** key twice to double space between the salutation and the body of the letter.

You have entered the date, the inside address, and the salutation of Karen's letter in a standard business letter format. Before you complete the letter, however, you should save what you have typed so far.

Saving a Document

The letter on which you are working is stored only in your computer's memory, not on a disk. If you were to exit WordPerfect, turn off your computer, or experience an accidental power failure, the part of Karen's letter that you just typed would be lost. For this reason, you should get in the habit of frequently saving your documents to a disk. Unless a document is very short, don't wait until you've typed the entire document before saving it. As a rule, you should save your work at least every 15 minutes.

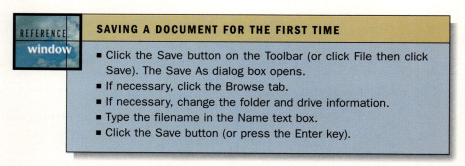

SAVING A DOCUMENT FOR THE FIRST TIME

- Click the Save button on the Toolbar (or click File then click Save). The Save As dialog box opens.
- If necessary, click the Browse tab.
- If necessary, change the folder and drive information.
- Type the filename in the Name text box.
- Click the Save button (or press the Enter key).

One advantage of Windows 95 over previous versions of Windows is the ability to use long filenames. You can, and should, use filenames that include a word that clearly identifies the type of document, for example, Letter, Report, Memo, or Agenda. You also should add other words to indicate the specific content of the document, for example, the addressee of a letter (Jackson, Cornell University, Mountain Fuel, and so forth). Finally, you might want to include what version of a document the file is, for example, Q3 (for a third-quarter report), June 99 (for a June 1999 invoice), 3 (for the third memo on a particular topic to a particular person).

Here are some sample filenames:

Annual Report 95
Mueller Thanks Letter
Company Policy Manual Chapter 1

A little thought in naming a file will save you a lot of time when you are searching for a specific file on your disk.

After you name your document, WordPerfect automatically appends the .wpd filename extension. This way, Windows 95 can identify the file as a Corel WordPerfect file. Depending on how Windows 95 is configured on your computer, you might not see .wpd. The filename extension is still part of the filename; it is just not displayed. These tutorials assume that filename extensions are hidden.

Although you haven't been working on this letter for 15 minutes yet, you should save the document now, just to be safe.

To save a document:

1. Insert your WordPerfect Student Disk into drive A. These tutorials assume that you have a hard disk (drive C) and at least one disk drive (drive A), and that you're using drive A. If you're using drive B, substitute "drive B" whenever you read "drive A" in these tutorials.

2. Click the **Save** button on the Toolbar. Because this is the first time you've saved the document, the Save As dialog box opens. See Figure 1-24.

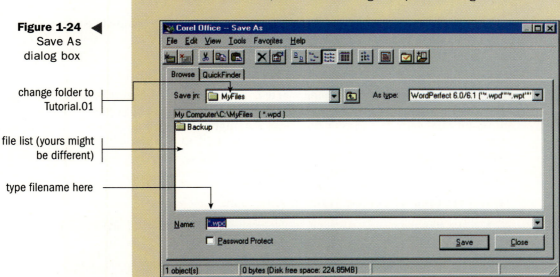

Figure 1-24 ◀
Save As dialog box

change folder to Tutorial.01

file list (yours might be different)

type filename here

The first time you save a document, WordPerfect opens the Save As dialog box so you can type a name for the document and specify the folder in which you want to save it. After you've saved a document once and then press the Save button, WordPerfect will save it using the filename and folder you entered in the Save As dialog box.

3. If necessary, click the **Browse** tab to make it the frontmost tab in the Save As dialog box.

4. Click the **Save in** list arrow, drag the **scroll box** to the top of the scroll bar, click **3½ Floppy (A)** or the drive in which your Student Disk is located, then double-click the **Tutorial.01** folder. The Tutorial.01 folder is now open for saving the file.

5. Click in the Name text box, then type **Tacoma Job Fair Letter** (the name you want to give your document). See Figure 1-25.

Figure 1-25 ◀
Save As dialog box with desired folder and filename

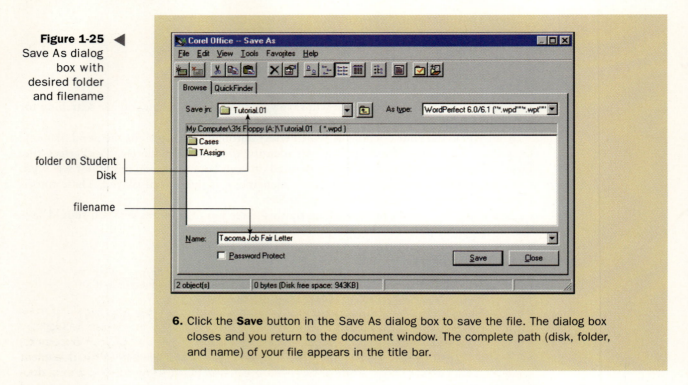

folder on Student Disk

filename

6. Click the **Save** button in the Save As dialog box to save the file. The dialog box closes and you return to the document window. The complete path (disk, folder, and name) of your file appears in the title bar.

With the letter saved to your Student Disk, you're ready to complete Karen's letter.

Observing Word Wrap

As you type the body of the letter, do not press the Enter key at the end of each line. Instead, WordPerfect will determine where to end one line and begin the next. When you type a word that extends into the right margin, both the insertion point and the word move automatically to the next line. This automatic line breaking of text is called **word wrap**. Word wrap ensures that each line of text fits between the left and right margins without you having to press the Enter key at the end of each line. You'll see how word wrap works as you type the body of Karen's letter.

To observe word wrap while typing a paragraph:

1. Make sure the insertion point is two lines below the salutation, at about Ln 4.74". If necessary, move it to that location by pressing the arrow keys.

2. Type the following sentence slowly, watching carefully when the insertion point automatically jumps to the next line: **Recently, you contacted our staff about the Chamber's decision to sponsor a job fair again this year.** WordPerfect automatically moved the word "year" to a new line. See Figure 1-26.

beginning of first paragraph

Figure 1-26 ◀
Wrapping text

word wrapped to new line

end of line after word wrap

> **TROUBLE?** If your line wrapped at a different word than shown in Figure 1-26 or the Ln value in your status bar does not match the one in Figure 1-26, don't be concerned. The word at which word wrap occurs and the status bar values might differ because fonts have varying letter widths and produce slightly different measurements on monitors. These slight variations are common. Continue with Step 3.
>
> 3. Press the **spacebar** twice to insert space before the next sentence, then type **We are interested in participating as we have done in the past.** to enter the rest of the first paragraph of the letter.
>
> 4. Press the **Enter** key to end the first paragraph, then press the **Enter** key again to double space between the first and second paragraphs.

You are ready to type the text of the second paragraph.

Scrolling

After finishing the last set of steps, the insertion point should be near the bottom of your document window. It might seem that no room is left in the document window to type the rest of Karen's letter. However, as you continue to add text at the end of your document, the text that you typed earlier will shift up and disappear from the top of the document window. This shifting up or down of text, called **scrolling**, allows you to view a long document one screen at a time. The entire document is still in the computer's memory and available for editing; you just can't see it all at once. Figure 1-27 illustrates scrolling.

Figure 1-27 ◀
Scrolling the document window

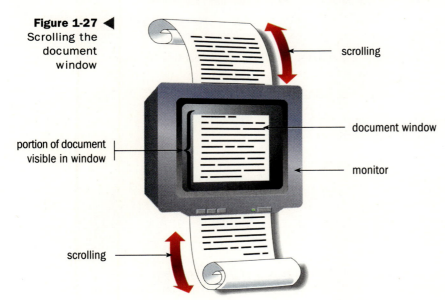

You'll see how scrolling works as you enter the final text of Karen's letter.

To observe scrolling while you're entering text:

> 1. Make sure the insertion point is at the end of the document.
>
> 2. Type the second paragraph, as shown in Figure 1-28, then press the **Enter** key twice to insert a blank line. Notice that as you type the paragraph, the date scrolls off the top of the document window. If you make a mistake in your typing, remember to use WordPerfect's Spell-As-You-Go feature to correct the misspelled word.

Figure 1-28
Text scrolled off the screen

date and part of inside address scrolled off screen

second and third paragraphs

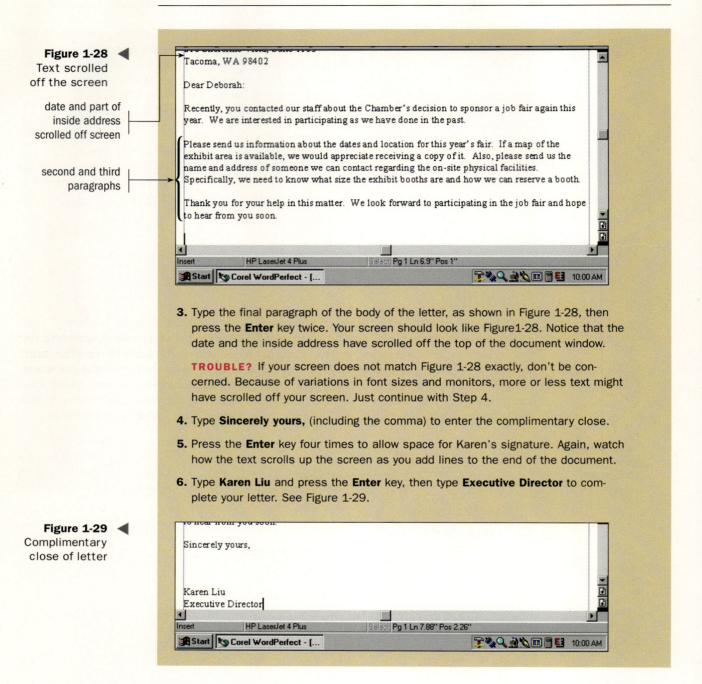

3. Type the final paragraph of the body of the letter, as shown in Figure 1-28, then press the **Enter** key twice. Your screen should look like Figure1-28. Notice that the date and the inside address have scrolled off the top of the document window.

   TROUBLE? If your screen does not match Figure 1-28 exactly, don't be concerned. Because of variations in font sizes and monitors, more or less text might have scrolled off your screen. Just continue with Step 4.

4. Type **Sincerely yours,** (including the comma) to enter the complimentary close.

5. Press the **Enter** key four times to allow space for Karen's signature. Again, watch how the text scrolls up the screen as you add lines to the end of the document.

6. Type **Karen Liu** and press the **Enter** key, then type **Executive Director** to complete your letter. See Figure 1-29.

Figure 1-29
Complimentary close of letter

In the last set of steps, you watched the text at the top of your document move off your screen. You can scroll this hidden text back into view so you can read the beginning of the letter. When you do, the text at the bottom of the screen will disappear or scroll out of view.

To scroll the text using the scroll bar:

1. Position the mouse pointer on the **Scroll Up** button ▲ at the top of the vertical scroll bar, then press and hold the mouse button to scroll the text. Notice that as one line of text reappears at the top of the document, one line of text disappears from the bottom of the document. When the text stops scrolling, you have reached the top of the document and can see the beginning of the letter.

2. Position the mouse pointer on the **Scroll Down** button ▼ on the vertical scroll bar, then press and hold the mouse button until the end of the letter is in view.

As you did with the letter, you can scroll to view any part of a document that is too long to fit within the document window. Now that you have finished typing the letter, you'll save the completed document.

Saving the Completed Letter

Although you saved the letter earlier, the text you typed since then exists only in the computer's memory. The version currently on your disk is incomplete. You must save your document after you complete it, even if you've saved the document one or more times while you created it. You should get into the habit of saving your document frequently while working and again just before you print. Then, if you experience problems that cause your computer to stop working while you are printing, you still will have a copy of the document on your disk.

To save the completed letter:

1. Make sure your Student Disk is still in drive A.
2. Click the **Save** button 💾 on the Toolbar.

Because you named and saved this file earlier, you can save the document without being prompted for information. The mouse pointer changes to ⌛ while the file is being written to the disk. Notice that the insertion point can be anywhere in the document window when you save a document.

Previewing and Printing a Document

Although you have completed the letter, you probably find it difficult to visualize how the letter fits on a page. The current document window displays the text, but you cannot see an entire page without scrolling or changing the margins. WordPerfect provides a method for viewing the full page of the letter before you print it, called **Full Page view**. You'll preview the full page of Karen's letter before printing it.

To preview the document:

1. Click the **Page/Zoom Full** button 🔍 on the Toolbar. The document shrinks in size so the page fits within the document window. Now you can see how the letter fits on the page. See Figure 1-30.

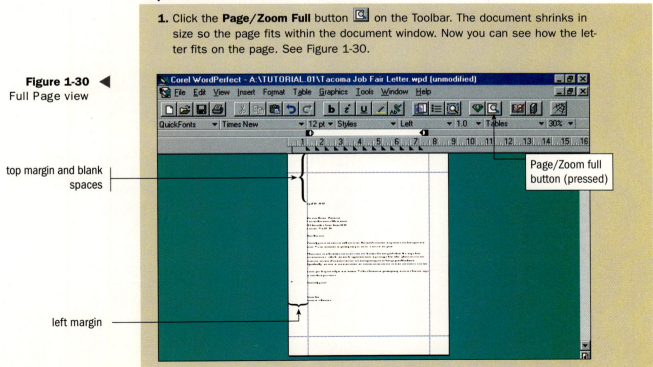

Figure 1-30 ◄
Full Page view

top margin and blank spaces

Page/Zoom full button (pressed)

left margin

> In concept, you can enter and edit text in Full Page view but usually the text is so tiny that, in practice, you have to return to Page view to work with the document.
>
> 2. Click [icon] again to return to Page view.

You've looked at how the letter will appear on the printed page. The text looks well spaced and the letterhead will fit at the top of the page. You're ready to print the letter.

The first time each session you print from a shared computer, you should check the settings in the Print dialog box, and make sure the number of copies is set to one.

To print a document:

> 1. Make sure your printer is turned on and has paper.
> 2. Click the **Print** button [icon] on the Toolbar. The Print dialog box opens. See Figure 1-31.

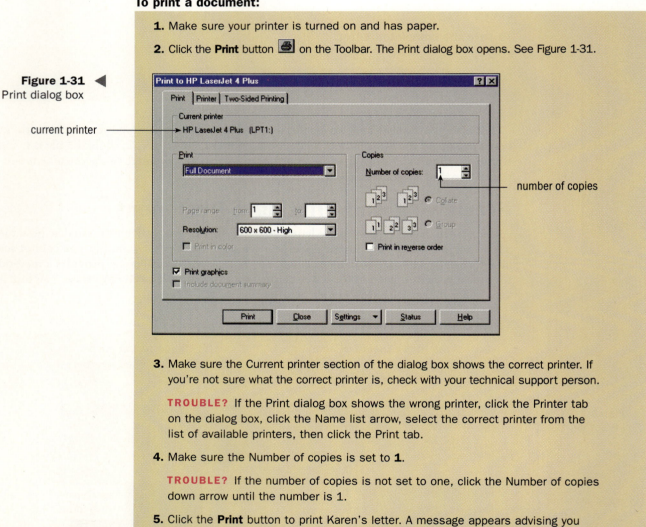

Figure 1-31
Print dialog box

current printer

number of copies

> 3. Make sure the Current printer section of the dialog box shows the correct printer. If you're not sure what the correct printer is, check with your technical support person.
>
>   **TROUBLE?** If the Print dialog box shows the wrong printer, click the Printer tab on the dialog box, click the Name list arrow, select the correct printer from the list of available printers, then click the Print tab.
>
> 4. Make sure the Number of copies is set to **1**.
>
>   **TROUBLE?** If the number of copies is not set to one, click the Number of copies down arrow until the number is 1.
>
> 5. Click the **Print** button to print Karen's letter. A message appears advising you that your document is being prepared for printing, and the mouse pointer changes to [icon].

Your printed letter should look similar to Figure 1-21 only without the Crossroads letterhead. The word wraps, or line breaks, might not appear in the same places on your letter because the size and spacing of characters can vary slightly with different printers, affecting the final output.

Printing an Envelope

You also need to prepare an envelope in which Karen can mail the letter to the Tacoma Chamber of Commerce. In WordPerfect, it is easy to address an envelope and print it. *Before you attempt to print the envelope, check with your instructor or technical support person to make sure you can print envelopes.* If not, whenever you are instructed to print an envelope, just print on an 8½ × 11-inch sheet of paper.

To set up and print an envelope:

1. Click **Format** then click **Envelope**. The Envelope dialog box opens. See Figure 1-32.

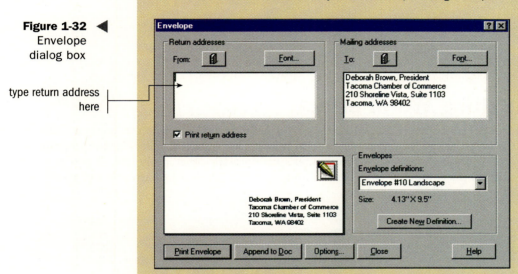

Figure 1-32 ◀
Envelope dialog box

type return address here

The address for Deborah Brown appears automatically in the Mailing addresses section of the dialog box. The information in the Return addresses section will vary, depending on who installed WordPerfect on your computer.

If you were using an envelope on which your company's return address already was printed, you would print the envelope without typing a return address. However, your envelope doesn't have the Crossroads return address.

2. If necessary, click the **Print return address** check box to select it.

3. Click anywhere in the From text box. If necessary, press the **Delete** key and the **Backspace** key to delete any text currently in the text box.

4. Type the following, pressing the **Enter** key after each line:

   Karen Liu followed by your name in parentheses
   Crossroads
   1414 East Bellingham S.W.
   Suite 318
   Tacoma, WA 98402

5. Make sure a piece of paper or a blank envelope is correctly positioned in your printer, then click the **Print Envelope** button.

   TROUBLE? If the font on the text of the envelope is the wrong size, click the Font button in the Return addresses section, make sure the font is set to 12-point Times New Roman, then click the OK button. Repeat this procedure to set the proper font in the Mailing addresses section.

Your envelope prints and should look like the envelope shown in Figure 1-33, except that your name will appear in parentheses after Karen Liu.

Figure 1-33
Printed envelope

Exiting WordPerfect

You have finished typing and printing the letter and envelope to the Tacoma Chamber of Commerce, and you're ready to **exit**, or quit, WordPerfect. Closing the program when you're finished frees up the computer's memory for other programs. If you're going to turn off the computer, you always should exit WordPerfect and any other program as part of your shutdown procedure.

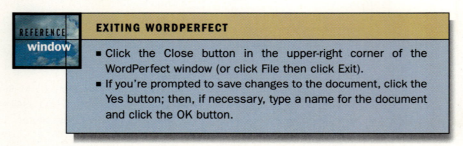

REFERENCE window

EXITING WORDPERFECT

- Click the Close button in the upper-right corner of the WordPerfect window (or click File then click Exit).
- If you're prompted to save changes to the document, click the Yes button; then, if necessary, type a name for the document and click the OK button.

Because you've completed the first draft of Karen's letter, you'll exit WordPerfect.

To exit WordPerfect:

1. Click the **Close** button ✖ in the upper-right corner of the WordPerfect window. Because you haven't modified the document since you last saved it, WordPerfect closes and you immediately exit to the Windows 95 desktop.

   TROUBLE? If a dialog box opens with the message "Save changes to Tacoma Job Fair Letter?" you have made changes to the document since the last time you saved it. You should save the document again before exiting. Click the Yes button to save the current version and exit WordPerfect.

You give the letter and envelope for the Tacoma Chamber of Commerce to Karen for her to review.

1. Why should you save a document to your disk several times, even if you haven't finished typing it?

2. What is the difference between the Save and Save As commands?

3. How do you see the portion of the document that has scrolled from sight?

4. What is Full Page view and when should you use it?

5. What is the difference between scrolling and word wrap?

6. How often should you save a document?

7. How do you print an envelope?

8. How do you exit WordPerfect?

SESSION 1.3

In this session you will open and rename an existing document, edit the document, and insert and delete text. You'll also use WordPerfect's Help feature to get additional information on commands, features, and screen elements.

Opening an Existing Document

After you typed, saved, and printed the first draft of the letter to the Tacoma Chamber of Commerce, Karen reviewed the letter and made some edits, as shown in Figure 1-34. She added a note that you should ask how many people the Chamber of Commerce anticipates will attend the job fair this year and requests a couple of other changes. To make these changes to the letter, you need to open the document file from your Student Disk and store it in the computer's memory.

Figure 1-34
Job fair letter with Karen's corrections

You can open a document from the menu bar or the Toolbar. Also, the last six files you worked on are listed at the bottom of the File menu. You can open any of these six files by clicking the one you want to edit.

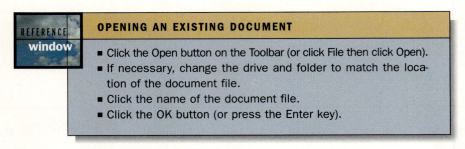

OPENING AN EXISTING DOCUMENT
- Click the Open button on the Toolbar (or click File then click Open).
- If necessary, change the drive and folder to match the location of the document file.
- Click the name of the document file.
- Click the OK button (or press the Enter key).

You'll open the letter to the Tacoma Chamber of Commerce so you can make Karen's changes.

To open an existing document:

1. Start WordPerfect as you did earlier in this tutorial (see the section called "Starting WordPerfect").

2. Make sure your Student Disk is in drive A or the appropriate disk drive.

3. Click the **Open** button on the Toolbar. The Open dialog box opens.

4. Click the **Look in** list arrow to display the list of available drives and files.

5. Click **3½ Floppy (A:)** or the letter of the drive containing your Student Disk. Notice that the window changes to reflect the contents of the selected drive.

6. Double-click the **Tutorial.01** folder to open the folder that contains the letter.

7. Click **Tacoma Job Fair Letter** to select it. In your list of files, the filename might appear with the ".wpd" filename extension. See Figure 1-35.

Figure 1-35
Open dialog box

folder on Student Disk

select this file

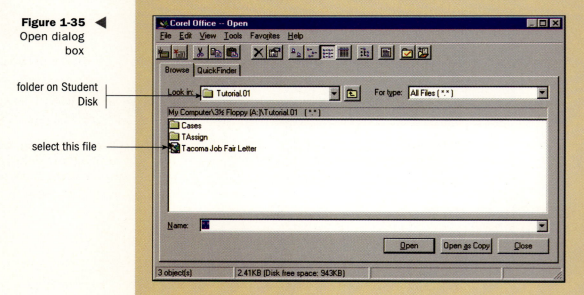

TROUBLE? If you can't find the file, make sure you're looking in the correct folder in the correct drive. If you're looking in the correct place but the letter isn't there, you might have saved the file to the hard disk of your computer. If you're working on the same computer as you were when you saved the document, check drive C. If you still can't locate your file, ask your technical support person for help.

8. Click the **Open** button to open the letter.

The letter opens in the document window and you can edit it.

Moving the Insertion Point

The insertion point is at the beginning of your letter to the Tacoma Chamber of Commerce, but for you to make Karen's changes it needs to be at a different point in the letter. One of the simplest ways to move the insertion point to a new location is to position the mouse pointer at the new location and click the mouse button. When the pointer is in the document window, you can tell its exact location within the text with the shadow pointer. Karen asked you to add new text to the letter, insert new text within the existing text, and edit the salutation.

You'll begin by moving the insertion point to the desired location and typing the new paragraph.

To move the insertion point and add the new paragraph:

1. Scroll the document until you see the end of the second paragraph.

2. Move the mouse pointer so the shadow pointer is immediately to the right of "...reserve a booth." at the end of the second paragraph, then click. The status bar changes to indicate the new position of the insertion point. See Figure 1-36.

Figure 1-36 ◀
Insertion point at end of second paragraph

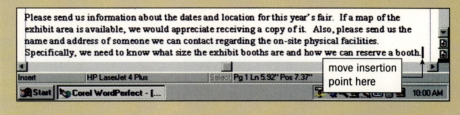

3. Press the **Enter** key twice to insert a blank line between the second and third paragraphs.

4. Type **In addition, we would like to know how many people you anticipate will attend this year's job fair.**

Now that you have typed the additional paragraph, you're ready to edit the previous paragraph by making changes to existing text.

Inserting Text

You can add new text into existing text without typing over or erasing it by using the **Insert mode**, WordPerfect's default typing mode. In Insert mode, the existing text shifts to the right as you add new text, and, if necessary, the line breaks change to accommodate the new text.

To insert new text into existing text:

1. Make sure WordPerfect is in Insert mode. The word "Insert" appears on the left edge of the status bar. If you see "Typeover" instead, press the **Insert** key.

2. If necessary, scroll to the first paragraph, then click to the left of the letter "a" in the word "again" in the first paragraph.

3. Type **in Tacoma** then press the **spacebar**. As you type the new text, the existing text moves to the right. The words "Tacoma" and "again" might temporarily wrap to the next line. After you press the spacebar, the line break probably will occur between "Tacoma" and "again."

4. Move the mouse pointer so the shadow pointer appears between the letter "t" in "past" and the period at the end of the first paragraph, then click.

5. Press the **spacebar** then type **three years**. As you type, the period moves to the right and WordPerfect inserts the new text. See Figure 1-37.

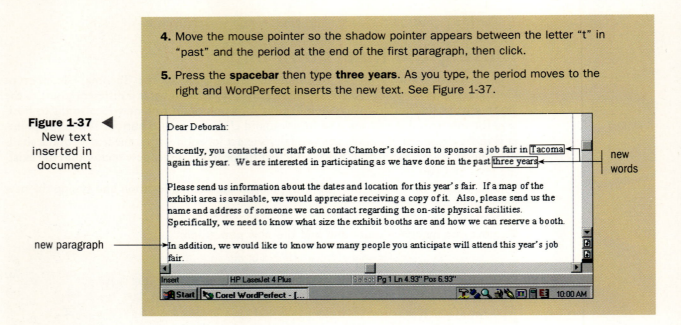

Figure 1-37
New text inserted in document

new paragraph

new words

It's as easy to remove text as it is to insert it.

Deleting Text

Next, you need to change a word in the first paragraph. Earlier, you deleted text to the left of the insertion point with the Backspace key. Now you'll use the Delete key to erase a space or character to the right of the insertion point.

To delete text using the Delete key:

1. Click the shadow pointer to the left of the "p" in "past" at the end of the first paragraph.

2. Press the **Delete** key to erase the "p." The remainder of the word, "ast," moves left to fill the space.

3. Type **l** to make the word "last." WordPerfect inserts the letter and the existing text moves to the right. See Figure 1-38.

Figure 1-38
Document window after making corrections

corrected word

Deleting text one character at a time is inefficient if you have more than one letter to erase. In WordPerfect, you can delete an entire word using a combination of keystrokes. Figure 1-39 summarizes the keystrokes you can use to delete text one character or word at a time.

Figure 1-39
Summary of deletion shortcut keys

Shortcut Key	Deletion
Backspace	Character to left of insertion point
Delete	Character to right of insertion point
Ctrl + Backspace	Word
Ctrl + Delete	From insertion point to end of line

Using Typeover Mode

Although Insert mode is WordPerfect's default typing mode, you can change WordPerfect to another mode of typing called **Typeover mode**. Typeover mode allows you to replace existing text as you type new text; it isn't used very often because it is easy to type over too much text and erase text you want to keep. However, Typeover mode works well for replacing numbers in columns. When you switch to Typeover mode, the word "Typeover" appears in the left corner of the status bar.

You'll use Typeover mode to change the name of the Tacoma Chamber of Commerce president.

To edit text using Typeover mode:

1. Scroll to view the salutation "Dear Deborah," then click the shadow pointer to the right of the "b" in "Deborah."

2. Press the **Insert** key to switch to Typeover mode. The word "Typeover" appears on the left edge of the status bar. See Figure 1-40.

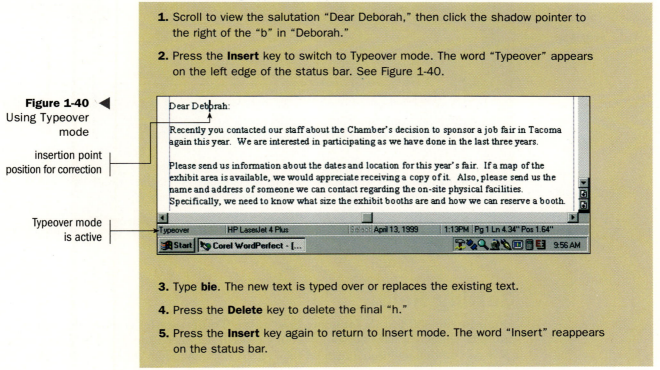

Figure 1-40
Using Typeover mode

insertion point position for correction

Typeover mode is active

3. Type **bie**. The new text is typed over or replaces the existing text.

4. Press the **Delete** key to delete the final "h."

5. Press the **Insert** key again to return to Insert mode. The word "Insert" reappears on the status bar.

You have edited the letter according to Karen's instructions and should save the completed letter so your file includes the most recent changes.

Saving a Document with a New Filename

Karen asked you to keep the original file intact, in case she decides she prefers the first version of the letter, and to save the revised version with a new name, Tacoma Job Fair Letter 2. You can change the save settings that you defined earlier for the letter from the Save As dialog box. First, you'll give a new name to the most recent version of the letter, then you'll print the edited document.

To save the edited letter with a different filename and print it

1. Click **File**, then click **Save As** to open the Save As dialog box. This is the same dialog box you used to save an unnamed file earlier.

2. Click after the "r" in "Letter" in the Name text box.

3. Press the **spacebar**, then type **2** to make the filename "Tacoma Job Fair Letter 2." This indicates that the current document is the second version of the letter. See Figure 1-41.

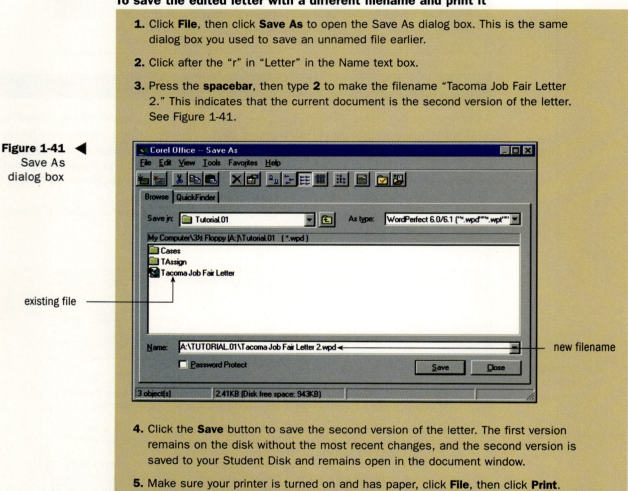

Figure 1-41 ◀
Save As
dialog box

existing file

new filename

4. Click the **Save** button to save the second version of the letter. The first version remains on the disk without the most recent changes, and the second version is saved to your Student Disk and remains open in the document window.

5. Make sure your printer is turned on and has paper, click **File**, then click **Print**.

The final copy of the letter is printed.

Getting Help

Although you will learn a lot about how to use WordPerfect by working through these tutorials, you might have questions about a procedure or need additional help on a topic. How do you find additional help on the Font Size command on the Power Bar? How do you learn more about Page view? You can use WordPerfect's Help system.

WordPerfect's online Help system provides quick access to information about commands, features, and screen elements. You can use Help to:

- get context-sensitive Help as you work
- look for general information with WordPerfect's Contents feature
- search for help on specific topics with the Index, Find, and Ask the PerfectExpert features

You'll try all three methods of getting help.

Using Context-Sensitive Help

To help you work more efficiently, WordPerfect provides context-sensitive Help. **Context-sensitive help** is information about commands and features currently on the screen. You'll use context-sensitive Help to learn about the Font Size feature on the Power Bar.

To use context-sensitive Help:

1. Press and hold down the **Shift** key, then press the **F1** key. This is the Shift + F1 key combination for the What Is? command, which provides context-sensitive Help. The mouse pointer changes to ?.

2. Click the **Font size** button on the Power Bar. A description of how to set the font size appears on the screen. See Figure 1-42.

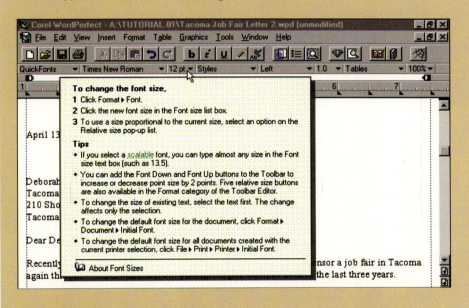

Figure 1-42 ◀
Help window with description of Font Size button

3. Read the information on changing fonts.

4. Click inside the information window. The information window closes.

You can use the What Is? pointer to get a definition or description of any portion of the WordPerfect screen.

Using the Help Topics Window

WordPerfect provides general information about many topics. You can look up a specific entry in the Index or ask a specific question in the Ask the PerfectExpert and select from a list of related topics. You'll use this window to find information about page views.

To use the Help Topics window:

1. Click **Help** then click **Help Topics**. The Help Topics dialog box opens.

2. If necessary, click the **Index** tab to make it active. If necessary, click in the text box at the top of the dialog box to move the insertion point there. See Figure 1-43.

Figure 1-43
Help Topics dialog box

Index tab is active

type help item here

3. Type **page**, the first word of the feature you're looking for. A list of topics related to "page" appears in the dialog box.

4. Click the **Scroll Down** button ▼ until you see the word "views" just above the word "palette (colors)."

5. Click **views**, then click the **Display** button. The Help window opens with information about the topic. See Figure 1-44.

Figure 1-44
Help window with description of page view

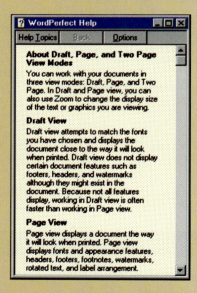

6. Read the description of page views, then click the **Close** button ☒ in the upper-right corner of the Help window to close the Help window and return to your document.

7. Click the **Close** button ☒ in the upper-right corner of the document window to close the letter.

You can use WordPerfect's Help feature any time you want more information about a command or feature.

You have now completed all the steps for producing a document: planning, typing and editing, formatting, and printing. You give the revised letter to Karen. She signs and mails it.

Quick Check

1. List three ways to open a document.
2. What is the quickest way to move the insertion point to another location in the document window?
3. What is the difference between the insertion point and the shadow pointer?
4. What is Typeover mode and when would you use it?
5. What is the difference between the Backspace key and the Delete key?
6. How do you save a document with a new filename?
7. Define context-sensitive Help and describe how it works.
8. How can you locate information about the Print command?

You have completed Tutorial 1. If you aren't going to work through the Tutorial Assignments now, you should exit WordPerfect.

Tutorial Assignments

Karen asks you to create a thank-you letter for people who donated to Crossroads and a memo to sign up Crossroads employees for the upcoming job fair. Start WordPerfect, if necessary, and make sure your Student Disk is in drive A. Check your screen to make sure your settings match those in the tutorials, then open the document DonLet in the TAssign folder in the Tutorial.01 folder on your Student Disk, then complete the following:

1. Save the file as My Donor Thanks Letter.
2. Delete the date and insert today's date using the Date command.
3. Replace the inside address with your name and address, as if the letter were being written to you.
4. Change the salutation to your first name.
5. Use Spell-As-You-Go to correct the misspelled words in the first paragraph, indicated by the hatched red lines.
6. Move to the left of the word "helps" in the second paragraph, press the spacebar, then insert: "is a nonprofit organization that".
7. Using Typeover mode, change the word "garments" in the third paragraph to "clothing."
8. Scroll to the beginning of the letter. Insert room for the letterhead by pressing the Enter key until the date is about 2.5 inches from the top of the page.
9. Save the document with the changes, then preview and print the letter.
10. Print an envelope on an 8½ × 11-inch sheet of paper.

11. Move the mouse pointer around the WordPerfect screen. Describe four shapes of the mouse pointer that you see.
12. Close the document.

13. Open the document DonLet by clicking the filename from the File menu. Close the file without saving changes to the document.

Use Figure 1-45 to complete Assignments 14 through 16.

Figure 1-45

> MEMORANDUM - Crossroads
>
> Date: July 31, 1999
>
> To: Staff Members
>
> From: Karen Lui
>
> Re: Dates for the 1999 Job Fair
>
> The 1999 Job Fair sponsored by the Tacoma Chamber of Commerce will be held September 15 through 20 from 10:00 A.M. to 5:30 P.M. This fair provides us with an opportunity to inform Tacoma residents about our services. In the past, we have each spent one day helping at the exhibit. Please let me know by tomorrow which day you would prefer to be at the exhibit.
>
> Thanks.

14. Create a new document.
15. Type the memo shown in Figure 1-45. (*Hint*: Press the Tab key after "Date:," "To:," "From:," and "Re:," then type the rest of each line.)
16. Insert today's date using the Date command.
17. After completing the memo, type your first name at the end of the memo. Use context-sensitive Help to find out about the Undo button ↶ on the Toolbar, then use the Undo command to undo the name you have typed.
18. Save the document as Fair Date Memo. View the memo in Full Page view, then print and close the memo.

Case Problems

1. Letter to Confirm a Conference Date As convention director for the Tallahassee Convention and Visitors Bureau, you and your staff are responsible for promoting and scheduling the convention center. The Southern Georgia chapter of the National Purchasing Management Association has reserved the convention center for its annual conference on October 24-25, 1999, and has requested a written confirmation of its reservation. The body of the letter already is written; you need only to insert specific information for this group.

Open the document Confirm from the Cases folder in theTutorial.01 folder on your Student Disk. Immediately save the document back to your Student Disk as Confirmation Letter NPMA and do the following:
1. Insert six blank lines at the beginning of the document to leave sufficient space for a letterhead.
2. Use the Date command to insert today's date at the insertion point.
3. Using the proper business letter format, type the inside address "Danetta Blackwelder, 618 Live Oak Plantation Road, Valdosta, GA 31355" four lines below the date.
4. Double space after the inside address, type the salutation "Dear Ms. Blackwelder:", then double space after the salutation.
5. Insert the date "October 24-25, 1999" at the end of the first paragraph.
6. Move the insertion point to the end of the document, insert a blank line, then type the complimentary close "Sincerely," (include the comma).
7. Add four blank lines to leave room for the signature, then type your name and title.

8. Use WordPerfect's Help feature to find out how to center a line of text, then center the date near the beginning of the letter.
9. Save the letter then preview it in Full Page view.
10. Print the letter then close it.

2. Letter to Request Information About a "Learning to Fly" Franchise Jeff and Seone Polychronis, who manage the UpTown Sports Mall, are interested in obtaining a franchise for "Learning to Fly," a free-fall bungee jumping venture marketed by Ultimate Sports, Inc. After reading an advertisement for the franchise, Jeff decides to write for more information. He already has written a draft of the letter and asks you to edit it.

Open the document Bungee from the Cases folder in the Tutorial.01 folder on your Student Disk. Immediately save the document back to your Student Disk as Bungee Request Letter then do the following:

1. Insert six blank lines at the beginning of the document to insert sufficient space for a letterhead.
2. Use the Date command to insert today's date.
3. Insert four blank lines after the date and, using the proper business letter format, type the inside address: "Ultimate Sports, Inc., 4161 Comanche Drive, Colorado Springs, CO 80906".
4. Insert a blank line after the inside address, type the salutation "Dear Franchise Representative:", and insert another blank line.
5. Correct any spelling errors.
6. Use WordPerfect's Help feature to learn how to insert bullets before typing text. (*Hint*: Look in the topic "bullets and numbers.") Insert the following between the first and second paragraphs: "Please answer the following questions:". Then press the Enter key, and type the following questions on separate lines (with a bullet in front of each one): "How much does your franchise cost?"; "Does the price include the cost for installing the 70-foot tower illustrated in your advertisement?"; "Does the price include the cost for purchasing the ropes and harnesses?"
7. Move the insertion point to the end of the document, insert a blank line, then type the complimentary close "Sincerely," (include the comma).
8. Insert four blank lines to leave room for the signature, type Jeff's full name and title, "Jeff Polychronis, Manager", then on the next line type "UpTown Sports Mall".
9. Save the letter with your changes.
10. Preview the letter using Full Page view then print the letter.
11. Print an envelope for this letter on an 8½ × 11-inch sheet of paper, then close the document.

3. Memo of Congratulations Glenna Zumbrennen is owner, founder, and president of Cuisine Unlimited. She was recently recognized as the 1999 New Hampshire Woman Business Owner of the Year by the National Association of Women Business Owners. She also was named to the 1999 Small Business Administration Advisory Council. Do the following:

1. Write a brief memo congratulating Glenna on receiving these awards. Remember to use the four-part planning process. You should plan the content, organization, and style of the memo, and use a standard memo format similar to the one shown in Figure 1-46.
2. Save the document as Awards Memo in the Cases folder in the Tutorial.01 folder on your Student Disk.
3. Preview the memo in Full Page view.
4. Print the memo then close it.

4. Writing a Personal Letter with the Letter Template WordPerfect provides **templates**, models with predefined formatting, to help you create documents quickly and effectively. For example, the Letter template helps you create letters with professional-looking letterheads and various letter formats. Do the following:

1. Click File then click New. The Select New Document dialog box opens.
2. Click <Main> in the Group list, click <Letter Expert> in the Select template list, then click the Select button. You might have to wait a few moments while WordPerfect opens the Letter Expert.

3. Fill in the Letter Expert information. Type a real or fictitious name and address for the inside (recipient's) name and address, type an appropriate salutation based on that name, then click the Finish button.
4. Include a sentence or two in the body of the letter explaining that you're using the WordPerfect Letter template to create this letter.
5. After typing the letter, make sure that you're listed as the person sending the letter. (Someone else's name might be listed if you're not using your own computer or the personal information already is entered into WordPerfect.)
6. Save the letter as My Template Letter in the Cases folder in the Tutorial.01 folder on your Student Disk, then preview it in full page view and print it.
7. Set up an envelope for this letter and print it on an 8½×11-inch sheet of paper.
8. Close the document.

Lab Assignment

This Lab Assignment is designed to accompany the interactive Course Lab called Word Processing. To start the Word Processing Lab, click the Start button on the Windows 95 taskbar, point to Programs, point to Course Labs, point to New Perspectives Applications, and click Word Processing. If you do not see Course Labs on your Programs menu, see your instructor or technical support person.

Word Processing

Word Processing software is the most popular computerized productivity tool. In this Lab you will learn how word processing software works. When you have completed this Lab, you should be able to apply the general concepts you learned to any word processing package you use at home, at work, or in your school lab.

1. Click the Steps button to learn how word processing software works. As you proceed through the Steps, answer all of the Quick Check questions that appear. After you complete the Steps, you will see a Quick Check summary report. Follow the instructions on the screen to print this report.
2. Click the Explore button to begin. Click File then click Open to display the Open dialog box. Click the file TIMBER.TEX, then press the Enter key to open the letter to Northern Timber Company. Make the following modifications to the letter, then print it. You do not need to save the letter.
   a. In the first and last lines of the letter, change "Jason Kidder" to your name.
   b. Change the date to today's date.
   c. The second paragraph begins "Your proposal did not include. . ." Move this paragraph so it is the last paragraph in the text of the letter.
   d. Change the cost of a permanent bridge to $20,000.
   e. Spell check the letter.
3. Using Explore, open the file STARS.TEX. Make the following modifications to the document, then print it. You do not need to save the document.
   a. Center and boldface the title.
   b. Change the title font size to 16-point Arial.
   c. Boldface the DATE, SHOWER, and LOCATION.
   d. Move the January 2-3 line to the top of the list.
   e. Number the items in the list 1., 2., 3., etc.
   f. Add or delete tabs to realign the columns.
   g. Double space the entire document.
4. Using Explore, compose a one-page double-spaced letter to your parents or to a friend. Make sure you date the letter and check your spelling. Print the letter and sign it. You do not need to save your letter on disk.

TUTORIAL 2

Editing and Formatting a Document

Investment Plan Description by Right-Hand Solutions

OBJECTIVES

In this tutorial you will:

- Move the insertion point around the document
- Delete words, sentences, and paragraphs
- Move text within the document
- Change margins and paragraph indents and justify text
- Set tabs to align columns
- Change fonts and adjust font sizes
- Emphasize points with bullets and numbering
- Create boldfaced, underlined, and italicized text
- Switch between open documents

CASE

Right-Hand Solutions

Reginald Thomson is a contract specialist for Right-Hand Solutions, a company that provides small businesses with financial and administrative services. Right-Hand Solutions contracts with independent insurance companies to prepare insurance plans and investment opportunities for their small business clients. Brandi Paxman, vice president of administrative services, asked Reginald to write a document that describes the tax-deferred annuity plan (an investment plan for pre-tax wages) for their clients' employee handbooks. After Brandi comments on and corrects the draft, Reginald asks you to make the necessary changes and print the document. He needs three copies—one for his files, one for Brandi, and one for the copy center, which will distribute the document to companies who contract with Right-Hand Solutions.

In this tutorial, you'll review Reginald's plan for preparing the document, then you'll edit the annuity plan description according to Brandi's comments.

In Session 2.1, you'll move the insertion point around the document, delete words, sentences, and paragraphs, and move text within the document. In Session 2.2, you'll use document- and paragraph-level formatting commands to change margins and tabs and to justify and align text. In Session 2.3, you'll use character-level formatting commands to create boldfaced, underlined, and italicized text, and to change font styles and sizes. Finally, you'll print a copy of the document.

SESSION 2.1

In this session you will see how Reginald planned his document, Annuity. Then you will edit the document by deleting words and sentences and by moving text within the document.

Planning the Document

Remember that planning a document means considering what you want to say and how you want to say it.

Content

The content of this document is a description of the tax-deferred annuity plan that Right-Hand Solutions offers its clients. This document contains a title and seven commonly asked questions along with their answers.

Organization

Right-Hand Solutions organizes each topic in its clients' employee handbooks into an overview followed by a brief explanation and questions employees commonly ask. Reginald followed this organization in his draft of the annuity plan description.

Style

The description is written in a conversational style with a minimum of legal and technical terms so employees can understand the content quickly and easily.

Presentation

For his draft of the document, Reginald used WordPerfect's default format settings: the left, right, top, and bottom margins set at 1 inch, and all text aligned along the left margin but ragged along the right margin. Later, you'll change the format of the document so it matches the presentation of the other documents in the employee handbook.

Opening the Document

Reginald planned the document, wrote his draft with WordPerfect, and then submitted it to Brandi. She later returned the draft to Reginald with her editing marks and notes, as shown in Figure 2-1.

Reginald asks you to prepare the final draft of the tax-deferred annuity plan description for him. You'll begin by opening the first draft of the description, which has the filename Annuity.

To open the document:

1. Start WordPerfect (if it's not already started) and complete the session checklist. In particular, make sure the Ruler appears below the Power Bar.
2. Insert your Student Disk into drive A or the appropriate disk drive.
3. Click the **Open** button on the Toolbar to open the Open dialog box.
4. Click the **Look in** list arrow. The list of drives and files appears.

Figure 2-1
Draft of annuity plan showing Brandi's edits

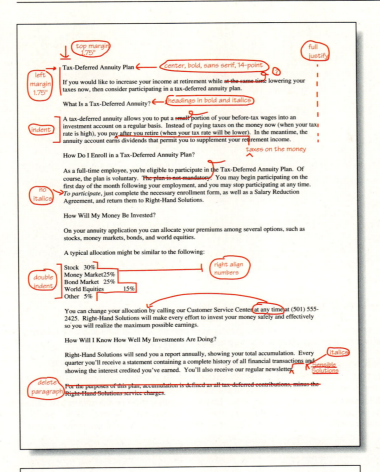
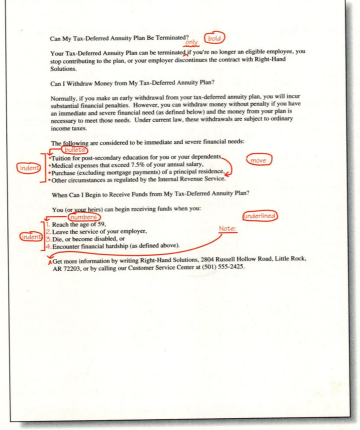

5. Click **3½ Floppy (A:)** or the letter of the drive that contains your Student Disk. Notice that the window changes to reflect the contents of your Student Disk.

6. Double-click the **Tutorial.02** folder to open the folder that contains the description of the tax-deferred annuity plan.

7. Click **Annuity** to select the file.

   TROUBLE? If you see Annuity.wpd in the folder instead of Annuity, Windows 95 might be configured to show filename extensions. Click Annuity.wpd then continue with Step 8. If you can't find the file with or without the filename extension, make sure you're looking in the Tutorial.02 folder and on the drive that contains your Student Disk. If you still can't locate the file, ask your technical support person for help.

8. Click the **Open** button in the Open dialog box. The document opens with the insertion point at the beginning of the document. See Figure 2-2.

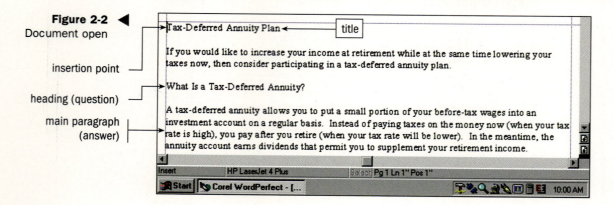

Figure 2-2
Document open

insertion point

heading (question)

main paragraph (answer)

Before you begin editing the description, Reginald asks you to work with a copy of the document.

Renaming the Document

To avoid altering the original disk file, Annuity, you'll save the document using the filename RHS Annuity Plan. Saving the document with another filename creates a copy of the file and leaves the original file unchanged in case you want to work through the tutorial again.

To save the document with a new name:

1. Click **File**, then click **Save As**. The Save As dialog box opens with the complete path, including the current filename, highlighted in the Name text box.

2. Click I to the left of the letter "A" in "Annuity," then type **RHS** and press the **spacebar**. Press the **Right Arrow** key (→) to move the insertion point to the right of the letter "y" in "Annuity," then press the **spacebar** and type **Plan** to change the filename to RHS Annuity Plan.wpd.

3. Click the **Save** button to save the document with the new filename and close the dialog box. The original file, Annuity, remains on your Student Disk in its original form and a copy of the file is saved to your Student Disk with the new filename.

Now you can edit Reginald's description of the tax-deferred annuity plan offered by Right-Hand Solutions. To make all of Brandi's edits, you'll want to quickly move the insertion point to any location in the document that Brandi has marked for editing.

Moving the Insertion Point

The arrow keys (←→↑↓) allow you to move the insertion point one character at a time to the left or right, or one line at a time up or down. While this is effective for moving short distances within a document, it can be time-consuming when you need to move the insertion point many characters or lines at once.

WordPerfect provides two ways to move the insertion point more than one character or one line at a time. You can point-and-click the pointer in other parts of the line or document, or you can press a combination of keys to move the insertion point. Either method will save you time when you need to work in a different part of your document. Throughout these tutorials, you'll use both methods; in time you might find you prefer one method over the other.

Figure 2-3 summarizes the keystrokes you can use to move the insertion point around the document.

Figure 2-3 ◄
Keystrokes for moving the insertion point

Press	To Move Insertion Point
← or →	Left or right one character at a time
↑ or ↓	Up or down one line at a time
Ctrl + ← or Ctrl + →	Left or right one word at a time
Ctrl + ↑ or Ctrl + ↓	Up or down one paragraph at a time
Home or End	To the beginning or end of the current line
Ctrl + Home or Ctrl + End	To the beginning or end of the document
PageUp or PageDown	To the previous or next screen
Alt + End or Alt + Home	To the top or bottom of the current page
Alt + PageUp or Alt + PageDown	To the beginning of the previous or next page

You'll use keystrokes to move the insertion point quickly to the beginning of the second page and to the end of the document.

To move the insertion point with keystrokes:

1. Press and hold down the **Alt** key while you press the **Page Down** key to move the insertion point to the beginning of the next page. Notice the status bar indicates that the insertion point is now on page 2.

2. Press ↑ twice to move to the previous page. Notice the document appears on two separate pages. See Figure 2-4.

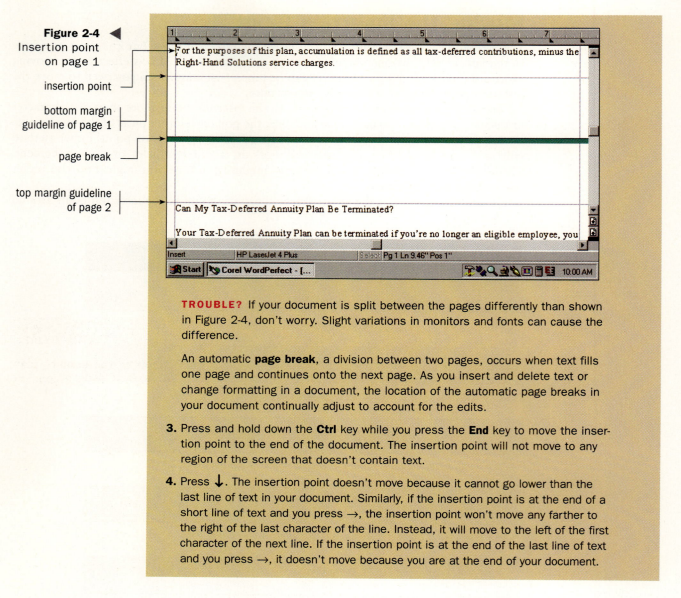

Figure 2-4
Insertion point on page 1

- insertion point
- bottom margin guideline of page 1
- page break
- top margin guideline of page 2

TROUBLE? If your document is split between the pages differently than shown in Figure 2-4, don't worry. Slight variations in monitors and fonts can cause the difference.

An automatic **page break**, a division between two pages, occurs when text fills one page and continues onto the next page. As you insert and delete text or change formatting in a document, the location of the automatic page breaks in your document continually adjust to account for the edits.

3. Press and hold down the **Ctrl** key while you press the **End** key to move the insertion point to the end of the document. The insertion point will not move to any region of the screen that doesn't contain text.

4. Press ↓. The insertion point doesn't move because it cannot go lower than the last line of text in your document. Similarly, if the insertion point is at the end of a short line of text and you press →, the insertion point won't move any farther to the right of the last character of the line. Instead, it will move to the left of the first character of the next line. If the insertion point is at the end of the last line of text and you press →, it doesn't move because you are at the end of your document.

Keystrokes quickly move the insertion point from one place to another in a document.

Selecting and Modifying Text

One of the most powerful editing tools in WordPerfect is the **select** feature, which allows you to select (highlight) a block or unit of text and then replace or change the look of that text. Selecting and then changing a block of text all at once is much more efficient than changing each character individually. You can quickly select and change any portion of your document—a single character, word, line, phrase, sentence, paragraph, page, or the whole document. For example, you can delete a block of text from the document, move a block of text from one location to another, change the text type from regular to bold or italic, or center the text.

You can select text using either the mouse or the keyboard; however, the mouse is usually more efficient and easier. You can quickly select a sentence, paragraph, page, or other units of text by clicking in the left margin of the document window. You quickly can select and change a paragraph by clicking the Paragraph Edit QuickSpot to open the Paragraph dialog box from which you can change the format of that paragraph. A **QuickSpot** is a gray button that appears in the left margin when you move the pointer into a paragraph. Figure 2-5 summarizes methods for selecting text with the mouse.

SELECTING AND MODIFYING TEXT **WP 51**

Figure 2-5
Methods for selecting text with the mouse

To Select	Do This
A word	Double-click in the word
A sentence	Click in the left margin next to the line or triple-click within the sentence
A paragraph	Quadruple-click in the paragraph or double-click in the left margin next to the paragraph
Multiple paragraphs	Double-click and drag in the left margin next to the paragraphs
Block of text (whole words)	Click at the beginning of a block, then press the Shift key and click at the end of the block, or drag the pointer over the text
Block of text (not whole words)	Press the Alt key and drag the pointer over the text

Usually you'll select text so you can make changes to it, such as deleting it.

Selecting and then Deleting Text

Brandi marked the word "small" in the second main paragraph of the annuity plan description for deletion. You'll select and then delete the word "small" from Reginald's draft.

To select and then delete a word:

1. Press and hold down the **Ctrl** key while you press the **Home** key to move the insertion point to the beginning of the document.
2. Double-click anywhere within the word **small**, located in the first line of paragraph 2, beneath the heading "What Is a Tax-Deferred Annuity?" to highlight the word. See Figure 2-6.

Figure 2-6
Word to delete

selected word

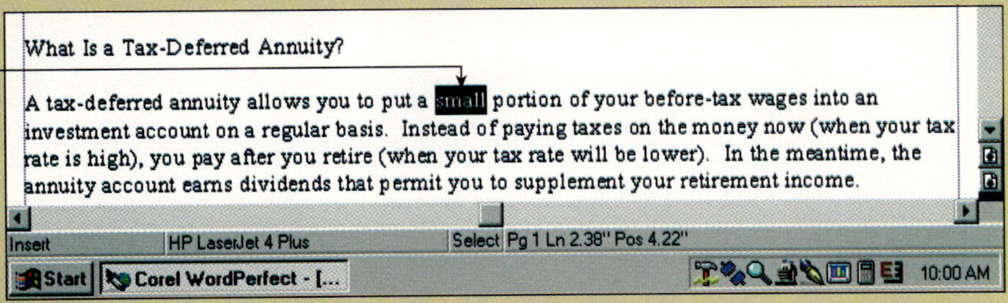

> What Is a Tax-Deferred Annuity?
>
> A tax-deferred annuity allows you to put a [small] portion of your before-tax wages into an investment account on a regular basis. Instead of paying taxes on the money now (when your tax rate is high), you pay after you retire (when your tax rate will be lower). In the meantime, the annuity account earns dividends that permit you to supplement your retirement income.
>
> Insert | HP LaserJet 4 Plus | Select Pg 1 Ln 2.38" Pos 4.22"
> Start | Corel WordPerfect - [...] | 10:00 AM

3. Press the **Delete** key. The word small and the space after it disappear from the document.

In the next paragraph, Brandi marked a complete sentence she wants deleted. You'll move to that paragraph and delete the sentence.

To select and then delete a sentence:

1. Scroll the text until you can see the next full paragraph, which is below the heading "How Do I Enroll...?"
2. Triple-click anywhere within the third sentence, "The plan is not mandatory." to highlight the entire sentence and the spaces after it. See Figure 2-7.

Figure 2-7
Sentence to delete

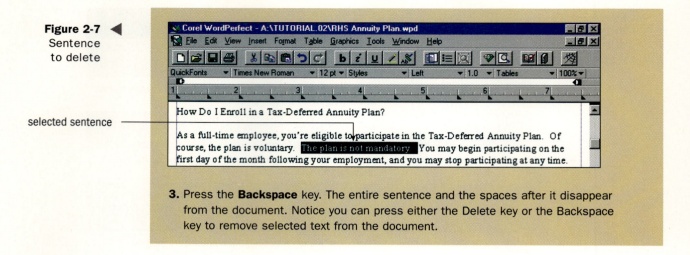

selected sentence

3. Press the **Backspace** key. The entire sentence and the spaces after it disappear from the document. Notice you can press either the Delete key or the Backspace key to remove selected text from the document.

You can see how easy it is to delete words and sentences in WordPerfect. It is just as easy to delete paragraphs. You'll remove the paragraph that Brandi wants deleted from the bottom of the first page.

To select and delete a paragraph:

1. Press and hold down the **Alt** key while you press the **End** key to move the insertion point to the last paragraph on page 1, which begins "For the purposes...." (From now on, key combinations like this will be shown as "Press **Alt** + **End**.")

   TROUBLE? If the paragraph is not the last paragraph on page 1, scroll the text until you locate it.

2. Move the pointer into the margin to the left of any line in the paragraph. The pointer changes to ⇘.

3. Double-click in the left margin, but don't click or double-click the Paragraph Edit QuickSpot. The entire paragraph is highlighted. See Figure 2-8.

Figure 2-8
Paragraph to delete

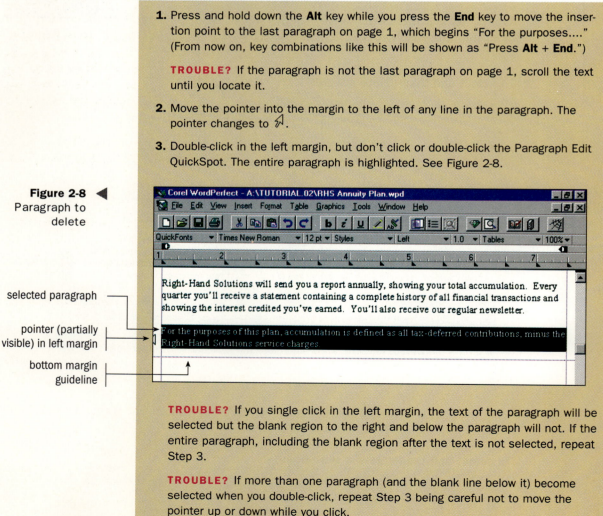

selected paragraph

pointer (partially visible) in left margin

bottom margin guideline

TROUBLE? If you single click in the left margin, the text of the paragraph will be selected but the blank region to the right and below the paragraph will not. If the entire paragraph, including the blank region after the text is not selected, repeat Step 3.

TROUBLE? If more than one paragraph (and the blank line below it) become selected when you double-click, repeat Step 3 being careful not to move the pointer up or down while you click.

4. Press the **Delete** key to delete the paragraph and the blank line below it.

As you have seen, you can quickly delete selected units of text such as words, sentences, and paragraphs. You'll use this method to delete the phrase "at the same time" in the first paragraph of the document.

To select and then delete a phrase:

1. Press **Ctrl** + **Home** to move to the beginning of the document.

2. Click and then drag the shadow pointer over the phrase "at the same time" located in the first line of the first paragraph. The phrase becomes highlighted. Notice that dragging the pointer over the second and successive words automatically selects entire words, which is much easier than selecting words and phrases one character at a time.

3. Press the **Delete** key. The phrase and the space after it disappear. The words "taxes now, then" from the second line wrap back to the first line and fill in the space left by the deleted phrase.

The phrase you deleted was an edit Brandi wasn't sure about. Reginald thinks the sentence should remain as it was. You could retype the text to put it back, but WordPerfect provides a much easier way to restore the phrase.

Undoing an Edit

If you delete text from a document and immediately change your mind, or you accidentally delete something you didn't mean to delete, you can restore that text with a single button click. WordPerfect's **Undo command** undoes (or reverses) the last editing action you performed. If you want to reinstate your original edit or change, the **Redo command** reverses the action of an Undo command (or redoes the Undo). The Undo and Redo commands work together to help you correct errors and undo mistakes.

The Undo command functions as follows:

- Undo reverses your last action immediately. No additional dialog box, beep, or prompt appears.

- Undo reverses any kind of action, including deletions and formatting changes.

- Undo reverses the action at its original location. For example, you can't delete a word or phrase and then undo it at a different location.

- Undo can reverse several previous actions. Click the Undo button several times to undo several actions in reverse order.

- Undo works in tandem with the Redo command. If you undo an action by mistake, you can choose the Redo command to reverse the undo.

Reginald decided that you should add the phrase "at the same time" back into the document; that is, you want to reverse your previous deletion. Rather than retyping the phrase, you'll reverse the edit using the Undo command.

To use the Undo command:

1. Click the **Undo** button on the Toolbar to restore the phrase that you deleted (your most recent operation). The phrase "at the same time" reappears in your document. Notice the Redo button becomes active.

   TROUBLE? If the phrase doesn't reappear in your document and something else changes in your document, you probably made another edit or change to the document (such as pressing the Backspace key) between the deletion and the undo. Click the Undo button on the Toolbar until the phrase reappears in your document.

> As you read the sentence, you decide it reads better without the phrase after all. Instead of selecting and deleting it again, you'll redo the undo.
>
> 2. Click the **Redo** button on the toolbar. The phrase "at the same time" again disappears from your document again.
>
> 3. Click the **Save** button on the Toolbar to save the annuity plan description.

You can also use WordPerfect's Undelete command to restore deleted text (a sentence, a paragraph, whatever). Undelete works the same as Undo, with three differences:

- Undelete restores a block of text to any location in the document, not just the location from which it was deleted. For example, you could delete a sentence from one paragraph, move the insertion point to another paragraph, and then use the Undelete command to insert the sentence in the new paragraph.
- From the Undelete dialog box, you can click the Restore button to restore the most recently deleted block of text to the location of the insertion point, even after you've performed other formatting or insertion-point-movement commands.
- From the Undelete dialog box, you can click Next or Previous to undelete any of your last three deletions.

> **REFERENCE window**
>
> **REVERSING EDITS WITH UNDO, REDO, OR UNDELETE**
>
> - Click the Undo button on the Toolbar (or click Edit then click Undo or press Ctrl + Z) to undo the previous action.
> - Click the Redo button on the Toolbar to reverse the undo.
> - Click Edit then click Undelete (or press Ctrl + Shift + Z) to restore deleted text at the insertion point.

You have edited the document by deleting all the text that Brandi marked for deletion. Now you're ready to make the rest of her editing suggestions.

Moving Text Within a Document

In addition to deleting text, one of the most important reasons to select text is to move it. You can move any amount of text from one location in a WordPerfect document to: another location in the same document, another WordPerfect document, or a different program document (such as Quattro Pro). For example, Brandi wants to reorder the four points Reginald made in the section "Can I Withdraw Money from My Tax-Deferred Annuity Plan?" on page 2 of his draft. You could reorder the list by deleting the sentence and then retyping it at the new location. A much more efficient approach, however, is to select and then move the sentence. WordPerfect has several ways to move text: drag and drop, cut and paste, copy and paste, and delete and undelete as described earlier. You'll use the first three methods to make Brandi's changes.

Dragging and Dropping Text

The easiest way to move text within a document is called drag and drop. With **drag and drop**, you select the text you want to move, press and hold down the mouse button while you drag the text to a new spot with the pointer, and then release the mouse button.

MOVING TEXT WITHIN A DOCUMENT   WP 55

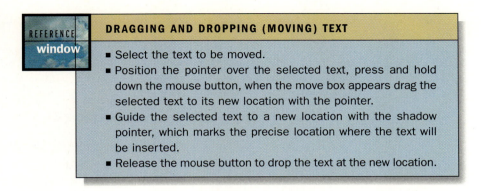

REFERENCE window

DRAGGING AND DROPPING (MOVING) TEXT
- Select the text to be moved.
- Position the pointer over the selected text, press and hold down the mouse button, when the move box appears drag the selected text to its new location with the pointer.
- Guide the selected text to a new location with the shadow pointer, which marks the precise location where the text will be inserted.
- Release the mouse button to drop the text at the new location.

Brandi suggested reordering of the bulleted list items on page 2 of Reginald's draft. You'll use the drag-and-drop method to reorder the items.

To move text using drag and drop:

1. Scroll through the document until you see "Tuition for post-secondary education…," the first in the list of "immediate and severe financial needs," which begins in the middle of page 2.

2. Double-click in the margin to the left of the line beginning "Tuition…" to select that paragraph of text. See Figure 2-9.

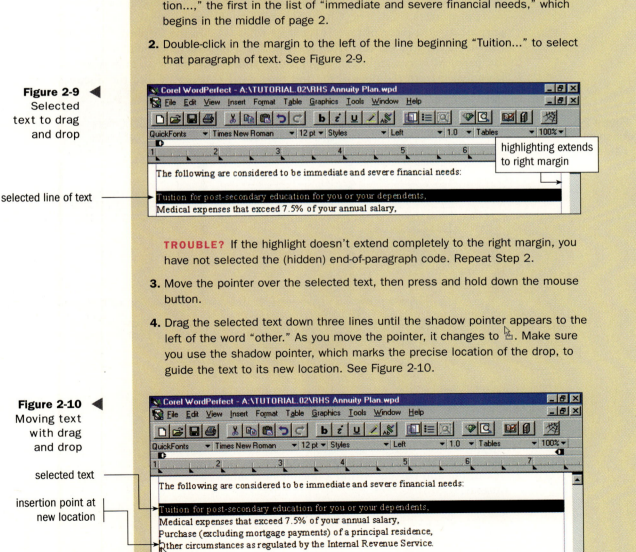

Figure 2-9
Selected text to drag and drop

selected line of text

highlighting extends to right margin

TROUBLE? If the highlight doesn't extend completely to the right margin, you have not selected the (hidden) end-of-paragraph code. Repeat Step 2.

3. Move the pointer over the selected text, then press and hold down the mouse button.

4. Drag the selected text down three lines until the shadow pointer appears to the left of the word "other." As you move the pointer, it changes to ⬚. Make sure you use the shadow pointer, which marks the precise location of the drop, to guide the text to its new location. See Figure 2-10.

Figure 2-10
Moving text with drag and drop

selected text

insertion point at new location

pointer

> 5. Release the mouse button. The selected text moves to its new location, and the list of items is reordered. The text remains selected.
>
>   **TROUBLE?** If the selected text moves to the wrong location, click the Undo button on the Toolbar, then repeat Steps 2 through 5, making sure you hold the mouse button until the insertion point appears in front of the word "other."
>
> 6. Deselect the highlighted text by clicking the pointer anywhere outside the selected text in the document window.

Dragging and dropping works well if you're moving text a short distance in a document; however, cut and paste works well for moving text either a short distance or beyond the current screen.

Cutting and Pasting Text

To **cut** means to remove text (or some other item) from the document and place it on the Windows Clipboard. The **Clipboard** is an area where text and graphics that have been cut or copied are stored. The Clipboard stores only one item at a time; when you cut a graphic or new piece of text, it replaces what was on the Clipboard. To **paste** means to transfer a copy of the text from the Clipboard into the document at the insertion point. To perform a cut-and-paste operation, you select the text you want to move, cut (remove) it from the document, and then paste (restore) it into the document in a new location, as shown in Figure 2-11.

Figure 2-11
Cut-and-paste operation

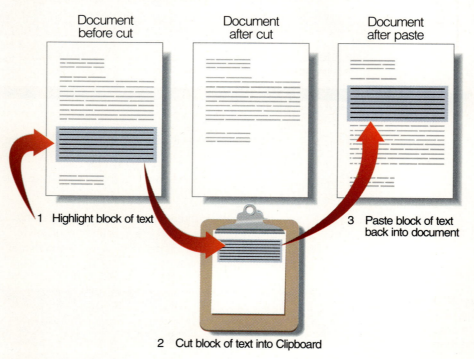

Cutting and pasting within a document is much easier than deleting and retyping a lot of text.

MOVING TEXT WITHIN A DOCUMENT   WP 57

> **REFERENCE window**
>
> **CUTTING AND PASTING (MOVING) TEXT**
> - Select (highlight) the text you want to move.
> - Click the Cut button on the Toolbar (or click Edit then click Cut or press Ctrl + X).
> - Move the insertion point to the location in the document where you want to move the text.
> - Click the Paste button on the Toolbar (or click Edit then click Paste or press Ctrl + V).

Brandi suggested moving the phrase "at any time" (in the paragraph beginning "You can change your allocation...") to a new location. You'll use cut and paste to move this phrase.

To move text using cut and paste:

1. Scroll the document up until you can see the paragraph just above the heading "How Will I Know...." near the bottom of page 1.

2. Position the shadow pointer immediately to the left of the phrase "at any time." Click and drag the pointer to the right to highlight the complete phrase, then release the mouse button. See Figure 2-12.

◀ **Figure 2-12**
Text to move using cut and paste

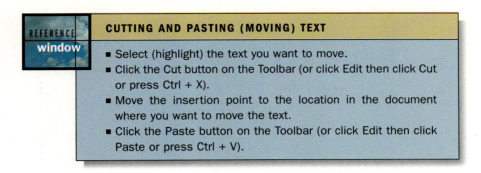

3. Click the **Cut** button ✂ on the Toolbar to cut, or remove, the selected text from the document. The deleted text is stored temporarily on the Clipboard.

4. Move the insertion point to the left of the letter "b" in "by calling," near the beginning of the same sentence. The insertion point marks the position where you want to move the text.

5. Click the **Paste** button 📋 on the Toolbar to restore the text to your document. The phrase "at any time" appears in its new location.

You might have noticed that before you cut the selected block of text, the Paste button on the Toolbar was dimmed or inactive. But once you cut the block of text to the Clipboard, the Paste button became active. The Paste button stays active even after you click it; you can paste additional copies of the phrase stored on the Clipboard throughout your document, until you cut or copy another block of text to the Clipboard.

Copying and Pasting Text

You can move a copy of a sentence, paragraph, or page to another part of your document with the **copy and paste** method, which works much the same way as cut and paste. When you copy text, however, the original text remains in the document and a duplicate of the selection is stored on the Clipboard. You can paste that text anywhere in your document, just as you would cut text. Although you could just retype the text, copy and paste is much quicker when you have more than one word to retype.

REFERENCE window

COPYING AND PASTING (COPYING) TEXT

- Select (highlight) the text you want to copy.
- Click the Copy button on the Toolbar (or click Edit then click Copy or press Ctrl + C).
- Move the insertion point to the location in the document where you want the copied text to appear.
- Click the Paste button on the Toolbar (or click Edit then click Paste or press Ctrl + V).

Brandi wants to repeat the phrase "taxes on the money" in the second paragraph to clarify the meaning of the sentence. You'll duplicate the phrase in the next line using copy and paste.

To copy and paste text:

1. Select the phrase "taxes on the money" but not the space following it in the second sentence beneath the heading "What Is a Tax-Deferred Annuity?" near the beginning of the document. See Figure 2-13.

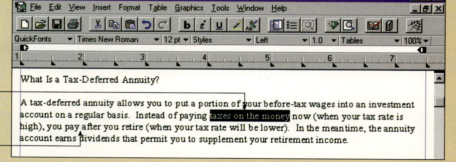

Figure 2-13 ◄ Phrase to copy

selected phrase

paste phrase here

2. Click the **Copy** button on the Toolbar.

   WordPerfect leaves the selected phrase intact within the document window, and places a copy of it on the Clipboard. (Because the Clipboard stores only the most recently cut or copied text, if you were to execute a second Cut or Copy command at this point, the phrase you just copied would be deleted from the Clipboard.) Now you need to move the insertion point where you want to place the copied phrase.

3. Click to the left of the phrase "after you retire" in the next line.

4. Click the **Paste** button on the Toolbar. A copy of the selected phrase appears at this new location. See Figure 2-14.

Figure 2-14 ◀
Phrase pasted into document

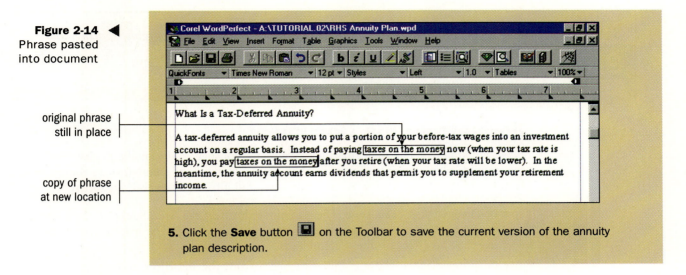

original phrase still in place

copy of phrase at new location

5. Click the **Save** button 🖫 on the Toolbar to save the current version of the annuity plan description.

You have completed the content changes Brandi suggested except those that also require changing the font. Next you'll format the document in a style that is consistent with the rest of the employee handbook.

1. Which key(s) do you press to move the insertion point to the end of the document? to the beginning of the document? to the beginning of the next page? to the beginning of the previous page?

2. If the insertion point is at the end of a short line of text and you press →, the insertion point won't go any farther to the right. Where will it move instead?

3. Which of the following is highlighted when you double-click in the left margin?
   a. a word
   b. a line
   c. a sentence
   d. a paragraph

4. What is the purpose of the Undo command? What is the purpose of the Redo command?

5. How can you restore deleted text to a new location in your document?

6. When you use the drag-and-drop method to move text, how do you know where the text will be positioned when it is dropped?

7. What is the difference between cut and paste and copy and paste?

If you aren't going to work through Session 2.2 now, you should close the document and exit WordPerfect. When you're ready to begin Session 2.2, start WordPerfect, open RHS Annuity Plan, and continue with the session.

SESSION 2.2

In this session you will use formatting commands to change the margins, spacing, and tabs, and to justify and align text.

Formatting the Document

Next, you'll implement the formatting changes Brandi suggested to make Reginald's draft of the annuity plan description consistent in format with other summaries in the employee handbook. WordPerfect's formatting commands fall into three general categories:

- **Document-layout commands**. These commands affect the overall layout of the entire document (for example, paper size and page orientation). The insertion point location has no effect on these commands.
- **Open commands**. These commands begin from the insertion point and continue until the end of the document or until the formatting feature is changed (for example, margin settings and justifying text). They are called "open commands" because they don't necessarily end at a later location. You can limit the scope of open commands by selecting text before executing the command.
- **Line and paragraph commands**. These commands affect only a single line or paragraph at the location of the insertion point (for example, indenting a paragraph). You can extend the effects of a line or paragraph command by selecting several lines or paragraphs. These commands affect all selected text before executing the command.

Reginald's summary of the annuity plan requires formatting of all three types.

Specifying the Page Size and Orientation

Changing the page size and orientation is an example of a WordPerfect document-layout command. You can leave the insertion point at any location in the document when you execute the command.

The employee handbook that Right-Hand Solutions distributes to its clients is printed on letter-size (8½ × 11-inch) paper. The handbook is positioned in **portrait** orientation, in which the page is taller than it is wide, rather than in **landscape** orientation, in which the page is wider than it is tall. See Figure 2-15.

Figure 2-15
Page orientations and available text area

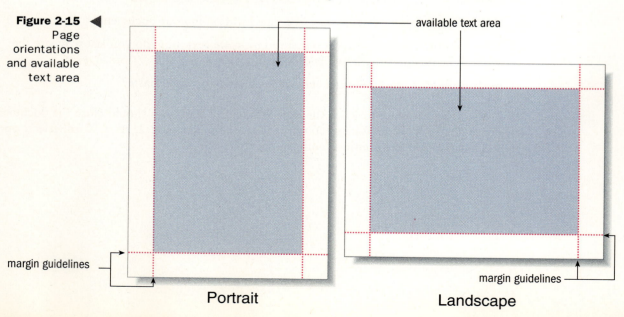

Portrait orientation is common for letters, reports, and other text documents while landscape orientation is often used for folded brochures and flyers.

CHANGING THE PAGE SIZE OR ORIENTATION OF THE DOCUMENT

- With the insertion point at any location in the document, click Format, point to Page, then click Page Size. The Page Size dialog box opens.
- Change the Page definition name to Letter for 8½ × 11-inch portrait pages, to Letter Landscape for 11 × 8½-inch landscape pages, or to the page size and orientation you want.
- Click the OK button in the Page Size dialog box.

Because the handbook uses Word Perfect's default settings for paper size and page orientation, you won't need to change them; however, you will change the margins in the document.

Changing the Margins

The default margins in WordPerfect are one inch for the left, right, top, and bottom margins. The Ruler, displayed below the Power Bar, shows the location of the left and right margins. The numbers on the Ruler indicate the distance in inches from the left edge of the paper, not from the left margin.

The margin commands are examples of open formatting commands. Changes you make to the margins will affect the text only from the current location of the insertion point to the end of the document. Because you want to change the margins for the entire annuity plan document, you need to move the insertion point to the beginning of the document.

CHANGING MARGINS

- Move the insertion point to the beginning of the document to change margins for the entire document or to the location where you want to begin changing the margins.
- Click the Page Margins button to open the Margins dialog box, adjust the margin values, then click the OK button.

or

- Drag the left or right margin marker on the Ruler to the new location.

or

- Drag the margin guidelines to the new locations.

You need to change the left and top margins to 1.75 inches, as suggested by Brandi. The left margin will be wider than usual to allow space for drilling holes so the document can be added to a three-ring binder.

To change the margins in the entire document:

1. Press **Ctrl** + **Home** to move the insertion point to the beginning of the document. This ensures that the new margin will affect the entire document.

2. At the location of the insertion point, position the pointer on the left margin guideline until it becomes ↔. (Make sure the pointer is not below the top line of the text.)

3. Press and hold down the mouse button to display a QuickTip with the current margin setting (1.0"), then drag the guideline to the right until the QuickTip reads **1.75"**. The dashed vertical line indicates the position of the new margin. See Figure 2-16.

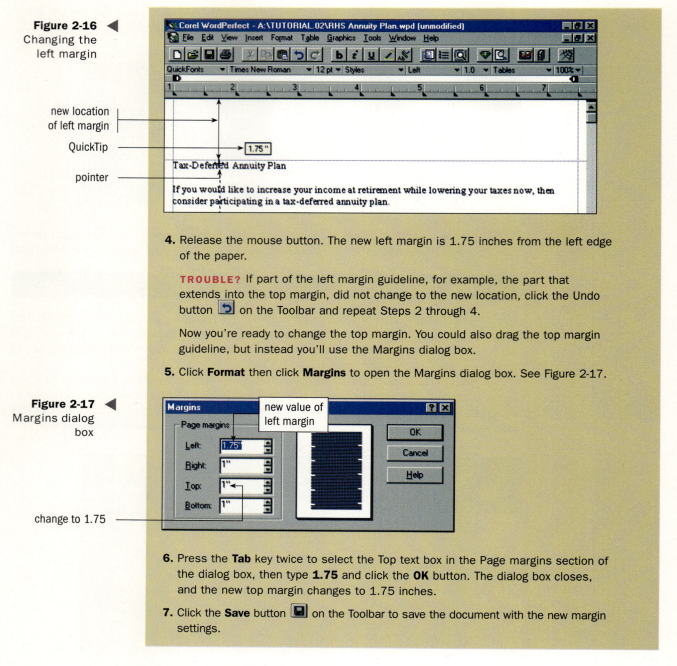

Figure 2-16 Changing the left margin

new location of left margin

QuickTip

pointer

Figure 2-17 Margins dialog box

new value of left margin

change to 1.75

4. Release the mouse button. The new left margin is 1.75 inches from the left edge of the paper.

   TROUBLE? If part of the left margin guideline, for example, the part that extends into the top margin, did not change to the new location, click the Undo button on the Toolbar and repeat Steps 2 through 4.

   Now you're ready to change the top margin. You could also drag the top margin guideline, but instead you'll use the Margins dialog box.

5. Click **Format** then click **Margins** to open the Margins dialog box. See Figure 2-17.

6. Press the **Tab** key twice to select the Top text box in the Page margins section of the dialog box, then type **1.75** and click the **OK** button. The dialog box closes, and the new top margin changes to 1.75 inches.

7. Click the **Save** button on the Toolbar to save the document with the new margin settings.

You have set the margins for the annuity plan description according to Brandi's specifications. Next, you'll justify the text.

Justifying Text

Justifying text is an open command in WordPerfect. Justification usually means adjusting the spacing between characters in any given line so text is aligned along the right margin as well as along the left. WordPerfect and other word processing programs, however, define justification more broadly: **Justification** is the process of aligning text relative to the left and right margins. Specifically, you can align text in a WordPerfect document in any of five ways: left, right, center, full, and all. Figure 2-18 shows these five types of justification and summarizes when you would use each type.

Figure 2-18
Five types of justification

Left Justification:
This paragraph is an example of *left* justification. The text is aligned along the left margin, but ragged along the right margin. This gives a less ordered look to the document but is generally easier to read than full justification. Left justification is the default setting in Word.

Right Justification:
This paragraph is an example of *right* justification. The text is aligned along the right margin, but ragged along the left margin. You would rarely use right justification in the body of a document because it is difficult to read; but you might use it for special effects.

Center Justification
This paragraph is an example of *center* justification. The text is centered between the left and right margins. You would never use center justification in the body of a document because it is difficult to read, but you would frequently use it for titles and headings.

Full Justification:
This paragraph is an example of *full* justification. The text is aligned along the left and right margins. This creates an ordered look, but it is generally more difficult to read because the spacing between words isnít consistent. Short or partial lines at the end of paragraphs are not aligned along the right margin. You would use full justification for professional documents.

All Justification:
This paragraph is an example of *all* justification. The text is aligned along the left and the right margins for all the lines in the paragraph, including the last line, even when the last line would normally be too short to reach the right margin. You would use all justification, therefore, only for s p e c i a l   e f f e c t s .

By default, a WordPerfect document is left justified, that is, the text is aligned along the left margin, but is ragged, or uneven, along the right margin.

JUSTIFYING TEXT

- Move the insertion point to the location where you want the justification to begin or select the text that you want to justify.
- Click the Align Text button on the Power Bar, then click Left, Right, Center, Full, or All.

or

- Click Format, point to Justification, then click Left, Right, Center, Full, or All.

or

- Press Ctrl + L to select Left justify, press Ctrl + R to select Right justify, press Ctrl + E to select Center justify, or press Ctrl + J to select Full justify. (All justification has no keyboard shortcut.)

Brandi indicated that she wants the main paragraphs of the annuity plan description to be full justified.

To full justify the text of the document:

1. Make sure the insertion point is still at the beginning of the document.
2. Click the **Align Text** button on the Power Bar to open a menu showing the five types of justification.
3. Click **Full**. The menu closes and the text in the main paragraphs becomes full justified. See Figure 2-19.

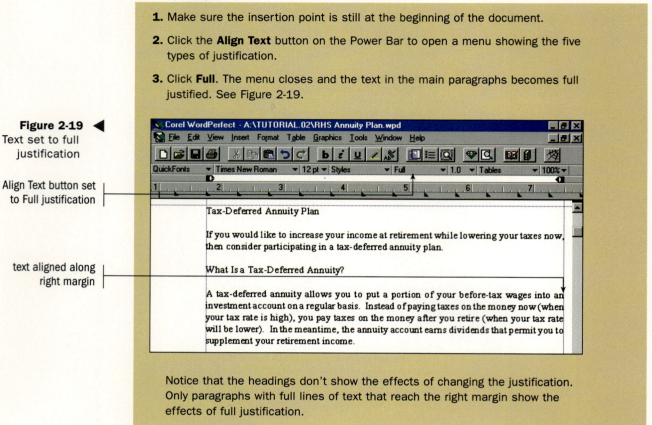

Figure 2-19
Text set to full justification

Align Text button set to Full justification

text aligned along right margin

Notice that the headings don't show the effects of changing the justification. Only paragraphs with full lines of text that reach the right margin show the effects of full justification.

You have full justified the document. Next you'll center the title, which is the first line of text in the document.

Formatting Lines and Paragraphs

So far you have seen how to use document-layout and open commands to format the text of a document. Now you'll use the third type of formatting command—line and paragraph commands.

Centering a Line of Text

The single-line title of the annuity plan description needs to be centered between the left and right margins. If you moved the insertion point to the title and applied center justification (an open command), the title as well as all the text in the document that follows it would become center justified. You could select the text of the title and then apply center justification, which indicates that you want to begin the open command at the beginning of the selected text and end it at the end of the selected text.

WordPerfect provides an easier way to center just one line of text: the center line command. The insertion point needs to be at the beginning of the line you want to center, then when you apply the center line command it affects only that line of text.

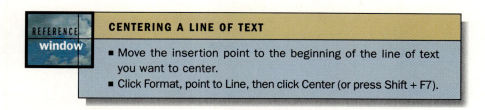

CENTERING A LINE OF TEXT
- Move the insertion point to the beginning of the line of text you want to center.
- Click Format, point to Line, then click Center (or press Shift + F7).

You'll center the title of the annuity plan description with the center line command.

To center a line of text:

1. Make sure the insertion point is immediately to the left of the title "Tax-Deferred Annuity Plan."

2. Press **Shift** + **F7**. The title becomes centered between the left and right margins. See Figure 2-20.

Figure 2-20 ◀
Centered title

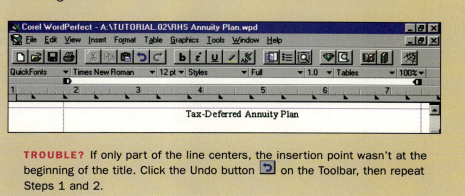

TROUBLE? If only part of the line centers, the insertion point wasn't at the beginning of the title. Click the Undo button on the Toolbar, then repeat Steps 1 and 2.

The title is centered. Later, you'll change the appearance of the text in the title. Indents are another way to distinguish text in your document.

Indenting Paragraphs

You can emphasize certain paragraphs in your document and improve their readability by changing their indentation. **Indentation** is a WordPerfect paragraph formatting command that moves certain lines of a paragraph away from the left margin. WordPerfect provides three main types of paragraph indentations—indents, hanging indents, and double indents—as shown in Figure 2-21.

Figure 2-21 ◀
Three types of paragraph indentation

> In this paragraph, called an **indent paragraph**, all of the lines are indented from the left margin to the next tab stop. You can create this type of indentation by positioning the insertion point at the beginning of the paragraph and pressing F7 or clicking Format, clicking Paragraph, and clicking Indent.
>
> In this paragraph, called a **hanging indent paragraph**, all lines except the first line are indented from the left margin to the next tab stop. You can create this type of indentation by positioning the insertion point at the beginning of the paragraph and pressing Ctrl + F7 or clicking Format, clicking Paragraph, and clicking Hanging Indent.
>
> In this paragraph, called a **double-indent paragraph**, all lines are indented from the left and right margins. You can create this type of indentation by moving the insertion point to the beginning of the paragraph and pressing Ctrl + Shift + F7 or clicking Format, clicking Paragraph, and clicking Double Indent.

When you choose any of these indent commands, the selected lines in the paragraph move to the next tab stop on the Ruler. You'll learn more about tab stops shortly. For now, you should know that default tab stops occur every half inch from the left margin, so if you indent a paragraph, the lines of the paragraph move to the right a half inch.

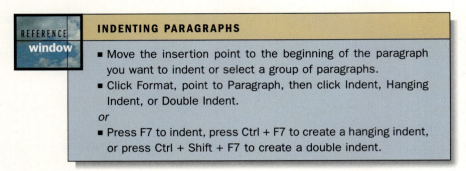

REFERENCE window

INDENTING PARAGRAPHS

- Move the insertion point to the beginning of the paragraph you want to indent or select a group of paragraphs.
- Click Format, point to Paragraph, then click Indent, Hanging Indent, or Double Indent.

or

- Press F7 to indent, press Ctrl + F7 to create a hanging indent, or press Ctrl + Shift + F7 to create a double indent.

Brandi indicated she wants all the main paragraphs indented one-half inch from the left margin. You'll indent the first paragraphs below the headings in the annuity plan document.

To indent the paragraphs:

1. Move the insertion point to the left of the phrase "A tax-deferred annuity allows" at the beginning of the paragraph below the first heading "What Is a Tax-Deferred Annuity?"

2. Press **F7**, the Indent shortcut key. All the lines in the paragraph become indented. See Figure 2-22.

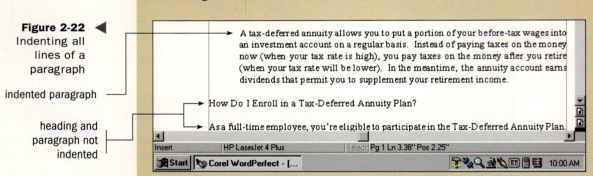

Figure 2-22 Indenting all lines of a paragraph

indented paragraph

heading and paragraph not indented

3. Move the insertion point to the beginning of the paragraph that begins "As a full-time employee" below the second heading.

4. Press **F7** to indent the paragraph.

5. Repeat Steps 3 and 4 for the first two paragraphs below the heading "How Will My Money Be Invested?"

Rather than continue indenting one paragraph at a time, you'll select several paragraphs and indent them at once.

6. Scroll until you can see the list of investment items, which begins with "Stock" and goes to "Other."

7. Click in the left margin to the left of "Stock" and while holding down the mouse button, drag the pointer to the line that begins "Other" to select the list of items.

   TROUBLE? If all the text in the five lines isn't selected, repeat Step 7.

8. Press **F7** to indent the selected paragraphs, then click anywhere outside the selected text. See Figure 2-23.

Figure 2-23
Indenting multiple paragraphs

group of indented paragraphs

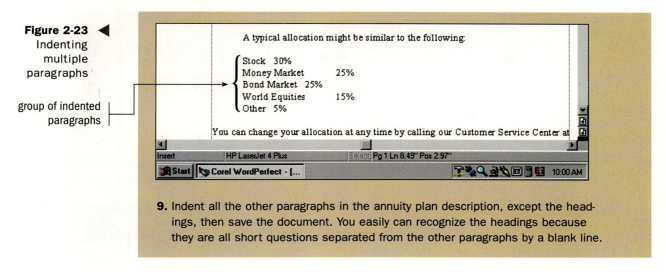

9. Indent all the other paragraphs in the annuity plan description, except the headings, then save the document. You easily can recognize the headings because they are all short questions separated from the other paragraphs by a blank line.

You should not confuse the indent command which indents every line in a paragraph, with the **first-line tab command**, which indents only the first line of a paragraph with the Tab key. You'll indent the first line of the first main paragraph below the title.

To indent the first line of a paragraph:

1. Move the insertion point to the beginning of the document so you can see the first paragraph below the title.

2. Move the insertion point to the beginning of the paragraph, which begins "If you would like to increase...."

3. Press the **Tab** key. The first line of the paragraph indents. See Figure 2-24.

Figure 2-24
First-line indented paragraph

first line tabbed

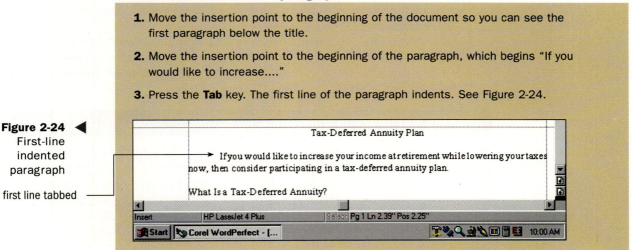

Rather than adding indentation to an existing document, as you did to the annuity plan description, you'll find it easier and less tedious to indent each paragraph as you type it.

Setting Tabs

In addition to indenting paragraphs, tabs are useful for vertically aligning text or numerical data in columns. A **tab** adds space between the text within a line and creates columns of text. A **tab stop** is the location where text moves when you press the Tab key.

WordPerfect's default tab stops are every one-half inch, as indicated by the small black triangles at the bottom of the Ruler shown in Figure 2-25. You set a new tab stop by clicking the bottom of the Ruler at a specific location. You remove a tab stop by dragging it off the Ruler.

Figure 2-25
Ruler with tab stops

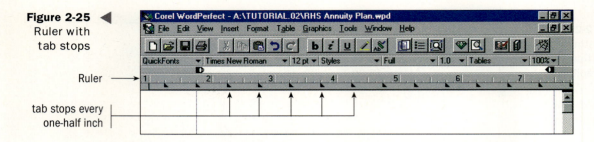

Ruler

tab stops every one-half inch

WordPerfect provides four types of tab stops: left, center, right, and decimal, as shown in Figure 2-26.

Figure 2-26
Tab stop styles

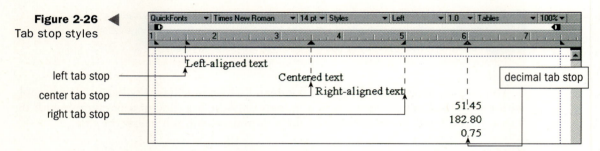

left tab stop
center tab stop
right tab stop

Each of these four styles also can appear with a **dot leader**, a dotted line that appears in the space created when you press the Tab key.

You should never try to align columns of text by adding extra spaces with the spacebar. Although the text might seem precisely aligned in the document window, it will move slightly when you print the document and not be precisely aligned. Always use tab stops and tabs or indent commands to align columns of text.

Aligning Vertical Columns

Brandi wants you to vertically align the right edges of the column of numbers that appear to the right of the phrases, "Stock," "Money Market," "Bond Market," "World Equities," and "Other," in the list below the heading "How Will My Money Be Invested?" You align the numbers by setting a right-align tab stop at a specific location, and then remove other tab stops that might be set in the spaces between the phrases and the numbers.

To right-align a column of numbers:

1. Scroll until you see the phrase "Stock 30%" under "A typical allocation...."

2. Select both columns of information, beginning with the phrase "Stock 30%" and ending with the phrase "Other 5%." See Figure 2-27.

Figure 2-27
Selected text for changing tab stops

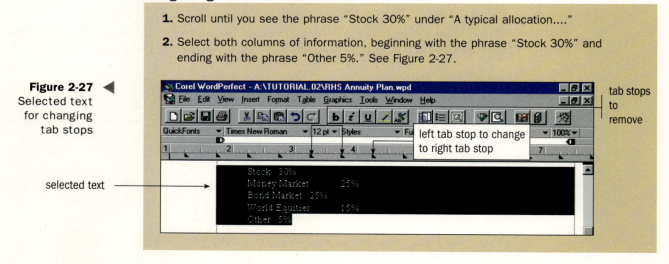

selected text

You'll indent these lines another half inch to separate them even more.

3. Press **F7** to left align the selected paragraphs at 2.75 inches on the Ruler.

Next you need to remove some of the tab stops and add a new right-aligned tab stop. When you remove a tab stop, any text following a tab will move to the next tab stop. In this case, you want to remove enough tab stops so all the numbers in the right column align along the same tab stop, then you can add the new tab stop.

4. Position ▷ over the tab stop at 3.25 inches on the Ruler, as indicated in Figure 2-27, then drag it from the Ruler into the document window. This removes the tab stop from the Ruler.

5. Repeat Step 4 for the tab stop at 3.75 inches. See Figure 2-28.

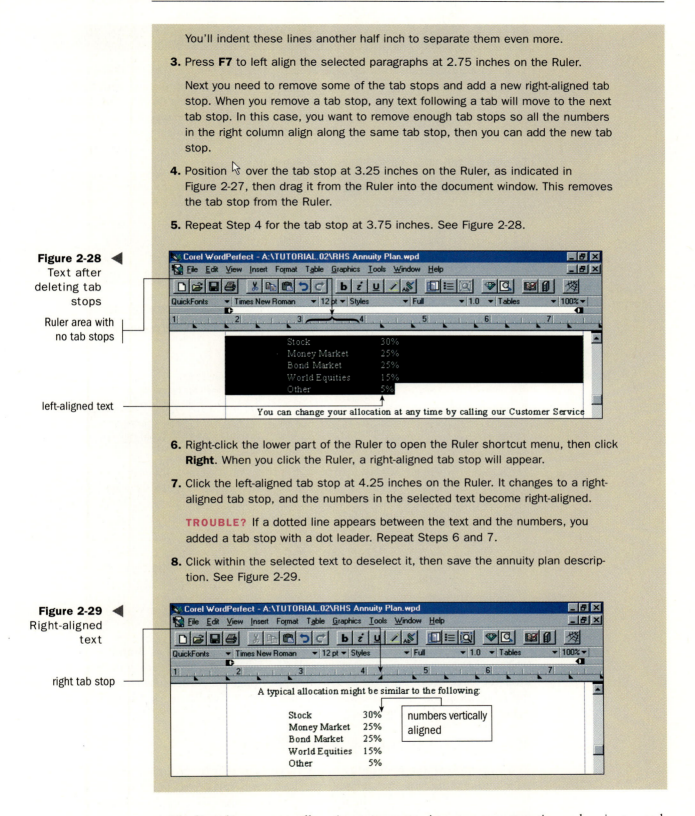

Figure 2-28 ◁
Text after deleting tab stops

Ruler area with no tab stops

left-aligned text

6. Right-click the lower part of the Ruler to open the Ruler shortcut menu, then click **Right**. When you click the Ruler, a right-aligned tab stop will appear.

7. Click the left-aligned tab stop at 4.25 inches on the Ruler. It changes to a right-aligned tab stop, and the numbers in the selected text become right-aligned.

   TROUBLE? If a dotted line appears between the text and the numbers, you added a tab stop with a dot leader. Repeat Steps 6 and 7.

8. Click within the selected text to deselect it, then save the annuity plan description. See Figure 2-29.

Figure 2-29 ◁
Right-aligned text

right tab stop

numbers vertically aligned

The list of investment allocation percentages is now more attractive and easier to read. When Reginald looks at the document, he suggests that the second column numbers would be even easier to read if the column was about one-quarter inch farther from the text in the first column.

Moving Tab Stops

You can adjust the location of a tab stop by dragging the tab stop marker to a new location. You'll move the right-aligned tab stop marker, as Reginald suggested, by dragging it to the new location. But instead of using the Ruler, you'll use a tab bar that appears when you click the Tab icon ⇨≣ in the left margin. The **tab bar** opens above the paragraph with the Tab icon and shows all the tab stops currently on the Ruler.

To move a tab stop marker using the tab bar:

1. If you can't see the left edge of the paper (that is, the entire left margin), drag the horizontal scroll box as far to the left as it can go. Notice Tab icons appear in the left margin.

2. Click the **Tab** icon ⇨≣ in the left margin, to the left of "Stock." A tab bar opens. See Figure 2-30.

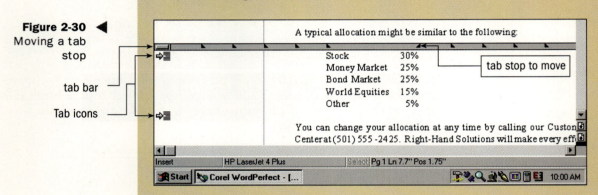

Figure 2-30 ◀ Moving a tab stop

tab bar

Tab icons

3. Click the right-aligned tab stop at 4.25 inches and drag it to 4.5 inches, the new location. Watch the yellow QuickTip to see the exact value of the tab stop location. When you release the mouse button, the column of numbers shifts right by one-quarter inch to the new location of the right-aligned tab stop.

4. Click anywhere in the document window to close the tab bar.

5. If necessary, drag the horizontal scroll box so you can see both the left and right margin guidelines.

6. Save the annuity plan description.

The two columns of information are positioned and aligned as Brandi requested.

You notice a problem. The paragraph that follows the last heading on page 1 appears after the page break on page 2. This is a poor page break because it separates the heading from its accompanying text. You'll use one of WordPerfect's "Keep Text Together" commands to solve the problem.

Keeping Lines of Text Together

You can improve the readability and flow of your text by grouping similar ideas on one page and making sure that related text does not break across pages in a distracting way. If possible, you should pair the following items on the same page: questions and answers, headings and lead paragraphs, and items in a list. Because you changed the margins and paragraph indents, and edited the text in the annuity plan description, the heading "How Will I Know How Well My Investments Are Doing?" appears at the bottom of page 1 and the answer to the question is at the top of page 2.

One solution to the problem would be to insert several additional blank lines just before the heading or to insert a command that forces a page break just before the heading. But if you later add or remove text before the heading, the extra lines or page break would be inappropriate. For example, if you inserted one or two blank lines to force the heading to the next page, and later add three or four lines of text on page 1, unwanted blank lines would appear on page 2, as shown by the incorrect formatting in Figure 2-31. Your screen should *not* look like this.

Figure 2-31
Document window with unwanted blank lines

page break

blank lines

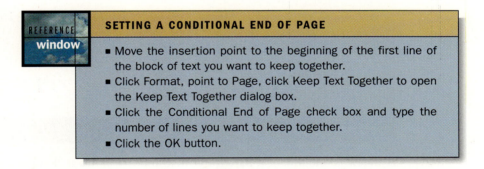

A better solution is to use WordPerfect's Conditional End of Page command. The **Conditional End of Page** command allows you to prevent WordPerfect from inserting a page break that would separate a particular block of text at an awkward position. For example, if you specify that four lines of text should be kept together and a page break falls within those lines, WordPerfect instead inserts the page break *above* the four lines.

REFERENCE window — SETTING A CONDITIONAL END OF PAGE

- Move the insertion point to the beginning of the first line of the block of text you want to keep together.
- Click Format, point to Page, click Keep Text Together to open the Keep Text Together dialog box.
- Click the Conditional End of Page check box and type the number of lines you want to keep together.
- Click the OK button.

You'll set a Conditional End of Page command to ensure the heading at the end of page 1 remains with the text on page 2.

To keep lines of text together on the same page:

1. Scroll the document window until you see the heading "How Will I Know...." An automatic page break splits the heading from the paragraph that follows. See Figure 2-32.

Figure 2-32
Heading isolated at bottom of page

insertion point

bottom margin guideline

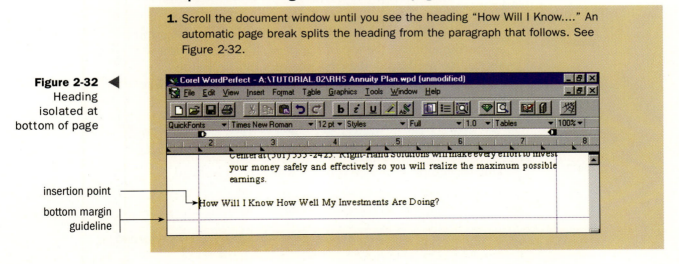

> **TROUBLE?** If the heading and paragraph aren't split between two pages in your document, don't worry. Differences in fonts and monitors change the number of lines of text that fit on each page. Just continue with Step 2.
>
> 2. Move the insertion point to the beginning of the heading "How Will I Know…," click **Format**, point to **Page**, then click **Keep Text Together**. The Keep Text Together dialog box opens.
>
> 3. Click the **Conditional end of page** check box, then type **4** in the Number of lines to keep together text box. This ensures that the heading, the space below it, and the first two lines of the paragraph below that always appear on the same page. See Figure 2-33.
>
>
>
> **Figure 2-33**
> Keep Text Together dialog box
>
> make sure this is checked
>
> set number of lines to 4
>
> 4. Click the **OK** button. Notice the automatic page break moves above the heading and the heading is positioned at the beginning of page 2.

In addition to headings being split from their corresponding text, a single line of a paragraph might appear isolated on a page.

Setting Widow/Orphan Protection

A **widow** is one line of a paragraph that appears alone at the top of a page. An **orphan** is one line of a paragraph that appears alone at the bottom of a page. Figure 2-34 shows a widow and orphan on a page.

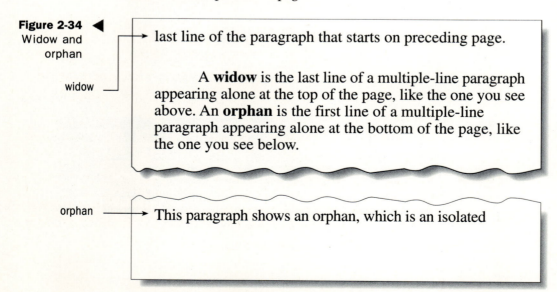

Figure 2-34
Widow and orphan

widow

orphan

Widows and orphans detract from the appearance and readability of a document. Fortunately, WordPerfect's Widow/Orphan protection (an open command) ensures that the first and last lines of a paragraph always remain with the rest of the paragraph.

SETTING WIDOW/ORPHAN PROTECTION

- Move the insertion point to the location where you want widow/orphan protection to begin.
- Click Format, point to Page, then click Keep Text Together. The Keep Text Together dialog box opens.
- Click the Widow/Orphan check box, then click the OK button.

You'll set widow/orphan protection for the entire annuity plan description.

To set widow/orphan protection for the entire document:

1. Press **Ctrl + Home** to move the insertion point to the beginning of the document because you want to set widow/orphan protection for the entire document.

2. Click **Format**, point to **Page**, then click **Keep Text Together**. The Keep Text Together dialog box opens.

3. If necessary, click the **Widow/Orphan** check box, then click the **OK** button. The dialog box closes and the protection is on. Now, your document will be free from widows and orphans.

4. Save the annuity plan description.

You have finished several of the formatting changes that Brandi marked on Reginald's first draft of the annuity plan description. Next you'll make character-level formatting changes.

Quick Check

1. What are the three categories of formatting commands?
2. A page that is longer than it is wide is in _____ orientation.
3. Name and describe the five types of justification.
4. What is the purpose of the decimal tab stop alignment?
5. What is the shortcut key to indent all the lines of a paragraph to the next tab stop?
6. What is the difference between a tab stop and a Tab icon? What happens when you click the Tab icon?
7. In general terms, describe how you would keep a paragraph and its corresponding heading from being split between two pages?
8. Why do you want to prevent widows and orphans from appearing in your document?

If you aren't going to work through Session 2.3 now, you should close the document and exit WordPerfect. When you're ready to begin Session 2.3, start WordPerfect, open RHS Annuity Plan, and continue with the session.

SESSION 2.3

In this session you will bold, underline, and italicize text and modify the font type and size. Then you will print the document.

Changing the Font

WordPerfect allows you to specify how the characters within your document look on the screen and on the printed page. A **character** is any letter, digit, punctuation mark, or typographical symbol in your document. You can specify certain **appearances**, or styles, of a character, such as font, size, style, and color.

All the remaining formatting changes that Brandi marked on the annuity plan description are for changing the font, font size, and style of some characters, and for adding special characters. You'll change the font of the title from 12-point Times New Roman to a 14-point bold, sans serif font, such as Arial, Swiss, Univers, or Futura. A **serif** is a small embellishment at the tips of the lines in a character, as shown in Figure 2-35. The text you're reading is a serif font called Sabon. **Sans** is French for "without"; thus a **sans serif** font is a font without the embellishments. Sans serif fonts are usually reserved for titles and headings, because in long lines of text, serif fonts are easier to read. The heading at the top of this section is a sans serif font called Franklin Gothic.

Figure 2-35
Serif and sans serif fonts

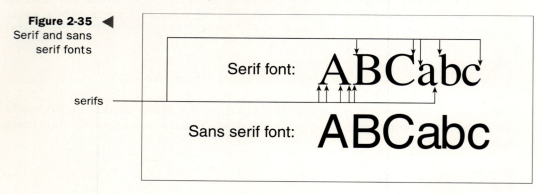

The size (height) of a font is measured in points (72 points to an inch). The larger the point size, the larger the font.

All the fonts that are available with your computer system are listed in the Font list box. Figure 2-36 lists some popular fonts. Your system might have only some of these fonts.

Figure 2-36
Sample fonts

Arial
Avant Garde
Bodoni
Bookman
Brush Script
Century Schoolbook
CG Times
Commercial Script
Courier
Futura

Garamond
Humanist
Letter Gothic
Old English
STENCIL
Swiss
Technical
Times New Roman
Univers
Zapf Calligraphic

Varying the choice of fonts and font sizes can improve the appearance of your document and convey your meaning to readers by helping them to distinguish headings from text, notes from text, and so on.

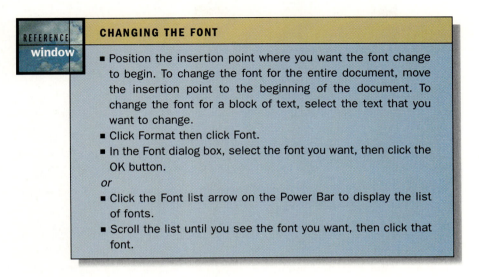

REFERENCE window

CHANGING THE FONT

- Position the insertion point where you want the font change to begin. To change the font for the entire document, move the insertion point to the beginning of the document. To change the font for a block of text, select the text that you want to change.
- Click Format then click Font.
- In the Font dialog box, select the font you want, then click the OK button.

or

- Click the Font list arrow on the Power Bar to display the list of fonts.
- Scroll the list until you see the font you want, then click that font.

Brandi wants you to change not only the font of the title, but also its size and style. To do this, you'll open the Font dialog box where you can make all these changes at once. The Font dialog box also shows a preview or example of the selected font. This is helpful if you're unsure about which font to choose.

To change the font appearance of the title using the Font command:

1. If necessary, press **Ctrl** + **Home** to move the insertion point to the beginning of the document, then select the title.

2. Click **Format** then click **Font** to open the Font dialog box. A list of available fonts appears in alphabetical order with the name of the current font highlighted in the Font face list box. See Figure 2-37. Your list of fonts might be different.

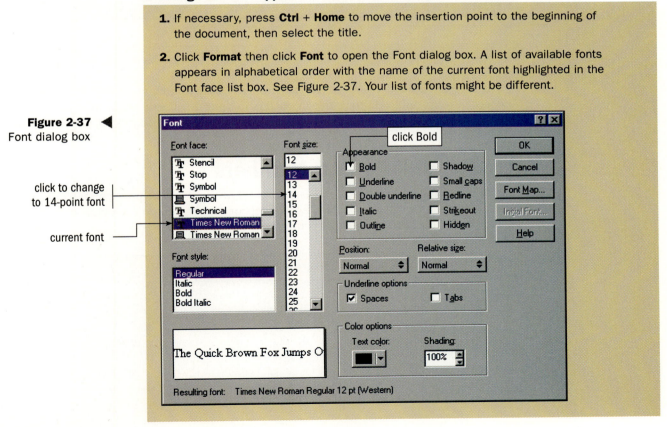

Figure 2-37
Font dialog box

click to change to 14-point font

current font

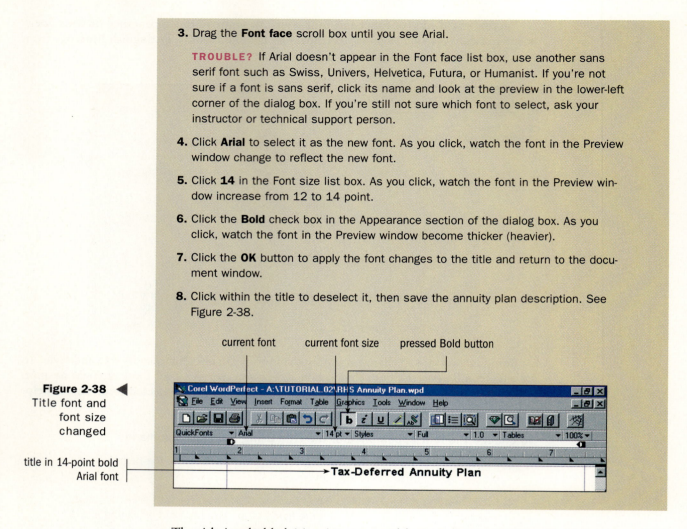

3. Drag the **Font face** scroll box until you see Arial.

   TROUBLE? If Arial doesn't appear in the Font face list box, use another sans serif font such as Swiss, Univers, Helvetica, Futura, or Humanist. If you're not sure if a font is sans serif, click its name and look at the preview in the lower-left corner of the dialog box. If you're still not sure which font to select, ask your instructor or technical support person.

4. Click **Arial** to select it as the new font. As you click, watch the font in the Preview window change to reflect the new font.

5. Click **14** in the Font size list box. As you click, watch the font in the Preview window increase from 12 to 14 point.

6. Click the **Bold** check box in the Appearance section of the dialog box. As you click, watch the font in the Preview window become thicker (heavier).

7. Click the **OK** button to apply the font changes to the title and return to the document window.

8. Click within the title to deselect it, then save the annuity plan description. See Figure 2-38.

Figure 2-38 ◀ Title font and font size changed

title in 14-point bold Arial font

The title is a bolded 14-point sans serif font, as shown in Figure 2-38. Because of differences in fonts and monitors, the characters in your document might look slightly different. Notice when the insertion point is in the title, the information in the Power Bar reflects the current font.

Adding Bullets and Numbers

Special characters or symbols, such as bullets (•) or numbers, help to emphasize particular words or a list of items. You can add bullets or numbers to an existing list or you can add bullets or numbers to a list as you type it.

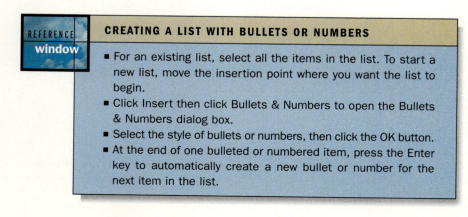

REFERENCE window

CREATING A LIST WITH BULLETS OR NUMBERS

- For an existing list, select all the items in the list. To start a new list, move the insertion point where you want the list to begin.
- Click Insert then click Bullets & Numbers to open the Bullets & Numbers dialog box.
- Select the style of bullets or numbers, then click the OK button.
- At the end of one bulleted or numbered item, press the Enter key to automatically create a new bullet or number for the next item in the list.

ADDING BULLETS, AND NUMBERS   WP 77

Brandi requested that you add bullets to the list of financial needs on page 2 to make them stand out as different items in a list.

To apply bullets to a list of items:

1. Scroll the document until you see the list of financial needs below the sentence "The following are considered to be immediate and heavy financial needs:"

2. Move the insertion point before "Medical expenses...," the first of four items that appear in the middle of page 2.

3. Click **Insert** then click **Bullets & Numbers** to open the Bullets & Numbers dialog box, then click **Large Circle**. See Figure 2-39.

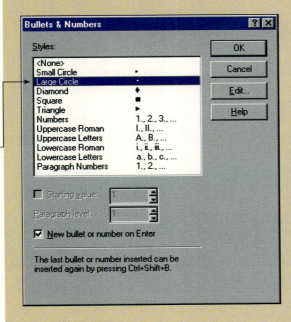

Figure 2-39
Bullets & Numbers dialog box

selected bullet style

4. Click the **OK** button.

A rounded bullet, a special character, appears before the first item in the list. WordPerfect also indents the item an additional ½ inch to the next tab stop.

5. Move the insertion point to the beginning of the next line, then click the **Insert Bullet** button on the Toolbar to insert a bullet and an indent.

6. Repeat Step 5 for the other two items in the list. See Figure 2-40.

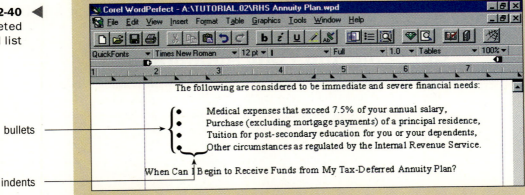

Figure 2-40
Completed bulleted list

bullets

indents

Brandi wants to emphasize how many ways employees can receive funds from their tax-deferred annuity plan by adding numbers to the list in the section below the bulleted list. You can do this in much the same way as you added bullets to the first list. WordPerfect's Bullets & Numbers feature automatically inserts consecutive numbers and aligns them. If you insert a new paragraph, delete a paragraph, or reorder the paragraphs, the numbers automatically adjust to remain consecutive.

To apply numbers to a list of items:

1. Scroll down to the next section and move the insertion point immediately to the left of the "R" in "Reach the age…," the first item in the list.

2. Click **Insert** then click **Bullets & Numbers**. The Bullets & Numbers dialog box opens.

3. Click **Numbers** in the Styles list box, then click the **OK** button. WordPerfect inserts the number 1, a period, and an indent at the beginning of the item.

4. Move the insertion point to the beginning of the next item (immediately to the left of the "L" in "Leave the service…"), then click the **Insert Bullet** button on the Toolbar, the same button you clicked to insert a bullet. WordPerfect automatically inserts the number 2, and again indents the paragraph to the next tab stop. Notice the Insert Bullets button inserts whatever you've set in the Bullets & Numbers dialog box.

5. Repeat Step 4 for the last two items in the list. Figure 2-41 shows the completed numbered list.

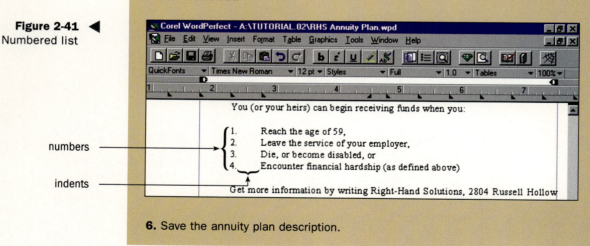

Figure 2-41 ◀
Numbered list

numbers
indents

6. Save the annuity plan description.

Another way to add emphasis and structure to a document is to change the font appearance of certain words and headings.

Changing the Font Appearance

You can emphasize a word in your document with bolding, underlining, or italicizing. These appearances help you make specific thoughts, ideas, words, or phrases stand out. Remember that adding too much emphasis can have the same effect as adding no emphasis—nothing will stand out.

CHANGING THE FONT APPEARANCE   WP 79

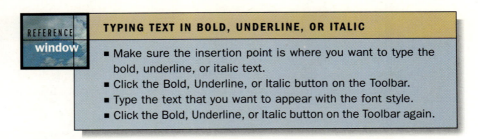

> **REFERENCE window**
>
> **TYPING TEXT IN BOLD, UNDERLINE, OR ITALIC**
> - Make sure the insertion point is where you want to type the bold, underline, or italic text.
> - Click the Bold, Underline, or Italic button on the Toolbar.
> - Type the text that you want to appear with the font style.
> - Click the Bold, Underline, or Italic button on the Toolbar again.

Brandi marked a few words on Reginald's draft that need to be in bold, underline, or italic text to add special emphasis.

Bolding Text

Brandi wants to make sure that clients' employees see that the tax-deferred annuity plan can be terminated only under certain conditions. You'll do this by typing the word "only" in boldface in the document. You could have typed the word, selected it, and then changed it to boldface, but typing the word directly in bold is more efficient in this case.

To type boldface text:

1. Move the insertion point immediately to the right of the word "terminated" in the first line of the paragraph beneath the question "Can My Tax-Deferred Annuity Plan Be Terminated?" near the top of page 2. This is where you'll add the bold-faced word, "only."

2. Press the **spacebar** to add a space between the word "terminated" and the word you'll insert.

3. Click the **Bold** button [b] on the Toolbar to turn on the Bold style. Notice [b] becomes pressed. Any new text you type will appear in boldface in the document and on your printed page.

4. Type **only** then click [b] again to turn off boldfacing. Notice [b] is no longer pressed. See Figure 2-42.

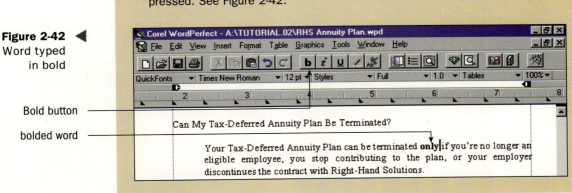

Figure 2-42 ◄ Word typed in bold

Bold button

bolded word

In the previous set of steps, you clicked the Bold button before you began typing to turn on the bold style, and you clicked it again after you finished typing to turn off the style. If you select the bolded word, the Bold button is pressed to show that the bold style is on. The Underline and Italic commands work the same way. All three commands are toggle switches. A **toggle switch** is any key or command that alternates between on and off.

Underlining Text

The Underline command works in the same way as the Bold command. Brandi's edits indicate that the word "Note" should be inserted and underlined at the beginning of the final paragraph. You'll make both of these changes at once using the Underline command.

To underline text:

1. Press **Ctrl + End** to move the insertion point to the end of the document, then move the insertion point to the left of the word "Get" in the first line of the final paragraph.

2. Click the **Underline** button [U] on the Toolbar to turn on underlining. Notice [U] is pressed. Now, whatever text you type will be underlined on your screen and in your printed document.

3. Type **Note** and then click [U] again to toggle off underlining. Notice [U] is no longer pressed, and the word "Note" is underlined.

4. Type **:** (a colon), then press the **spacebar** twice. See Figure 2-43.

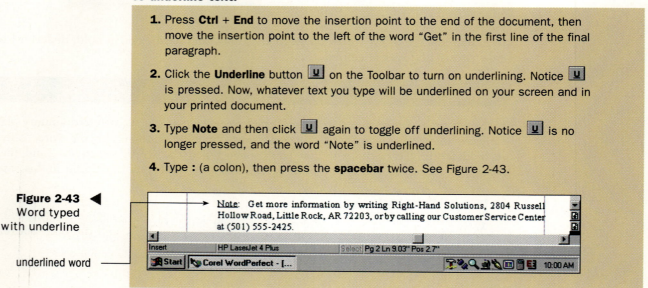

Figure 2-43
Word typed with underline

underlined word

The last font style Brandi wants you to add to the annuity plan description is italic text.

Italicizing Text

Like the Bold and Underline commands, the Italic command is a toggle switch; it works the same way as the other font appearance commands. Brandi wants to insert and italicize the name of the newsletter, *Sensible Solutions*, that Right-Hand Solutions produces and distributes to its clients. You'll do this by typing the italicized name into the text.

To type italicized text:

1. Scroll to the paragraph under the heading "How Will I Know How Well My Investments Are Doing?" at the beginning of page 2, and then move the insertion point between the letter "r" in the word "newsletter" and the period at the end of the sentence.

2. Type **,** (comma) then press the **spacebar** to insert a space.

3. Click the **Italic** button [i] on the Toolbar to toggle on the command.

4. Type **Sensible Solutions** then click elsewhere in that line. When you move the insertion point from the italicized text region, the Italic button automatically turns off.

5. Save the annuity plan description.

You have added new text in boldface, underline, or italics in just one step. You can also change the appearance of existing text. The select method is the quickest way to apply bold, underline, or italic to existing text. You'll make Reginald's document conform with the other documents that Right-Hand Solutions produces by italicizing and boldfacing each question (heading) in the document. This makes the document easier to read by clearly separating the sections. You'll begin with the first heading.

To italicize and boldface the first question heading:

1. Move to the beginning of the document and triple-click **What Is a Tax-Deferred Annuity?** to select the text of the first heading.

2. Click the **Italic** button on the Toolbar to toggle on the command. The heading changes from regular to italic text.

   With the heading still selected, you can easily apply the boldfacing.

3. Click the **Bold** button on the Toolbar to bold the heading. See Figure 2-44.

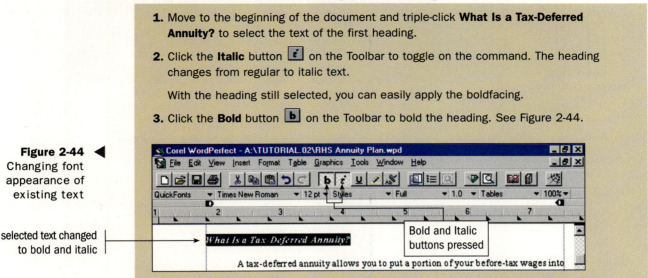

Figure 2-44 Changing font appearance of existing text

selected text changed to bold and italic

Bold and Italic buttons pressed

You need to italicize and boldface the other six questions (headings) in the document. Rather than select each one individually and then click the Italic and the Bold buttons, you'll use QuickFormat.

Using QuickFormat

QuickFormat is a feature that allows you to copy quickly and accurately all the formatting features of one paragraph to one or more other paragraphs. QuickFormat saves you time because you make all the formatting changes for a paragraph once and then copy the formats to the rest of your document. You'll use QuickFormat to italicize and boldface the other headings.

To apply formatting with QuickFormat:

1. Make sure the first heading "What Is a Tax-Deferred Annuity?" is still selected.

2. Click the **QuickFormat** button on the Toolbar. The QuickFormat dialog box opens.

3. Click the **Headings** radio button, then click the **OK** button. The pointer becomes.

4. If necessary, scroll so you can see the second heading, "How Do I Enroll in a Tax-Deferred Annuity Plan?"

5. Click anywhere in the second heading. The heading immediately becomes italicized and boldfaced.

6. Repeat Steps 4 and 5 for the remaining five question headings. After formatting the last heading, your document window looks like Figure 2-45.

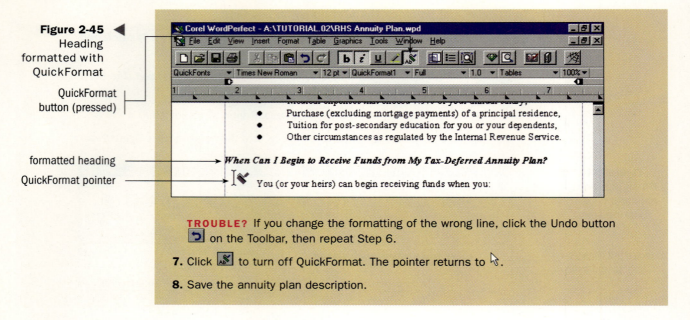

Figure 2-45 Heading formatted with QuickFormat

QuickFormat button (pressed)

formatted heading
QuickFormat pointer

> **TROUBLE?** If you change the formatting of the wrong line, click the Undo button on the Toolbar, then repeat Step 6.
>
> 7. Click to turn off QuickFormat. The pointer returns to .
> 8. Save the annuity plan description.

The italicized and boldfaced headings stand out from the rest of the text and help give the document a visual structure.

Revealing Format Codes

Whenever you execute WordPerfect commands, WordPerfect inserts invisible format codes into your document. These codes tell WordPerfect how to format the document on the screen as well as how to print it. When you're typing a document, you usually do not need to see these format codes. But sometimes you need to reveal them—for instance, when you've pressed the wrong key or you want to delete a format code. WordPerfect's **Reveal Codes** feature displays the format codes so you can:

- Find the exact location of open format commands, that is, where a particular formatting feature begins.

- See spaces between words more easily because the spaces appear as diamond characters. Sometimes it's difficult to tell if you have accidentally included an extra space between words or omitted a space if you're using a small font (such as 10-point Times Roman).

- Determine the cause of formatting problems, which are often due to incorrectly placed formatting codes.

- Delete codes to remove a particular format.

- Adjust precisely which characters you format a certain way; this is especially valuable when formatting is difficult to see on the monitor.

You'll show the formatting codes in the annuity plan description so you can see some of the advantages of Reveal Codes.

To reveal hidden format codes:

> 1. Click **View** then click **Reveal Codes**. WordPerfect divides the document window into two parts. The upper part is the main document window and the lower part is the Reveal Codes window.
>
> 2. Press **Ctrl + Home** to move the insertion point to the beginning of the document and to display the format codes that appear there. See Figure 2-46.

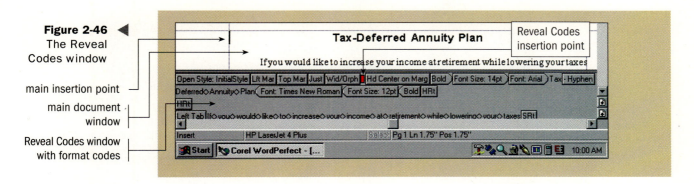

Figure 2-46
The Reveal Codes window

main insertion point

main document window

Reveal Codes window with format codes

Notice in Figure 2-46 each gray button contains a formatting code. The Open Style: InitialStyle button in the upper-left corner of the Reveal Codes window is a formatting code that sets the initial format of the document. The next two buttons, labeled Lft Mar and Top Mar, are the codes for the left and top margin changes that you made earlier.

Some codes mark the location of a format change but do not specify a value. For example, the Top Mar button indicates a margin change but doesn't show the new value of the top margin. To see the value, you must move the insertion point to the left of the code button.

The insertion point in the Reveal Codes window is marked with a red rectangle. Therefore Figure 2-46 contains two insertion points, the usual one in the document window and the red rectangular one in the Reveal Codes window. The two insertion points move together.

You'll move the insertion point in the Reveal Codes window to the left of the Top Mar code so you can read the top margin value.

To move the insertion point to a particular code:

1. Click the **Top Mar** button in the Reveal Codes window. The insertion point immediately moves to the left of the code. The button expands so you can read the top margin's value. See Figure 2-47.

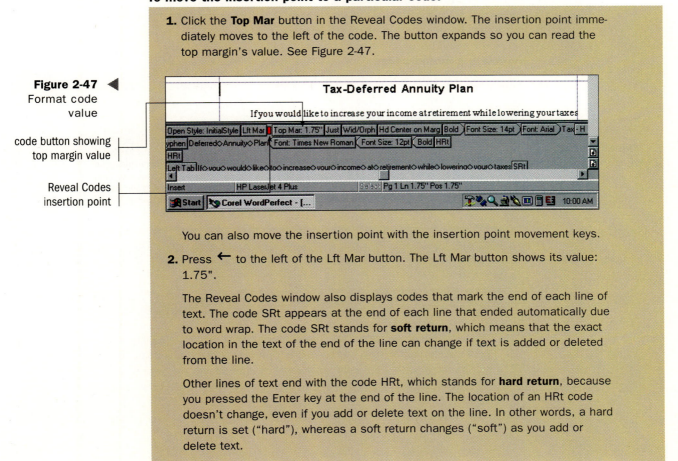

Figure 2-47
Format code value

code button showing top margin value

Reveal Codes insertion point

You can also move the insertion point with the insertion point movement keys.

2. Press ← to the left of the Lft Mar button. The Lft Mar button shows its value: 1.75".

The Reveal Codes window also displays codes that mark the end of each line of text. The code SRt appears at the end of each line that ended automatically due to word wrap. The code SRt stands for **soft return**, which means that the exact location in the text of the end of the line can change if text is added or deleted from the line.

Other lines of text end with the code HRt, which stands for **hard return**, because you pressed the Enter key at the end of the line. The location of an HRt code doesn't change, even if you add or delete text on the line. In other words, a hard return is set ("hard"), whereas a soft return changes ("soft") as you add or delete text.

3. Press ↓ several times so the text scrolls up through the Reveal Codes window. As you can see, every line of text ends with SRt or HRt.

4. Move the insertion point to the beginning of the first line of text below the heading "How Do I Enroll in the Tax Deferred Annuity Plan?" See Figure 2-48.

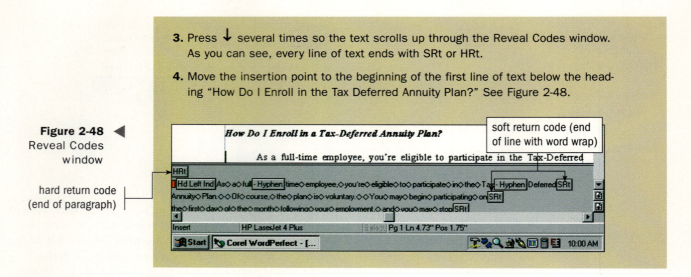

Figure 2-48
Reveal Codes window

hard return code (end of paragraph)

soft return code (end of line with word wrap)

With the Reveal Codes window open, you can insert, edit, and format text exactly as you did before. The only difference is that you can see the format codes as WordPerfect inserts them into your document. This way if you want to remove a certain format, you can do so by deleting its code button.

Deleting Format Codes

Reginald had italicized the phrase "To participate" in the third paragraph of the document, but it should be in regular text. Because bold, underline, and italic are toggle switches, you can remove the style easily by selecting the text and then clicking the appropriate button to remove the style. Alternatively, you can delete the beginning or ending format code in the Reveal Codes window to change the font appearance. You'll remove the italics by deleting the format code.

To delete a format code:

1. Move the insertion point to the left of the italicized phrase "To participate" in the paragraph below the third heading, "How Do I Enroll in a Tax-Deferred Annuity Plan?" See Figure 2-49.

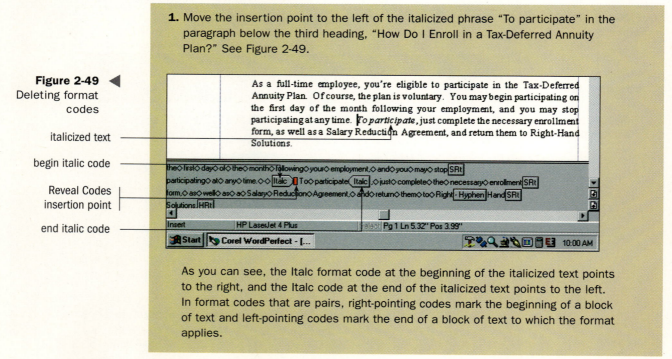

Figure 2-49
Deleting format codes

italicized text

begin italic code

Reveal Codes insertion point

end italic code

As you can see, the Italc format code at the beginning of the italicized text points to the right, and the Italc code at the end of the italicized text points to the left. In format codes that are pairs, right-pointing codes mark the beginning of a block of text and left-pointing codes mark the end of a block of text to which the format applies.

2. With the Reveal Codes insertion point to the right of the beginning Italc code button, press the **Backspace** key to delete the code. Both the beginning and ending codes are deleted, and the text is no longer italicized. When format codes appear in pairs, you automatically delete both codes when you delete either one.

3. Click **View** then click **Reveal Codes** to close the Reveal Codes window.

4. Save the annuity plan description.

You have made all the editing and formatting changes that Brandi requested for the annuity plan description. You're ready to print a copy of the document. Before you do, however, Reginald asks you to check if the document meets the guidelines for all documents produced by Right-Hand Solutions.

Getting Document Properties

Right-Hand Solutions publishes writing guidelines for the various types of documents produced by its employees. One of those guidelines is that benefits descriptions should contain fewer than 550 words. You need to ensure that the final annuity plan description fits within this word limit. You'll determine the document's length (in words) using WordPerfect's Document Properties feature.

To determine a document's properties:

1. Click **File**, point to **Document**, then click **Properties** to open the Properties dialog box.

2. Click the **Information** tab to display statistics for the document. See Figure 2-50. Because every computer is different, some of the statistics for your document might differ from those shown in Figure 2-50.

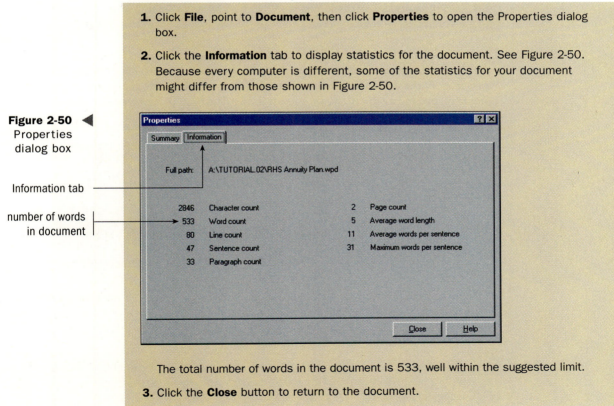

Figure 2-50
Properties dialog box

Information tab

number of words in document

The total number of words in the document is 533, well within the suggested limit.

3. Click the **Close** button to return to the document.

Reginald is pleased that the annuity plan description fits within the word limit. He is curious about how the word count changed from his earlier draft and asks you to check the word count of the unedited document.

Switching Between Documents

Currently, only the document you saved and edited as RHS Annuity Plan is open. With WordPerfect, you can have as many documents open at one time as your computer's memory can handle. There are many reasons you might want or need more than one document open at a time. For example, you might want to compare two versions of a document as Reginald asked you to do, cut and paste text from one document to another, or refer to one document while you're working on another.

When you open a document, it appears in the document window and its name is listed on the title bar. When you open two or more documents at once, you can view only one document at a time in the document window; this is the **active document**. The Window menu contains a list of all the open WordPerfect documents. You can switch between open documents (or change the active document) by choosing a document from this list.

You'll open the unedited version of the annuity plan, Annuity, which is still on your Student Disk, so you can check its word count and see how it differs from the edited version, RHS Annuity Plan.

To open another document:

1. With the document RHS Annuity Plan in the document window, click the **Open** button on the Toolbar. The Open dialog box opens.

2. If necessary, click the **Look in** list arrow, click **3½ Floppy (A:)** or the appropriate drive, then double-click the **Tutorial.02** folder.

3. Click **Annuity** to select the unedited file, then click the **Open** button. The document opens, with the insertion point at the beginning of the unedited document.

Although you now have two documents open (Annuity and RHS Annuity Plan), you can work in only the active document, Annuity. You can tell which document is the active document by looking at the filename shown in the title bar. To work on the edited RHS Annuity Plan, you must make it the active document.

REFERENCE window	SWITCHING BETWEEN OPEN DOCUMENTS
	▪ Click Window then click the name of the document you want to make active.
	or
	▪ Press Ctrl + Shift + F6 until the document you want active appears in the document window.

You'll switch between the two open documents—the unedited document, Annuity, and the edited version, RHS Annuity Plan.

To switch between the open documents:

1. Click **Window** to open the Window menu. Both document names appear at the bottom of the Window menu. A check mark by **Annuity** indicates that it is the active document.

2. Click **RHS Annuity Plan**. The Window menu closes and **RHS Annuity Plan** becomes the active document. You can see the edited title and formatted paragraphs.

3. Click **Window** again to open the Window menu, then click **Annuity** to make it the active document.

4. Open the **Properties** dialog box and click the **Information** tab to check the word count of **Annuity**, just as you did earlier for **RHS Annuity Plan**. The word count is 550, right at the recommended word count for Right-Hand Solutions documents. Close the Properties dialog box.

5. Click **File** then click **Close** to close **Annuity** without saving changes. If the message Save changes to...?," appears, click the **No** button to indicate that you don't want to save any changes to the document. **RHS Annuity Plan** again becomes the active document because it is the only open document.

Reginald is pleased that the word count dropped a bit between the two versions of the annuity plan description. You are ready to print the document.

Printing the Document

Reginald originally asked you to print three copies of the edited annuity plan description—one for Brandi, one for himself, and one for the copy center that will print and distribute the final document to the company's clients. You could print multiple copies by selecting the Print command three times or you could change the Number of copies in the Print dialog box. However, new company policy suggests printing only one copy of a document and photocopying the original to make additional copies. This leaves the printer available to more people and reduces the amount of time you spend waiting for your document to print.

Reginald suggests that you give him one printed copy and he'll make the needed photocopies. You need to check that the Print dialog box is set to print only one copy.

To print one copy of the document using the Print dialog box:

1. Click the **Print** button on the Toolbar to open the Print dialog box.

2. Make sure the Number of Copies box in the Copies section of the dialog box is set to **1**. If you wanted to print more than one copy of the document, you would type the appropriate number in the Number of Copies text box.

3. Click the **Print** button. After a few moments, your printer will print a copy of the annuity plan description.

4. Click **File** then click **Exit** to close your document and exit WordPerfect.

You have a hard copy of the final annuity plan description, as shown in Figure 2-51. You give the hard copy to Reginald, who makes two photocopies—one for Brandi and one for the copy center, which copies and distributes the document to all clients of Right-Hand Solutions.

Figure 2-51
Final version of RHS Annuity Plan

Tax-Deferred Annuity Plan

If you would like to increase your income at retirement while lowering your taxes now, then consider participating in a tax-deferred annuity plan.

What Is a Tax-Deferred Annuity?

A tax-deferred annuity allows you to put a portion of your before-tax wages into an investment account on a regular basis. Instead of paying taxes on the money now (when your tax rate is high), you pay taxes on the money after you retire (when your tax rate will be lower). In the meantime, the annuity account earns dividends that permit you to supplement your retire

How Do I Enroll in a Tax-Deferred Annuity Plan?

As a full-time employee, you're eligible to parti Annuity Plan. Of course, the plan is voluntary. You the first day of the month following your emplo participating at any time. To participate, just comple form, as well as a Salary Reduction Agreement, and Solutions.

How Will My Money Be Invested?

On your annuity application you can allocate you options, such as stocks, money markets, bonds, and

A typical allocation might be similar to the followi

Stock	30%
Money Market	25%
Bond Market	25%
World Equities	15%
Other	5%

You can change your allocation at any time by ca Center at (501) 555-2425. Right-Hand Solutions wil your money safely and effectively so you will rea earnings.

How Will I Know How Well My Investments Are Doing?

Right-Hand Solutions will send you a report annually, showing your total accumulation. Every quarter you'll receive a statement containing a complete history of all financial transactions and showing the interest credited you've earned. You'll also receive our regular newsletter, *Sensible Solutions*.

Can My Tax-Deferred Annuity Plan Be Terminated?

Your Tax-Deferred Annuity Plan can be terminated **only** if you're no longer an eligible employee, you stop contributing to the plan, or your employer discontinues the contract with Right-Hand Solutions.

Can I Withdraw Money from My Tax-Deferred Annuity Plan?

Normally, if you make an early withdrawal from your tax-deferred annuity plan, you will incur substantial financial penalties. However, you can withdraw money without penalty if you have an immediate and severe financial need (as defined below) and the money from your plan is necessary to meet those needs. Under current law, these withdrawals are subject to ordinary income taxes.

The following are considered to be immediate and severe financial needs:

- Medical expenses that exceed 7.5% of your annual salary,
- Purchase (excluding mortgage payments) of a principal residence,
- Tuition for post-secondary education for you or your dependents,
- Other circumstances as regulated by the Internal Revenue Service.

When Can I Begin to Receive Funds from My Tax-Deferred Annuity Plan?

You (or your heirs) can begin receiving funds when you:

1. Reach the age of 59,
2. Leave the service of your employer,
3. Die, or become disabled, or
4. Encounter financial hardship (as defined above).

Note: Get more information by writing Right-Hand Solutions, 2804 Russell Hollow Road, Little Rock, AR 72203, or by calling our Customer Service Center at (501) 555-2425.

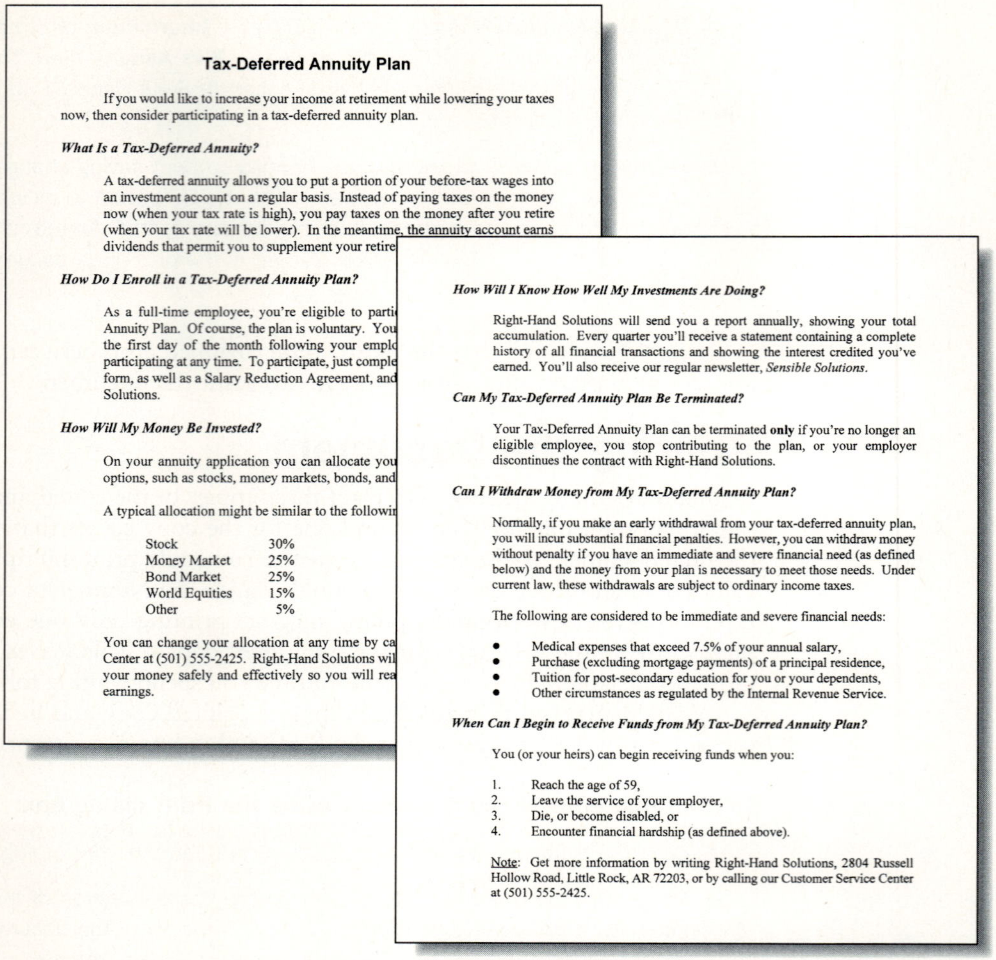

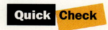

Quick Check

1. Define the following in your own words:
   a. character
   b. styles
2. True or False: The larger the point size, the smaller the font that will be displayed and printed.
3. In your own words, explain the difference between a serif and a sans serif font.
4. How do you apply numbers to a list of items?
5. What is a toggle switch? Name three toggle switches.
6. Describe an instance in which you would use italics in a document.
7. Describe Reveal Codes and explain its purpose.
8. List one method for determining the length (in words) of a document.

Tutorial Assignments

Start WordPerfect, and if necessary, make sure your screen matches those in the tutorial. Open RHSQuart from the TAssign folder from the Tutorial.02 folder on your Student Disk, save the document as RHS Quarterly Report, then complete the following:

1. Make all edits and formatting changes marked on Figure 2-52.

Figure 2-52 ◀

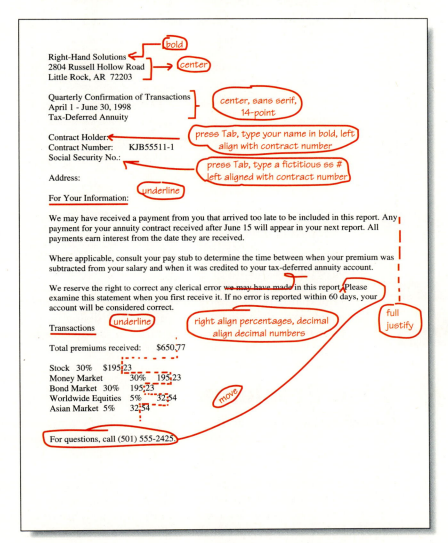

2. Save the document and print it.
3. Determine the number of words in the document, and then write that number in the upper-right corner of the printout.
4. Close the document.

Open the file RHSPort from the TAssign folder from the Tutorial.02 folder on your Student Disk, save the file as RHS Portfolio Changes, then complete the following:

5. Make all the edits and formatting changes marked on Figure 2-53.

Figure 2-53

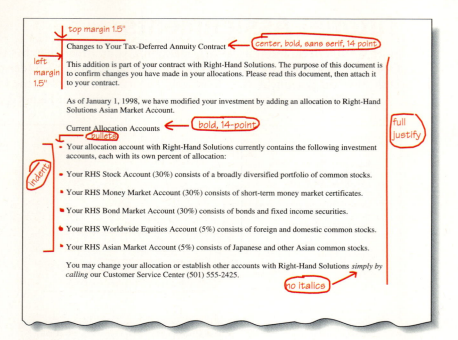

6. Turn on Reveal Codes, then delete the italic codes from the last paragraph.
7. Save the document.
8. Print two copies of the document. (*Hint*: Change the Number of copies in the Print dialog box.) After you've printed the document, reset the Number of copies to 1, then click Cancel in the Print dialog box.
9. Determine the number of *paragraphs* in the document, then write that number in the upper-right corner of one printout.
10. Close the document.

Case Problems

1. Raleigh Rentals Michele Stafford manages Raleigh Rentals, a storage facility in Huntsville, Alabama. She has written the draft of a tenant information sheet outlining Raleigh Rental's policies for new customers. She asks you to edit and format her tenant information sheet.

Open the file Raleigh from the Cases folder in the Tutorial.02 folder on your Student Disk, save it as Raleigh Rental Policies, then do the following:

1. Delete the word "general" from the first sentence of the first full paragraph.
2. Delete the sentence that begins "If you renew your contract..." from the end of the second paragraph.
3. Insert the bolded sentence "A bill will not be sent to you." after the first sentence under the "Rental Payments" heading.
4. Delete the second paragraph under the "Rental Payments" heading.
5. Move the heading "Fees" and the sentence below it after the "Rental Charges" section.
6. Delete the phrase "not negotiable, and are" from the first sentence under the "Rental Charges" heading.
7. Change all the margins (top, bottom, left, and right) to 1.5 inches for the entire document.
8. Change the justification for the entire document to full.
9. Align the first column (unit sizes) of the rental charges using a right-aligned tab stop.

10. Align the second column of the rental charges using a decimal-aligned tab stop.
11. Bold the phrase "in writing" in the last sentence under the "Termination" heading.

12. Add bullets to the list under the "Delinquent Accounts" heading.
13. Change both lines of the title to 16-point Arial (or some other sans serif font).
14. Center and bold both lines of the title.
15. Boldface and italicize the first heading, then use QuickFormat to boldface the subsequent headings.
16. If necessary, keep the heading "Termination" and the paragraph that follows it on the same page.
17. Save and print the rental information sheet.
18. Write the number of words in the document in the upper-right corner of the printout, then close the document.

2. Synergy Synergy provides productivity training for large companies across the country. Matt Patterson is Synergy's marketing director for the Northeast region. Matt wants to provide interested clients with a one-page summary of Synergy's productivity training.

Open the file Synergy from the Cases folder in the Tutorial.02 folder on your Student Disk, save it as Synergy Training Summary, then do the following:

1. Change the title at the beginning of the document to a 14-point sans serif font.
2. Center and bold the title.
3. Delete the word "main" from the second sentence of the first paragraph after the document title.
4. Add bullets to the list of training components following the first paragraph.
5. Delete the second sentence from the first paragraph under the heading, "Personal Productivity Training Seminar."
6. Delete the phrase, "in attendance at the seminar," from the first sentence in the second paragraph under the heading "Personal Productivity Training Seminar."
7. In the first paragraph under "Management Productivity Training," move the second sentence beginning with "As a result..." to the end of the paragraph.
8. Switch the order of the paragraphs under the "Field Services Technology and Training" heading.
9. Change the top margin to 1.5 inches and the left margin to 1.75 inches.

10. Format the first paragraph as a hanging indent.
11. Bold the first heading then use QuickFormat to bold the subsequent headings.
12. Align the training costs at the end of the document using a right-aligned tab stop for the second column.

13. Keep the "Costs for Synergy's Productivity Training" heading, the paragraph below it, and the columns explaining the training costs together on the same page. (*Hint*: Select the text then apply block protection.)
14. Bold the word "free" both times in the second paragraph under the "Field Services Technology and Training" heading.
15. Save and print Synergy Training Summary, then close the file.

3. RecTech Ralph Dysktra is vice president of sales and marketing at RecTech, an outdoor and gear store in Conshohocken, Pennsylvania. Each quarter, Ralph and his staff mail a description of new products to RecTech's regular customers. Ralph has asked you to edit and format the first few pages of this quarter's new products description.

Open the file RecTech from the Cases folder in the Tutorial.02 folder on your Student Disk, save it as RecTech Backpackers Guide, then do the following:

1. Delete the word "much" from the first sentence of the paragraph below the heading "Snuggle Up to These Prices."
2. Reverse the order of the last two paragraphs under the heading, "You'll Eat Up the Prices of This Camp Cooking Gear!"
3. Move the last sentence of the document to the end of the first full paragraph.
4. Reorder the "RecTech Gear Up Ideas" by moving the first two product ideas to the end of the list. Some product ideas contain more than one sentence and span more than one line.

5. Add Large Circle bullets to the Gear Up product ideas. (*Hint*: Select all the text (but not the blank lines) below the sentence that begins "Here are some other product ideas," and above the last line of the document, then apply the bullets.)

6. Change the top margin to 2 inches and the left margin to 1.75 inches.
7. Use a first line indent of 0.75 inch for the first paragraph.
8. Change the alignment for the entire document to full justification.

9. Apply a 14-point, bold, script font to each heading. (*Hint*: Use QuickFormat.) Examples of script fonts are Commercial Script, Coronet, Embassy, Murray Hill, Park Avenue, and Zapf Chancery. If your system doesn't have a script font, use another font.
10. Change the font and appearance of the title to match the headings, except set the size to 16 point.
11. Center both lines of the title.
12. Bold the names and prices for all of the brand-name products in the RecTech Backpackers Guide.
13. Turn on widow/orphan protection. If necessary, set a Conditional End of Page for each heading that might appear alone at the bottom of a page.
14. Save and print the document, then close the file.

4. Movie Review Your student newspaper has asked you to review four films currently showing in your area. Write a brief summary (one to two paragraphs) and provide a rating for each movie. Save the document as Movie Review in the Cases folder in the Tutorial.02 folder on your Student Disk and print it, then edit and format your document by doing the following:

1. Rearrange the order in which you discuss the movies to alphabetical order.
2. Change the top margin to 2 inches.
3. Set the left and right margins to 1.75 inches.
4. Add a title to your review and center it.
5. Indent the first line of each paragraph and set the paragraph alignment to full justification.
6. Italicize the title of each movie.
7. If your document is more than one page, turn on widow/orphan protection.
8. Save the edited document as Edited Movie Review, then print it.
9. Determine the number of words in your document and write the number in the upper-left corner of your printout.
10. Close your document.

TUTORIAL 3

Creating a Multiple-Page Report

Writing a Recommendation Report for AgriTechnology

OBJECTIVES

In this tutorial you will:

- Find and replace text
- Use the Spell Checker, Thesaurus, and Grammatik
- Center text vertically on a page
- Create headers and footers
- Number the pages in a document
- Create footnotes and endnotes
- Change line spacing in a document
- Define and apply styles
- Save styles in a separate file for use in other documents

CASE

AgriTechnology

Brittany Jones works for AgriTechnology, a biotechnology company that develops genetically engineered foods. Recently, AgriTechnology began shipping the EverRipe tomato to supermarkets. The EverRipe tomato is genetically engineered to stay ripe and fresh nearly twice as long as other varieties. Because of its longer shelf life and vine-ripened taste, supermarkets are eager to stock the new tomato, and the demand has been high. Unfortunately, the EverRipe tomato also is more susceptible to bruising than usual varieties. Nearly 20% of the first year's crop was unmarketable due to shipping and handling damage. AgriTechnology's vice president, Ramon Espinoza, appointed Brittany to head a task force to determine how to increase the profitability of the EverRipe tomato. The task force is ready to present the results of their study to him and other executives at AgriTechnology in the form of a recommendation report. Brittany asks you to help prepare the report.

In this tutorial, you'll review Brittany's plan for the task force's recommendation report and then edit and format the report for her.

In Session 3.1, you'll learn how to move the insertion point directly to a particular word or phrase, find and replace a word or phrase in the text, and use WordPerfect's Spell Checker, Thesaurus, and Grammatik features to correct errors and improve the readability of the text. In Session 3.2, you'll create headers and footers and use WordPerfect's Footnote feature. In Session 3.3, you'll create and apply styles to automatically format the document, then you'll print it.

SESSION 3.1

In this session you will see how Brittany planned the task force's recommendation report. You will edit the document by replacing words and sentences, checking the spelling of the document, finding synonyms for words, and checking the grammar.

Planning the Document

As head of the task force, Brittany divided the responsibility for the report among the members. Each person gathered information about one aspect of the problem and wrote the appropriate section of the report. Now Brittany must compile all the findings into a coherent and unified report. She also must follow the company's style guidelines for the content, organization, style, and format of the report.

Content

The content of the report is the results of the study—obtained from employee interviews, and visits to the packaging and distribution plant, trucking company, and so forth—and recommendations for action.

Organization

Because Brittany knows some executives prefer a brief synopsis of the entire report, she includes an executive summary. The body of the report provides an in-depth statement of the problem and recommended solutions.

Style

The report follows established standards of business-writing style, emphasizing clarity, simplicity, and directness.

Presentation

In accordance with AgriTechnology's style guidelines, Brittany's report will begin with a title page with the text centered between the top and bottom margins. The text in the body of the report will be double-spaced and full justified. Every page, except the title page, will include a header with the name of the report and the page number. Every page, including the title page, will include a footer with the company name and the date will be included on every page (even the title page).

Opening the Draft of the Report

Brittany and the other members of the task force already have combined their individual sections into a draft of the report. She asks you to edit the report, as shown in Figure 3-1, to correct errors and improve the readability, to check the grammar of a section of the text, and to format the report according to AgriTechnology's style guidelines.

Figure 3-1 ◀
Initial draft of task force's report with edits

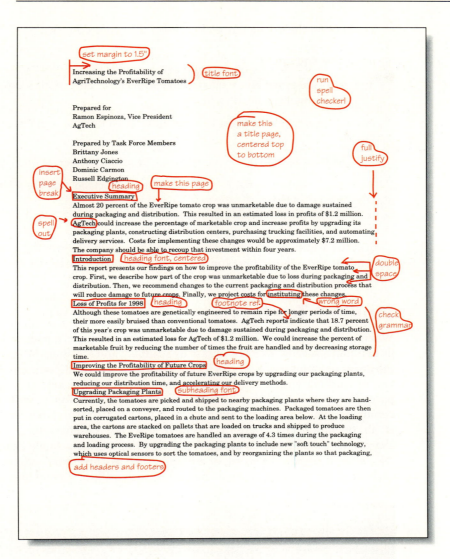

You'll open the document and perform the required tasks.

To open the document:

1. Start WordPerfect and conduct a screen check to make sure your screen matches the figures in this tutorial.
2. Click **View** then click **Page** to make sure your document is in Page view, not Draft view.
3. Open the **EverRipe** document from the **Tutorial.03** folder on your Student Disk.
4. To avoid overwriting the original file, save the document as **EverRipe Report** to the same folder.

Brittany wants you to insert the word "handheld" before the word "computers" near the end of the report, but you don't know exactly where to find "computers" in the document.

Finding Text

When you're working with a short document (for example, a page or less in length) you easily can find a specific word or phrase by scanning and scrolling the text. Then, you can move the insertion point to the word's location with the insertion-point movement keys. But when you're working with a longer document, usually the quickest and easiest way to locate a particular word or phrase or move to a specific location is with the **Find and Replace** command, which searches your document for a search string that you can replace. A **search** is an operation that finds a specified sequence of characters, formatting, or special characters, called a **search string**. A search string can be a single character, such as "T" or "4"; a word, a part of a word, or a phrase, such as "inventory" or "feasibility"; formatting, such as a font or italics; special characters, such as ¶; or a combination of these.

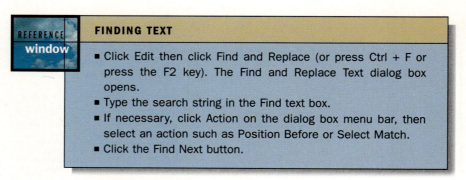

REFERENCE window

FINDING TEXT

- Click Edit then click Find and Replace (or press Ctrl + F or press the F2 key). The Find and Replace Text dialog box opens.
- Type the search string in the Find text box.
- If necessary, click Action on the dialog box menu bar, then select an action such as Position Before or Select Match.
- Click the Find Next button.

You need to insert the missing word "handheld" before the word "computers" in the paragraph above the heading "Cost of the Changes," as shown in Figure 3-2.

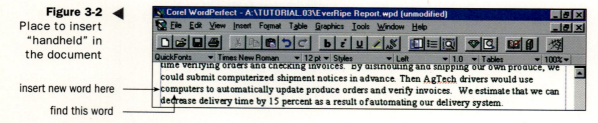

Figure 3-2
Place to insert "handheld" in the document

insert new word here

find this word

You'll use the Find and Replace command to move the insertion point quickly to the word "computers."

To find the word "computers" in the report:

1. Make sure the insertion point is at the beginning of the document so you can search the entire report. Usually, search operations start from the current location of the insertion point and move to the end of the document.

2. Click **Edit** then click **Find and Replace** to open the Find and Replace Text dialog box. Notice the dialog box contains a menu bar from which you can select options, just as you would select commands from the menu bar in the document window. See Figure 3-3.

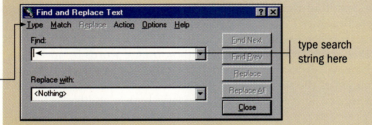

Figure 3-3 ◀
Find and Replace Text dialog box

dialog box menu bar

type search string here

   TROUBLE? If the Find text box already has text in it, someone already has used WordPerfect to locate a word. The text is highlighted so the old string will be replaced when you type your search string. Continue with Step 3.

3. Type the search string **computers** in the Find text box.

   Now you want to specify the action WordPerfect should take when it finds the search string.

4. Click **Action** on the dialog box menu bar, then click **Position Before** so the insertion point moves before the found search string.

5. Click the **Find Next** button to begin the search. WordPerfect searches the document until it finds the first (and in this report only) occurrence of the word "computers" and then positions the insertion point to its left. You might not be able to see the insertion point until you close the dialog box.

   TROUBLE? If WordPerfect stopped at the word "computerized," you might have typed the word "computer" in the Find text box. Any word that contains the search component, in this case the word "*computer*ized," is usually found during a search unless you specify otherwise. Change the search string to "computers" and then click the Find Next button until "computers" is highlighted.

6. Click the **Close** button in the Find and Replace Text dialog box. Now you can see the insertion point.

7. Type **handheld** then press the **spacebar** to add the missing word.

8. Click the **Save** button on the Toolbar to save the report.

As you work with long documents, you'll discover that using the Find and Replace command to move the insertion point to specific locations is usually much faster than scrolling or using the insertion-point movement keys.

Finding and Replacing Text

Brittany wants you to find and change any occurrence of the word "AgTech" to the company's full name, which is more appropriate for a formal report. You can make all the changes at once with the Find and Replace command. The complete Find and Replace command searches through a document for a search string and then substitutes one or more occurrences of the string with a replacement string. Like the search string, the **replacement string** can be any combination of characters, words, or formatting. You can stop at each occurrence of the search string and decide when to substitute the replacement string by clicking the Replace button, or you can click the Replace All button to substitute every occurrence of the search string with the replacement string all at once.

WordPerfect looks for every instance of the search string you specify, even if it occurs within another word. For example, if your company initials were "ABI" and you wanted to substitute the full name "American Budget Insurance," WordPerfect would replace "profitability" (which contains the letters "abi") with "profitAmerican Budget Insurancelity," which makes no sense. You can avoid stopping at words that contain the search string or replacing text with nonsense words by specifying that you want to match whole words to the search string. You also can specify to match the exact case (capitalization) of the search string. If the Find and Replace command causes problems in your document, immediately click the Undo button and try again.

FINDING AND REPLACING TEXT

- Click Edit then click Find and Replace (or press Ctrl + F or press the F2 key). The Find and Replace Text dialog box opens.
- Type the search string in the Find text box.
- If necessary, click Match, then select one or more match criteria, such as Whole Word or Case.
- Type the replacement string in the Replace with text box.
- If necessary, click Action then click Select Match so WordPerfect selects the found search string.
- Click the Replace button to find the next occurrence of the search string, or click the Replace All button to replace all occurrences of the search string with the replacement string.
- If you clicked the Replace button (not the Replace All button), click Replace to make the replacement and find the next occurrence of the search string, or click the Find Next button to skip the current occurrence and find the next occurrence.

Brittany used the company nickname "AgTech" throughout the document. You'll use the Find and Replace command to find and replace every "AgTech" in the document with "AgriTechnology."

To find and replace text:

1. Move the insertion point to the beginning of the document, click **Edit** then click **Find and Replace** to open the Find and Replace Text dialog box again. The contents of the Find text box (your previous Find and Replace operation) is highlighted. Any text you type replaces the highlighted text.

2. Type **AgTech** in the Find text box, then press the **Tab** key to move the insertion point to the Replace with text box.

   Notice that pressing the Tab key in a dialog box moves the insertion point from one text box to another. In the document window, pressing the Tab key inserts an invisible tab code and moves the text and insertion point to the next tab stop.

TROUBLE? If you pressed the Enter key instead of the Tab key after typing "AgTech," WordPerfect found the next occurrence of the search string, highlighted it, and left the Find and Replace Text dialog box open. Press the Tab key to move the insertion point to the Replace with text box, and proceed to Step 3.

3. Type **AgriTechnology** in the Replace with text box. See Figure 3-4. "AgTech" is the new search string and "AgriTechnology" is the new replacement string.

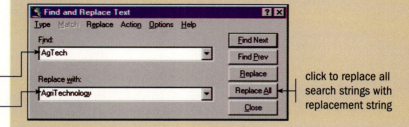

Figure 3-4 ◀
Find and Replace Text dialog box

search string

replacement string

click to replace all search strings with replacement string

4. Click the **Replace All** button to change all occurrences of "AgTech" to "AgriTechnology."

   TROUBLE? If you pressed the Enter key or clicked the Find Next button, WordPerfect stopped at the first occurrence of "AgTech." Click the Replace All button to make this and all other replacements.

5. Click the **Close** button to return to the document window. The insertion point is positioned after the last replacement.

As you look through the document, you see that "AgriTechnology" replaced all occurrences of "AgTech."

When Brittany read the draft of the report, she noticed the word "changes" appears too often in the report. She asks you to substitute the word "improvements" in some places to avoid the repetition. The choice of when or when not to change a word is based on whatever reads well to you, not on any rules.

To replace some occurrences of the search string with the replacement string:

1. Move the insertion point to the beginning of the report, then press the **F2** key to open the Find and Replace Text dialog box.

2. Type **changes** in the Find text box to replace the previous search string.

   Because you want to find every occurrence of the search string, not just those in lowercase letters, you'll make sure Case isn't selected on the Match menu.

3. Click **Match** on the dialog box menu bar, then if necessary click **Case** to deselect it. If Case is not checked, click **Match** again to close the menu.

4. Press the **Tab** key to highlight the previous replacement string, then type the new search string, **improvements**, in the Replace with text box.

5. Click the **Replace** button to find the next occurrence of the search string. WordPerfect highlights the first "changes," located in the executive summary. See Figure 3-5.

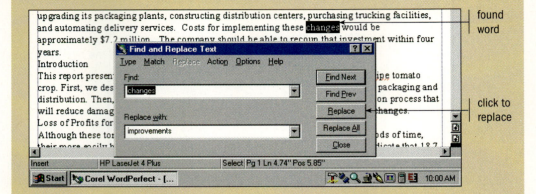

Figure 3-5
First occurrence of "changes"

TROUBLE? If you can't see the highlighted word, the Find and Replace Text dialog box is probably covering it. Drag the dialog box by its title bar to another part of the screen.

You can click the Replace button to substitute the replacement string for that word or you can click the Find Next button to skip that occurrence and find the next occurrence of "changes."

6. Click the **Replace** button. WordPerfect replaces the first occurrence of "changes" with "improvements" and highlights the next occurrence of the search string.

7. Click the **Replace** button to replace the second occurrence, click the **Find Next** button to skip the third occurrence. Click the **Replace** button to accept the replacement in the heading of the final paragraph. Click the **Find Next** button to skip the first replacement in the final paragraph, then click the **Replace** button to replace the final occurrence in the last sentence of the document.

When you have looked at every occurrence of the word "changes" in the report, a message dialog box displays: "changes" Not Found.

8. Click the **OK** button to close the message dialog box, then click the **Close** button to close the Find and Replace Text dialog box.

9. Scroll to the heading "Cost of the Improvements" near the end of the document to see the last few changes you have made. See Figure 3-6.

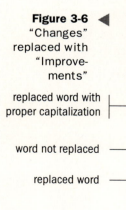

Figure 3-6
"Changes" replaced with "Improvements"

replaced word with proper capitalization

word not replaced

replaced word

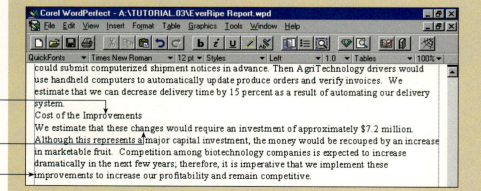

Notice in the heading, the word "Improvements" replaced "Changes" and is capitalized automatically. Because you found every occurrence of the search string regardless of case, WordPerfect automatically matches the case of the replacement string to the original word.

Brittany wants you to check the spelling of the report. At first you think this is unnecessary because she corrected all the misspellings marked by Spell-As-You-Go. But, as you'll see, WordPerfect's Spell Checker is still important.

Running the Spell Checker

The **Spell Checker**, sometimes called **Speller**, verifies the spelling of all the words in your document against the spelling of words in WordPerfect's dictionary, which is a file on your computer. Just like Spell-As-You-Go, if a word doesn't appear as it does in the dictionary or if it isn't in the dictionary (for example, a person's name), then the Spell Checker will flag it.

Even if you corrected spelling errors with Spell-As-You-Go, you should run the Spell Checker after you have completed writing your documents because the Spell Checker helps you spell words consistently. For example, you might ignore Spell-As-You-Go when it marks "AgriTechnology" in the report because you know the word is not in the dictionary. But the Spell Checker will catch such typographical errors as "Agritechnology" (case error) or "AgriTecnology" (misspelling).

The Spell Checker together with Spell-As-You-Go helps ensure that your documents are free from typing and spelling errors.

REFERENCE window

CORRECTING SPELLING

- With the insertion point anywhere within the document, click the Spell Check button on the Toolbar (or click Tools then click Spell Check).
- When the Spell Checker stops at a word that isn't in the dictionary, click the Replace button to replace the misspelled word with a suggested word; click the Skip Once button to skip the word this time; or click the Skip Always button to skip that spelling for the remainder of the document.
- When a message appears that spell checking is complete, click the Yes button.

You'll run the Spell Checker to find and correct duplicated words and inconsistent spellings.

To run the Spell Checker:

1. Click the **Spell Check** button on the Toolbar. WordPerfect immediately begins checking the spelling from the beginning of the document.

    TROUBLE? If a dialog box opens before WordPerfect begins spell checking, click the Start button on the Spell Checker dialog box.

    The Spell Checker first stops at the word "AgriTechnology's" and highlights "AgriTechnology" because this word is not in WordPerfect's dictionary. See Figure 3-7. You'll tell WordPerfect to always skip that word because, in fact, it is spelled correctly.

Figure 3-7
Spell Checker with flagged word

word not in WordPerfect's dictionary

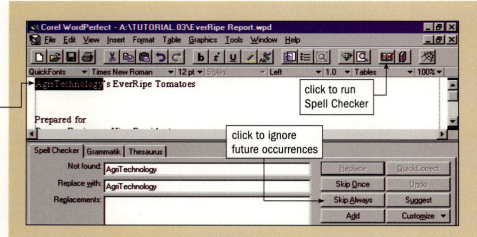

2. Click the **Skip Always** button. From now on, the Spell Checker will skip any occurrence of "AgriTechnology."

   Next the Spell Checker stops at "EverRipe." Again, this correctly spelled word doesn't appear in WordPerfect's dictionary.

3. Click the **Skip Always** button. The Spell Checker will no longer mark "EverRipe."

   The Spell Checker next stops at "Espinoza." Although many common names appear in WordPerfect's dictionary, most last names don't.

4. Click the **Skip Always** button for "Espinoza" and again for each name near the beginning of the report.

   The Spell Checker flags "EveRipe," a typographical error that should be "EverRipe." Because earlier you skipped "EverRipe" (which is similar to the flagged word), Spell Checker places that word in the Replace with text box as a substitution option.

5. Click the **Replace** button to change "EveRipe" to "EverRipe."

   Next the Spell Checker stops at the duplicated words "to to." Because the words are split onto two lines, the repetition is difficult to detect. See Figure 3-8.

Figure 3-8
Duplicate word located by Spell Checker

highlighted double word

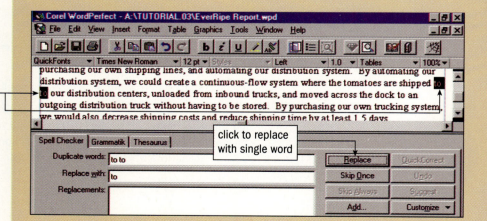

6. Click the **Replace** button to remove one occurrence of "to."

   WordPerfect displays the message, "Spell check completed. Close Spell Checker?"

7. Click the **Yes** button then click the **Save** button 🖫 on the Toolbar to save the report.

You should always run the Spell Checker before you print a document to catch errors that Spell-As-You-Go might have missed.

Brittany wants you to change one more word in the report. She thinks the word "instituting" in the Introduction doesn't seem quite right; however, she isn't sure what word to use in its place. She asks you to use WordPerfect's Thesaurus to find a better word.

Using the Thesaurus

The **Thesaurus** is a WordPerfect feature that contains a list of words with their synonyms and antonyms. Similar to a thesaurus reference book, you can look up a specific word in WordPerfect's Thesaurus, find its synonyms and antonyms, and reference related words.

The Thesaurus lists the following types of words:

- **Synonyms**. These are words with meanings similar to the word you're looking up. Not all words have synonyms. For example, the Thesaurus does not list a synonym for "school" because no word with the precise meaning of "school" exists.

- **Related words**. These are approximate synonyms. For example, the Thesaurus lists "college" and "university" among others as related words for "school."

- **Is a Type of**. These are more general terms for the word you're looking up. For example, the Thesaurus shows that "school" is a type of "educational institution."

- **Has Types**. These are words for parts that make up the whole of the term you're looking up. For example, for the word "school," the Thesaurus lists the terms "Sunday school," "academy," and "conservatory" among others, because these are types of schools.

- **Antonyms**. These words have a meaning opposite to the word you're looking up. For example, if you look up the word "curse," you'll find among others the antonym "bless."

The Thesaurus is a good editing tool to help make your word choices varied and exact.

USING THE THESAURUS
- Move the insertion point to the word you want to replace.
- Click Tools then click Thesaurus.
- If necessary, scroll the replacement word into view.
- Click the replacement word, then click the Replace button.

You'll use the Thesaurus to find a synonym for the word "instituting" in the introduction.

To find a synonym with the Thesaurus:

1. Move the insertion point within the word "instituting," which appears just above the heading "Loss of Profits for 1998." The insertion point must be within the word or immediately to its left or right.

2. Click **Tools** then click **Thesaurus** to highlight "instituting" and open the Thesaurus dialog box below the document window. The highlighted word "instituting" appears in the Replace With text box along with definitions for "institute," and several synonyms of "institute" appear in the Replacements list box. See Figure 3-9.

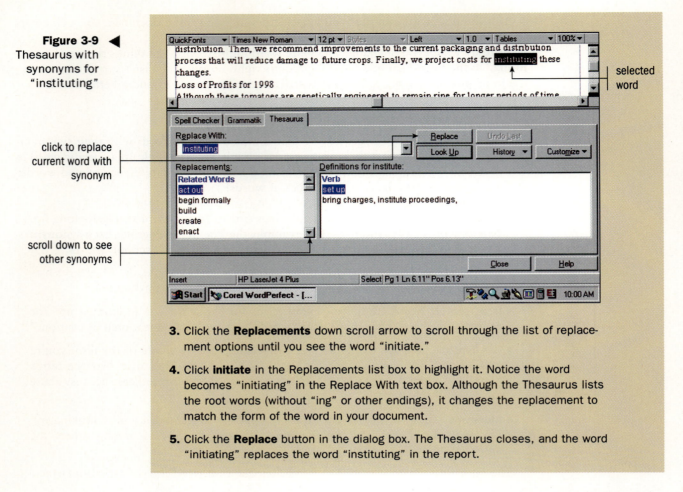

Figure 3-9
Thesaurus with synonyms for "instituting"

3. Click the **Replacements** down scroll arrow to scroll through the list of replacement options until you see the word "initiate."

4. Click **initiate** in the Replacements list box to highlight it. Notice the word becomes "initiating" in the Replace With text box. Although the Thesaurus lists the root words (without "ing" or other endings), it changes the replacement to match the form of the word in your document.

5. Click the **Replace** button in the dialog box. The Thesaurus closes, and the word "initiating" replaces the word "instituting" in the report.

The Thesaurus can help you increase your word power as you write. WordPerfect's grammar checker is another good editing tool.

Using Grammatik

WordPerfect's grammar checker, called **Grammatik** (rhymes with "dramatic"), searches selected text, or your entire document, for common grammar and style errors, such as incorrect subject-verb agreement and passive voice. It also explains the potential problem, and often suggests a correction. Although Grammatik can help you catch and fix grammatical and stylistic problems, it is by no means a cure-all. It might suggest changes appropriate for your document, but other suggested changes might not be applicable. You need to review each suggestion and determine whether to accept or ignore it.

Grammatik might suggest changes to your writing style; sometimes certain conventions are appropriate in one document but not another. Again, you need to decide. However, you can set Grammatik to search your document using a writing style that is appropriate for the type of document you're writing (formal, informal, fiction, technical, other types of writing, or a writing style of your choice). For example, in formal writing, Grammatik flags any contractions (for example, "can't"), clichés (for example, "mad as a hornet"), and colloquial language (for example, "bonehead"). On the other hand, in informal writing, Grammatik ignores these same constructions.

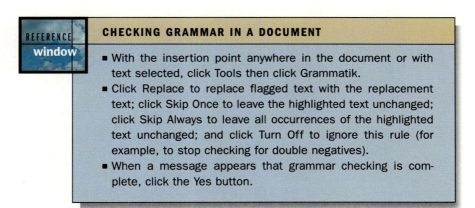

CHECKING GRAMMAR IN A DOCUMENT

- With the insertion point anywhere in the document or with text selected, click Tools then click Grammatik.
- Click Replace to replace flagged text with the replacement text; click Skip Once to leave the highlighted text unchanged; click Skip Always to leave all occurrences of the highlighted text unchanged; and click Turn Off to ignore this rule (for example, to stop checking for double negatives).
- When a message appears that grammar checking is complete, click the Yes button.

After Brittany checked all the grammar of the report, she added the paragraph following the heading "Loss of Profits for 1998," so she asks you to check that paragraph. First you'll make sure the writing style is set to formal writing, then you'll check the paragraph.

To set the writing style and check the grammar:

1. Select the paragraph following the "Loss of Profits for 1998" heading.
2. Click **Tools** then click **Grammatik**. WordPerfect highlights an error in the first sentence, and the Grammatik dialog box opens. See Figure 3-10.

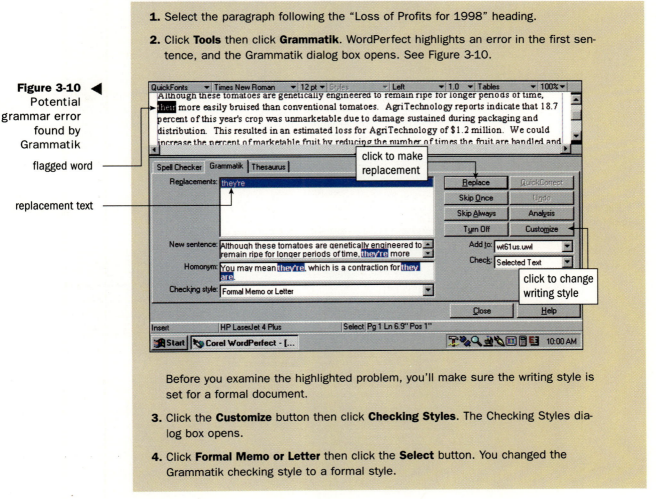

Figure 3-10 ◄
Potential grammar error found by Grammatik

flagged word

replacement text

Before you examine the highlighted problem, you'll make sure the writing style is set for a formal document.

3. Click the **Customize** button then click **Checking Styles**. The Checking Styles dialog box opens.
4. Click **Formal Memo or Letter** then click the **Select** button. You changed the Grammatik checking style to a formal style.

Now you're ready to look at the first potential problem in the paragraph: the word "their." The suggested change appears in the Replacements text box; the change in context of the current sentence appears in the New sentence text box; and an explanation appears in the Homonym text box. Because the word Brittany used is incorrect, you'll replace "their" with "they're."

To check and correct grammar:

1. Click the **Replace** button. Grammatik changes "their" to "they're" in the report.

   Next Grammatik flags the phrase "these tomatoes are genetically engineered" because it contains the passive voice. The Replacements text box shows various forms of the active voice. To get an explanation of the active voice, you can click the green text "active voice" in the Passive Voice text box.

2. Click on **active voice** in the Passive Voice text box to open the Grammatik Help on Grammar and Writing window, read the explanation, then click the **Close** button.

   Although active voice usually is preferable to passive voice, passive voice is appropriate when you're describing a process and want to emphasize the process rather than the person doing the process. Because passive voice is appropriate in this instance and throughout the paragraph, you'll ignore the rule for this flagged error.

3. Click the **Turn Off** button. Grammatik will ignore any future occurrence of passive voice in the selected text. Grammatik stops at the phrase "periods of time." This is repetitious. Replacing "periods of time" with "periods" gives the same meaning in fewer words.

4. Click the **Replace** button to accept the suggestion. Next, Grammatik flags "AgriTechnology" because the word isn't in the dictionary. You want Grammatik to ignore any instance of this "misspelling."

5. Click the **Skip Always** button so Grammatik will skip any occurrence of AgriTechnology. Grammatik flags the word "indicate," because it is overstated, and suggests the simpler word "show."

6. Click the **Replace** button to replace "indicate" with "show." Grammatik flags the next potential error, "fruit are," a problem of subject-verb agreement. See Figure 3-11.

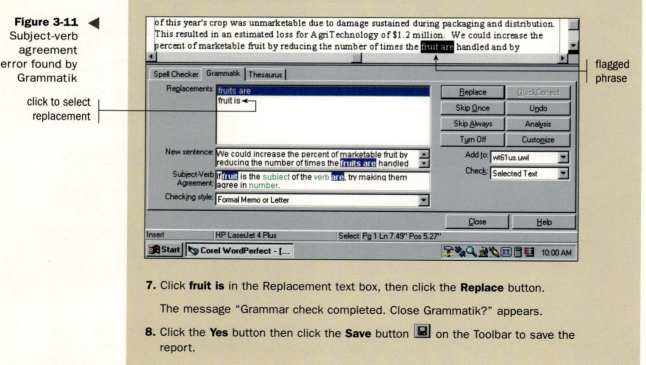

Figure 3-11 ◄
Subject-verb agreement error found by Grammatik

click to select replacement

flagged phrase

7. Click **fruit is** in the Replacement text box, then click the **Replace** button.

   The message "Grammar check completed. Close Grammatik?" appears.

8. Click the **Yes** button then click the **Save** button on the Toolbar to save the report.

You have completed the editing suggestions Brittany made for the document and are ready to format it.

Quick Check

1. How do you locate a specific word or words in a document?
2. What is a search string? What is a replacement string?
3. Why do you need to run the Spell Checker if you use Spell-As-You-Go?
4. How do you replace every instance of "IRS" with "Internal Revenue Service" in a document? How do you avoid having "Internal Revenue Service" inserted into the middle of the word "first"?
5. List four synonyms WordPerfect's Thesaurus provides for the word "placed."
6. How does Grammatik indicate a potential grammar error? How do you bypass Grammatik's suggestion for improving the grammar of the marked text? How do you accept Grammatik's suggestion for improving the grammar of the marked text?
7. What is the difference between the formal and informal writing styles in Grammatik?

If you aren't going to work through Session 3.2 now, you should close the report and exit WordPerfect. When you're ready to begin Session 3.2, start WordPerfect, open EverRipe Report, then continue with the session.

SESSION 3.2

In this session you will format the task force's report by vertically centering the title page, adding headers and footers, and inserting footnotes.

Centering a Page Vertically

AgriTechnology requires a separate title page at the beginning of a report. The text on the title page also needs to be centered vertically on the page, which means the text should be centered between the top and bottom margins. Right now the title, subtitle (for whom the report is prepared), and the names of the task force members appear on the same page as the body of the report. You need to split the title page from the body of the report with a **hard page break**, a code that you insert manually to move text to a new page even if the previous page isn't filled.

CENTERING A PAGE VERTICALLY

- If necessary, press Ctrl + Enter below the text you want to center to insert a hard page break.
- Move the insertion point to the beginning of the page you want to center.
- Click Format, point to Page, click Center, click the Current page radio button, then click the OK button.

To make the report title page meet the company's style guidelines, you'll center the lines of text between the top and bottom margins.

To insert a page break and vertically center text:

1. Position the insertion point immediately to the left of "E" in the heading "Executive Summary." You want the text above this heading to become a separate title page and the executive summary to begin the second page of the report.

2. Press **Ctrl + Enter** to insert a hard page break. Now the title page is on its own separate page.

3. Press **Ctrl + Home** to move the insertion point to the beginning of the report and the page you want to center.

4. Click **Format**, point to **Page**, then click **Center**. The Center Page(s) dialog box opens.

5. Click the **Current page** radio button, then click the **OK** button. The text of the page becomes centered between the top and bottom margins.

6. Click the **Page/Zoom Full** button on the Toolbar to switch to Full Page view and see how the text looks on the page. See Figure 3-12.

Figure 3-12
Title page centered vertically

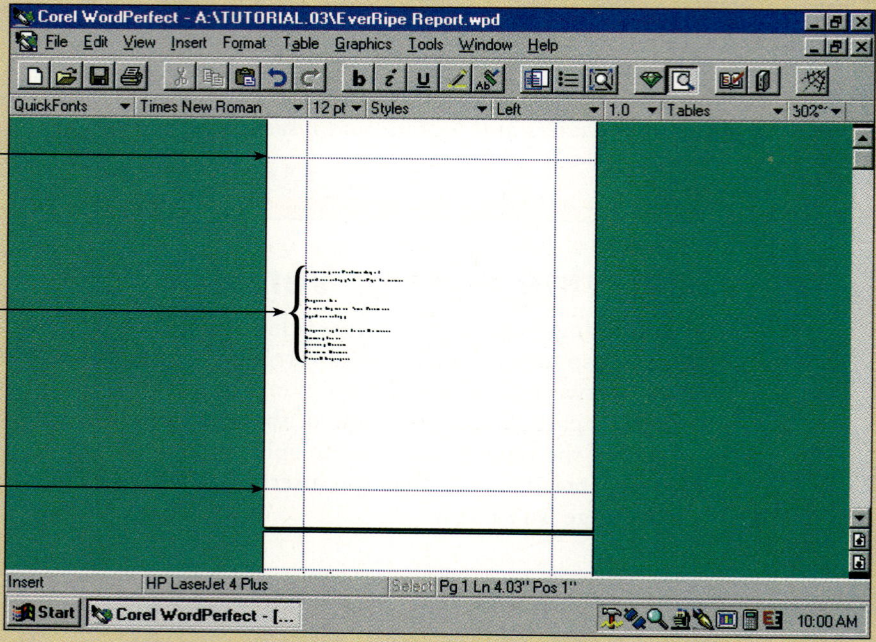

top margin guideline

centered text

bottom margin guideline

7. Click again to return to Page view.

You have centered the title page. Next you'll add the name of the report and the page number at the top of every page after the title page.

Adding Headers and Footers

The AgriTechnology style guidelines require specific information to be printed at the top and bottom of each page of a report. Text that is printed at the top of every page is called a **header**. For example, the page number and section name printed at the top of the page you're reading is a header. Similarly, a **footer** is text that is printed at the bottom of every page.

REFERENCE window

INSERTING A HEADER OR FOOTER

- Move the insertion point to the beginning of the page where you want the header or footer to begin.
- Click Format then click Header/Footer. The Headers/Footers dialog box opens.
- Click the Header A radio button or the Footer A radio button. (If you were creating different headers or footers for odd and even pages, you might choose Header B or Footer B.)
- Click the Create button.
- Type the text for the header or footer.
- Click the Close button on the Header/Footer feature bar.

AgriTechnology wants the title of the report and a page number printed on every page of the report, except the title page, to make it easy for a reader to refer to specific pages of the report.

Creating a Header with Automatic Page Numbering

When you create a header you can type text as well as add a code that automatically inserts the correct page number for each page. This way, the numbering will adjust to account for text you might add or remove after inserting the page number. You'll create a header for the body of the report that prints "EverRipe Recommendation Report" at the left margin and the page number at the right margin.

To insert a header beginning from page 2:

1. Move the insertion point immediately to the left of "Executive Summary" at the beginning of page 2.

2. Click **Format** then click **Header/Footer**. The Headers/Footers dialog box opens.

3. If necessary, click the **Header A** radio button to select it, then click the **Create** button. WordPerfect creates a header box, with violet margin guidelines, places the insertion point in the header box, and opens the Header/Footer feature bar below the Power Bar. See Figure 3-13.

Figure 3-13
Creating a header

Header/Footer feature bar

header box

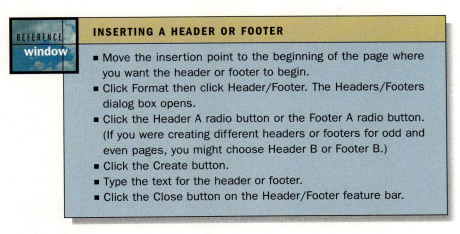

TROUBLE? If you don't see violet margin guidelines above and below the header box, you need to turn on guidelines. Click View, click Guidelines, click the Header/Footer check box, then click the OK button. Click the Close button on the Header/Footer feature bar, then repeat Steps 1 through 3.

You're ready to insert the text into the header.

4. Type **EverRipe Recommendation Report** so the report title will appear on all pages in the main body of the report.

Now you want to insert automatic page numbering at the right margin. For this you'll use the Flush Right command, which causes the insertion point to move to the right margin and allows you to insert text from that point to the left.

5. Click **Format**, point to **Line**, then click **Flush Right**. The insertion point moves to the right margin, where you want to insert a code for the page number. You don't want to actually type the page number because then every page will display the same number.

6. Click the **Number** button on the Header/Footer feature bar, then click **Page Number**. The page number "2" appears at the right margin. See Figure 3-14.

Figure 3-14
Text of header

It might appear as if you simply typed the number 2, but you actually inserted a page number code. If you were to turn on Reveal Codes, you would see the Page Number Display format code.

You decide to add a horizontal line below the text of the header to give the report a more formal appearance.

To insert a horizontal line in the header:

1. With the insertion point to the right of the page number, press the **Enter** key to move the insertion point below the header text.

2. Click the **Insert Line** button on the Header/Footer feature bar. A horizontal line appears below the text of the header.

3. Click the **Close** button on the Header/Footer feature bar. The toolbar closes and the insertion point returns to the main document window. You'll look at the headers in Two Page view, which displays two full pages at once.

4. Click **View** then click **Two Page**. WordPerfect switches to Two Page view. See Figure 3-15. You can see the headers on pages 2 and 3.

ADDING HEADERS AND FOOTERS   WP 111

Figure 3-15
Report in Two Page view

header on both pages after the title page

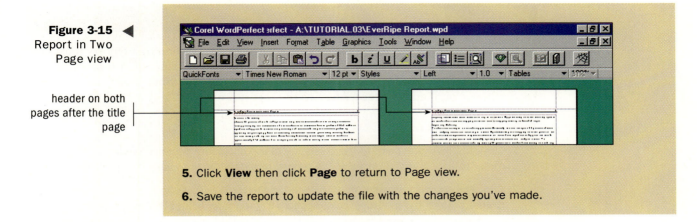

5. Click **View** then click **Page** to return to Page view.
6. Save the report to update the file with the changes you've made.

The recommendation report now has the header that Brittany asked you to add.

Changing the Page Numbering

The header you created will print the name of the document and page numbers on all pages of the report except the title page. By default, WordPerfect starts numbering pages from the first page of a document even if the page numbers won't print on all pages. In this case, WordPerfect includes the title page (the first page of the document) in the page numbering and begins the body of the report (the second page of the document) with page number 2. According to the AgriTechnology style guidelines, title pages of reports shouldn't be numbered and the body of the report should begin on page 1. You'll fix the page numbering so the first page of the report after the title page (the second page of the document) is numbered as page 1.

To change the page numbering:

1. Make sure the insertion point is still at the beginning of page 2, just below the header, then click **Format**, point to **Page Numbering**, and click **Value/Adjust**. The Value/Adjust Number dialog box opens. If necessary, click the **Page** tab to make it the frontmost tab. See Figure 3-16.

Figure 3-16
Value/Adjust Numbering dialog box

click to change to 1

2. Click the **Set page number** down arrow to change the page number from 2 to **1**, then click the **OK** button. As you can see in the header and on the status bar, the current page number is now 1.

The header of the recommendation report will now print the report name and page numbers beginning with page 1 starting at the body of the report. Next, you need to add a footer that will print on every page of the report, including the title page.

Inserting a Footer

The footer that prints at the bottom of each page of AgriTechnology reports must contain the company name and the date the report is presented. You add a footer the same way you added the header, except that you type text into the footer box rather than the header box. You'll add the footer text to the report now.

To insert a footer:

1. Move the insertion point to the beginning of the document because you want the footer to appear on all pages of the report, including the title page.

2. Click **Format**, click **Header/Footer**, click the **Footer A** radio button, then click the **Create** button. The insertion point appears in the footer box at the bottom of the first page of the report.

3. Type **AgriTechnology**, click **Format**, point to **Line**, then click **Flush Right** to move the insertion point to the right margin. You're ready to insert a code for the current date.

4. Click **Insert**, point to **Date**, then click **Date Code**. The current date appears. Because the date is a code, like the page numbers in the header, it will automatically update to the current date each time you print the report. See Figure 3-17.

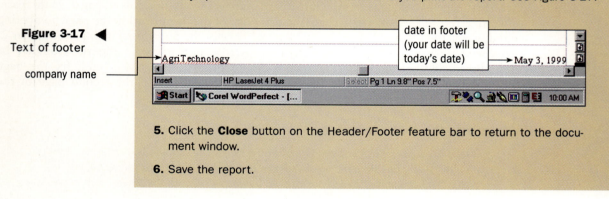

Figure 3-17 ◀
Text of footer

company name

5. Click the **Close** button on the Header/Footer feature bar to return to the document window.

6. Save the report.

The footer you created will print on all pages of the report.

Adding Footnotes and Endnotes

Earlier, Brittany printed and distributed a copy of the recommendation report to each task force member, one of whom suggested minor revisions. Anthony Ciaccio suggested that the report include two footnotes: the first indicating the source of the information for income loss, and the second explaining that estimates for construction are based on construction costs as of July 1999.

Numbered notes often are added to documents to reference a source of information or expand on a point by adding information that is secondary to the main point. **Footnotes** are notes that print at the bottom of the page on which the paragraph or sentence they reference appears. When all notes for a document are gathered together and printed at the end of the document, they are called **endnotes**. Usually a document will contain footnotes or endnotes, but not both.

The Footnote/Endnote feature provides several benefits over just typing notes at the bottom of a page or end of a document, such as:

- Footnotes or endnotes automatically are numbered. If you add a note anywhere in the document, delete a note, or move a note, WordPerfect automatically renumbers all the remaining footnotes or endnotes consecutively.

ADDING FOOTNOTES AND ENDNOTES   WP 113

- WordPerfect automatically formats the footnote text at the bottom of the page or the endnote text at the end of the document.
- You can edit a footnote or endnote at any time by clicking the note and editing it as you would any other text.

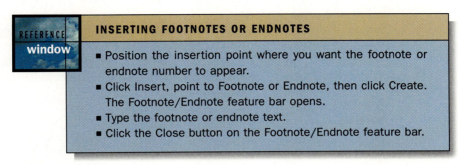

REFERENCE window

INSERTING FOOTNOTES OR ENDNOTES
- Position the insertion point where you want the footnote or endnote number to appear.
- Click Insert, point to Footnote or Endnote, then click Create. The Footnote/Endnote feature bar opens.
- Type the footnote or endnote text.
- Click the Close button on the Footnote/Endnote feature bar.

You'll insert the notes that Anthony suggested as footnotes using the Footnote command.

To insert footnotes:

1. Position the insertion point after the phrase "AgriTechnology reports" at the beginning of the second sentence under the heading "Loss of Profits for 1998" in the middle of the new page one. This is where you want to add the first footnote number.

2. Click **Insert**, point to **Footnote**, then click **Create**. The Footnote/Endnote feature bar opens above the document window, inserts the footnote number into the text, and positions the insertion point just above the footer.

3. Without pressing the spacebar or the Tab key at the beginning of the line, type the text of the first footnote as shown in Figure 3-18. Do not press the Enter key at the end of the note. When you're done, your screen should match Figure 3-18.

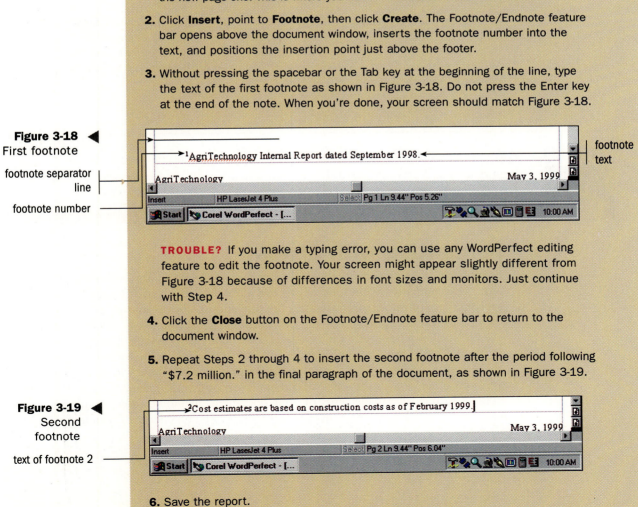

Figure 3-18 ◀ First footnote

footnote separator line

footnote number

footnote text

TROUBLE? If you make a typing error, you can use any WordPerfect editing feature to edit the footnote. Your screen might appear slightly different from Figure 3-18 because of differences in font sizes and monitors. Just continue with Step 4.

4. Click the **Close** button on the Footnote/Endnote feature bar to return to the document window.

5. Repeat Steps 2 through 4 to insert the second footnote after the period following "$7.2 million." in the final paragraph of the document, as shown in Figure 3-19.

Figure 3-19 ◀ Second footnote

text of footnote 2

6. Save the report.

You can delete or move a note just as easily as you added it.

Deleting or Moving a Footnote or Endnote

To delete a footnote or endnote, just highlight the footnote or endnote number in your document and press the Delete key. When you delete the number, WordPerfect automatically removes the text of the footnote or endnote and renumbers the remaining notes consecutively.

You can move a footnote or endnote using the cut-and-paste method. Just highlight the note number and cut it from the document, then paste it anywhere in your document. Again, WordPerfect automatically renumbers the notes consecutively.

Quick Check

1. Why would you insert a hard page break into a document?
2. Define center a page vertically in your own words.
3. What is the difference between a header and a footer?
4. How do you insert the page number at the right margin in a header?
5. How do you insert a horizontal line below the header text?
6. What is the difference between a footnote and an endnote?
7. List three benefits to using the Footnote/Endnote feature.

You have completed all the document-level formatting changes Brittany wanted for the document. You're ready to make paragraph-level formatting changes. If you aren't going to work through Session 3.3 now, you should close the document and exit WordPerfect. When you're ready to begin Session 3.3, start WordPerfect, open EverRipe Report, then continue with the session.

SESSION 3.3

In this session you will make the additional formatting changes to your document using the Styles feature in WordPerfect. You will also edit the header and print the completed report.

Formatting with Styles

Brittany asked you to format the document so it conforms to AgriTechnology's style guidelines. The company requires all reports to follow the same format to make it easier to find specific types of information, such as the title and executive summary. You need to make the title page and executive summary conform to AgriTechnology's specifications; you also need to format paragraphs and headings consistently throughout the document.

The best way to accomplish these formatting tasks is with styles. A **style** is a set of character- or paragraph-level formatting features that you save with a specific name and apply to other text in the same document or in other documents. Using styles, you can quickly format all the elements of your document, including titles, headings, numbered lists, and other features you encounter frequently as you create a document.

Formatting with styles offers several advantages:

- **Efficiency**. After you specify the format of a style, you can apply that style to every similar element in the document. For example, when you create the style for a heading in the recommendation report, you need to change the font face and size, center the heading, and bold the text only once. Then you can apply that style to all other headings in the report.

- **Consistency**. You don't need to remember exactly how you formatted a particular element in your document. Just select the appropriate style name for that element, and WordPerfect will apply the same format you used earlier. For example, with styles you can be confident that all level-1 headings in the recommendation report will have the same format—Arial, 16 point, center, bold, etc., the required style for AgriTechnology reports.

- **Flexibility**. If you decide to modify the formatting of a style, you need to make the change only once; all parts of the document that use the style automatically will change. For example, if after you applied the heading style to every heading in the recommendation report, you decide that they should be underlined instead of bold, you would make the formatting change once and all the headings automatically would switch from bold to underlined text. If you didn't use styles, you would have to scroll through the entire document and change each heading individually.

Four types of styles exist in WordPerfect:

- **Character (paired)**. A character style includes any combination of character-level formats from the Font command (such as the font type, appearance, and size) that you can save and apply to other text. Character styles can be applied to new text or to existing selected text. The word "paired" indicates that this type of style requires both beginning and ending style format codes.

- **Paragraph (paired)**. A paragraph style is any combination of formats (such as font attributes, tab settings, line spacing, and indents) that you can save and apply to other paragraphs. Paragraph styles can be applied to the paragraph that contains the insertion point or to selected paragraphs.

- **Paragraph (paired-auto)**. This style is similar to the Paragraph (paired) style except that when you change the format of a paragraph to which this type of style has been applied, all other paragraphs with that same style automatically change accordingly.

- **Document (open)**. This type of style changes the formatting from the location of the insertion point to the end of the document.

In WordPerfect, the term **paragraph** means any unit of text that ends with a hard return, including titles, headings, and text that wrapped automatically to more than one line.

When you create a paragraph style, you can choose either Paragraph (paired) or Paragraph (paired-auto). If you wanted to create a title or heading style, you usually would choose paired-auto, because then if you change the format of one of the headings, the format of all headings also automatically will change. This ensures consistency among all the headings tagged with the Paragraph (paired-auto) style. On the other hand, if you wanted to create a paragraph style, for example, to italicize certain paragraphs, you might choose paired rather than paired-auto, so if you decide to bold one of the italicized paragraphs, you won't also inadvertently bold all the other paragraphs formatted with that style.

Every WordPerfect document opens with a set of predefined or **system styles**, which include styles for five levels of headings, numbered lists, bulleted lists, and the initial document format. You can create your own styles (called **user styles**) to customize the formatting of a document. You also can modify any of the system or user styles to suit the needs of your document. Although you can delete user styles, you cannot delete system styles.

The style of the current paragraph appears on the Styles button on the Power Bar. If the text has no style applied to it, the Styles button is labeled "Styles."

Applying Styles

You'll begin by applying several system styles to the recommendation report. Later you'll modify these system styles to meet the AgriTechnology's format specifications.

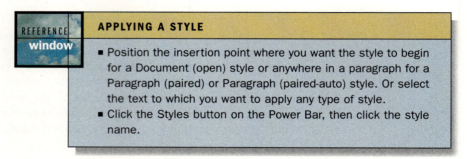

REFERENCE window

APPLYING A STYLE

- Position the insertion point where you want the style to begin for a Document (open) style or anywhere in a paragraph for a Paragraph (paired) or Paragraph (paired-auto) style. Or select the text to which you want to apply any type of style.
- Click the Styles button on the Power Bar, then click the style name.

First, you'll apply the Heading 1 system style to the title of the report. The default format of the Heading 1 is very large, bold, Times New Roman font, centered between the left and right margins. In WordPerfect, a **very large** font size is 1.5 times the initial (default) font. In the recommendation report, the initial font size is 12 points, so the very large size is 18 points. After you apply Heading 1 to the title, you'll apply the Heading 2 style to each of the five main headings and the Heading 3 style to three subheadings.

To apply system styles to existing text:

1. Move the insertion point to the beginning of the document, then select the first two lines (the title) on the title page. You want to apply the Heading 1 style to both lines (paragraphs) of the title.

2. Click the **Styles** button [Styles] on the Power Bar, then click **Heading 1**. The two lines of the title switch to the Heading 1 style. Deselect the text. See Figure 3-20.

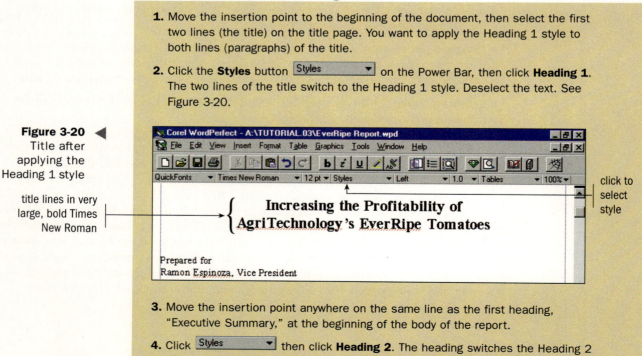

Figure 3-20 ◄
Title after applying the Heading 1 style

title lines in very large, bold Times New Roman

click to select style

3. Move the insertion point anywhere on the same line as the first heading, "Executive Summary," at the beginning of the body of the report.

4. Click [Styles] then click **Heading 2**. The heading switches the Heading 2 style, which is large (1.2 times the initial font, or 14.4 points if the initial font is 12 points) Times New Roman.

5. Repeat Steps 3 and 4 for the other four main headings in the document: "Introduction," "Loss of Profits for 1998," "Improving the Profitability of Future Crops," and "Cost of the Improvements."

6. Repeat Steps 3 and 4 for the three subheadings below the heading "Improving the Profitability of Future Crops," except use Heading 3 instead of Heading 2. The subheadings are "Upgrading Packaging Plants," "Improving Distribution Methods," and "Improving Delivery." Your last page now looks like Figure 3-21.

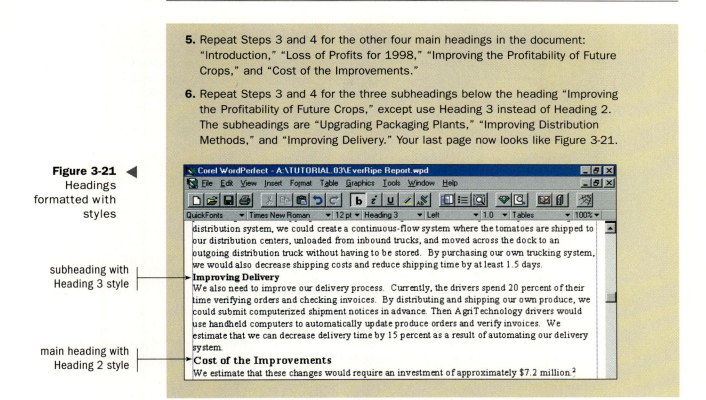

Figure 3-21
Headings formatted with styles

subheading with Heading 3 style

main heading with Heading 2 style

You have applied the Headings 1, 2, and 3 styles to existing text. Applying styles to new text is similar. Just move the insertion point to where you want to insert the new text, select the appropriate style from the Styles button on the Power Bar, then type the text. Next, Brittany wants you to change the Headings 1, 2, and 3 system styles.

Modifying Styles

You can change any formatting attribute of a system style or user style at any time. When you modify a style, WordPerfect automatically updates any text to which you have applied that style. WordPerfect supports two methods for modifying a style:

- **Using an existing paragraph as an example.** This works only for Paragraph (paired-auto) styles. All the heading styles, including Headings 1 and 2, are paired-auto styles.

- **Using the Styles Editor.** In this method, you insert format codes into the contents box of the Styles Editor.

You'll use both methods to modify styles for the recommendation report.

Modifying a Style by Example

Modifying a style by example often is easier than using the Styles Editor because you can make most font and formatting changes in the document window using the Toolbar and Power Bar buttons; however, the Styles Editor provides more options.

MODIFYING A PAIRED-AUTO STYLE BY EXAMPLE

- Select a paragraph formatted with the style you want to modify.
- Make all necessary formatting changes to the selected paragraph. WordPerfect automatically updates all the text to which the style has been applied.

You'll modify the Headings 1, 2, and 3 styles by example to match Brittany's specifications.

To modify styles by example:

1. Select the first line of the title at the beginning of the title page.

2. Change the font to 14-point Arial. When you change the font size, you don't remove the Very Large formatting code, so that a 14-point base font becomes a 21-point font (14 × 1.5 = 21) in your report.

   Notice that, although you modified only the first line of the title, the second line automatically becomes reformatted. This is because the Heading 1 style is a Paragraph (paired-auto) style, where the "auto" means if you edit one paragraph having that style, all the paragraphs with the style automatically modify the same way.

3. Select the "Executive Summary" heading at the beginning of the next page.

4. Change the font to Arial, then center the text between the left and right margins. You can use the Center Line command or the Center Justify command. Notice as you change the format of this first heading, WordPerfect automatically changes the format of all headings tagged with that same style (Heading 2). See Figure 3-22.

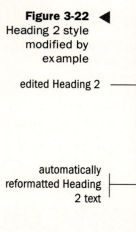

Figure 3-22
Heading 2 style modified by example

edited Heading 2

automatically reformatted Heading 2 text

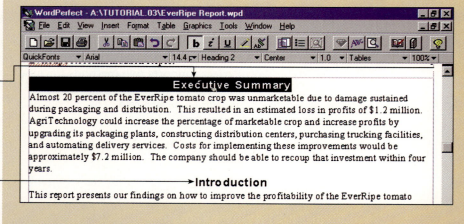

5. Select a heading with the Heading 3 style, such as the heading "Upgrading Packaging Plants."

6. Change the font to Arial italics, keeping the default font size (12 points) and the boldfacing. Don't change the justification. See Figure 3-23.

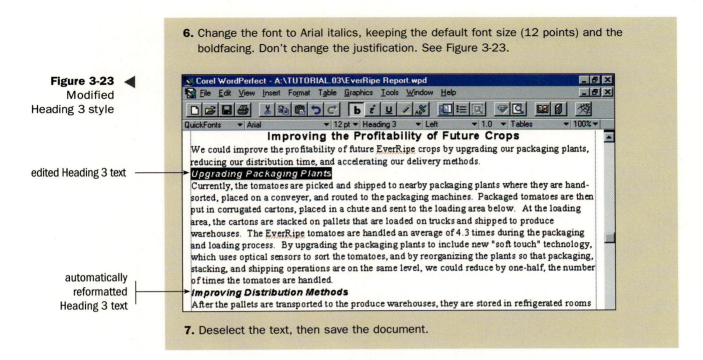

Figure 3-23
Modified Heading 3 style

edited Heading 3 text

automatically reformatted Heading 3 text

7. Deselect the text, then save the document.

You have changed the style of all three headings. Next, you'll change the Initial Codes Style using the Styles Editor.

Modifying a Style with the Styles Editor

The Initial Codes Style sets the initial (default) format codes for the document. For example, Brittany wants all AgriTechnology reports to be double-spaced and full justified. You could put the double-space and full-justification codes at the beginning of the document, but then the codes would apply only to this document and not become part of the AgriTechnology styles file for all future reports. You'll use the Styles Editor to change the initial codes.

To change the Initial Codes Style:

1. Click **Format**, point to **Document**, then click **Initial Codes Style**. The Styles Editor dialog box opens.

   The Contents box in the Styles Editor dialog box is similar to the Reveal Codes window. It contains codes that will apply to the style you're currently editing.

2. Click **Format** on the dialog box menu bar, point to **Line**, then click **Spacing** to open the Line Spacing dialog box. Change the line spacing to **2** and click the **OK** button. The Ln Spacing format code appears in the Contents box of the Styles Editor dialog box.

   TROUBLE? If, when you click Format, WordPerfect doesn't respond except for giving a sound to indicate that you're trying an unavailable command, you tried to use the main menu bar, the Toolbar, or the Power Bar. Click Format on the menu bar in the Styles Editor dialog box.

3. Click **Format** on the dialog box menu bar, point to **Justification**, then click **Full**. The Just format code appears in the Contents box.

   You have added the codes for line spacing and full justification. Now you'll add codes to set widow/orphan protection and a new left margin.

4. Click **Format**, point to **Page**, click **Keep Text Together** to open the Keep Text Together dialog box, click the **Widow/Orphan** check box, then click the **OK** button. WordPerfect inserts the Wid/Orph format code into the Contents box. Now the report will be protected against widows and orphans.

5. Click **Format**, click **Margins** to open the Margins dialog box, set the left margin to **1.5"**, then click the **OK** button. See Figure 3-24.

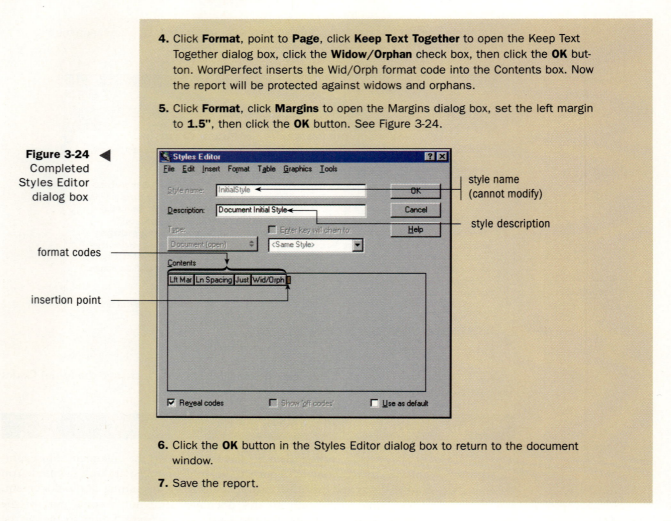

Figure 3-24
Completed Styles Editor dialog box

6. Click the **OK** button in the Styles Editor dialog box to return to the document window.

7. Save the report.

Brittany wants the text below the title on the title page to be 14-point Arial font and centered between the left and right margins. Because she wants all AgriTechnology reports to have this same format for the "Prepared for" and "Prepared by" text, you'll create a new style with these formatting features.

Creating Styles

WordPerfect provides two methods for creating styles: you can use either the Styles Editor or a feature called QuickStyle. With **QuickStyle**, you format the paragraph or text with the attributes you want, and then name and describe the style. The obvious advantage of QuickStyle is that it's fast and easy; the disadvantage is that some formatting features, such as centering, don't become incorporated into the style.

REFERENCE window	CREATING A NEW STYLE WITH THE STYLES EDITOR

- Click Format then click Styles to open the Style List dialog box.
- Click the Create button. The Styles Editor dialog box opens.
- Type a name in the Style name text box and type a description in the Description text box.
- Specify the type of style using the Type button.
- Specify the style that will follow this style (that is, the default style of the paragraph following the current style when you press the Enter key) by using the Enter key will chain to check box and list box.
- In the Content box, insert the format codes for your style.
- Click the OK button to close the Styles Editor dialog box.
- Click the Close button to close the Style List dialog box.

Because you want to ensure that all formatting features become part of the style, you'll use the Styles Editor to create the style for the nontitle text on the title page.

To create a new style using the Styles Editor:

1. Click **Format** then click **Styles** to open the Style List dialog box, then click the **Create** button to open the Styles Editor dialog box.

2. With the insertion point in the Style name text box, type **Nontitle Text**, the name you want to give the style, press the **Tab** key to move the insertion point to the Description text box, then type **For- and by-line text on title page**.

3. Make sure the **Type** of style is set to **Paragraph (paired)**, the **Enter key will chain to** check box is checked, and the text box below it has **<Same Style>** selected. This ensures that, while you're inserting the nontitle text on the title page using this style, the same style will automatically be applied to the next paragraph when you press the Enter key. You're ready to insert the format codes for this new style.

4. Click **Format**, point to **Justification**, click **Center** to center any text to which this style is applied. WordPerfect inserts the Just format code.

5. Set the font to 14-point Arial. This inserts the Font and Font Size format codes. See Figure 3-25.

Figure 3-25 ◀
Styles Editor dialog box with user style

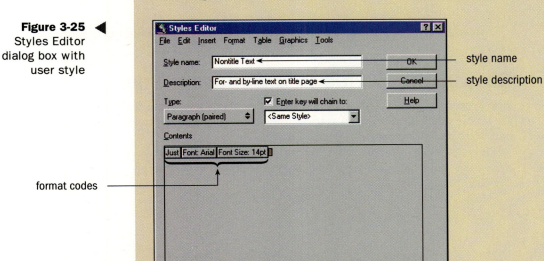

format codes

6. Click the **OK** button to close the Styles Editor dialog box.

7. Click the **Close** button to close the Style List dialog box.

Having created the new style, you're ready to apply it to the text below the title on the title page.

To apply the new style:

1. Select all the text on the title page, except the title itself, beginning with the phrase "Prepared for" and ending with the name "Russell Edgington."

2. Click the **Styles** button [Styles] on the Power Bar, then click **Nontitle Text**, the name of your new style. The selected text becomes 14-point Arial and centered.

3. Click anywhere outside the selected text to deselect it. Your title page looks like Figure 3-26.

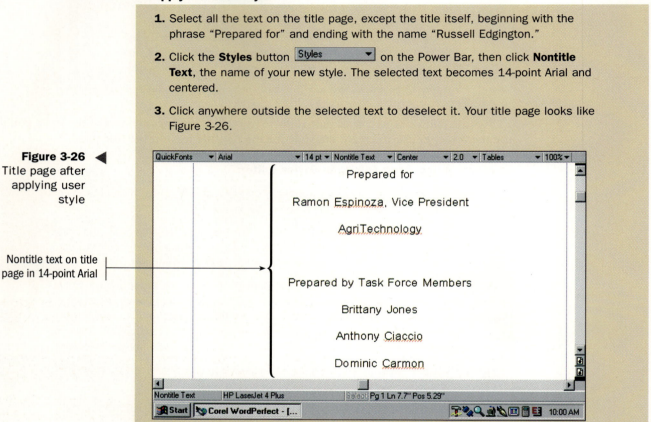

Figure 3-26
Title page after applying user style

Nontitle text on title page in 14-point Arial

You've finished modifying the styles that apply to all AgriTechnology reports. Brittany asks you to save the styles so she can use them for other reports.

Saving the Styles in a Separate File

After you create a set of styles, you can save them in a separate file. Then, when you create a new document, you can retrieve the styles into the document and use them to format your new document.

Having created a set of styles to format the recommendation report, you want to save the styles in a separate file so Brittany can retrieve and apply them to future AgriTechnology reports.

REFERENCE window

SAVING STYLES IN A SEPARATE FILE

- Click Format then click Styles.
- Click the Options button then click Save As.
- Select the folder in which you want to save the styles file.
- Type the name of the file including the filename extension .sty, if necessary.
- Click the OK button, then click the Close button.

You'll save the set of styles in a styles file named AgTech Report.

To save the styles in a separate file:

1. Click **Format** then click **Styles** to open the Style List dialog box.
2. Click the **Options** button then click **Save As**.
3. Click the **Filename** folder button to open the Select File dialog box. If necessary, change the **Look in** folder to **Tutorial.03** on your Student Disk.
4. Type **AgTech Report.sty** in the Name text box, then click the **Select** button.
5. Click the **OK** button in the Save Styles To dialog box.
6. Click the **Close** button in the Style List dialog box to return to the document window.
7. Save the report.

Whenever AgriTechnology employees create a report, they can use the styles in AgTech Report.sty to format the document. They just have to retrieve the styles file into their document.

Retrieving a Styles File

Whenever you want to use the styles in the AgTech Report.sty, you must retrieve the file into your document. Then you can apply those styles to existing or new text, and modify the styles as necessary for that document.

REFERENCE window

RETRIEVING A STYLES FILE

- Click Format then click Styles. The Style List dialog box opens.
- Click the Options button then click Retrieve. The Retrieve Styles From dialog box opens.
- In the Filename text box, type the path and filename of the styles file you want to use, then click the OK button.
- If asked if you want to overwrite current styles, click the Yes button.
- Click the Close button in the Style List dialog box, then apply the styles to the document.

You don't need to retrieve the styles file into a document right now, but you do need to fix a problem in the header.

Editing the Header

You notice a problem has occurred because of the codes you added to the Initial Codes Style: the header is double-spaced. This leaves an unwanted blank line between the text of the header and the horizontal line. The footer does not have this problem because it is only one line. You'll edit the header to fix this problem.

To edit the header:

1. Click **Format** then click **Header/Footer** to open the Headers/Footers dialog box.

2. Make sure the **Header A** radio button is selected, and then click the **Edit** button. WordPerfect opens the Header/Footer feature bar and moves the insertion point to the beginning of the header.

3. Click the **Line Spacing** button 1.0 on the Power Bar, then click **1.0** to change the spacing from 2.0 (double spacing) to 1.0 (single spacing). The space between the text and the horizontal line in the header disappears. See Figure 3-27.

Figure 3-27 ◄
Edited header

header changed to single spacing

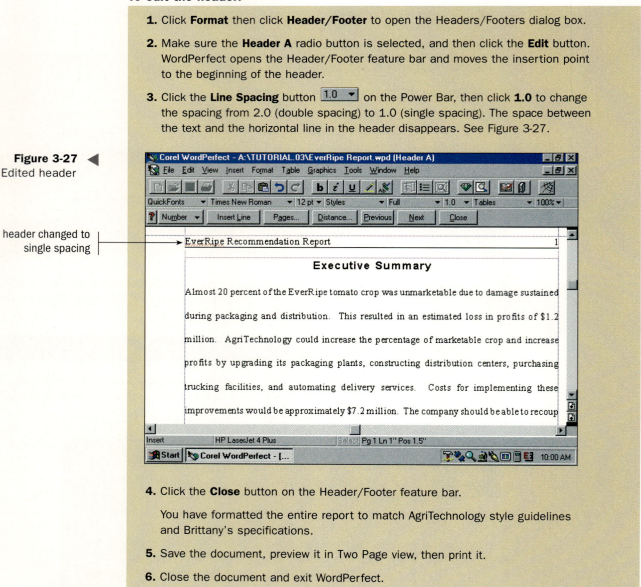

4. Click the **Close** button on the Header/Footer feature bar.

   You have formatted the entire report to match AgriTechnology style guidelines and Brittany's specifications.

5. Save the document, preview it in Two Page view, then print it.

6. Close the document and exit WordPerfect.

Your report should look like Figure 3-28.

Figure 3-28
Final version of recommendation report

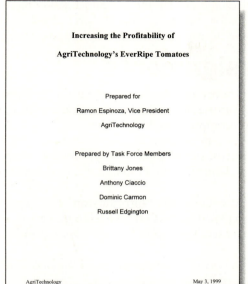

Quick Check

1. Define the following in your own words:
   a. style
   b. Character (paired) style
   c. Paragraph (paired) style
   d. Paragraph (paired-auto) style

2. List three advantages to using styles.

3. How do you apply a style?

4. What is the simplest way to modify a paired-auto style?

5. How do you create a style that requires format codes for justification, margins, and line spacing?

6. What is a styles file and why would you want to use one?

You have edited, formatted, and printed the recommendation report for Brittany. You also have saved a new template for creating reports at AgriTechnology. She thanks you for your help and goes to copy the report so she can distribute it to the company executives.

Tutorial Assignments

Start WordPerfect, and if necessary, conduct a screen check. Open StatRep from the TAssign folder from the Tutorial.03 folder on your Student Disk, save the document as AgTech Status Report, then complete the following:

1. Find and replace every instance of "the company" with "AgriTechnology."
2. Using the Thesaurus, substitute a synonym for the word "conventional" in your document. (*Hint*: Use the Find and Replace command to locate the word.)
3. Select the body text under the "Introduction" heading and run Grammatik with the checking style set to Formal Memo or Letter. Accept the changes WordPerfect suggests. Then run the Spell Checker and make any necessary corrections.
4. Insert a hard page break after the names of the task force members so the executive summary begins on a new page.
5. Center the first page (title page) of the document vertically.

6. Create a header that reads "EverRipe Status Report" at the left margin, centers the page number, prints in 12-point Arial bold, and doesn't appear on the title page.

7. Create a footer that aligns your name at the left margin, the date at the right margin, and prints on every page. Also include a horizontal line above the text of the footer.
8. Insert the footnote, "Internal report dated September 15, 1998," after the words "AgriTechnology reports" in the second sentence of the paragraph following "Loss of Profits for the EverRipe Crop." Insert a second footnote, "Task Force Report dated January 15, 1999," after "$7.2 million." in the second sentence of the paragraph following "Cost of the Improvements."
9. Retrieve the styles file, AgTech Report.sty.
10. Apply the Heading 1 style to the three title lines at the beginning of the report.
11. Apply the Nontitle Text style to the other text on the title page.
12. Apply the Heading 2 style to the headings "Introduction," "Loss of Profits for the EverRipe Crop," "Efforts to Improve Profitability," "Cost of the Improvements,"and "Other Factors Influencing Profitability."
13. Apply the Heading 3 style to the subheadings "Upgraded Packaging Plants," "Improved Distribution Methods," and "Improved Delivery."

14. Create a new style named "Exec Text" for the paragraph below the heading "Executive Summary." Give the style the description "Executive Summary Text." The style should include format codes to make the text 12-point Arial, single-spaced, and left-justified.
15. Apply the Exec Text style to the paragraph of the Executive Summary.

16. Create a new style named "Exec Summ" with the description "Executive Summary Heading." Make the text single-spaced, 13-point Times New Roman, left-justified, and double-indented. Apply the style to the heading "Executive Summary."
17. Save the styles in a separate file called AgTech Report Styles.sty in the TAssign folder of the Tutorial.03 folder on your Student Disk.
18. Save the document, print then close it.

Case Problems

1. Ocean Breeze Bookstore Annual Report As manager of Ocean Breeze Bookstore in San Diego, California, Reed L. Paige must submit an annual report to the Board of Directors. Open OceanRep from the Cases folder in the Tutorial.03 folder on your Student Disk, save the document as Ocean Breeze Report, then complete the following:

1. Find and replace every instance of "book store" with "bookstore."
2. Use the Thesaurus to substitute a synonym for the word "finest" in at least two instances in the annual report document. (*Hint*: Use the Find and Replace command to locate the word.)
3. Run Grammatik on the text in the "Company Philosophy" section with the checking style set to Formal Memo or Letter. Ignore the suggestion to change passive voice, but accept the others.
4. Create a new page after the phrase "Ocean Breeze Bookstore" and then center the title page vertically.
5. Create a header that aligns "Ocean Breeze Annual Report" on the left margin, aligns the date on the right margin, and prints on every page except the title page.
6. Insert the endnote "Mission Statement adopted May 29, 1967" after the first sentence in the "Mission Statement" paragraph. Insert a second endnote "Board of Director's Meeting, May 29, 1998" after the last sentence of the document.
7. Apply the Heading 1 style to the title (the first line of the document).
8. Apply the Heading 2 style to the headings "Introduction," "Mission Statement," "Company Philosophy," "Organization," "Autograph Signing," "Children's Story Hour," "Summer Reading Contest," "Home Delivery," and "Summary."
9. Apply the Heading 3 style to the headings "Board of Directors" and "Store Management and Personnel."
10. Define a style named "Left Indent8" with the following formatting options: 12-point Book Antiqua, full justification, line spacing set to 1.5. If you don't have Book Antiqua on your computer, use a different serif font.
11. Apply the newly defined Left Indent8 style to the text of every paragraph that isn't a heading.
12. Save, print, and close the document.

2. Ultimate Travel's "Europe on a Budget" Report As director of Ultimate Travel's "Europe on a Budget" tour, Bronwyn Bates is required to write a report summarizing this year's tour. Open Europe from the Cases folder in the Tutorial.03 folder on your Student Disk, save the document as Europe Tour Report, then complete the following:

1. Find and replace at least one instance of "baggage" with "luggage."
2. Use the Thesaurus to substitute a synonym for the second "typical" in the text under the heading "Accommodations."
3. Run Grammatik on the text under the "General Planning and Preparation" heading (ending with the word "packet:"). Accept those suggestions that are appropriate.
4. Replace all occurrences of the word "suggest" that are in boldface with the word "recommend" not in boldface. (*Hint*: Use the Match menu to add formatting to the search string.)
5. Create a title page from the beginning of the document to the phrase "Tour Director," then center the page vertically.
6. Create a footer that aligns "Evaluation Report" on the left margin, aligns the page number on the right margin, and appears only after the title page. For the page number, use the text and format "page x or y" (where x means the current page and y means the total number of pages in the document). (*Hint*: Use the Number button on the Header/Footer feature bar to insert code for the total number of pages.)

7. Start the body of the report with page 1.
8. Insert the footnote, "Travel Tips for Tourists, May 1987, published by the U.S. Department of Health and Human Services," after the phrase "three phases," in the "General Planning and Preparation" section.

9. Create a style called "BullList" with the description "Bulleted List." The style should contain codes to insert a bullet at the beginning of each line of the paragraph with the rest of the paragraph indented. The style also should include 12-point Arial text and full justification.
10. Apply the BullList style to each paragraph that begins "Packet #."
11. Apply the Heading 2 style to all the headings.
12. Define a style named "Title1" for the title of the report. Font formatting for the Title1 style should be 22-point, bold Arial; paragraph formatting should include center justification. Apply the Title1 style to the title of your document.
13. Define a style named "Title2" for the subtitle of the report. Formatting for the Title2 style should be 18-point, bold Arial; center justification. Apply the Title2 style to the remainder of the text in section 1.
14. Add codes for double spacing to the Initial Codes Style.

15. Set the initial font to 10-point Times New Roman. The initial font will affect not only the text in the body of the document but also footnotes, endnotes, headers, and so forth. (*Hint*: Use the Format, Initial Font command.)
16. Save, print, and close the document.

3. 2010 Olympic Bid Committee Report Ardell Barratt is chair of the Lake Tahoe, Nevada, 2010 Olympic Bid Committee. Recently, she was asked to submit a report on the feasibility of an Olympic bid to leaders of the state legislature. Open Olympic from the Cases folder in the Tutorial.03 folder on your Student Disk, save the document as Olympic Bid Report, then complete the following:

1. Find the words "foster national winter sports" and insert the words "and international" between "national" and "winter."
2. Find the words "3.6 million" and insert a "$" before "3.6."
3. Use the Thesaurus to substitute a synonym for the word "organized" in the "Organization of the Bid Committee" section.
4. Run Grammatik on the paragraphs in the "Organization of the Bid Committee" section with the checking style set to Formal Memo or Letter. Accept the appropriate changes and ignore the others.
5. Start a new page after the words "Lake Tahoe, Nevada" and after the summary paragraph ending, "a successful Olympic bid."
6. Center the text of the first page between the top and bottom margins.
7. Insert the endnote, "Lake Tahoe Carrier, January 15, 1999," following the words "a poll." Insert a second endnote, "*Los Angeles Times*, October 1998," following the words "$60 million."
8. Create a header that prints "Olympic Bid Report" at the left margin and the page number at the right margin and prints on all but the first two pages of the report. Make the font of the header 10-point Arial.
9. Apply the Heading 1 style to the first line (title) of the first page.
10. Create a heading style that includes a 6-line Conditional End of Page (so the heading can't appear alone at the bottom of a page), a boldface, 14-point, sans serif font, and centers between the left and right margins. Name the style "Main Heading" and apply it to all the headings.
11. Set the Initial Codes Style to double spacing, full justification, and widow/orphan protection.
12. Save, print, and close the document.

4. Advisory Letter on a Tuition Increase Your school wants to raise tuition beginning next term. As head of the Student Advisory Board, you must submit a letter to the school's president about the increase. Write a one-page letter explaining: what the current tuition or fees are at your school, what the new current tuition and fees will be, and three reasons why the school should wait for another year to increase tuition. Do the following:

1. At the top margin, insert today's date, then using the appropriate format for a letter, type a return address, inside address, salutation, body, and complimentary close.
2. Save your document in the Cases folder in the Tutorial.03 folder on your Student Disk as Tuition Letter.
3. Run Grammatik with the checking style set to Formal Memo or Letter. Accept the reasonable suggestions, and ignore the others.

4. Using the Initial Font command on the Format menu, change the initial font to 12-point Arial.
5. Using the Initial Codes Styles, change the left and right margins to 1.25 inches, and set the justification to full.
6. Create a footnote (with fictitious information, if necessary) to document some of the numbers you quoted.

7. Create a Character (paired) style called "My Letterhead," with the description "Letterhead Format," that includes codes *and text* to format and display your name, address, and phone number. Use at least two fonts in the style and make sure the text appears on at least two lines (for example, one line for your name and another for your address and phone number).
8. Apply your style above the date at the top of the document.

9. Save your style in a separate document called Letterhead.sty in the Cases folder in the Tutorial.03 folder on your Student Disk. When you save the styles file, save only the user styles, not the system styles.
10. Run the Spell Checker, then save, print, and close your letter.

TUTORIAL 4

Creating Outlines, Tables, and Tables of Contents

Writing a Business Plan for EstimaTech

OBJECTIVES

In this tutorial you will:

- Create and edit an outline
- Suppress the header on a page
- Create and modify tables
- Sort information in a table
- Perform a mathematical calculation in a table
- Move text between two open documents
- Format tables with Table SpeedFormat
- Change table border, cell lines, and cell fill
- Generate a table of contents

CASE

EstimaTech

Chui Lee Hwang and Robert Camberlango recently developed a computer program called EstimaQuote. Architects and construction companies use this program to estimate the cost of restoring or renovating buildings and homes. Now they are writing a business plan for EstimaTech—the new company that will market the software. A **business plan** is a report that details all aspects of starting a business, including market, operations, financial information, and personnel. One purpose of their business plan is to secure a $475,000 loan from Commercial Financial Bank of New England for the start-up of EstimaTech. Chui Lee and Robert have written a draft of the entire plan and have asked you to help them complete Chapter 2, "Industry Analysis," in time for their meeting with the bank. Specifically, they want you to organize the chapter sections more logically, summarize the results of recently completed market research in tables, and create a table of contents for the chapter.

In this tutorial, you'll create and modify an outline for the Industry Analysis chapter, open and review the chapter, create informational tables, and generate a table of contents. In Session 4.1, you'll create and edit an outline, suppress the header on a page, and create and modify a table. In Session 4.2, you'll create a table using the Create command from the Table menu, transfer data between documents, and format tables by aligning text within cells and adding borders, rules, and shading. In Session 4.3, you'll format tables automatically, center a table, add captions, and generate a table of contents. Finally, you'll print the chapter for the business plan.

> **SESSION 4.1**
>
> *In this session you will see how Robert and Chui Lee planned their report. Then you will create and edit an outline of the business plan, suppress the header on the first page of the report, and create a table using the Table button on the Power Bar.*

Planning the Document

A thorough business plan informs prospective investors about the purpose, organization, goals, and projected profits of a proposed business.

Content

Chapter 2 of the business plan discusses the market research about EstimaTech's new cost-estimating software and potential customers.

Organization

Following standard business plan organization, the market analysis begins with an explanation of how the research was compiled, followed by a summary of the results. Because numerical information is easier to understand when organized in tabular form, Chui Lee and Robert want you to summarize the results of the market research in tables. They also want you to include a table of contents for the chapter.

Style

Chui Lee and Robert use facts and statistics in their business plan to convince potential investors that the company will be profitable and that the cost-estimating software will fill an existing need in the marketplace. They write in a formal, business style.

Presentation

Chui Lee and Robert already formatted the document with the appropriate font, margins, header, and styles. However, they still need to add the tables summarizing their market research and create the table of contents.

Creating an Outline

Chui Lee and Robert want you to logically organize the chapter of their business plan. Before you begin, you'll create an **outline**—a list of basic points to discuss and the order in which to present them—of their business plan with WordPerfect's Outline feature. This way you can see the general organization of the chapter and decide how to move material.

In an outline, each paragraph is preceded by "paragraph numbers," which can be either numerals or letters. As shown in Figure 4-1, paragraph numbers represent the outline **levels**: level-1 paragraphs (major ideas) usually are preceded by Roman numerals (I, II, III, ...); level-2 paragraphs (supporting ideas) by uppercase letters (A, B, C, ...); level-3 paragraphs by Arabic numerals (1, 2, 3, ...); level-4 paragraphs by lowercase letters (a, b, c, ...); and so forth. WordPerfect's Outline feature uses this standard hierarchy and allows up to eight levels of paragraph numbers.

Figure 4-1
Standard outline paragraph levels and numbers

```
I.   Level 1, first paragraph
     A.  Level 2
         1.  Level 3
         2.  Level 3
     B.  Level 2
         1.  Level 3
             a.  Level 4
             b.  Level 4
         2.  Level 3
II.  Level 1, second paragraph
     A.  Level 2
     B.  Level 2
III. Level 1, third paragraph
```

When Outline is on and you press the Enter key to end one paragraph and start a new one, WordPerfect automatically inserts the appropriate paragraph number (or letter) for the next item in the outline. With a simple click of the mouse, you can change a paragraph number to the previous or next level. When you move a paragraph or group of paragraphs in the outline, WordPerfect automatically renumbers them.

REFERENCE window

CREATING AND EDITING OUTLINES

- Click Tools then click Outline to open the Outline feature bar.
- Click the Outline Definition list arrow, then click Outline. WordPerfect automatically inserts a level-1 paragraph number (Roman numeral I).
- Type the text of the level-1 paragraph, then press the Enter key.
- To switch from a higher level to a lower level (such as level 1 to level 2), click the Promote button or press the Tab key. To switch from a lower to a higher level, click the Demote button or press Shift + Tab.
- To change the order of text, click the Move Up button or the Move Down button.
- To end the outline, move the insertion point to a blank line below the outline, click the Text button then click the Close button.

You'll create and modify the outline for chapter 2 of Robert and Chui Lee's business plan. You'll begin by typing the title.

To insert the title for the outline:

1. Start WordPerfect, if necessary, and conduct a quick screen check.
2. Close the Ruler to make more space on your screen. You won't need the Ruler to work on the business plan chapter.
3. Make sure a blank document window appears on the screen.
4. Set the justification to **Center**, type **OUTLINE**, press the **Enter** key, type **EstimaTech Business Plan**, press the **Enter** key, type **Chapter 2. Industry Analysis**, then press the **Enter** key.

5. Set the justification to **Left**, then press the **Enter** key to double space after the title. The insertion point is in position for the first numbered paragraph of the outline. See Figure 4-2.

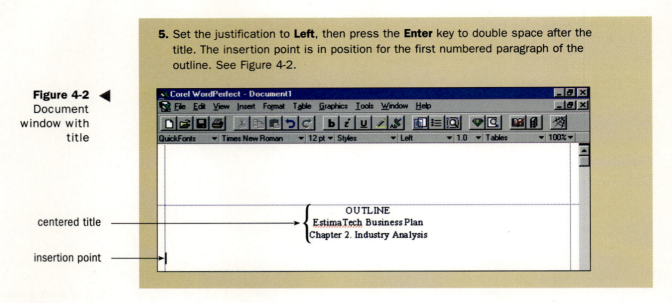

Figure 4-2 ◀ Document window with title

centered title

insertion point

You're ready to create an outline for chapter 2 of the business plan.

To create an outline:

1. Click **Tools** then click **Outline** to open the Outline feature bar and insert the first paragraph number, 1.

   On the right side of the Outline feature bar, the current outline definition type appears. WordPerfect supports nine types of outlines, including: Numbers (which is normal paragraph numbering), Legal 2 (which is paragraph numbering for legal documents), and Outline (which is normal outline numbering). You want to make sure the definition type is Outline.

2. If necessary, click the **Outline Definition Type** list arrow, then click **Outline**. The first paragraph number changes to Roman numeral I.

   You're ready to type the text of the first outline paragraph.

3. Type **Chapter 2.**, press the **spacebar** twice, type **Industry Analysis**, then press the **Enter** key. See Figure 4-3.

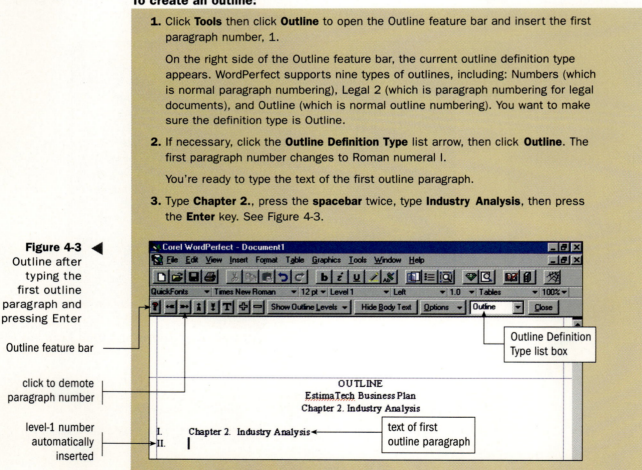

Figure 4-3 ◀ Outline after typing the first outline paragraph and pressing Enter

Outline feature bar

click to demote paragraph number

level-1 number automatically inserted

Outline Definition Type list box

text of first outline paragraph

When you press the Enter key, WordPerfect automatically inserts the next level-1 number, Roman numeral II. Because you want this to be the level-2 number A, you should demote the paragraph. To **demote** an outline paragraph means to decrease the level, for example, to change a level-1 paragraph to level-2. To **promote** an outline paragraph means to increase the level, for example, to change a level-2 paragraph to a level-1.

To demote outline paragraphs:

1. Click the **Demote** button on the Outline feature bar to indent the current number to the next tab stop and change the paragraph number from II to A.

2. Type **Market Research** then press the **Enter** key. Again, WordPerfect automatically inserts a paragraph number at the same level (in this case, level 2). Therefore, when the current paragraph number is A and you press the Enter key, the new paragraph number becomes B.

3. Type **Phases of the Market Research**, press the **Enter** key, type **Market Definition**, then press the **Enter** key.

   The paragraph number at the insertion point is D, but you want to type subparagraphs under "Market Definition." Again you'll demote the paragraph.

4. Click to indent the paragraph to the next tab stop. The new paragraph number is the Arabic numeral 1.

   TROUBLE? If you accidentally click the Promote button, click twice. If you click too many times, click until the current paragraph number is 1.

5. Type the subparagraphs below "Market Definition" as shown in Figure 4-4.

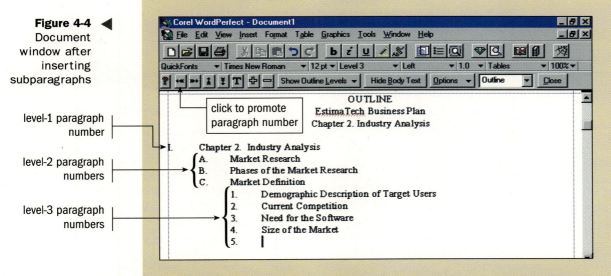

Figure 4-4 ◄
Document window after inserting subparagraphs

level-1 paragraph number

level-2 paragraph numbers

level-3 paragraph numbers

6. Correct any typographical errors, if necessary, then adjust any paragraphs to the correct outline level by clicking or the Promote button on the Outline feature bar.

In order to complete the outline, you need to promote the current outline paragraph from paragraph number 5 to D.

To promote a paragraph number:

1. If necessary, move the insertion point after paragraph number 5, then click the **Promote** button on the Outline feature bar. The current paragraph number becomes D.

2. Type **Customer Needs** then press the **Enter** key.

3. Type **Market Trends** then press the **Enter** key.

You have completed the outline and need to convert the current line (with the paragraph number F) to normal (non outline) text.

4. Click the **Text** button [T] on the Outline feature bar. WordPerfect erases the paragraph number and marks the line of text with a T in the left margin.

5. If necessary, click the **Left Scroll Arrow** [◄] in the lower-left corner of the screen to see the outline symbols in the left margin. See Figure 4-5.

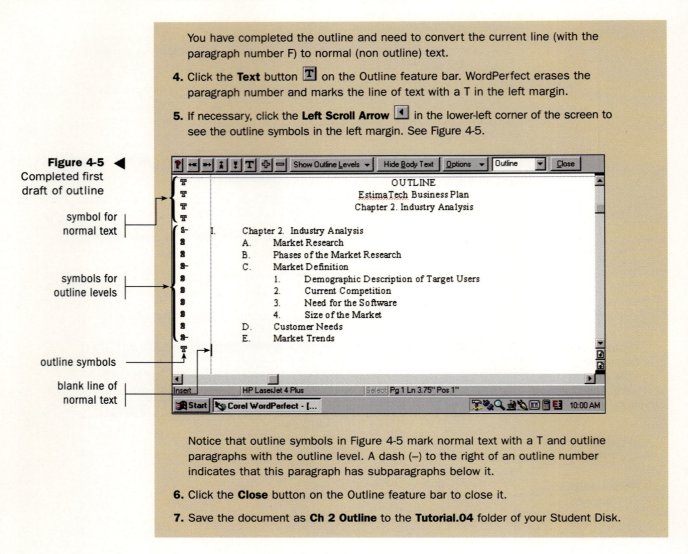

Figure 4-5 ◄ Completed first draft of outline

symbol for normal text

symbols for outline levels

outline symbols

blank line of normal text

Notice that outline symbols in Figure 4-5 mark normal text with a T and outline paragraphs with the outline level. A dash (–) to the right of an outline number indicates that this paragraph has subparagraphs below it.

6. Click the **Close** button on the Outline feature bar to close it.

7. Save the document as **Ch 2 Outline** to the **Tutorial.04** folder of your Student Disk.

You review the outline for chapter 2 of the business plan to determine how to better organize the material.

Modifying an Outline

After reviewing the outline of chapter 2, you realize that the topic "Current Competition" should be a level-2 paragraph and appear after the topic "Market Trends." You also decide the topic "Size of the Market" should appear before "Demographic Description of Target Users." The Outline feature provides commands for easily reordering the text in the outline.

Moving Outline Paragraphs Up and Down

You can rearrange the outline paragraphs in two ways: dragging the outline symbols in the left margin or clicking the Move Up or Move Down buttons on the Outline feature bar. When you move an outline paragraph, WordPerfect automatically renumbers all the paragraphs so they remain sequential. You'll move "Current Competition" to follow the "Market Trends" section.

OPENING THE BUSINESS PLAN   WP 137

To move outline paragraphs:

1. Place the insertion point anywhere in the "Current Competition" paragraph, click **Tools**, click **Outline** to open the Outline feature bar, then click the **Move Down** button on the Outline feature bar. The outline paragraph shifts down one line to follow the "Need for the Software" paragraph.

2. Move the pointer to the outline symbol 3 in the left margin next to "Current Competition." The pointer becomes ↕.

3. Press and hold down the mouse button to highlight the paragraph, then drag the pointer until the horizontal line marks the new location just below the last outline paragraph. See Figure 4-6.

Figure 4-6 ◀
Moving an outline paragraph

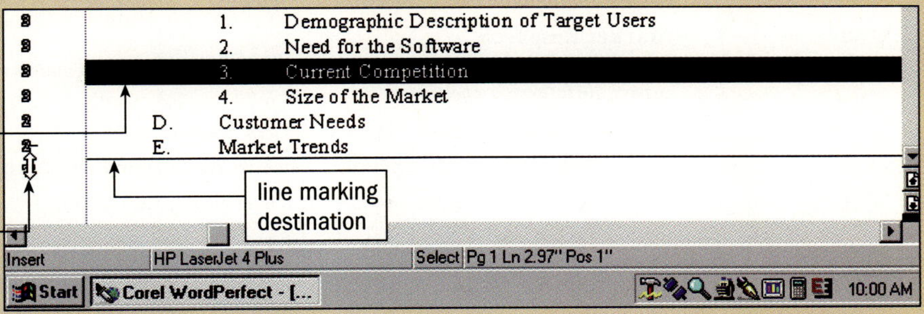

selected paragraph

pointer for moving up or down

```
      1.   Demographic Description of Target Users
      2.   Need for the Software
      3.   Current Competition
      4.   Size of the Market
   D.   Customer Needs
   E.   Market Trends
```
line marking destination

4. Release the mouse button. As you can see, you can drag-and-drop an outline symbol the same as you would other text.

   You also can drag-and-drop an outline family. An **outline family** is a group of outline paragraphs that includes the paragraph containing the insertion point and all its subordinate levels. An outline symbol followed by a dash (–) marks an outline family; just click this symbol to select the entire outline family.

5. Click the **Promote** button on the Outline feature bar to change the Current Competition section to a level-2 paragraph.

   Next, you'll move the level-3 paragraph "Size of the Market" above "Demographic Description of Target Users."

6. Place the insertion point anywhere in the heading "Size of the Market," then click the **Move Up** button on the Outline feature bar twice. The paragraph shifts up two lines to become the first subparagraph (level-3 paragraph) under "Market Definition."

7. Save the completed outline, then close the document.

You have used the Outline feature to create and modify an outline.

Opening the Business Plan

Chui Lee and Robert have revised their draft of chapter 2 of the business plan based on your outline. They give you a copy of the revised business plan to work with. You'll open and modify chapter 2 of the business plan.

To open the document:

1. Open **Industry** from the **Tutorial.04** folder on your Student Disk.

2. Save the document to the same folder as **Ch 2 Industry Analysis** to avoid overwriting the original file.

3. Make sure your document is in Page view and the Ruler is closed. See Figure 4-7.

Figure 4-7
Business plan in Page view

header (to be suppressed on this page)

Heading 1 style

Heading 2 style

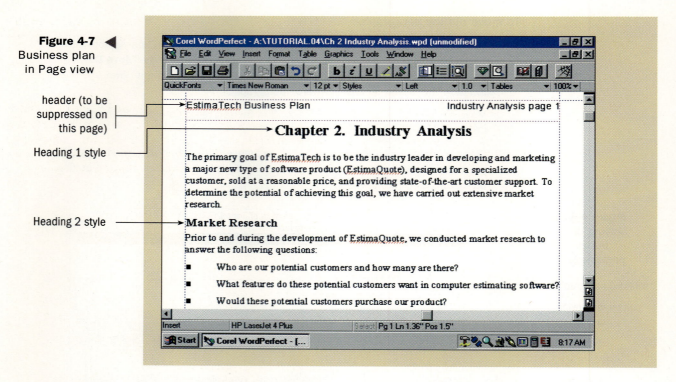

As you look through the document you see the current version of the document includes the text, margins, headings (in modified system styles), and a header.

Suppressing Headers

Often, when you create headers, footers, and other page elements, you move the insertion point to the beginning of the document so these elements will occur throughout the document. But what if later you decide you don't want one or more of these elements to appear on a particular page, such as the title page? Fortunately, you can use the **Suppress command** to hide page elements on one or more pages.

As you can see in Figure 4-7, the header appears on the first page of the chapter. Usually, you want headers to appear only after the first page. You'll suppress the header on this page to make the business plan document conform to this standard.

To suppress the header on the first page:

1. Make sure the insertion point is at the beginning of the document, the page where you want to suppress the header.

2. Click **Format**, point to **Page**, then click **Suppress**. The Suppress dialog box opens. See Figure 4-8.

Figure 4-8
Suppress dialog box

click to suppress header on first page

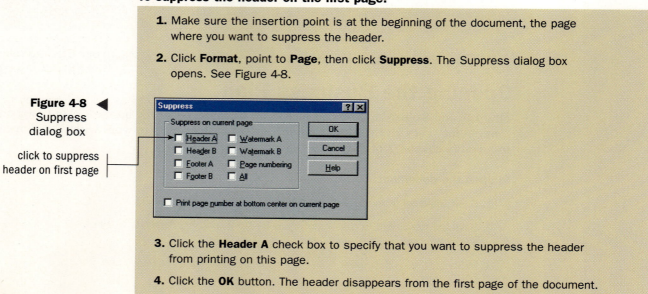

3. Click the **Header A** check box to specify that you want to suppress the header from printing on this page.

4. Click the **OK** button. The header disappears from the first page of the document.

You can use this same command to suppress other page elements, such as footers and page numbering. This chapter doesn't contain these other page elements, so you'll add the information about EstimaTech's potential customers.

Inserting Tables

Earlier, you learned how to align text in columns using tabs. Tabs work well if you have only two or three columns with three or four rows of information, but tabs and columns become tedious and difficult to work with when you need to organize a larger amount of more complex information. WordPerfect's Table feature allows you to quickly organize data, and to place text and graphics in a more readable format. Figure 4-9 summarizes the elements of a WordPerfect table.

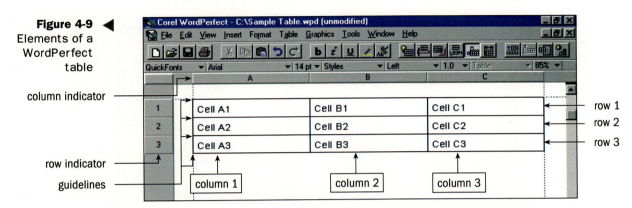

Figure 4-9 Elements of a WordPerfect table

A **table** is information arranged in horizontal **rows** and vertical **columns**. Each row is labeled with a number—row 1 at the top, row 2 below row 1, and so forth. Each column is labeled with a letter—column A on the far left, column B to the right of column A, and so forth.

The area where a row and column intersect is called a **cell**. Each cell is identified by a column and row label. For example, the cell in the upper-left corner of a table is cell A1 (column A, row 1), the cell to the right of that is cell B1, the cell below cell A1 is A2, and so forth. Cells provide a structure for the table; the structure is indicated by table **guidelines**, which outline the rows and columns on the screen. Although the guidelines themselves do not print, you can add or remove lines that print around the table or individual cells. With WordPerfect's Table feature, you can create a blank table and then insert information into it, or you can convert existing text into a table.

Creating a Table Using the Table Button

The easiest way to create a table is by moving the insertion point to the location in your document where you want a table, clicking the Table button on the Power Bar, and then specifying the number of rows and columns you need in your table. WordPerfect inserts a blank table structure with the number of rows and columns you specified.

Chui Lee and Robert want you to create a table that summarizes the information on EstimaTech's potential customers. You'll use the Table button to create that table.

To create a blank table using the Table button:

1. Scroll until you see the paragraph entitled "Size of the Market" near the bottom of page 1. Position the insertion point immediately after the phrase "... in renovation cost estimates."

2. Press the **Enter** key twice to double space before the table. WordPerfect will insert the table at the location of the insertion point. The insertion point will probably be at the beginning of page 2.

TROUBLE? If your insertion point isn't at the top of page 2, don't worry. Differences in fonts and printers could cause your insertion point to appear near the bottom of page 1 or after a few lines of text on page 2.

3. Click the **Table** button [Tables] on the Power Bar and hold down the mouse button. A grid resembling a miniature table appears on the screen, with the label "No Table." You'll drag the pointer in the grid so it extends three columns and seven rows.

4. Drag the pointer down and across the grid until you highlight three columns and seven rows. As you drag the pointer across the grid, the size of the table (columns by rows) appears at the top of the grid. See Figure 4-10.

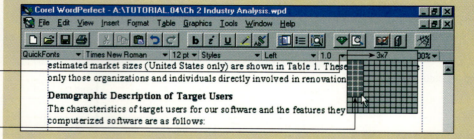

Figure 4-10
Table button on Power Bar

table dimensions (columns × rows)

selected number of columns and rows

5. Release the mouse button. An empty table, three columns by seven rows, appears in your document with the insertion point blinking in the upper-left corner (cell A1). Lines mark the boundaries between all the rows and columns. If you don't change them, lines will print on all four sides of each cell. The Toolbar changes to the Tables toolbar with 10 new buttons, nine dealing with tables.

6. Click the **Row/Column Indicators** button on the Tables toolbar; scroll the document window so you can see the entire table. The row indicators appear to the left of the document window and the column indicators appear above the document window. See Figure 4-11. Notice the status bar below the document window indicates the cell in which the insertion point is located.

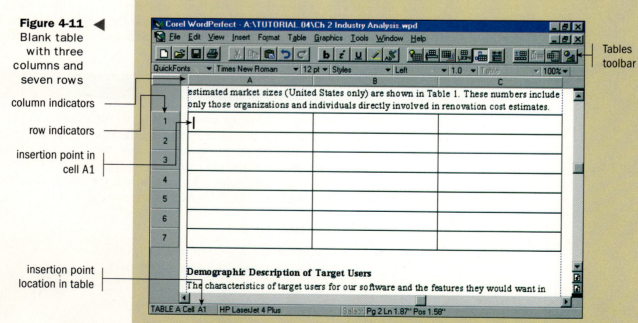

Figure 4-11
Blank table with three columns and seven rows

column indicators

row indicators

insertion point in cell A1

insertion point location in table

Tables toolbar

7. Save the document with the empty table.

Now that you've created the table, you're ready to enter the customer data Robert gave you.

Entering Text in a Table

You can enter text in a table by moving the insertion point to a cell and typing. If the text takes up more than one line in the cell, WordPerfect automatically wraps the text to the next line and increases the height of that cell and all the cells in that row. To move the insertion point to the next cell to the right, you can either click in that cell or press the Tab key. If you want to return to the previous cell, you can press and hold the Shift key while you press the Tab key. You also can move around the table using the usual cursor-movement arrow keys.

Now that you've created the table, you can insert the information Robert gave you about the number of potential EstimaQuote customers.

To insert text into the table:

1. Make sure the insertion point is in cell **A1** of the table.

2. Type **Potential Customers**.

3. Press the **Tab** key to move to cell B1.

   TROUBLE? If you accidentally pressed the Enter key instead of the Tab key, WordPerfect created a new paragraph within cell A1 rather than moving the insertion point to cell B1. Click the Undo button on the Toolbar to remove the hard return, then repeat Step 3.

4. Type **Percent**, then press the **Tab** key to move to cell C1.

5. Type **Number**, then press the **Tab** key to move the insertion point from cell C1 to cell A2. Notice when you press the Tab key in the last column of a row, the insertion point moves to the first column in the next row.

   You have entered the **header row**, the row that identifies the information in each column.

6. Type the remaining information for the table, as shown in Figure 4-12, pressing the **Tab** key to move from cell to cell.

Figure 4-12
Table with all data entered

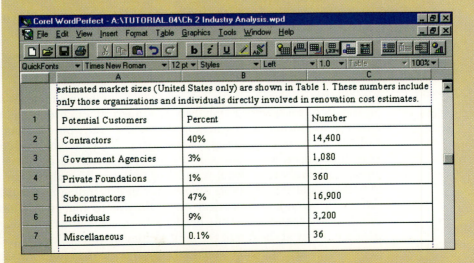

TROUBLE? If a new row (row 8) appeared in your table, you pressed the Tab key after entering text in cell C7, the last cell in the table. Click the Undo button on the Toolbar to remove row 8 from the table.

As you look at the data in the table, you realize it should be ordered differently.

Editing a Table

You can edit text within a table the same way you edit text in the rest of the document. Many of the methods you've used to edit a document, such as the Backspace key, the copy-and-paste feature, the Undo button, the QuickCorrect feature, and the Thesaurus, work the same way in a table. Just like in a paragraph, you must select text within a table in order to edit it.

Selecting Text in a Table

To make editing changes in a table, you can select text within a cell just as you would select text within a paragraph. In addition, WordPerfect provides special techniques to quickly highlight an entire cell, row, column, or table. Figure 4-13 lists the methods for selecting each element of a table.

Figure 4-13 ◄
Methods for selecting elements of a table

To Select	Do This
a cell	Click ⇦ on the left edge or ⇧ on the top edge of the cell.
a row	Click the row indicator or double-click ⇦ on the left edge of any cell of the row.
a column	Click the column indicator or double-click ⇧ on the top edge of any cell of the column.
the entire table	Click ⇨ on the gray button in the upper-left corner of the row/column indicators, or triple-click the edge of any cell in the table, or click Edit, click Select, and click Table.

As you move the pointer to the left edge of a cell (but not onto the guideline), the pointer changes to ⇦. When you move the pointer to the top edge of a cell (but not onto the guideline), the pointer changes to ⇧. Once the pointer has changed, you can click, double-click, or triple-click to make a selection.

You entered the data into the table in the order that Robert provided. You decide to reorder the data in a more logical manner. You can manually cut and paste rows in the table, but it is much easier to reorganize the table by sorting the rows.

Sorting Rows in a Table

WordPerfect allows you to sort the rows or columns in a table. To **sort** means to rearrange information in a specified alphabetical, numerical, or chronological order. The most common use for sorting is to rearrange rows in a table, but you can use the Sort feature to sort any list of information. For example, in the table you just created, which is Table 1 in the document, you could sort the list of potential customers alphabetically in ascending alphabetical order (from A to Z) or in descending alphabetical order (from Z to A). You also could sort the table numerically in descending numerical order (highest to lowest) or in ascending numerical order (lowest to highest). When you sort table data, WordPerfect does not sort the header row into the other information, but instead leaves the header row at the top of the table as long as you indicate you have used a header row.

You think arranging the potential customers in the table in descending numerical order, from the highest percentage to the lowest percentage, best emphasizes who most likely will purchase EstimaQuote. Before you perform the sort, you'll specify the top row as the header row.

EDITING A TABLE **WP 143**

To specify the header row in the table:

1. Click the row indicator for row 1 to select that row.

2. Click the **Table Format** button on the Tables toolbar to open the Properties for Table Format dialog box, then click the **Row** tab, if necessary. See Figure 4-14.

Figure 4-14
Properties for Table Format dialog box

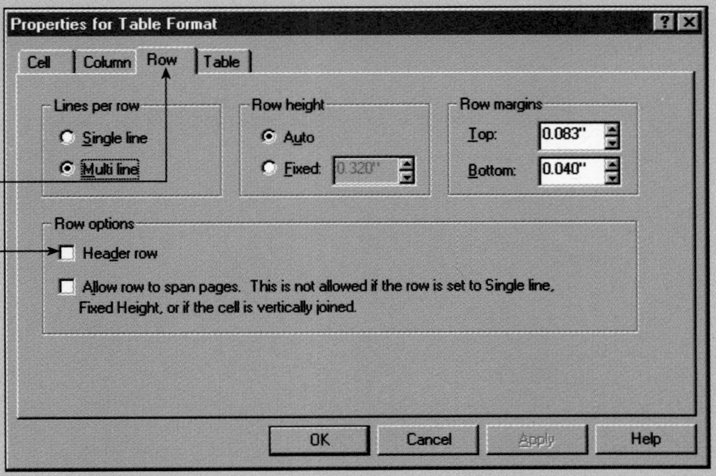

Row tab selected

click to set selected row as header row

3. Click the **Header row** check box in the Row options section to identify the selected row as the header row, then click the **OK** button.

4. Deselect the row by clicking in any other cell of the table.

Now when you sort the table, WordPerfect will keep row 1 at the top of the table. Moreover, if the table spans two or more pages, the header row will appear at the top of the table on all pages.

To sort the table in descending numerical order:

1. With the insertion point anywhere within the table, click **Tools**, then click **Sort**. The Sort dialog box opens with the Defined sort "First cell in a table row" selected. This would sort your table alphabetically by the first cell in each row. However, you want to sort by the second cell in each row, so you'll use a User Defined Sort.

2. Click the **Options** button then, if **Allow Undo** is not checked, click it. This permits you to use the Undo feature in case you make a mistake in sorting the table.

3. Click the **New** button. The New Sort dialog box opens.

You want to set the User Defined Sort so WordPerfect will sort the rows of the table using the second column as the sort key. A **sort key** is a column, line, word, or some other text element that specifies the order of priority in which a list is sorted. You can set as many as nine keys in a sort definition. If you set multiple keys, WordPerfect sorts the list using the first key. Then, if two or more items in the list have the same first key, WordPerfect sorts those items by the second key. If some of those items also have the same second key, then WordPerfect sorts by the third key, and so forth. Because Table 1 is small and each row has a unique percentage, you need to use only one key to sort the table.

4. If necessary, click the **Table row** radio button in the Sort by section so that WordPerfect will sort the rows in Table 1.

5. For Key 1, if necessary, click the **Type** button, then click **Numeric**. This specifies that you want to sort numerically, not alphabetically.

6. If necessary, click the **Sort order** button for Key 1, and set the order to **Descending**, which will sort the numbers highest to lowest.

7. Set the Column text box value to **2** so WordPerfect will sort the table using the numbers in column 2.

8. Make sure the Line text box is set to **1** and the Word text box is set to **1**. The dialog box should match Figure 4-15.

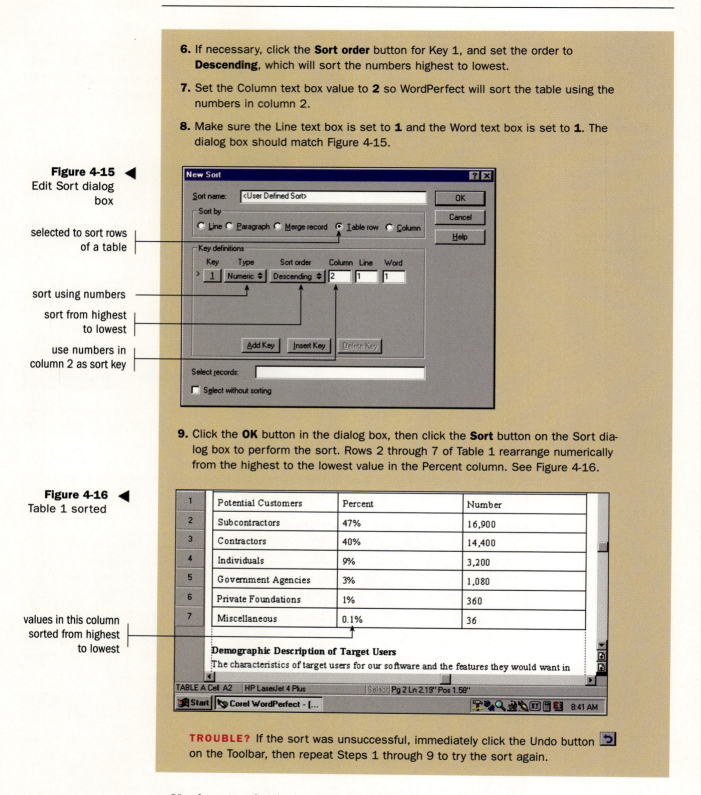

Figure 4-15
Edit Sort dialog box

- selected to sort rows of a table
- sort using numbers
- sort from highest to lowest
- use numbers in column 2 as sort key

9. Click the **OK** button in the dialog box, then click the **Sort** button on the Sort dialog box to perform the sort. Rows 2 through 7 of Table 1 rearrange numerically from the highest to the lowest value in the Percent column. See Figure 4-16.

Figure 4-16
Table 1 sorted

- values in this column sorted from highest to lowest

TROUBLE? If the sort was unsuccessful, immediately click the Undo button on the Toolbar, then repeat Steps 1 through 9 to try the sort again.

You have just finished sorting the information in the table, when Chui Lee stops by and asks you to total columns B and C. You'll need to modify the structure of the table so that you can show totals for the data.

Modifying an Existing Table Structure

Often, when you create a table you're unsure how many rows or columns you'll actually need. You might need to delete extra rows and columns, or, as in this case, you might need to add them. Either way, you can easily modify or change an existing table structure. Figure 4-17 summarizes ways to insert or delete rows and columns in a table.

Figure 4-17 ◀
Ways to insert or delete table rows or columns

To	Do This
Insert a row or column within a table	Move the insertion point to the row or column before or after which you want to insert a row or column, click Table, click Insert, select the number of rows or columns, select Before or After the current row or column, and click the OK button.
Insert a row at the end of the table	Move the insertion point to the last cell in the bottom row, then press the Tab key.
Delete a row or column	Select the row or column, click Table, click Delete, and click the OK button.

You'll need to insert an extra row in Table 1.

Inserting Additional Rows in a Table

In WordPerfect, you can insert additional rows within the table or at the end of a table. In Table 1 of the business plan, you need to insert a row for totals at the end of the table.

To insert a row at the bottom of Table 1:

1. Click in cell **C7**, the last cell of the last row in Table 1, which contains the number 36.

2. Press the **Tab** key. A blank row is added to the bottom of the table similar to the rows above it. You might need to scroll to see the entire table.

   TROUBLE? If a blank row is not added to the bottom of the table, click the Undo button on the Toolbar, make sure the insertion point is in the last cell of the last row, then press the Tab key.

3. Type **Totals** in cell A8.

Before you total columns B and C, you decide to delete row 7 from Table 1 because the numbers in the Miscellaneous customers category are so small that they represent an insignificant portion of EstimaQuote's potential customers.

Deleting Existing Rows in a Table

With WordPerfect, you can delete either the contents or the structure of the cells. You'll delete the row using the Table shortcut menu, which contains frequently used table commands.

To delete a row using the Table shortcut menu:

1. Select row **7** ("Miscellaneous") by clicking the row indicator.

2. With the pointer anywhere over the selected text, click the right mouse button. The Table shortcut menu opens.

3. Click **Delete** to open the Delete dialog box, make sure the **Rows** radio button is selected, then click the **OK** button. The selected row is deleted from the table. See Figure 4-18.

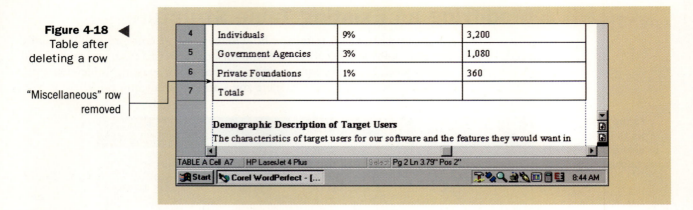

Figure 4-18
Table after deleting a row

"Miscellaneous" row removed

You have modified the structure of the table in the business plan by inserting and deleting rows. Now you're ready to insert the totals for the data in the table. Rather than adding up the columns on a calculator and typing in the totals, you'll use WordPerfect's Table Formula command to calculate the totals automatically.

Performing Mathematical Calculations in Tables

Tables are especially effective for displaying the results of a mathematical calculation. Table formulas perform a wide variety of simple calculations (such as adding, subtracting, multiplying, dividing, averaging, and finding percentages), as well as complex calculations (such as mathematical and financial functions). In fact, WordPerfect tables provide many of the same functions found in spreadsheet programs, such as Quattro Pro.

Having WordPerfect perform calculations is much more efficient than doing them yourself. If you modify the table or change the calculations, WordPerfect will update the results when you execute the Calculate command from the Tables menu, or you can specify that WordPerfect automatically updates the results any time you change cell contents.

As Chui Lee requested, you need to calculate the total values for the number of potential customers for EstimaTech's new software. Because simple summations are so common, WordPerfect provides a special command called **QuickSum** that automatically inserts a function to sum a column or row of numbers.

To calculate the total number of potential customers in Table 1:

1. Place the insertion point in cell **B7**, the last cell of the second column in Table 1.

2. Click **Table**, then click **QuickSum**. WordPerfect automatically inserts the number 1 (which is equal to 100%) into cell B7. Now you'll set the number to a percentage and specify the number of digits you want to the right of the decimal point.

3. Click the **Numeric Format** button on the Tables toolbar to open the Properties for Table Numeric Format dialog box. See Figure 4-19.

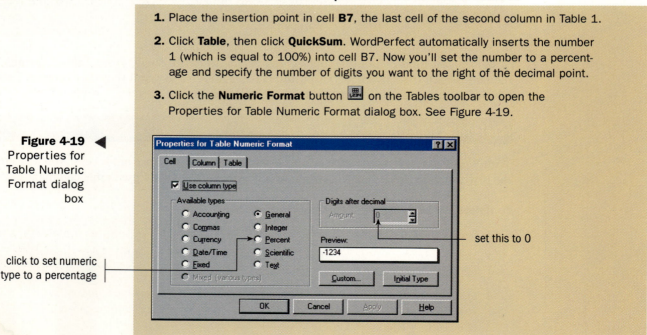

Figure 4-19
Properties for Table Numeric Format dialog box

click to set numeric type to a percentage

set this to 0

4. Click the **Percent** radio button, set the Digits after decimal Amount text box to **0** because you want to round to the nearest 1% rather than to the nearest 0.01%, then click the **OK** button. The number in cell B7 becomes 100%.

5. Press the **Tab** key to move the insertion point to cell C7 and repeat Steps 2 through 4, except set the numeric format to **Commas** rather than Percent. The total number of potential customers (35,940) appears in cell C7.

6. Save the document with the changes you have made to the table.

You have created Table 1, sorted the data, and totaled columns. Later, you'll format Table 1, but first you'll create the other tables in the business plan.

Quick Check

1. What is the purpose of WordPerfect's Suppress command?
2. How do you begin an outline in WordPerfect?
3. What does it mean to promote an outline paragraph? demote an outline paragraph?
4. Define table and table guidelines in your own words.
5. List two ways to move the insertion point from cell A1 to cell A2 in a table. List two ways to move from cell B7 to cell B6.
6. How do you insert a row in the middle of a table?
7. What happens when you delete an existing row?
   a. Only the text within that row disappears from the table.
   b. The entire row, including the text within it, disappears from the table.
   c. The entire table disappears from the document.
   d. Only the guidelines around that cell disappear from the table.
8. How would you change the format of a number from a decimal to a percentage?

If you aren't going to work through Session 4.2 now, you should close the business plan and exit WordPerfect. When you're ready to begin Session 4.2, start WordPerfect, open Ch 2 Industry Analysis, and continue with the session.

SESSION 4.2

In this session you will create a table using the Create command from the Table menu, enter data into the table by transferring it from another document, and then you will format both tables.

Creating a Table with the Table Create Command

Earlier, you created a table using the Tables button on the Power Bar; you can also create tables using the Create command on the Table menu. With the Create command, WordPerfect opens the Create Table dialog box, in which you can specify the number of columns and rows of the table.

> **REFERENCE window**
>
> **INSERTING A TABLE WITH THE TABLE CREATE COMMAND**
> - Click Table then click Create.
> - Set the number of rows and columns you want.
> - Click the OK button.

Chui Lee likes the table of potential customers you created and wants you to create a table that summarizes the results of the customer needs survey.

To insert a table using the Create command:

1. Scroll until you see the heading "Customer Needs" in the middle of page 2, then place the insertion point at the end of the first paragraph after the phrase, "...sample results in Table 2." Press the **Enter** key twice to insert a blank line between the end of the paragraph and the beginning of the table.

2. Click **Table** then click **Create**. The Create Table dialog box opens. Click the **Table** radio button in the Create section to select it, if necessary. Next, you'll specify the number of columns and rows in the dialog box.

3. Click the **Columns** up arrow until the text box reads **4**.

4. Click the **Rows** up or down arrow until the text box reads **4**.

5. Click the **OK** button to close the Create Table dialog box. A blank 4 × 4 table appears on the screen with the insertion point blinking in cell A1. The columns are of equal width.

6. Make sure the column/row indicators appear above and to the left of the document window, then enter the customer needs survey results shown in Figure 4-20 into the table. Leave the cells below "Statement" blank.

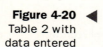
Figure 4-20
Table 2 with data entered

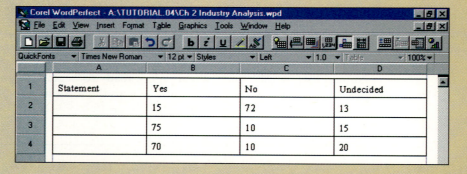

7. Save the document with the new table.

You're ready to enter Chui Lee and Robert's survey statements into the table. Rather than retyping the text into the table, you can take advantage of the Windows system's ability to open more than one document at a time and move information between them.

Transferring Data Between Documents

You have moved or copied text *within* a document, using both the cut-and-paste (or copy-and-paste) method and the drag-and-drop method. You also can move or copy text *between* two WordPerfect documents, using the same techniques. That is, you can either cut and paste (or copy and paste) or drag and drop to move text from one document to another. Opening more than one document and transferring text between them saves time and typing, and insures accuracy.

Copying and Pasting Between Documents

Robert has given you the file that contains the original customer survey. You need to transfer the survey statements from the original survey document into the business plan document.

> **REFERENCE window**
>
> **TRANSFERRING DATA BETWEEN DOCUMENTS**
>
> - Open both documents you want to transfer between.
> - Select text you want to transfer.
> - Click the Cut button or Copy button on the Toolbar.
> - Move the insertion point to the location in the other document where you want to transfer the data.
> - Click the Paste button on the Toolbar.

You'll use the copy-and-paste command to move the text.

To transfer the survey statements using copy and paste:

1. Open **Survey** from the **Tutorial.04** folder on your Student Disk. The file Ch 2 Industry Analysis remains open but is not visible.

2. Scroll through the document to read the survey statements, then select survey statement 5 by clicking the shadow pointer before the word "I" and dragging across to select the rest of the statement. Do not include the statement number, but do include the period at the end. See Figure 4-21.

Figure 4-21 ◄
Text to copy from one document to another

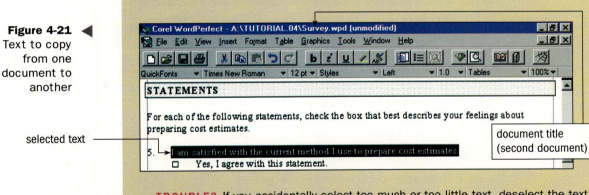

selected text

document title (second document)

TROUBLE? If you accidentally select too much or too little text, deselect the text and try again.

3. Click the **Copy** button 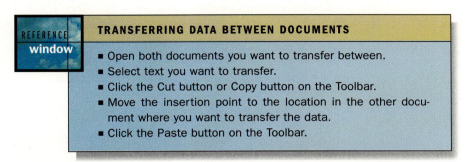 on the Toolbar to place survey statement 5 on the Clipboard.

Now you need to paste the copied statement from the Clipboard to cell A2 of Table 2 in the business plan. But first, you must make the business plan the active document.

4. Click **Window** then click **A:\TUTORIAL.04\Ch 2 Industry Analysis** to make it the active document. Notice the insertion point is in the same location it was before you switched documents. The Survey document is still open, but it is not visible.

5. Move the insertion point to cell **A2**, just below the "Statement" heading.

6. Click the **Paste** button on the Toolbar. The survey statement is pasted from the Clipboard to cell A2 in Table 2. Notice the row height increases to fit the new text. See Figure 4-22.

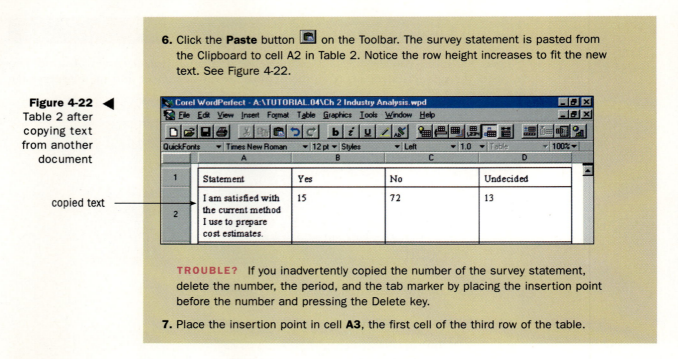

Figure 4-22
Table 2 after copying text from another document

copied text

TROUBLE? If you inadvertently copied the number of the survey statement, delete the number, the period, and the tab marker by placing the insertion point before the number and pressing the Delete key.

7. Place the insertion point in cell **A3**, the first cell of the third row of the table.

You've moved text between two open documents, but it's somewhat cumbersome to continually switch between the documents using the Window menu. WordPerfect provides a way to view both documents at once.

Viewing Two Document Windows

WordPerfect lets you arrange the screen to show two or more document windows at once. Each open document window is reduced so all open document windows can fit on your screen. Only one document is active at a time, but you can just click an inactive document to make it active rather than using the Window menu. This function makes it much easier to work with two or more documents at the same time. When you're finished, you can close the documents you no longer need, or maximize one document window so that you can't see the other documents, although they remain open.

You still need to transfer more survey statements into Table 2, but first you'll arrange the document window so you can view both documents at once.

To view both open documents on the screen:

1. Click **Window** to open the Window menu. **Ch 2 Industry Analysis** and **Survey** should be the only two documents listed in the lower part of the menu.

    TROUBLE? If another document is listed, click its name to make it the active document, close it, then repeat Step 1.

2. Click **Tile Top to Bottom**. Each document appears in its own document window. Ch 2 Industry Analysis is the active document; you can tell because the active document has a highlighted title bar and scroll bars, while the inactive document does not. See Figure 4-23.

Figure 4-23
Two documents visible at once

active document title bar

inactive document title bar

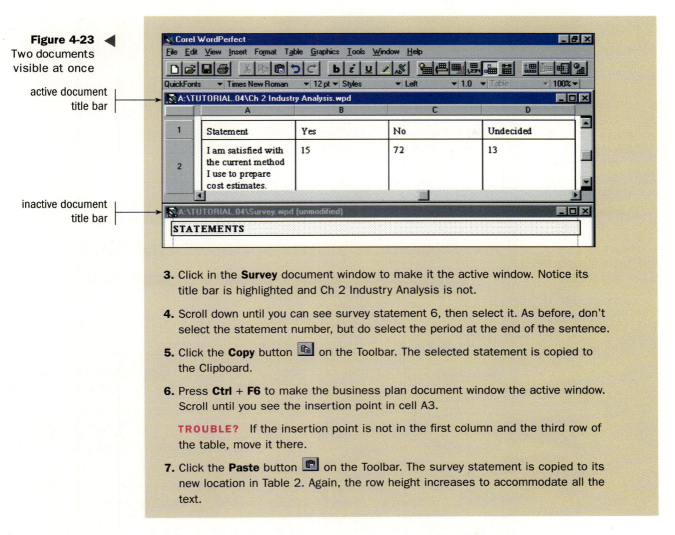

3. Click in the **Survey** document window to make it the active window. Notice its title bar is highlighted and Ch 2 Industry Analysis is not.

4. Scroll down until you can see survey statement 6, then select it. As before, don't select the statement number, but do select the period at the end of the sentence.

5. Click the **Copy** button on the Toolbar. The selected statement is copied to the Clipboard.

6. Press **Ctrl** + **F6** to make the business plan document window the active window. Scroll until you see the insertion point in cell A3.

   TROUBLE? If the insertion point is not in the first column and the third row of the table, move it there.

7. Click the **Paste** button on the Toolbar. The survey statement is copied to its new location in Table 2. Again, the row height increases to accommodate all the text.

You have one more survey statement to copy to Table 2. This time you'll drag and drop the survey question into the business plan document.

Dragging and Dropping Between Documents

You've used the drag-and-drop method to move text within a document. You also can use it to copy text between documents, if the two document windows are both visible at once. Just select text in one window, press and hold down the Ctrl key while you drag the text into the other window, then finally release the mouse button. Recall that when you use the drag-and-drop method to move text, the selected text is not placed on the Clipboard.

Now you'll transfer the last survey statement from the original survey document into the business plan document using the drag-and-drop method.

To copy text between the two documents using drag and drop:

1. Click in cell **A4** in Table 2 of Ch 2 Industry Analysis. You might need to scroll the window to see the blank cell A4.

2. Press **Ctrl** + **F6** to make Survey the active window, then select survey statement 7, including the period at the end of the sentence but not the statement number.

3. Move the pointer over the selected text.

4. Press and hold the **Ctrl** key while you press and hold down the mouse button. The pointer changes to 🖱 to indicate that you're copying the selected text rather than moving it. Do not release the Ctrl key yet.

5. Drag the pointer until the insertion point is in cell **A4** of Table 2 in Ch 2 Industry Analysis. See Figure 4-24.

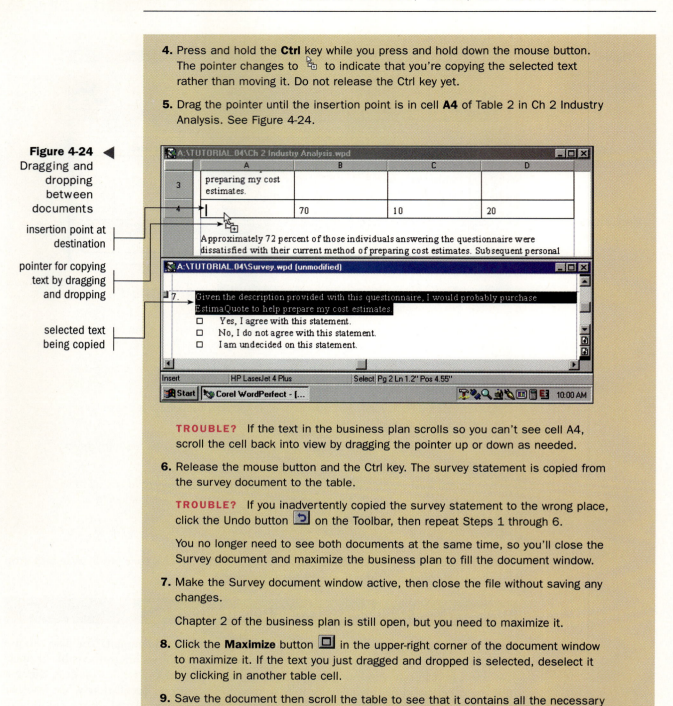

Figure 4-24
Dragging and dropping between documents

- insertion point at destination
- pointer for copying text by dragging and dropping
- selected text being copied

TROUBLE? If the text in the business plan scrolls so you can't see cell A4, scroll the cell back into view by dragging the pointer up or down as needed.

6. Release the mouse button and the Ctrl key. The survey statement is copied from the survey document to the table.

TROUBLE? If you inadvertently copied the survey statement to the wrong place, click the Undo button ↶ on the Toolbar, then repeat Steps 1 through 6.

You no longer need to see both documents at the same time, so you'll close the Survey document and maximize the business plan to fill the document window.

7. Make the Survey document window active, then close the file without saving any changes.

Chapter 2 of the business plan is still open, but you need to maximize it.

8. Click the **Maximize** button ◻ in the upper-right corner of the document window to maximize it. If the text you just dragged and dropped is selected, deselect it by clicking in another table cell.

9. Save the document then scroll the table to see that it contains all the necessary information. Your table will probably span from the bottom of page 2 to the top of page 3.

You have created Table 2 and added text by transferring it from another document, just like Chui Lee wanted. However, you can see that the table is not formatted attractively and the information is difficult to read. You need to format Table 2 to give it a more professional appearance and make it easier to read.

Formatting Tables

Like other text in your document, WordPerfect provides a variety of ways to enhance the appearance of the tables you create: you can alter column widths and row heights; change the text alignment within cells or the alignment of the table between the left and right margins; and place borders around cells, parts of a table, or the entire table.

The tables in Chapter 2 of the business plan need formatting to make them more attractive and easier to read.

Changing Column Width

Sometimes you want to adjust the column widths in a table to improve the readability of the text or to improve the appearance of the table. If you want to modify the width for a column, you can use the Table Format button or you can simply drag the desired vertical guideline to a new position.

You'll drag guidelines within Table 2 to make it more readable. The first column is too small to fit all the text attractively, and the rest of the columns don't need to be so large. Increasing the width of the first column, and shrinking the other column widths will help make the table more attractive and easier to read.

To change column widths by dragging the guidelines:

1. Place the insertion point anywhere in Table 2. Make sure you do not select any cells.

2. Move the pointer over the guideline between columns C and D. The pointer changes to ↔. When you click a guideline with this pointer, WordPerfect displays a QuickTip, showing the column widths to the left and right of the guideline.

3. Click and drag the guideline to the right, until the QuickTip indicates that the left column (column C) is **2"** and the right column (column D) is **1"**. See Figure 4-25. Then release the mouse button.

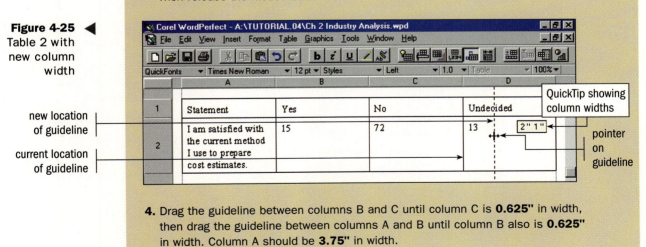

Figure 4-25 ◄
Table 2 with new column width

4. Drag the guideline between columns B and C until column C is **0.625"** in width, then drag the guideline between columns A and B until column B also is **0.625"** in width. Column A should be **3.75"** in width.

Table 2 takes up less space on the page and looks much better with its new column widths. Now, you'll align the text in Tables 1 and 2 to make them more attractive.

Justifying Text Within Cells

Justifying text within table cells makes the information easier to understand and the table more attractive. For example, right-justifying numbers and percentages within table columns helps the reader to quickly determine the place value of the numbers. Centering the headings makes the columns more visually appealing. You can align text within the cells by using the Table Format button on the Tables toolbar or using the Align Text button on the Power Bar.

The survey results (the data in cells B2 through D4) in Table 2 and the dollar and percentage amounts in Table 1 would be much easier to read if you right-aligned the numbers. Both tables will also look better with the text of the header row centered.

To right-justify the numeric data and center the headings:

1. Select cells **B2** through **D4** in Table 2, the nine cells that contain the survey results. See Figure 4-26.

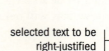

Figure 4-26
Justifying text

selected text to be right-justified

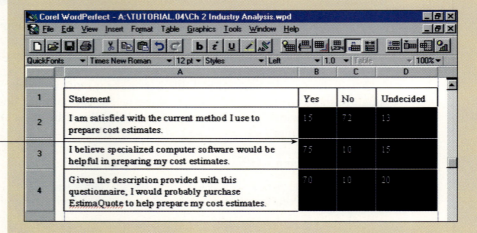

TROUBLE? If your table spans two pages, you will need to scroll so you can see at least the first row that you're going to select (row 2). Click the pointer on the row 2 indicator, then drag the pointer slowly down until the pointer selects the row 3 and row 4 indicators.

2. Click the **Table Format** button on the Tables toolbar, then if necessary, click **Column** to make it the frontmost tab.

3. In the dialog box, click the **Justification** button, click **Right**, then click the **OK** button. The numbers line up along the right edge of the cell.

TROUBLE? If more than just the number amounts right-align within the table, click the Undo button on the Toolbar, then repeat Steps 1 through 3.

4. Select cells **A1** through **D1** (the header row in Table 2) click the **Align Text** button on the Power Bar, then click **Center**. The text becomes centered between the left and right cell boundaries in each cell.

TROUBLE? If more than just the header row centered, click the Undo button on the Toolbar, then repeat Step 4.

Now you'll align the percentage and number amounts in Table 1.

5. Scroll up until you see Table 1 in your document window, then select cells **B2** through **C7**, the 12 cells that contain the total percentage and number of potential EstimaQuote customers.

TROUBLE? If the headings in the top row or the text in the first column highlight, click within the table to deselect the text, then repeat Step 5.

6. Set the justification to **Right**. The highlighted percentage and number amounts become right-justified.

7. **Center** the text in cells **A1** through **C1** (the header row in Table 1), then deselect the cells of the table. See Figure 4-27.

Figure 4-27
Justified text in Table 1

center-justified cells

right-justified columns

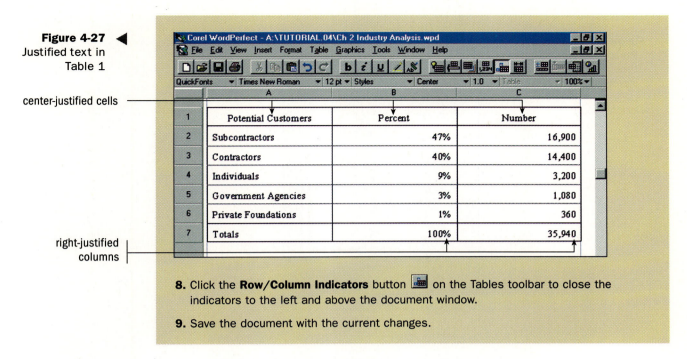

8. Click the **Row/Column Indicators** button on the Tables toolbar to close the indicators to the left and above the document window.

9. Save the document with the current changes.

The tables look better with header rows centered and the numbers right-aligned. You decide to format the tables even more. But first you'll add a shaded border to the chapter title to make it match the rest of the business plan chapters.

Adding Borders, Rules, and Shading to Paragraphs

WordPerfect allows you to add borders, rules, and shading to tables and text. A **border** is a box that frames tables and table cells, text, or graphics; it is made up of four rules. A **rule** is a horizontal or vertical line that you use to set off a portion of your document to enhance its appearance or improve its readability. Rules can be placed to the right, left, top, or bottom of table cells, text, or graphics. **Shading** is a gray or colored background on which text is printed. Shading often is placed within a border to make the text or cell stand out even more.

When you add a border around text, you also can add a drop shadow. A **drop shadow** is a shaded box, usually behind and slightly below and to the right of the border, that looks like a shadow of the box.

Chui Lee and Robert have placed a border with a drop shadow around the titles of every chapter in their business plan and separated each chapter introduction from the first heading with a rule. You need to do this in chapter 2.

To create a border with a drop shadow around the chapter title:

1. Scroll to the beginning of page 1 and place the insertion point anywhere within "Chapter 2. Industry Analysis."

2. Click **Format**, point to **Border/Fill**, then click **Paragraph**. The Paragraph Border/Fill dialog box opens.

3. Click the **Border** tab, if necessary, then click the box with the drop shadow in the Available border styles section, as shown in Figure 4-28.

Figure 4-28
Paragraph Border/Fill dialog box

select this border style

drop shadow style

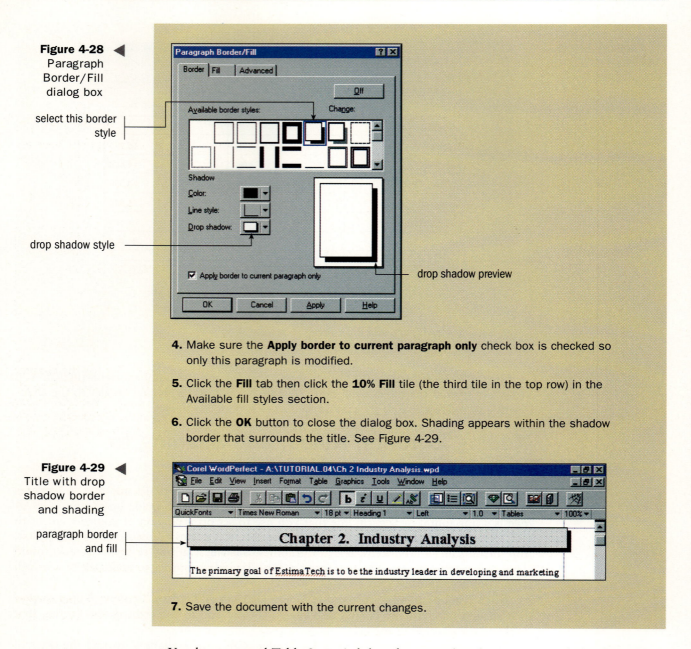

drop shadow preview

4. Make sure the **Apply border to current paragraph only** check box is checked so only this paragraph is modified.

5. Click the **Fill** tab then click the **10% Fill** tile (the third tile in the top row) in the Available fill styles section.

6. Click the **OK** button to close the dialog box. Shading appears within the shadow border that surrounds the title. See Figure 4-29.

Figure 4-29
Title with drop shadow border and shading

paragraph border and fill

7. Save the document with the current changes.

You have created Table 2, copied data from another document, justified cell contents, and formatted the chapter title. Next, you'll format Tables 1 and 2, convert existing text into a table, and create a table of contents for chapter 2 of the business plan.

1. Describe two methods of creating a table.

2. When you have two documents open and visible on the screen at once, how do you know which one is the active window?

3. How do you adjust column widths in a table?

4. When you drag a vertical guideline in a table, how do you know the width of the columns?

5. Why would you usually decimal-align numbers in a table?
   a. To quickly see the place value of the numbers.
   b. To make the table look more attractive.
   c. To make the table easier to understand.
   d. all of the above

6. What is a drop shadow?

If you aren't going to work through Session 4.3 now, you should close the business plan and exit WordPerfect. When you're ready to begin Session 4.3, start WordPerfect, open Ch 2 Industry Analysis, then continue with the session.

SESSION 4.3

In this session you will use the SpeedFormat command to format Tables 1 and 2 automatically, center Table 1, add captions to the tables, and generate a table of contents for chapter 2 of the business plan.

Formatting Tables Automatically

You can add borders, rules, and shading to tables just as you did earlier for the chapter title. Just select the table or table cells to which you want to add borders, rules, or shading, then choose the appropriate options from the Properties of Table Lines/Fill dialog box. However, WordPerfect provides a way to create professionally formatted tables automatically—the SpeedFormat command. **SpeedFormat** allows you to quickly apply one of many predefined formats to a table.

REFERENCE window

FORMATTING TABLES AUTOMATICALLY

- Click Table then click SpeedFormat.
- In the Table SpeedFormat dialog box, select a predefined format,
- Click the Apply button.

You want to modify the borders and add shading to both Tables 1 and 2 to make them more attractive and easier to read. You'll use SpeedFormat to choose a predefined format, then apply it to Tables 1 and 2 automatically.

To modify the table format automatically:

1. Place the insertion point anywhere in Table 2, click the **Table SpeedFormat** button on the Tables toolbar. The Table SpeedFormat dialog box opens.

2. Scroll to the end of the **Available styles** list, then click **Fancy Header** and look at a sample of the format in the Preview window. You like the style, but don't think it's appropriate for the professional look of a business plan.

3. Click **Ledger Header** in the Available styles list. Look at the sample in the Preview window. This format seems perfect for the business plan. See Figure 4-30.

Figure 4-30
Table SpeedFormat dialog box

select this predefined style

preview of table with selected style

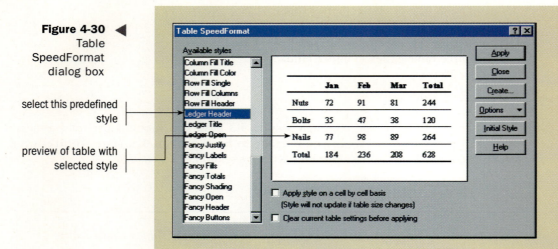

4. Click the **Apply** button to close the Table SpeedFormat dialog box and format Table 2 with the predefined format. Notice the table splits between pages 2 and 3, that the header row appears on both pages, and that all the vertical guidelines appear as dashed lines because the table has no vertical rules. The dashed lines only mark the location of the boundaries between columns and do not print.

Now you'll format Table 1.

5. Click in Table 1, click 🔲 to open the Table SpeedFormat dialog box again.

6. Click **No Lines Totals** in the Available styles list, then click the **Apply** button. Most of the horizontal rules in the table disappear, leaving only the dashed guidelines.

The table still is not well-formatted because most of the columns are too wide. You can solve the problem quickly with the Size Column to Fit command.

7. Select row **1**, the header row, then click the **Size Column to Fit** button 🔲 on the Tables toolbar. Deselect the header row. The column widths shrink so each column is only as wide as the text in the header row.

If you wanted the columns to be as wide as the widest item in each column (not just as wide as the text in the header row), you would select the entire table before clicking the Size Column to Fit button.

Table 2 still extends across the entire page width, but Table 1 no longer does.

Centering a Table

If a table doesn't fill the entire page width, you can center it between the left and right margins. The Center Justify command centers only text within each selected cell, not the table across the page. To center a table across the page (between the left and right margins), you need to use the Table position command in the Properties for Table Format dialog box.

Table 1 is much smaller now that it is formatted. You think it will stand out and look better if it is centered between the left and right margins.

To center Table 1 across the page:

1. Place the insertion point anywhere within Table 1, but do not select any cells, then click the **Table Format** button 🔲 on the Tables toolbar. The Properties for Table Format dialog box opens.

2. Click the **Table** tab, if necessary, to display the table information in the dialog box.

3. Click the **Table position** button in the dialog box, then click **Center**.

4. Click the **OK** button to close the dialog box. Table 1 centers across the top of page 2. See Figure 4-31.

Figure 4-31 ◄
Centered, formatted, and sized Table 1

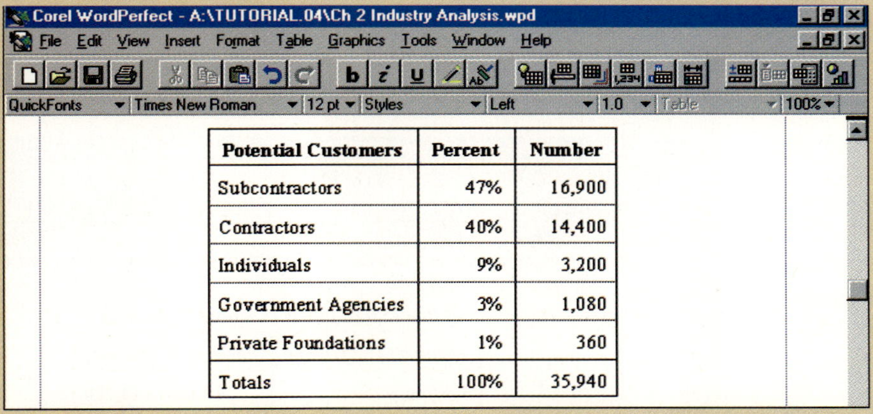

Potential Customers	Percent	Number
Subcontractors	47%	16,900
Contractors	40%	14,400
Individuals	9%	3,200
Government Agencies	3%	1,080
Private Foundations	1%	360
Totals	100%	35,940

5. Save the changes you have made to the tables.

Although you automatically formatted the tables, you decide to make the header row in Table 1 stand out more than it does in the predefined format.

Modifying a Table Format

Sometimes a predefined format doesn't exactly meet your needs or you want to adapt a predefined format to your own taste. You can modify a table to which you have applied a predefined format, just as you would any other table.

For the business plan, you want to adapt the No Lines Totals format by adding shading to the cells in the header row.

To add shading to the header row of Table 1:

1. Select the top (header) row in Table 1.
2. Click the **Lines/Fill** button on the Tables toolbar to open the Properties for Table Lines/Fill dialog box, and if necessary, click the **Cell** tab.
3. In the Cell fill section of the dialog box, change the Fill text box to **10% Fill**.
4. Click the **OK** button, then deselect the top row.

The header row is shaded. Now that the tables are formatted to your satisfaction, you decide to label each table.

Adding Captions

You like the formatting of the tables, but you can improve their usefulness by adding captions. A **caption**, which is text that identifies a table or figure with a number and name, allows a reader to quickly determine the content of tabular material or other figures. For a graphics figure in WordPerfect, you can right-click the figure, click Caption, and type a caption, which WordPerfect then automatically numbers. But for tables, you just type captions right in the document, just as you would any other text.

For the business plan, Chui Lee and Robert have been placing captions above the tables. You'll add captions above both Tables 1 and 2.

To add table captions:

1. Move the insertion point to the blank line immediately above Table 1, the location where you want to insert the caption for Table 1.

2. Press **Enter** to double space between the paragraph above the table and the caption.

3. Press **Shift** + **F7** to center the insertion point between the left and right margins, click the **Bold** button [b] on the Toolbar, then type **Table 1. Number of Potential Customers**, as the caption of Table 1. See Figure 4-32.

Figure 4-32 ◀
Caption for Table 1

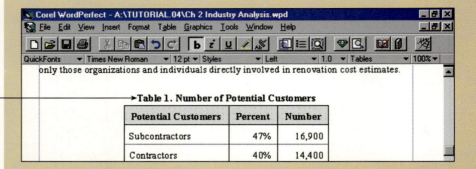

caption centered above table

4. Scroll to Table 2, place the insertion point in the blank line immediately above Table 2, then repeat Steps 2 and 3 to create the caption **Table 2. Results of Survey of 100 Potential Customers** for the second table.

This chapter of the business plan is almost finished now that you have added captions to both tables. All that remains is to compile a table of contents.

Generating a Table of Contents

Many reports, particularly long business reports, typically provide a **table of contents**, which lists the main topics in the report and the page numbers on which they begin. The table of contents helps a reader quickly locate a topic without having to read the whole report.

Although this chapter of the business plan is relatively short, the entire business plan is quite lengthy so Chui Lee and Robert want to include a table of contents. Right now, they are generating a table of contents for each chapter rather than the entire report.

WordPerfect will generate a table of contents for any report as long as you have applied heading styles in the form of Heading 1, Heading 2, Heading 3, and so forth. WordPerfect quickly creates a table of contents in the style you choose and inserts the page numbers based on the page breaks of your document at that time.

REFERENCE window

GENERATING A TABLE OF CONTENTS

- Make sure heading styles are applied in the form of Heading 1, Heading 2, Heading 3, etc.
- Move the insertion point to the location where you want the table of contents to appear.
- Click Tools, point to Generate, then click Table of Contents.
- Click the Define button on the Table of Contents feature bar, specify the number of levels, the style, and the position of the page numbers, then click the OK button.
- Click the Generate button to compile the table of contents, then click the Close button.

GENERATING A TABLE OF CONTENTS **WP 161**

You'll generate a table of contents for chapter 2 of Chui Lee and Robert's business plan and insert it just below the title of the chapter.

To generate the table of contents for chapter 2:

1. Move the insertion point to the blank line immediately below the chapter title on page 1. First you'll type the heading for the table of contents.

2. Press the **Enter** key to insert another blank line, click the **Bold** button [b] on the Toolbar, type **Contents**, click [b] again to turn off boldface, then press the **Enter** key. The insertion point is located where you want to insert the table of contents.

3. Click **Tools**, point to **Generate**, then click **Table of Contents** to open the Table of Contents feature bar.

4. Click the **Define** button on the Table of Contents feature bar to open the Define Table of Contents dialog box.

   Because the document has Heading 1 through Heading 4 styles, you'll set the number of levels to 4.

5. Type **4** in the **Number of levels** text box. See Figure 4-33.

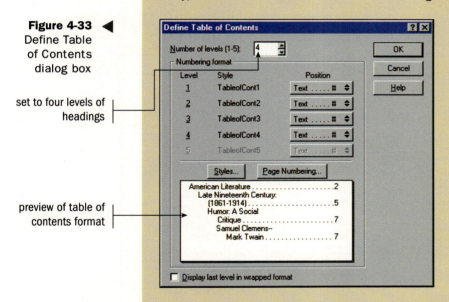

Figure 4-33
Define Table of Contents dialog box

set to four levels of headings

preview of table of contents format

TROUBLE? If the dialog box doesn't look like Figure 4-33, make any necessary changes.

6. Click the **OK** button. WordPerfect inserts the message "<<Table of Contents will generate here>>" at the insertion point.

7. Click the **Generate** button on the Table of Contents feature bar to open the Generate dialog box, then click the **OK** button. (Because your document doesn't have subdocuments or hypertext links, you don't need to worry about the two check boxes in the dialog box.) WordPerfect generates the table of contents. See Figure 4-34.

Figure 4-34
Table of contents for chapter 2

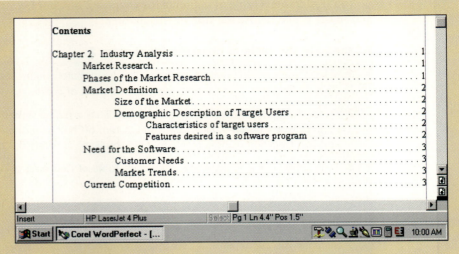

8. Click the **Close** button on the Table of Contents feature bar.
9. Save the final version of Chapter 2 of the business plan, print it, then close the business plan document and exit WordPerfect. See Figure 4-35.

Figure 4-35
Final version of chapter 2 of the business plan

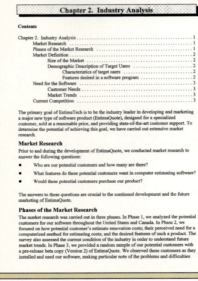
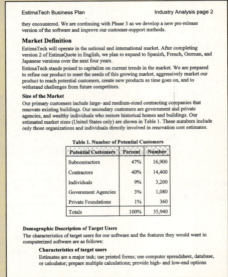

You take the hard copy of the final Chapter 2 of the business plan to Robert and Chui Lee. They think it looks great. They add it to the rest of their business plan chapters for EstimaTech, and rush off to meet with a loan officer at the bank.

1. What is the advantage of using the Table SpeedFormat command?
2. True or False: If you use the Table SpeedFormat command, you cannot place additional borders or shading on the table.
3. What is the purpose of the Size Column to Fit button on the Tables toolbar?
4. True or False: You can center the text within a table, but you cannot center a table between the left and right margins of the page.
5. In general, how do you generate a table of contents automatically?
6. How do you decide how many levels of headings to include in the definition of the table of contents?

Tutorial Assignments

Start WordPerfect, if necessary, and conduct a screen check. Open Training from the TAssign folder from the Tutorial.04 folder on your Student Disk, save the document as Training Courses, then complete the following:

1. Open a blank document window, then, using the headings in the training document, create an outline for this document.
2. Promote the paragraph "Using Technical Support" to a first-level heading.
3. Save the document as Training Outline, print it, then close the document.
4. Change the heading "Using Technical Support" from a Heading 3 to a Heading 2 style.
5. Create a table (three columns by three rows) after the first paragraph below the "Training" heading. Insert a blank line between the text and the top of the table.
6. Enter the data shown in Figure 4-36 into the table.

Figure 4-36 ◄

EstimaQuote Beginner	Installation, How to Get Started, Making Estimates, Printing Reports	January 21-23, 1998
EstimaQuote Intermediate	Making On-Site Estimates, Tips and Tricks	February 26-27, 1998
EstimaQuote Advanced	Styles, Script Files, Interfacing with Project Management Programs	March 26-27, 1998

7. Insert one row at the top of the table.
8. Type the text for the cells in the new row in the following order: "Class," "Topics," "Dates."
9. Format the table using the predefined Column Fill Single format.
10. Set the widths of the three columns A, B, and C to 2, 2.75, and 1.75 inches, respectively.
11. Insert "Table 1. Schedule of Training Courses" as the bolded caption immediately above the table.
12. Insert a table (four columns by four rows) directly above the note explaining the cost per year of the Gold and Platinum plans. Leave a blank line above the table.

13. Type the text shown in Figure 4-37 into the table.

Figure 4-37

Bronze	1	Telephone support during regular business hours.	$200
Gold	4	Same as Silver plus two on-site visits for installation and training	$2,400
Platinum	10	Same as Gold plus five on-site visits for installation and training	$5,000
Silver	1	Toll-free telephone support, 24 hours a day, six days a week	$600

14. Insert an additional row above the table, then type the headings for the first row in the following order: "Name," "Minimum Licenses," "Description," "Cost Per Year."

15. Sort the rows in the table in ascending numerical order, from Bronze $200 to Platinum $5,000. Make sure you set the header row before you perform the sort.
16. Set the widths of columns A through D to 0.875, 0.875, 3.75, and 1 inches, respectively.
17. Center the number of minimum licenses within the cells; right-justify the cost per year numbers within the cells.

18. Format the table using the predefined Header Fill Column table style.
19. Insert "Table 2. Technical Support Plans" as the bolded caption immediately above the table.
20. Insert a boldfaced heading, "Contents," immediately following the title and company address and phone numbers. Below the heading, generate a table of contents for the document.
21. Save your document, preview and print it, then close the file.

Case Problems

1. Mountainland Nursery Raynal Stubbs is sales manager of Mountainland Nursery in Steamboat Springs, Colorado. Twice each year he provides sales representatives with guidelines for helping customers with their planting needs. Raynal has asked you to help him prepare this year's list of spring-blooming perennials. Open Flowers from the Cases folder in the Tutorial.04 folder on your Student Disk, save the document as Mountainland Flowers, then complete the following:

1. Insert an additional row for headings at the top of the existing table.
2. Type the following boldface column headings in the cells of the new row: "Common Name," "Name," "yellow," "red," "blue," "white."

3. Move the Name column to the first column in the table. (*Hint:* Select a column and drag it to new location. You might have to experiment. If you make a mistake, click the Undo button, and try again.)
4. Sort the table alphabetically by Name (the new first column). Remember to specify the header row before the sort.
5. Insert a row following the flower Aurinia saxatilis and type "Bellis perennis" in the first cell and "English Daisy" in the second cell.
6. Delete the row containing the flower Cynoglossum amabile.

7. Insert another row at the top of the table. Highlight the cells above the flower colors and join them into one cell. (*Hint:* Use the Join command on the Table menu.)

CASE PROBLEMS **WP 165**

8. Type the following boldface heading in the newly created cell above the flower colors: "Blossom Color."
9. Center the text in the top two rows (all the headings) and bold the text in row 2.
10. Using Table SpeedFormat, apply the style Single Lines to the table.
11. Remove the top and left border lines from cells A1 and B1, as shown in Figure 4-38.

Figure 4-38 ◀

		Blossom Color			
Name	**Common Name**	**yellow**	**red**	**blue**	**white**
Aquilegia	Columbine				
Aster	Aster				
Aurinia saxatilis	Basket-of-Gold				
Bellis perennis	English Daisy				
Cymbidium	Terrestrial Orchids				
Digitalis	Foxglove				
Iberis sempervirens	Evergreen Candytuft				
Viola cornuta	Tufted Pansy				
Viola odorata	Sweet Violet				

12. Add 20% shading to the cells, as shown in Figure 4-38.
13. Insert a table of contents for the document above the introduction. Above the table of contents, create a heading with the bolded word "Contents."
14. Save, print, then close the document.

2. Classical CD Sales at The Master's Touch Austin Cornelius is purchasing agent for The Master's Touch, a music store in Little Rock, Arkansas. Each month Austin publishes a list of the classical CDs on sale at The Master's Touch. He has asked you to create a table showing this month's list of sale items. Open Classics from the Cases folder in the Tutorial.04 folder on your Student Disk, save the document as Classical Music CDs, then do the following:

1. Change the column widths of the table to improve readability and appearance.
2. Insert an additional row for headings at the top of the table.
3. Add the following headings in the order given: "Title," "Artist," "Label," "#CDs," and "Price."
4. Insert a row after "The Best of Chopin," then type the following in the cells: "Beethoven Piano Sonatas," "Alfred Brendel," "Vox," "2," "18.95."
5. Sort the rows in the table in ascending alphabetical order by the CD titles. Make sure you set the header row before sorting.
6. Center the number of CDs within the cells.
7. Decimal-align the price within the cells.

8. Format the table using the predefined Row Fill Header style.
9. Save your changes to the document then print it.
10. Format the table using the predefined Column Fill Header table style.
11. Save the newly formatted table as Classical Music CDs 2.
12. Open Prices from the Cases folder in the Tutorial.04 folder on your Student Disk.
13. Arrange the document window so you can view both open documents at once. Remember to close any other open documents before tiling the documents.

14. Copy the new prices for the sale CDs (column B) from the Prices document to your formatted table.
15. Close the Prices document without saving changes. Save the Classical Music CDs 2 document, print it, then close it.

3. The Business of Basketball As part of the requirements for your advanced English composition class, your group has written a term paper on "The Business of Basketball." Your assignment is to create the preliminary outline, format the document with appropriate heading styles, format a table, and generate a table of contents for the final paper. Start WordPerfect, if necessary, and conduct a quick screen check. Open Business from the Cases folder in the Tutorial.04 folder on your Student Disk, save the document as Business of Basketball, then complete the following:

1. Open a new document window, type the two-line title "Outline" and "Business of Basketball," double space, then create an outline of your paper. The first three level-1 outline paragraphs are "Abstract," "Introduction," and "Profitability: Who is Hot and Who is Not." For the other outline paragraphs, see the end of the document Business of Basketball. The level-1 paragraphs are flush with the left margin and the level-2 paragraphs are indented. *(Hint:* You can copy the text from the report to the outline and then use promote and demote commands to create the outline from the normal text. You will have to delete the tabs at the beginning of the level-2 paragraphs.
2. Reorder the outline so that "Team Philosophy" follows "Management Style."
3. Demote the section "Marketing" to make it a level-2 paragraph.
4. Save the outline as Outline Business of Basketball, print and close it.
5. In the report, apply Heading 1 and Heading 2 styles to the appropriate headings, including those after the table. You should delete the tabs at the beginning of the level-2 headings.
6. Sort the table by franchise value in descending numerical order.
7. Format the table with the predefined Double Border Header table style.
8. Insert a row at the top of the table.

9. Remove the border lines above row 2. (*Hint:* Select row 2, then click the Lines/Fill button.)
10. Join all the cells in row 1 except the cell above the NBA Team column. (*Hint:* Use the Join command on the Table menu.)
11. Type the heading "Millions of Dollars" in the merged cell, then center it.
12. Center the text of all the headings in the second row of the table.
13. Decimal-align all of the numbers in the cells.
14. Create a box border with drop shadow and 20% shading around the title "The Business of Basketball" on the title page.
15. Suppress the header on the title page.
16. Add your name to the list of authors.
17. Insert a page break to begin a new page following the date on the title page.
18. Create a table of contents for the report to appear on its own page following the title page.
19. Save and print your report, then close it.

4. Monthly Menu Deciding what to cook each night can be difficult when it's dinnertime and you're hungry. To avoid making spaghetti every night next month, you'll plan next month's dinner menu now. Open a new document window and complete the following:

1. Create a 7 × 7 table.
2. Join the top row of cells. (*Hint:* Use the Join command on the Table menu.)
3. Type the name of the current month and year in the merged cell in a 16-point, sans serif font of your choice.
4. Center and bold the month and year in the merged cell.
5. In row 2 of the table, type the days of the week in 12-point font, using the same sans serif font as you did in row 1.
6. Adjust the column widths so the name of each day of the week is on one line.
7. Center the days of the week headings in the cells.
8. Type the number of each day of the month in a cell, press the Enter key to place the number on its own line, then press the Tab key to move to the next cell. For example, if September 1 is a Tuesday, type "1" in cell C3, press the Enter key, then press the Tab key. Repeat for the remaining days of the month.

9. Select rows 3 through 7, then set the row height to one inch. (*Hint:* In the Properties for Table Format dialog box, on the Row tab set the Row height to Fixed 1".)
10. Place the insertion point on the line below the date, then type the name of a main dish in each cell of the table for the first two weeks of the month.
11. Copy and paste seven dinners to the third week to repeat meals.
12. Fill in the remaining cells by copying menus from the rest of the month using drag and drop.
13. Format the table using the predefined table style of your choice or using your own formatting.
14. Save the menu as Monthly Menu in the Cases folder in the Tutorial.04 folder on your Student Disk.
15. Print the document then close it.

TUTORIAL 5

Creating Form Letters and Mailing Labels

Writing a Sales Letter for The Pet Shoppe

OBJECTIVES

In this tutorial you will:

- Create, edit, and format a merge data file
- Create, edit, and format a merge form file
- Sort records in a data file
- Merge files to create personalized form letters
- Create, format, and print mailing labels
- Create a telephone list from a data file

CASE

The Pet Shoppe

Alicia Robles is vice president of sales for The Pet Shoppe, a chain of superstores based in Colorado Springs, Colorado. The Pet Shoppe sells a wide variety of pets, pet food, supplies, and services. The Pet Shoppe is celebrating its tenth anniversary. Alicia wants to send, as a promotional tool, a letter to all customers on the store's mailing list telling them about the chain's 10th Anniversary Celebration and offering them a discount if they purchase a product or service anytime during the anniversary month.

Alicia needs to send the same information to many customers, but because of the large number of The Pet Shoppe customers, she and her staff don't have the time to write a personal letter to each customer. Instead, she creates a **form letter** that contains the information she wants to send to all customers. She adds personal information for each customer, such as their name, address, type of pet, and so on, in specific places. To do this manually would be very time-consuming. Fortunately, WordPerfect provides a time-saving method that simplifies this job. By using WordPerfect's Merge feature, you can produce multiple copies of the same letter yet personalize each copy with the customer's name, address, type of pet, and so forth, in about the same amount of time it takes to personalize just one letter. You also could use this feature to create such documents as catalogs, directories, and contracts.

Alicia has already written the letter she wants to send, but she needs to add the personal information for each customer. She asks you to create the form letters with the personal information and put together mailing labels for the envelopes.

In this tutorial, you'll help Alicia create a form letter and mailing labels using WordPerfect's Merge feature. In Session 5.1, you'll create a data file document that contains specific information for each customer, such as name and address. In Session 5.2, you'll insert the merge instructions into the form letter and create a merged document. In Session 5.3, you'll create mailing labels for the letter and a telephone list.

SESSION 5.1

In this session you will see how Alicia planned her letter. Then you will create a document that contains the customer information to be merged into the form letter.

Planning the Document

Alicia hopes to generate sales for The Pet Shoppe chain by announcing a 10 percent discount on the purchase of any product or service as part of the company's 10th Anniversary Celebration. An effective sales letter can convince customers to purchase a product or service.

Content

The sales letter will inform current customers about The Pet Shoppe's 10th Anniversary Celebration and offer them a special discount on products and services.

Organization

Alicia organized her letter to capture the reader's attention. First she cites a few examples of the need The Pet Shoppe fills, then she briefly describes The Pet Shoppe's services and products, and finally she offers a discount to encourage the customer to visit the store.

Style

Alicia writes in a persuasive style, using informal language. She illustrates the need and quality of The Pet Shoppe's services by including personal experiences of current customers.

Presentation

Alicia wants to send a professional-looking, personalized letter to each customer on The Pet Shoppe's mailing list. She uses a standard business letter format and will print the letters on company letterhead.

The Merge Process

Alicia asks you to use WordPerfect's Merge feature to generate the form letters. In general, a **merge** combines information from two separate documents to create many final documents (or many final pages in one document), each of which contains customized information that makes it slightly different from the others. In WordPerfect, the two separate documents are called a form file and a data file.

A **form file** is a document (such as a letter or a contract) that, in addition to text, contains placeholder text (called merge codes) to mark where variable information (such as a name or an address) will be inserted. While merging a form letter, for example, the variable information (the name and the address) is different in each resulting letter, but the remaining text is constant, that is, the same in all the resulting letters. Alicia's form file is a letter that looks like Figure 5-1, except that merge codes for the customer's name, address, and other data will replace the underlined text, which represents the variable information. All the text not underlined is constant, so it will be the same in all letters to the customers.

Figure 5-1 ◀
Alicia's form letter

> # The Pet Shoppe
> 121 Sillitoe Avenue • Colorado Springs, CO 80901
> Phone: (719) 555-5555 • Fax: (719) 555-5556
>
> Date
>
> First Name Last Name
> Address
> City, CO Postal Code
>
> Dear First Name :
>
> Ten years ago, Stephen Mueller was unable to find suitable grooming facilities for his dog, Rusty. Maria Fuentes drove 100 miles to buy food for her cat, Sneakers. And Carole Cochran only dreamed of owning an armadillo lizard. Today, Stephen, Maria, and Carole are among The Pet Shoppe's loyal customers.
>
> Established in 1988, The Pet Shoppe chain provides a complete line of high quality yet affordable pet supplies and services for customers throughout Colorado. We're committed to helping you meet the needs of your Kind of Pet in a caring manner.
>
> We invite you and your pet to join us in our 10th Anniversary Celebration. Just bring this letter to The Pet Shoppe in the Branch anytime during the month of November and you'll receive a 10% discount on the purchase of any product or service. And remember to register Name of Pet for our month-long "Purrfect Pet" drawing. We'll be giving away over $1,000 worth of prizes and services each week.
>
> We look forward to seeing you at The Pet Shoppe.
>
> Sincerely yours,
>
>
> Alicia Robles
> Vice President, Sales

A **data source** is information, such as customers' names and addresses, that will be merged into the form file. A data source can consist of a data file, an address book, or keyboard input. A **data file** is a WordPerfect document that contains information for use in merge operations, and can be a **text file**, which organizes information in lines of text, or a **table file**, which organizes information in a table. Although a WordPerfect merge operation uses a WordPerfect data file directly, the data itself might have originated in a spreadsheet program (such as Quattro Pro), a database program (such as Paradox), or from some other source. Alicia's data source will be a data text file, created with WordPerfect, of The Pet Shoppe customers.

Merging information from a data source into a form file produces a final document, called a **merged document**. Figure 5-2 illustrates how a data source and form file combine to form a merged document.

Figure 5-2
A form file merges with a data source to create a merged document

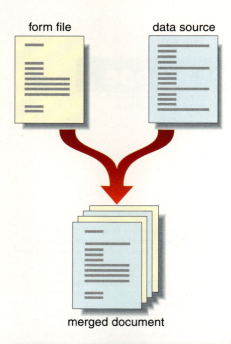

Merge Codes

During a merge, **merge codes** (the placeholders for text that changes in the form file) instruct WordPerfect to retrieve specific information from the data file or from some other source, such as the computer's clock or from the keyboard. For example, one merge code in the form file might retrieve a name from the data file, while another merge code might retrieve an address. Figure 5-3 lists some sample merge codes.

Figure 5-3
Sample WordPerfect merge codes

Merge Codes	Action
DATE	Inserts current date
KEYBOARD	Displays a prompt during merge; text typed from the keyboard is inserted into the merged document
IF	Performs a task only if a specific condition is met
FIELD	Extracts information from the source document and inserts it into the merged document

You can distinguish merge codes from the other text of a form file or data file because each merge code name appears as red, uppercase letters, often followed by a set of parentheses.

For each complete set of data (in this instance, a name and address) in the data file, WordPerfect will create a new, separate page in the merged document. For example, if Alicia has five sets of customer names and addresses in her data file, the merge will produce one document with five pages; each page contains the same letter but with a different customer name and address in the appropriate places.

Data Files and Records

The data file for a merge consists of fields and records, as shown in Figure 5-4. The set of information about one individual or object in the data file is called a **record**. Each item within a record is called a **field**. A field replaces the merge code in the form file. As in Figure 5-4, one field might be the first name of a customer, another field the customer's address, another field the customer's city, and so forth. For a merge to work properly, every record in the data file must have the same set of fields.

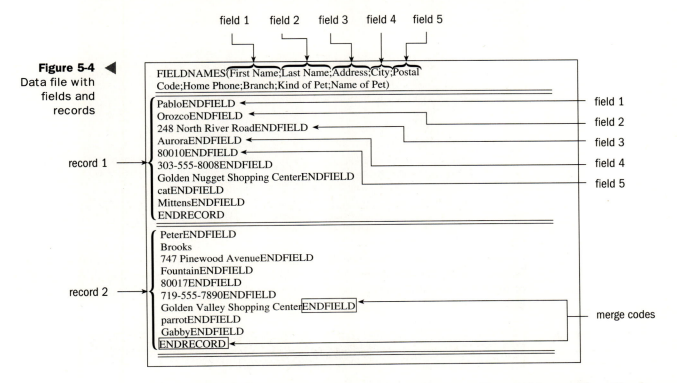

Figure 5-4 Data file with fields and records

Data files are not limited to records about customers. You could create data files from inventory records, records of suppliers, records of equipment, and so forth. After you become familiar with managing and manipulating records in a data file, you'll be able to use them for many purposes.

Creating a Data File

The data file for The Pet Shoppe letter will be a WordPerfect document that begins with the FIELDNAMES merge code. This code specifies the names of individual fields in a data file record. For example, you'll use "First Name" to label the field that contains the first names of The Pet Shoppe customers.

You must follow several conventions when choosing field names:

- Each field name must be unique. That is, you cannot have two fields with the same name.
- Field names can be as long as 40 characters.
- Field names can begin with any letter, digit, or character.
- Field names can contain spaces and other characters.

Although the order of field names in the data file doesn't affect their placement in the form file, you'll want to arrange the field names in a logical order. This way, you can enter information quickly and efficiently. For example, you probably want the first and last name fields adjacent or the city, state, and postal code fields adjacent.

The rest of the data file consists of actual records, where each field takes up one line of text and ends with the ENDFIELD merge code, and the set of fields for one customer ends with the ENDRECORD merge code.

> **REFERENCE window**
>
> **CREATING A DATA FILE**
>
> - Click Tools then click Merge to open the Merge dialog box.
> - In the Data source section of the Merge dialog box, click the Place records in a table check box to select it. If you want to create a data table file, then click the Data File button.
> - Type the names of the fields you want in each record of the data file, click the Add button after typing each field name, then click the OK button to accept the Field name list and open the Quick Data Entry dialog box.
> - Enter information into the data fields for each record, then click the OK button.
> - Click the Yes button to save the file, enter a filename, then click the OK button.

You need to create a data file that contains all the necessary information about The Pet Shoppe's customers to merge into Alicia's form letter. Alicia has given you a list of the type of information you'll merge into the letter and the field names you should use, as shown in Figure 5-5.

Figure 5-5
Field names for data source records

Field Name	Description
First Name	Customer's first name
Last Name	Customer's last name
Address	Customer's street address
City	Customer's city (in Colorado)
Postal Code	Customer's ZIP code
Home Phone	Customer's phone number
Branch	Location of The Pet Shoppe branch
Kind of Pet	The kind of pet owned by the customer
Name of Pet	The name of the customer's pet

Alicia doesn't have an existing data file document, so you'll create one.

To create a data file:

1. Start WordPerfect and make sure a blank document window appears on the screen.
2. Click **Tools** then click **Merge**. WordPerfect opens the Merge dialog box. See Figure 5-6.

Figure 5-6
Merge dialog box

click to create data file

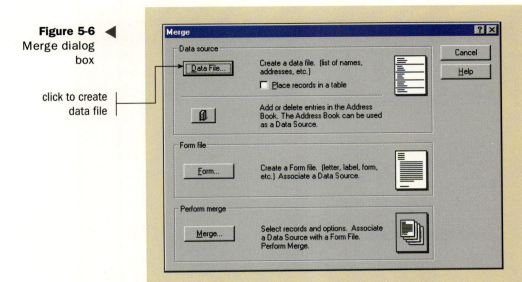

3. Make sure the Place records in a table check box is *not* checked. For The Pet Shoppe data file, you want to create a text file rather than a table file, although a table file would work just as well.

4. Click the **Data File** button in the Data source section of the Merge dialog box. The Create Data File dialog box opens so you can insert the FIELDNAMES merge codes. The Field name list box is blank because you haven't specified any field names yet. See Figure 5-7.

Figure 5-7
Create Data File dialog box

type field name

list of field names will appear here

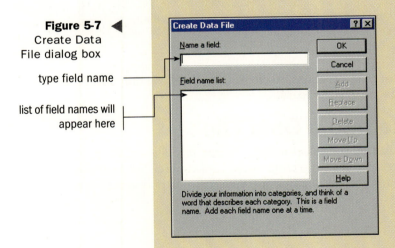

To create the data file, you'll use field names based on information cards that customers complete to join the mailing list. The form letter will include the first and last name, address, city, postal code, and phone number of the customer, the store branch, type of pet, and name of the pet.

5. Type **First Name** in the Name a field text box, then click the **Add** button. The field name "First Name" appears in the Field name list. This specifies that the first field in each record will contain the first name of the client.

   TROUBLE? If you made a typing mistake, click the mistyped word in the Field name list box to move it back to the Name a field text box, edit the name, then click the Replace button.

6. Type **Last Name** in the Name a field text box, then press the **Enter** key to add the second field name to the list. Notice that pressing the Enter key while in the dialog box has the same function as clicking the Add button.

7. Add the names of the remaining fields **Address**, **City**, **Postal Code**, **Home Phone**, **Branch**, **Kind of Pet**, and **Name of Pet** to the Field name list. See Figure 5-8. Check the Field name list carefully to make sure your field names are identical to the ones in Figure 5-8.

Figure 5-8 ◀
Completed Create Data File dialog box

completed list of field names

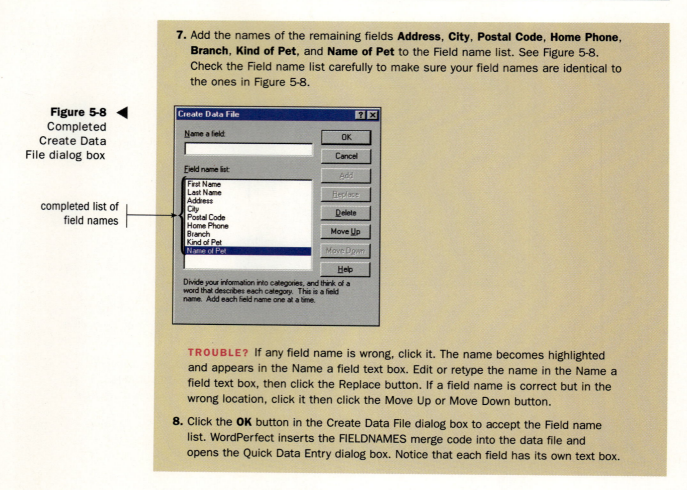

TROUBLE? If any field name is wrong, click it. The name becomes highlighted and appears in the Name a field text box. Edit or retype the name in the Name a field text box, then click the Replace button. If a field name is correct but in the wrong location, click it then click the Move Up or Move Down button.

8. Click the **OK** button in the Create Data File dialog box to accept the Field name list. WordPerfect inserts the FIELDNAMES merge code into the data file and opens the Quick Data Entry dialog box. Notice that each field has its own text box.

The data file you just created contains no records yet; you have only named each field. You need to enter the data for each record.

Entering Data into a Data File

The Pet Shoppe staff uses customer information cards to collect data from their customers. As shown in Figure 5-9, each section of the card contains information for a field in the data file. You'll add the information for three customers (the first three records) into the data file document.

Figure 5-9 ◀
Sample card for gathering customer information to make records in data source

You'll use the Quick Data Entry dialog box to enter information about three of The Pet Shoppe's customers into the data file. Whatever text you type in the Quick Data Entry dialog box will appear in the form letter, including spaces or symbols.

To enter data into a record:

1. With the insertion point in the First Name text box, type **Sarah** to enter the first customer's first name. Make sure you don't press the spacebar after you finish typing any entry; otherwise, the merged documents will have extraneous spaces in them. You'll add the necessary spaces in the text of the form file, not in the data file.

2. Press the **Enter** key to move the insertion point to the Last Name text box. You also could click in that text box, click the Next Field button, or press the Tab key to move the insertion point to the next field's text box. You would click the Previous Field button or press Shift + Tab to move to the previous text box.

3. Type **Sorenson** then press the **Enter** key to insert the customer's last name and move the insertion point to the next field name.

4. Type **585 Pikes Peak Road** then press the **Enter** key to insert the customer's street address and move the insertion point to the next field name.

5. Type **Denver** then press the **Enter** key to insert the city where the customer lives and move the insertion point to the next field name.

6. Type **80207** and press the **Enter** key to insert the customer's ZIP code (or postal code) and move to the next field name.

7. Type **303-555-8976** and press the **Enter** key, type **High Prairie Mall** and press the **Enter** key, then type **dog** and press the **Enter** key.

   You have inserted the customer's home phone number, the branch location of The Pet Shoppe, and the kind of pet the customer owns. The insertion point is now in the text box of the last field, Name of Pet.

8. Type **Rascal** but do *not* press the Enter key yet. See Figure 5-10.

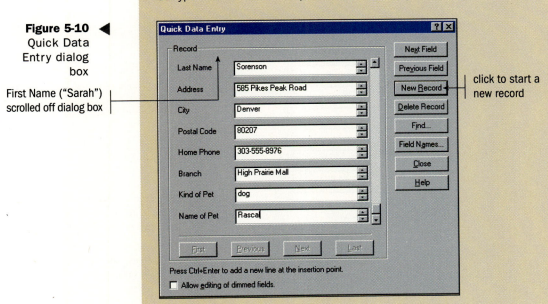

Figure 5-10 ◄
Quick Data Entry dialog box

First Name ("Sarah") scrolled off dialog box

click to start a new record

You have completed the information for the first record of the data file document. Now you're ready to enter the information for the two remaining records.

To create additional records in the data file:

1. With the insertion point still at the end of the last field of the first record, click the **New Record** button to insert the new record into the data file and open a blank Quick Data Entry dialog box.

2. Type **Joel** then press the **Enter** key to enter the first name, and then enter the rest of the information for the second record, as shown in Figure 5-11.

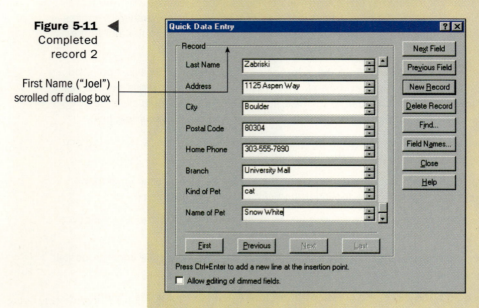

Figure 5-11
Completed record 2

First Name ("Joel") scrolled off dialog box

3. After entering data into the last field press the **Enter** key to open a new Quick Data Entry dialog box.

4. Enter the information for the third record, as shown in Figure 5-12, then press the **Enter** key and type **Geronimo** as the name of pet.

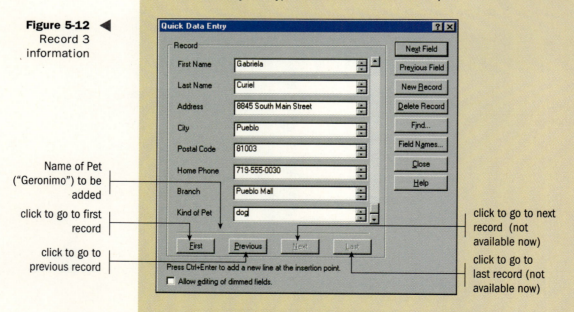

Figure 5-12
Record 3 information

Name of Pet ("Geronimo") to be added

click to go to first record

click to go to previous record

click to go to next record (not available now)

click to go to last record (not available now)

5. Press the **Enter** key to insert the record into the data file and to open a new blank Quick Data Entry dialog box.

You have entered the information for three customers. You should proofread each record to make sure you typed the information correctly. Any misspelled names or other typos will print in the final letters and reflect poorly on The Pet Shoppe. You can move between individual records within the data file by using the Record buttons. You'll begin by proofreading the first data record.

To move to the first record within the data file:

1. Click the **First** button at the bottom of the Quick Data Entry dialog box to move to the first data record.

2. Proofread the data by comparing your information with Figure 5-10. Make any necessary corrections by selecting and retyping the text.

3. Click the **Next** button at the bottom of the Quick Data Entry dialog box to move to the next record. The information for the second data record appears. Compare your record to Figure 5-11.

4. Click the **Next** button to review the third record. Compare your record to Figure 5-12. Make corrections where necessary.

5. Click the **Close** button. When asked if you want to "Save the changes to disk?" click the **Yes** button.

6. Make sure the **Tutorial.05** folder of your Student Disk is open, type **Pet Shoppe Data** in the Name text box, then click the **Save** button. WordPerfect automatically adds the filename extension ".dat" to indicate that this is a data file.

You have entered and edited the three records using the Quick Data Entry dialog box. You also can add and edit records in the data file while viewing the records as a WordPerfect table.

Krishan, an employee of The Pet Shoppe, has created a WordPerfect table with the other records you'll need to add to the data file. You'll add those records now.

To add new records to the data file:

1. Move the insertion point to the end of the document, onto the blank line below the last record in the data file.

2. Click **Insert** then click **File**. The Insert File dialog box opens.

3. Make sure the **Tutorial.05** folder on your Student Disk is selected, click the filename **ShopDat**, then click the **Insert** button. WordPerfect automatically combines the data table file from ShopDat into the data file in the Pet Shoppe Data document.

    Now that you have inserted additional customer records, you should save the data file document.

4. Click the **Save** button on the Toolbar. WordPerfect saves the file using the current filename, Pet Shoppe Data.

Alicia's data file eventually will contain hundreds of records for all customers of The Pet Shoppe. The current data file, however, contains only the records Alicia wants to work with now.

Quick Check

1. Define the following in your own words:
   a. form letter
   b. form file
   c. data file
   d. merge code

2. In a data source, what is the difference between a text file and a table file?

3. All the information about one individual or object in a data file is called a _____.

4. True or False: For a merge to work properly, every record in the data file must have the same set of fields.

5. What is the purpose of the Quick Data Entry dialog box?

6. How do you move to individual records within the Quick Data Entry dialog box?

You have created a data file for a merge. Next you'll insert the merge codes into the form file and create the merged document. If you aren't going to work through Session 5.2 now, exit WordPerfect, then click the Yes button when you're asked if you want to save changes to the file, Pet Shoppe Data. When you're ready to begin Session 5.2, start WordPerfect, then continue with the session.

SESSION 5.2

In this session you will create, edit, and insert merge codes into a form file, then you will merge the form file and the data file. You'll also sort the data file and merge it with the form file, then you will set conditions for selecting certain records in the data file, edit the form file, and merge the two.

Creating a Form File

A form file contains the text that will appear in all the letters, as well as the merge codes that tell WordPerfect where to insert the information from the data file. In the first step of the merge process, you must indicate which document you intend to use as the form file. You can either create a new document or use an existing document as the form file. Then you **link**, or associate, a data file to it so that WordPerfect will know where to find the information you want inserted into the form file.

REFERENCE window

CREATING A FORM FILE

- Click Tools then click Merge to open the Merge dialog box.
- Click the Form button in the Form file section of the dialog box, then click the Use file in active window radio button or click the New Document Window button.
- Click the Associate a data file radio button in the Create Form File dialog box, select the data file that you want to associate, then click the OK button.
- Edit or create the text of the form file; add merge codes into the form file by clicking the Insert Field or Merge Codes button on the Merge feature bar.

Alicia has already written the letter she wants to send out to all customers of The Pet Shoppe. So you don't need to create a new document; instead, you'll modify an existing document to create the form file.

To create the form file:

1. Open **PetShopp** from the **Tutorial.05** folder on your Student Disk. This is the text of the letter that Alicia wrote to send to The Pet Shoppe customers and will become the form file of your form letter.

2. Click **Tools** then click **Merge**. The Merge dialog box opens.

3. Click the **Form** button in the Form file section. The Create Merge File dialog box opens.

4. If necessary, click the **Use file in active window** radio button to select it, then click the **OK** button. The Create Form File dialog box opens. See Figure 5-13.

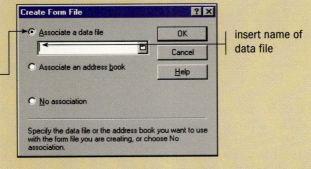

Figure 5-13
Create Form File dialog box

make sure this is selected

insert name of data file

5. If necessary, click the **Associate a data file** radio button to select it, then type **a:\Tutorial.05\Pet Shoppe Data**, the path and filename of the data file, and click the **OK** button.

6. Click **File** then click **Save As**, delete the current filename and extension (".wpd"), then save the document to your Student Disk as **Pet Shoppe Form Letter** (without typing a filename extension). WordPerfect automatically adds the filename extension ".frm" to indicate that this is a form file.

7. Click the **Save** button in the Save As dialog box.

Next you'll edit the form file to include the proper WordPerfect and merge codes for the form letter.

Editing a Form File

Alicia created her sales letter earlier, but didn't enter any of the merge codes. With the text of the letter in the document window, you're ready to edit the sales letter.

Inserting Merge Codes

The date should print below the company letterhead. Instead of just typing today's date, you'll insert a DATE code. By entering the DATE merge code, you won't have to modify the form file each time you send it; the DATE code will automatically insert the current date when you print the document.

To insert the DATE merge code:

1. Make sure the insertion point is on the first blank line of the form letter, then press the **Enter** key six times to leave enough space for the company letterhead.

   Now, rather than typing today's date, you'll insert the DATE merge code so that no matter when you print the document, the current date will appear.

2. Click the **Date** button on the Merge feature bar to insert the DATE code into the form file. See Figure 5-14.

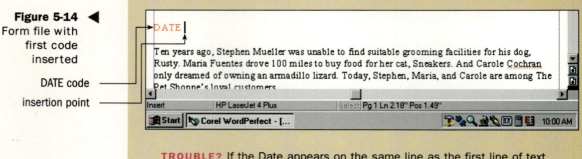

Figure 5-14
Form file with first code inserted

DATE code

insertion point

TROUBLE? If the Date appears on the same line as the first line of text, press the Enter key twice to double space between the date and the letter text.

The DATE code appears in the document in red, uppercase letters. This is to remind you that "DATE" is not a typed word but rather a merge code, such that when you perform the merge, the current date will appear at this location in the document.

The sales letter is a standard business letter, so the customer's name and address need to print below the date. You'll use FIELD merge codes for the fields for the customer's first name, last name, address, city, and ZIP code to create the inside address of the form letter. As you insert these merge codes into the form file, you must enter proper spacing and punctuation around the codes so the information in the merged document will be formatted correctly.

To insert FIELD merge codes:

1. Press the **Enter** key four times to leave three blank lines between the date and the first line of the inside address.

2. Click the **Insert Field** button on the Merge feature bar. The Insert Field Name or Number dialog box opens listing all the field names you created in the data file. See Figure 5-15.

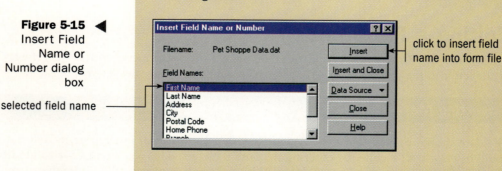

Figure 5-15
Insert Field Name or Number dialog box

selected field name

click to insert field name into form file

3. Click **First Name** in the Field Names list, then click the **Insert** button in the dialog box. WordPerfect inserts the merge code for the field name First Name in the form letter at the location of the insertion point.

   TROUBLE? If you make a mistake and insert the wrong merge code, select the entire merge code, press the Delete key, then repeat Step 3.

When you merge the form file with the data file, WordPerfect will retrieve the first name from the data file and insert it into the letter at the First Name merge code location. Now you're ready to insert the merge codes for the rest of the inside address. You'll add appropriate spacing and punctuation to the form file as well.

To insert the remaining merge codes for the inside address:

1. Press the **spacebar** to insert a space after the First Name field, click **Last Name** in the Field Names list, then click the **Insert** button. WordPerfect inserts the Last Name merge code into the form letter. Notice the dialog box remains open when you type in the document window.

2. Press the **Enter** key to move the insertion point to the next line, click **Address** in the Field Names list, then click the **Insert** button. WordPerfect inserts the Address merge code into the form letter.

3. Press the **Enter** key to move the insertion point to the next line, click **City** in the Field Names list, then click the **Insert** button. WordPerfect inserts the City merge code into the form letter.

4. Type **,** (a comma), press the **spacebar** to insert a space after the comma, then type **CO** to insert the abbreviation for the state of Colorado.

   Because all customers of the Pet Shoppe live in Colorado, you can type the state name directly in the form letter. If The Pet Shoppe had a significant number of customers outside Colorado, you would create a State field name in the data file and insert a State merge code in the form file.

5. Press the **spacebar** to insert a space after the state abbreviation, click **Postal Code** in the Field Names list, then click the **Insert** button. WordPerfect inserts the Postal Code merge code into the form letter. See Figure 5-16.

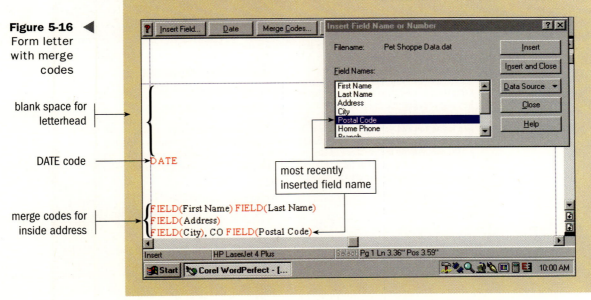

Figure 5-16 Form letter with merge codes

The inside address is set up to match the form for a standard business letter. You can now add the salutation for the letter.

To insert the merge code for the salutation:

1. Press the **Enter** key twice to double space between the inside address and the salutation, then type **Dear** and press the **spacebar**.

2. Click **First Name** in the Field Names list, then click the **Insert** button. WordPerfect inserts the First Name merge code into the form letter.

3. Type **:** (a colon) to complete the salutation.

Alicia wants her customers to know that The Pet Shoppe values its customers and remembers them and their pets. You'll personalize the letter even further by including the kind of pet each customer owns and the pet's name.

To finish personalizing the letter:

1. Scroll to the second paragraph of the letter, select the phrase **[kind of pet]** (including the brackets) in the second paragraph of the form letter, then press the **Delete** key.

   You'll replace this phrase with a merge code.

2. Press the **spacebar**, scroll down the Field Names list in the Insert Field Name or Number dialog box, click **Kind of Pet**, then click the **Insert** button. WordPerfect inserts the Kind of Pet merge code into the form letter. Make sure there is a space before and after the field code.

3. Select **[branch]** (including the brackets) in the third paragraph of the form letter, then press the **Delete** key.

4. Press the **spacebar**, click **Branch** in the list of fields, then click the **Insert** button. WordPerfect inserts the Branch merge code into the form letter. Again, make sure there is a space before and after the merge code.

5. Similarly, replace **[pet's name]** in the third sentence of the third paragraph of the form letter with the Name of Pet field. See Figure 5-17.

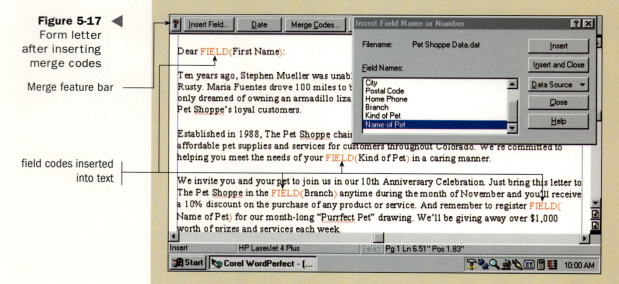

Figure 5-17
Form letter after inserting merge codes

Merge feature bar

field codes inserted into text

6. Carefully check your document to make sure all the field names and spacing are correct.

   TROUBLE? If you see errors, use WordPerfect's editing commands to delete the error, then insert the correct merge code or spacing.

7. Click the **Close** button in the Insert Field Name or Number dialog box. Scroll up so you can see the inside address and salutation. Carefully check over the letter to make sure the text and format are correct. In particular, check to make sure that the spaces before and after the merged data are correct because it is easy to omit spaces or add extra spaces around merge codes. The merged form letters will print with the same spacing you see in the form file.

8. Save the form file.

The form letter (form file) of the merge is complete. As you saw while creating the form file, merge codes are easy to use and very flexible:

- You can use merge codes anywhere in the form file. For example, in Alicia's form letter, you inserted fields for the inside address and you inserted fields within the body of the letter.
- You can use the same merge code more than once. For example, Alicia's form letter uses the First Name field in the inside address and in the salutation.
- You don't have to use all the fields from the data file in your form file. For example, Alicia's form letter doesn't use the Home Phone field.

Now that you have created the form letter (form file) and the list of customer information (data file), you're ready to merge the two files and create personalized letters to send to The Pet Shoppe's customers.

Merging the Form File and Data File

Because the data file consists of 14 records, you'll create a merged document with 14 pages, one letter per page. You could merge the data file and form file directly to the printer, which is often quicker and doesn't require disk space. However, Alicia wants to keep a copy of the merged document on disk for her records. So you'll merge the data file and form file to a new document on disk.

MERGING A FORM FILE AND DATA FILE

- Make sure the form file and the Merge feature bar are open.
- Click the Merge button on the Merge feature bar.
- Click the Output button then click New Document.
- Click the Merge button.

You'll merge all the records of the data file with the form file.

To merge a form file and a data file:

1. With **Pet Shoppe Form Letter** as the active document, click the **Merge** button on the Merge feature bar. The Perform Merge dialog box opens.

   Because the current form file is associated with the **Pet Shoppe Data** data file, that name appears in the Data source text box.

2. If necessary, click the **Output** button then click **New Document**.

3. Click the **Merge** button on the Merge feature bar to perform the merge. WordPerfect creates a new document with 14 pages.

   TROUBLE? If your merge generated 15 pages, scroll to the beginning of page 15 so you can see the inside address, which probably has no data. With the insertion point anywhere in page 15, click Edit, point to Select, click Page, press the Delete key to delete the selected text, then press the Backspace key to delete the extra page break. Now the merged document has only 14 pages.

4. Save the merged document as **Pet Shoppe Form Letters1** to the **Tutorial.05** folder on your Student Disk, then close the document.

Figure 5-18 shows what one of the merged form letters will look like when Alicia prints it on company letterhead.

Figure 5-18
One page of the merged document

The Pet Shoppe
121 Sillitoe Avenue • Colorado Springs, CO 80901
Phone: (719) 555-5555 • Fax: (719) 555-5556

October 8, 1999

Amelia Gutierrez
623 Heather Drive
Lamar, CO 81052

Dear Amelia:

Ten years ago, Stephen Mueller was unable to find suitable grooming facilities for his dog, Rusty. Maria Fuentes drove 100 miles to buy food for her cat, Sneakers. And Carole Cochran only dreamed of owning an armadillo lizard. Today, Stephen, Maria, and Carole are among The Pet Shoppe's loyal customers.

Established in 1988, The Pet Shoppe chain provides a complete line of high quality yet affordable pet supplies and services for customers throughout Colorado. We're committed to helping you meet the needs of your dog in a caring manner.

We invite you and your pet to join us in our 10th Anniversary Celebration. Just bring this letter to The Pet Shoppe in the Olde West Shopping Center anytime during the month of November and you'll receive a 10% discount on the purchase of any product or service. And remember to register Nieve for our month-long "Purrfect Pet" drawing. We'll be giving away over $1,000 worth of prizes and services each week.

We look forward to seeing you at The Pet Shoppe.

Sincerely yours,

Alicia Robles
Vice President, Sales

You have completed the merge and generated a merged document. Alicia stops by to see how the letters are coming.

Sorting Records

As Alicia looks through the letters to The Pet Shoppe customers in the merged document, she notices one problem—the letters are not grouped by ZIP codes. Currently, the letters are in the order in which customers were added to the data file. She is going to use bulk mailing rates to send her letters, but the U.S. Postal Service requires bulk mailings to be separated into groups according to ZIP code. She asks you to sort the data file by ZIP code (the Postal Code field) and to merge the form file with the sorted data file. You can sort information in a data file just as you sort any information. Recall that **sort** means to rearrange a list or a document in alphabetical, numerical, or chronological order. You can sort information in **ascending** order (A to Z, lowest to highest, or earliest to latest) or in **descending** order (Z to A, highest to lowest, or latest to earliest).

REFERENCE window

SORTING A DATA FILE

- Make sure the data file is in the document window.
- Click the Options button on the Merge feature bar, then click Sort to open the Sort dialog box.
- Click the New button to open the New Sort dialog box, then specify the sort conditions.
- Click the OK button, then click the Sort button in the Sort dialog box.

You'll sort the records in ascending order by the Postal Code field in Pet Shoppe Data.

To sort the data file by ZIP code:

1. With the form file still in the document window, click the **Go to Data** button on the Merge feature bar. If the Pet Shoppe Data file isn't open, WordPerfect will open it; if it is open, WordPerfect will make it the active document.

   TROUBLE? If the Merge feature bar isn't open, you might not have closed the merged Pet Shoppe Form Letters1. Click File, then click Close to close the file, then repeat Step 1.

2. On the Merge feature bar, click the **Options** button, then click **Sort**. The Sort dialog box opens.

   Because none of the sort options listed will sort the data by ZIP code, you will have to define a new sort.

3. Click the **New** button in the Sort dialog box. The New Sort dialog box opens. If necessary, click the **Merge record** radio button in the Sort by section to indicate that the data to be sorted are in merge records.

4. Type **Sort by ZIP code** in the Sort name text box.

5. For Key 1 in the Key definitions section, click the **Type** button then click **Numeric**, click the **Sort order** button then click **Ascending**, click in the **Field** text box then type **5**. This defines an ascending numerical sort by the Postal Code field. See Figure 5-19.

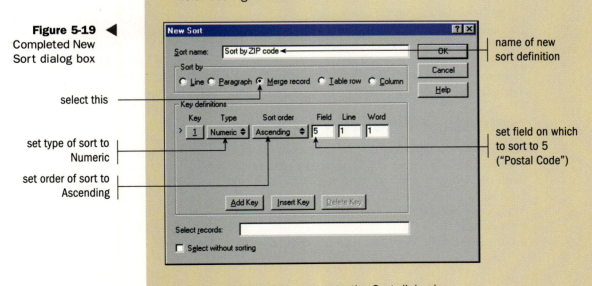

Figure 5-19 Completed New Sort dialog box

6. Click the **OK** button to return to the Sort dialog box.

7. Make sure **Sort by ZIP code** is selected, then click the **Sort** button. WordPerfect sorts the data table from lowest ZIP code number to highest.

When you merge the data file with the form letter, the letters will appear in the merged document in order of the ZIP codes.

8. Save the data file. You have to save the document before you perform the merge because WordPerfect uses the data file on the disk during the merge, not the data file in the document window.

With the data file sorted and saved, you're ready to perform the merge.

To merge the sorted data file and the form letter:

1. Click the **Go to Form** button on the Merge feature bar to switch to Pet Shoppe Form Letter.

2. Click the **Merge** button on the Merge feature bar, then click the **Merge** button in the Perform Merge dialog box.

    WordPerfect generates the new merged document with 14 letters, one letter per page, as before, but this time the first letter is to Pablo Orozco, who has the lowest ZIP code (80010).

    TROUBLE? If your merge generated 15 pages, scroll to the beginning of page 15 so you can see the inside address, which probably has no data. With the insertion point anywhere in page 15, click Edit, point to Select, click Page, press the Delete key to delete the selected text, then press the Backspace key to delete the extra page break. Now the merged document has only 14 pages.

3. Scroll through the letters in the new merged document to see that they are in ascending order by ZIP code. Click and drag the scroll box in the vertical scroll bar to move quickly from letter to letter.

    TROUBLE? If the letters in the merged document are not sorted by ZIP code, you probably did not save the data file before you performed the merge. Switch to the Pet Shoppe Data window, make sure the records are sorted, then save the file and repeat Steps 1 through 3.

4. Save the new merged document as **Pet Shoppe Form Letters2** in the **Tutorial.05** folder on your Student Disk.

5. Close the merged document.

As Alicia requested, you created a merged document with the letters to The Pet Shoppe customers sorted by ZIP code. She stops back to tell you that the letters to customers who frequent one branch of The Pet Shoppe need additional information.

Selecting Records to Merge

The Pet Shoppe is going to offer additional savings on certain surplus items at the High Prairie Mall in Denver. Alicia wants to modify the form letter slightly and then merge it with only those records of customers of The Pet Shoppe in the High Prairie Mall.

You can select specific records from the data file to merge with the form file by specifying conditions for one or more fields. A **condition** is an expression that restricts the selection of records based on values or attributes of the field in the records. Figure 5-20 shows examples of some conditions for selecting records during a merge.

SELECTING RECORDS TO MERGE   WP 189

Figure 5-20 ◄
Examples of conditions for selecting records

With Field Set To	And Condition Set To	These Records Will Be Selected
Salary	-$30,000 or<=$30,000	all with salary less than or equal to $30,000
Salary	$30,000- or>=$30,000	all with salary greater than or equal to $30,000
Last Name	Jones-Smith	all whose last names fall between Jones and Smith
Last Name	A*-M*	all whose last names begin with A to M (* = match anything)
State	!TX	all except those whose state is Texas (! = NOT)
ZIP Code	802?5	any with a ZIP code that matches this pattern, where ? = any character (80205, 80215, 80225, etc., match; 80204 doesn't match)

To select certain records to print with the revised sales letter, you'll set the Branch field so that it is equal to "High Prairie Mall." That way, WordPerfect will select records only of customers who shop at the High Prairie Mall branch of The Pet Shoppe and omit other records. First, you'll modify the form letter.

To edit the form letter:

1. Move the insertion point to the right of the phrase "10% discount on the purchase of any product or service" in the third paragraph of the form letter.

2. Press the **spacebar** then type **and a 25% discount on the purchase of selected items**. See Figure 5-21.

Figure 5-21 ◄
Form letter with inserted text

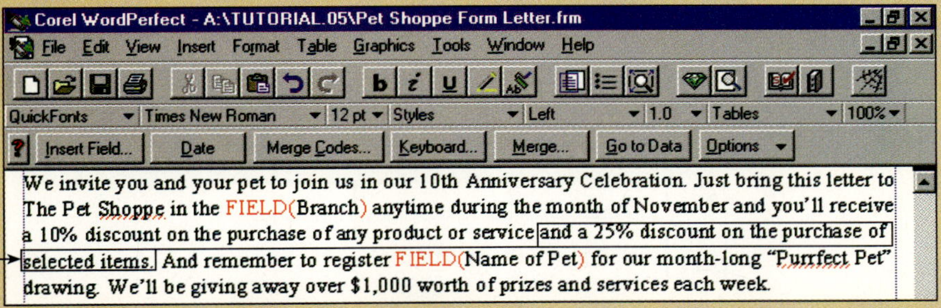

added phrase

Alicia wants to send this version of the letter only to customers of the High Prairie Mall store. You'll specify the Select Records conditions to select only those records for High Prairie Mall, then you'll merge the revised form letter with the records in the data file that match the selection conditions.

To select records for a merge:

1. If necessary, click the **Go to Form** button on the Merge feature bar to make Pet Shoppe Form Letter the active document window, then click the **Merge** button on the Merge feature bar. The Perform Merge dialog box opens.

2. Click the **Select Records** button in the center of the Perform Merge dialog box. The Select Records dialog box opens. See Figure 5-22.

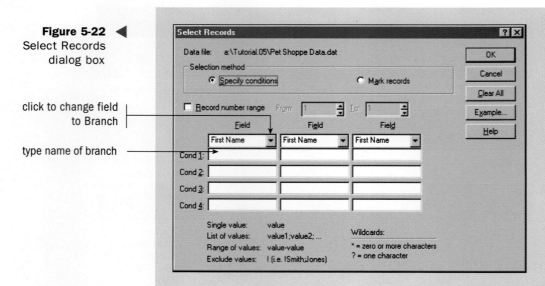

Figure 5-22
Select Records dialog box

click to change field to Branch

type name of branch

3. If necessary, click the **Specify conditions** radio button in the Selection method section of the dialog box. Now you'll specify the conditions.

4. Click the **Field** list arrow in the first Field column, click the **Branch** field name, click in the **Cond 1** text box, then type **High Prairie Mall**. This tells WordPerfect to select only those files in which the Branch field name is equal to "High Prairie Mall." Be careful to spell the store branch exactly as shown. If any character or space differs, WordPerfect won't match any records. This is the only condition that you need to select the desired records. See Figure 5-23.

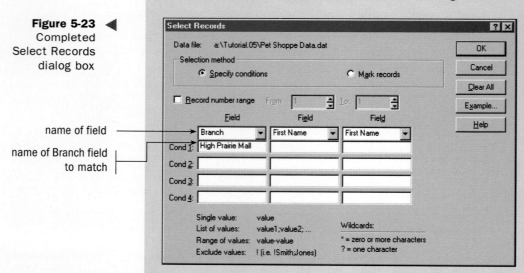

Figure 5-23
Completed Select Records dialog box

name of field

name of Branch field to match

5. Click the **OK** button to accept the selection conditions and return to the Perform Merge dialog box, make sure Output is set to **New Document**, then click the **Merge** button.

WordPerfect performs the merge and creates a new document that merges the modified form letter with all the records that match the selection conditions. Notice the document is only three pages because only three records list High Prairie Mall in the Branch field.

6. Scroll through the merged document to see the three letters, those to Julia Akin, Randall Ure, and Sarah Sorenson—customers of The Pet Shoppe in the High Prairie Mall. See Figure 5-24.

Figure 5-24
Last page of merged document after selecting records

only three pages

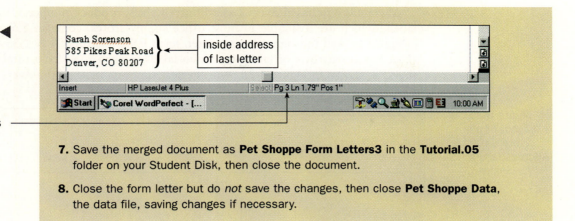

7. Save the merged document as **Pet Shoppe Form Letters3** in the **Tutorial.05** folder on your Student Disk, then close the document.

8. Close the form letter but do *not* save the changes, then close **Pet Shoppe Data**, the data file, saving changes if necessary.

You give the completed file to Alicia, who will print the letters on company letterhead.

Quick Check

1. What is the purpose of a DATE code in a form file?
2. How do you insert a merge code into a form file?
3. How can you distinguish a merge code from the rest of the text in a form file?
4. Define the following in your own words:
   a. merged document
   b. sort
   c. Select Records condition
5. Suppose one of the fields in a data file contains the salary of your employees. How would you select only the records of those employees whose salary is less than $15,000?
6. If your form file is a form letter and you have 23 records in your data file, how many letters will the merged document create?

You have created merged documents for a sorted data file, selected records in a data file, and edited a form file. Next you'll create mailing labels and a telephone list of The Pet Shoppe's customers. If you aren't going to work through Session 5.3 now, you should exit WordPerfect. When you're ready to begin Session 5.3, start WordPerfect and continue with the session.

SESSION 5.3

In this session you will create and print mailing labels for the form letter and create a telephone list of The Pet Shoppe's customers.

Creating Mailing Labels

Now that you have created personalized sales letters, Alicia is ready to print them on company letterhead while you prepare envelopes in which to mail the letters. You could print the names and addresses directly onto envelopes or you could create mailing labels to attach to the envelopes. The latter method is easier because 14 labels come on each sheet, and you don't have to feed envelopes through the printer one by one. You decide to create mailing labels.

Alicia has purchased Avery Laser Printer Labels, product number 5162 Address. These labels, which are available in most office supply stores, come in 8.5 × 11-inch sheets designed to feed through a laser printer. Each label measures 4 × 1.33 inches, and each sheet has seven rows of labels with two labels in each row, for a total of 14 labels per sheet, as shown in Figure 5-25. WordPerfect supports most of the Avery label formats.

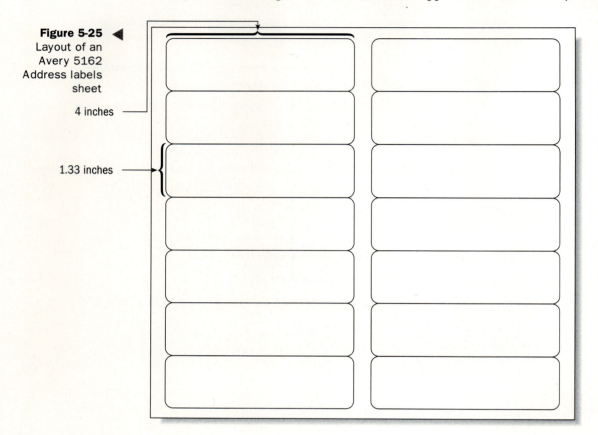

Figure 5-25
Layout of an Avery 5162 Address labels sheet

You can use the same data file (Pet Shoppe Data) as you did earlier, but you'll have to create a new form file.

CREATING MAILING LABELS

- Click Format then click Labels. The Labels dialog box opens.
- Click the appropriate label form name from the Labels list.
- Click the Select button.
- Make the document window a form file, associate a data source, insert the appropriate merge codes, then merge the labels form file with the data source.

You'll begin creating the mailing labels by specifying the form file and data file.

To create a form file for mailing labels:

1. Make sure a blank document window appears on the screen.
2. Click **Format** then click **Labels**. The Labels dialog box opens.
3. Scroll down the Labels list box until you see Avery 5162 Address, click **Avery 5162 Address**, then click the **Select** button. The document is formatted for Avery 5162 Address labels. You're ready to make the document a merge file.

CREATING MAILING LABELS   WP 193

4. Click **Tools**, click **Merge**, then click the **Form** button on the Merge dialog box to open the Create Merge File dialog box.

5. Make sure the **Use file in active window** radio button is selected, then click the **OK** button.

6. Associate the data file **Pet Shoppe Data**, then click the **OK** button in the Create Form File dialog box. The Merge feature bar opens.

You can insert the field codes into the labels form file.

To insert field codes:

1. Click the **Insert Field** button on the Merge feature bar. The Insert Field Name or Number dialog box opens. Double-click **First Name** in the Field Names list to insert the FIELD(First Name) merge code.

2. Press the **spacebar**, double-click **Last Name** in the Field Names list to insert the FIELD(Last Name) merge code, then press the **Enter** key. Continue inserting the FIELD merge codes and formatting the label exactly as shown in Figure 5-26.

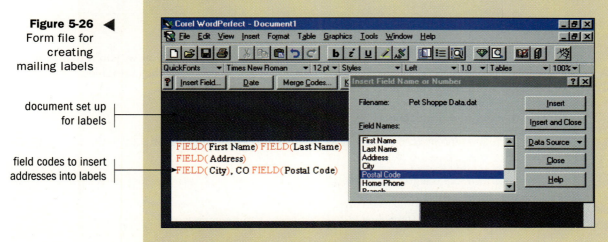

Figure 5-26
Form file for creating mailing labels

document set up for labels

field codes to insert addresses into labels

3. Close the Insert Field Name or Number dialog box.

4. Save the file **Pet Shoppe Labels Form** to the **Tutorial.05** folder on your Student Disk.

You have specified the form file, which is the blank document in the document window, and the data file, which is the file Pet Shoppe Data. You're ready to create the merged document of labels and select the type of labels.

To merge the files:

1. Click the **Merge** button on the Merge feature bar. The Perform Merge dialog box opens.

2. Make sure Form file is set to **Current Document**, and the Output is set to **New Document**.

3. Click the **Select Records** button then click the **Clear All** button to remove any conditions. This ensures that all records are merged with the labels form file. Click the **OK** button.

4. Click the **Merge** button to perform the merge. WordPerfect merges the form and data files to produce the address labels shown in Figure 5-27.

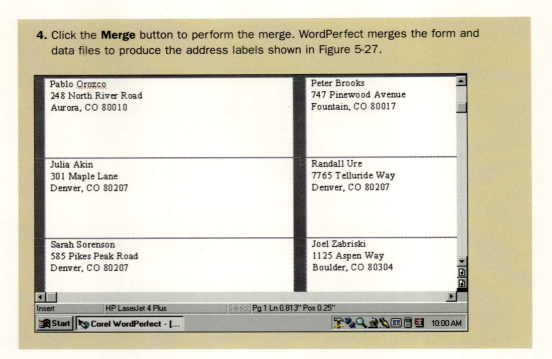

Figure 5-27 ◀
Merged document showing address labels

You're ready to save the document and print the labels. For now, you'll just print the labels on an 8½ × 11-inch sheet of paper so you can see what they look like. Later, Alicia will print them on a sheet of labels.

To save and print labels:

1. Save the merged document as **Pet Shoppe Labels** to the **Tutorial.05** folder on your Student Disk.
2. Print the merged document of labels just as you would print any other document.

    TROUBLE? If you're printing on a sheet of labels, ask your instructor or technical support person how to feed the sheet into the printer.

3. Close the merged document, then close the labels form file.
4. If necessary, close the data file, but do not exit WordPerfect.

As your final task, Alicia wants you to create a telephone list for all the customers in the data file.

Creating a Telephone List

Alicia asked some of the sales personnel to call customers and remind them of The Pet Shoppe's anniversary sale; the sales personnel will call all the customers on the telephone list you create.

You'll begin by setting up a merge as before, except this time you'll create a list type of form file rather than a letter.

To prepare for creating the telephone list:

1. If necessary, click the **New** button on the Toolbar to open a new blank document.

2. Click **Tools**, click **Merge**, click the **Form** button in the Merge dialog box, associate the data file **Pet Shoppe Data**, then click the **OK** button in the Create Form File dialog box.

You're ready to create the form file for the telephone list and merge the form file with the data file. The format of the telephone list is the customer's name (last name first) at the left margin of the page and the phone number at the right margin. You'll set up the form file so that the phone number is preceded by a dot leader. A **dot leader** is a dotted line that extends from the last letter of text on the left margin to the beginning of text aligned at a tab stop.

To create the form file:

1. With the insertion point in a blank document window, insert the **Last Name** merge code, type **,** (a comma), press the **spacebar**, then insert the **First Name** merge code.

   Now you'll use the Flush Right command with a dot leader.

2. Click **Format**, point to **Line**, then click **Flush Right with Dot Leaders** to create a dot leader and move the insertion point to the right margin.

3. Insert the **Home Phone** merge code at the location of the insertion point. Notice the dot leader shortened to accommodate the inserted text.

4. Close the Insert Field Name or Number dialog box, then press the **Enter** key. You inserted a hard return so that each name and telephone number will appear on a separate line. The completed form file looks like Figure 5-28.

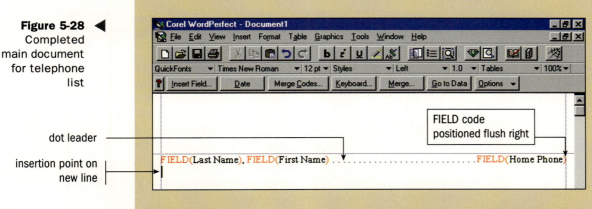

Figure 5-28 ◀ Completed main document for telephone list

dot leader

insertion point on new line

FIELD code positioned flush right

5. Save the document as **Pet Shoppe Phone Form** to the **Tutorial.05** folder on your Student Disk.

You're almost ready to merge this file with the data file, except that you want the name and telephone numbers list to be alphabetized by the customers' last names. You need to sort the data file, then you can merge the files.

To sort the data file by last name:

1. Click the **Go to Data** button on the Merge feature bar. WordPerfect opens the data file and makes it the active document window.

2. Click the **Options** button on the Merge feature bar, then click **Sort**. The Sort dialog box opens.

3. Click the **New** button to open the New Sort dialog box.

4. Type **Alphabetize by Last Name** in the Sort name text box, then click the **Merge record** radio button in the Sort by section.

5. In the Key definitions section of the dialog box, click the **Type** button then click **Alpha**, click the **Sort order** button then click **Ascending**, and type **2** in the Field text box. See Figure 5-29.

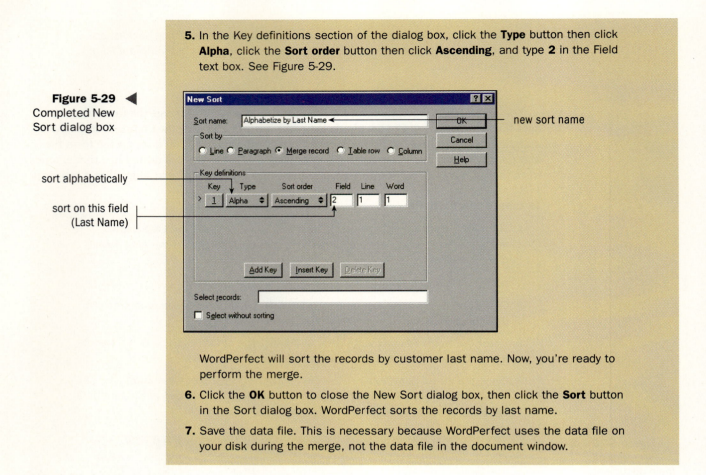

Figure 5-29
Completed New Sort dialog box

sort alphabetically

sort on this field (Last Name)

new sort name

WordPerfect will sort the records by customer last name. Now, you're ready to perform the merge.

6. Click the **OK** button to close the New Sort dialog box, then click the **Sort** button in the Sort dialog box. WordPerfect sorts the records by last name.

7. Save the data file. This is necessary because WordPerfect uses the data file on your disk during the merge, not the data file in the document window.

You'll return to the form file to perform the merge.

To perform the merge to create the telephone list:

1. Click the **Go to Form** button on the Merge feature bar to go to Pet Shoppe Phone Form.

2. Click the **Merge** button on the Merge feature bar. The Perform Merge dialog box opens. You need to tell WordPerfect not to put each record on a different page, as when you merged the letters.

3. Click the **Options** button, click the **Separate each merged document with a page break** check box to deselect it, then click the **OK** button. When you perform the merge, the merged document will not have page breaks between the records.

4. Click the **Merge** button in the Perform Merge dialog box. WordPerfect generates the telephone list. See Figure 5-30.

Figure 5-30
Merged telephone list document

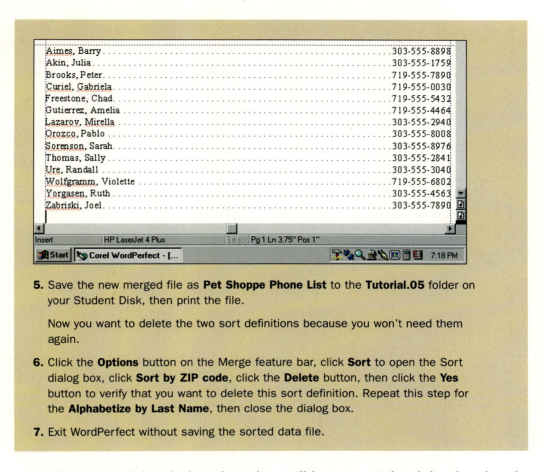

5. Save the new merged file as **Pet Shoppe Phone List** to the **Tutorial.05** folder on your Student Disk, then print the file.

   Now you want to delete the two sort definitions because you won't need them again.

6. Click the **Options** button on the Merge feature bar, click **Sort** to open the Sort dialog box, click **Sort by ZIP code**, click the **Delete** button, then click the **Yes** button to verify that you want to delete this sort definition. Repeat this step for the **Alphabetize by Last Name**, then close the dialog box.

7. Exit WordPerfect without saving the sorted data file.

You have created the telephone list. Alicia will have it copied and distributed to the appropriate sales personnel. She thinks that The Pet Shoppe's 10th Anniversary Celebration will be a great success.

1. True or False: To create mailing labels you can use the same data file you used for a form letter.
2. Describe the general process for creating mailing labels from a data file.
3. True or False: WordPerfect automatically inserts a page break after each merged record of a form file.
4. What is a dot leader?
5. How do you sort a data file using the Last Name field so that all the customers are arranged in descending alphabetical order (Z to A)?

Tutorial Assignments

Start WordPerfect and open the document PetVacc from the TAssign folder in the Tutorial.05 folder on your Student Disk, then save it as Pet Shoppe Vaccines. Complete the following:

1. Create a new data file document, using the filename Pet Vaccine Data, with the following eight field names: First Name, Last Name, Address, City, Postal Code, Branch, Kind of Pet, and Name of Pet.

2. Create records using the following information:
   Elmo Zoulek, 1771 Levan Drive, Boulder, CO 80307, University Mall, dog, Ringo
   AnnaClair Smuin, 927 S. Crestview, Cortez, CO 81321, Cortez, dog, Charity
   Percy Burnside, 1037 Wilderness Ave., Greeley, CO 80631, Rocky Mountain Mall, cat, Buffy
   Armand Walborsky, 21 Parkway Circle #202, Denver, CO 80204, High Prairie Mall, cat, Zorba
3. Sort the data file by postal code from the lowest to the highest, then save the data file.
4. Create a merge form letter using Pet Shoppe Vaccines as the form file.
5. In the form file replace the text of the field names in brackets with actual merge codes. Save the changes to the form file.

6. Merge those records for only customers who own a dog, save the merged document as Pet Vaccine Letters to the TAssign folder in the Tutorial.05 folder on your Student Disk, then print the letters.
7. Close all documents, saving changes as needed.

Open the file Payroll from the TAssign folder in the Tutorial.05 folder on your Student Disk, then save the file as Payroll Memo.

8. Create a new data file, called Payroll Data, with the following field names: First Name, Last Name, Office Number, Work Phone, and Exemptions.
9. Create a record for each of the following The Pet Shoppe employees working at company headquarters:
   Leslie Knecht, B-141, 555-1121, 3
   Mei-Young Soh, B-333, 555-1818, 2
   Cesar Velarde, B-353, 555-1811, 2
   Scott Coe, B-147, 555-1135, 1
10. Create a form letter using Payroll Memo as the active file, then edit the form file.
11. To the right of "TO:," press the Tab key and insert the First Name field (for the employee's first name), then press the spacebar and insert the Last Name field (for the employee's last name).
12. To the right of "DATE:" in the memo, press the Tab key and insert the WordPerfect DATE code.
13. In the body of the memo, immediately before the word "exemptions," insert the Exemptions field. Make sure the field code has a space on each side. Save the form file with the changes.

14. In one merge operation, select only the records of employees with two or more exemptions, send the merged information to the printer (*Hint:* Set the Output to Printer), and print an envelope for the memo on an 8½ × 11-inch sheet of paper. (*Hint:* In the Perform Merge dialog box, click Envelope then use the Field button to insert field codes into the mailing addresses section of the dialog box.)
15. Close all documents, saving any changes. Open a new, blank document window and create a form file for generating a one-page telephone list. Use Payroll Data as the data file.
16. Create an employee telephone list by inserting the Last Name and First Name fields at the left margin. Insert the Work Phone field at the right margin with a dot leader.
17. Format the form file so each telephone number appears on a separate line, then sort the data file alphabetically in ascending order.
18. Generate a one-page telephone list and save the new merged file as Employee Phone List in the TAssign folder in the Tutorial.05 folder on your Student Disk.
19. Print the telephone list, then close all documents, saving changes as needed.

Case Problems

1. DeeDee Sandau for Mayor DeeDee Sandau is preparing to run for the office of mayor of Jefferson City, Missouri. DeeDee's campaign staff is creating a data file of prospective supporters of her campaign.

Open the document Campaign from the Cases folder in the Tutorial.05 folder on your Student Disk, then do the following:

1. Make the Campaign document a merge form file, then save the document as Campaign Form Letter to the Cases folder in the Tutorial.05 folder on your Student Disk.
2. Create a data file with the following field names: Full Name, Nickname, Title, Company, Address, Phone, and Party.
3. Enter the following four records into the data file. Each line is one record. The fields in each record are separated by commas. (Don't include the commas in the records.)

    Maria De Jesus, Maria, Chief Medical Officer, Jefferson Medical Center, 1577 Lancelot Drive, 555-7740, Republican

    Randall Dakota, Randy, President, Dakota Appraisal Services, 633 Wentworth, 555-1095, Democrat

    Leilani Kinikini, Lani, Business Manager, Nolan and Ash Architects, 4424 Bedford, 555-9850, Independent

    David Bezzant, Dave, Chief Financial Officer, Midtown Missouri State Bank, 844 Heatherton Rd, 555-0180, Republican

4. Save the data file document as Supporters Data to the Cases folder in the Tutorial.05 folder on your Student Disk.
5. Switch to the form file, then at the beginning of the form letter, insert the DATE code then add three blank lines.
6. Insert merge codes for the complete inside address. Include fields for each person's name, title, company, and street. All the inside addresses should include the city (Jefferson City), the abbreviation for the state (MO), and the ZIP code (65101).
7. Double space after the inside address, then create the salutation of the letter. Use the Nickname field in the salutation. Make sure there is a blank line between the salutation and the body of the letter.
8. In the third paragraph, replace the words in brackets with the actual merge codes.
9. Save the edited form file, then merge the files to create a set of letters to prospective contributors.
10. Save the letters file as Campaign Letters to the Cases folder in the Tutorial.05 folder on your Student Disk, then print the first letter.
11. Create a telephone list of prospective contributors. Use a dot leader to separate the name on the left from the phone number on the right.
12. Save the telephone list form file as Campaign Phone Form to the Cases folder in the Tutorial.05 folder on your Student Disk.
13. Alphabetize the records in ascending order, then merge the phone list onto one page.
14. Save the merged document of the telephone list as Campaign Phone List to the Cases folder in the Tutorial.05 folder on your Student Disk.
15. Print the telephone list, then close the documents.

2. Gina's Gems Gina Lujan owns a small jewelry store in White Plains, New York. She frequently notifies her regular customers of upcoming sales. She decides to prepare personalized form letters to mail to all her regular customers one month before their birthdays. She will mail the letters in manila envelopes along with a two-page color catalog and a gift certificate. Do the following:

1. Create a data file with the following field names: First Name, Last Name, Address, City, State, Postal Code, Birth Day, Birth Month, and Birth Stone.

2. Save the data file as Gems Data to the Cases folder in the Tutorial.05 folder on your Student Disk.
3. Enter the following five records into the data file. Each line is one record. The fields in each record are separated by commas. (Don't include the commas in the records.) Enter months by numbers (1, 2, 3) not names (January, February, March) so you can sort in chronological order.

   John, Pataki, 426 Hudson Way, White Plains, NY, 10602, 23, January, garnet

   Allison, Mandelkern, 11812 Westbrook Way, Croton-on-Hudson, NY, 10520, 31, August, sapphire

   Susan, Gardner, 804 Lake Placid Road, West Haven, CT, 06156, 14, June, pearl

   Garth, Poduska, 77 Catskill Circle, Lake Carmel, NY, 10512, 7, January, garnet

   Donald, Truong, 4055 Empire Road, Scarsdale, NY, 10583, 22, August, sapphire

4. Insert the document Gems from the Cases folder in the Tutorial.05 folder on your Student Disk into the blank form file, and save the form file document to the disk as Gems Form Letter.
5. At the beginning of the form file, insert the DATE code and other merge codes for the inside address and salutation. Use the customer's first name in the salutation.
6. In the body of the letter, insert the Birth Month, Birth Day, and Birth Stone fields at the locations indicated by the bracketed words.
7. Save the form letter then sort the data file in descending alphabetical order by customer last name.

8. Select only those records for customers whose birthdays are in January, then merge the form file with the data file.
9. Save the merged document as Gem Letters to the Cases folder in the Tutorial.05 folder on your Student Disk, then print the letters.
10. Create a form file for generating mailing labels on sheets of Avery 5162 Address labels.
11. Save the document as Gem Labels Form to the Cases folder in the Tutorial.05 folder on your Student Disk.
12. Print the labels on an 8½ × 11-inch sheet of paper.

13. Create a form file for generating a list of customers. Use the following example to format your merge codes (press the Enter key after the last line):

    Name: Garth Poduska
    Address: 77 Catskill Circle, Lake Carmel, NY, 10512
    Birth date: 1/7
    Birth stone: garnet

14. Save the form file as Gems Customer List Form to the Cases folder in the Tutorial.05 folder on your Student Disk.

15. Sort the data file in ascending order by birth month then by birth day.
16. Merge the customer list form with the data file; then save the file as Gems Customer List to the Cases folder in the Tutorial.05 folder on your Student Disk.
17. Print the list, then close the files.

3. Heritage Auto Sales Joe Whitlock is the customer relations manager for Heritage Auto Sales in Cadillac, Michigan. After a customer purchases a new car, Joe sends out a Sales Satisfaction Survey accompanied by a personalized letter. Do the following:

1. Create a data file with the following field names: First Name, Last Name, Address, City, Postal Code, Make of Car, Model of Car, Sales Rep, and Purchase Price.
2. Save the data file as Auto Sales Data to the Cases folder in the Tutorial.05 folder on your Student Disk.

3. Enter the following five records into the data file. Each line is one record. The fields in each record are separated by commas. (Don't include the commas in the records.)

   Patty, Muelstein, 4102 Apple Avenue, Detroit, 48235, Honda, Civic, Carl, 17,840

   Delbert, Greene, 875 Gunnison Road, Ecorse, 48229, Toyota, Camry, Audry, 21,331

   Li, Du, 2221 Wolverine Drive, Kentwood, 49508, Honda, Accord, Michael, 19,242

   Art, Zupan, 301 Maple Avenue, Walker, 49504, Toyota, Corolla, Carl, 14,875

   Dina, Webb, 772 West University Drive, Detroit, 48238, Honda, Civic, Michael, 16,421

4. Open the file AutoSale from the Cases folder in the Tutorial.05 folder on your Student Disk, then save the document as Auto Sales Form Letter.
5. Edit the form file to include the following in the letter: date, inside address, and salutation. (*Hint:* You'll need to add the state as text.)
6. Edit the body of the form letter to replace words in brackets with their corresponding merge code names, then save the form letter.
7. Sort the data file in ascending alphabetical order by the last name.

8. Merge the form letter with the data file, selecting only those records for which the sales price is between $17,000 and $18,000 and the make of car is a Honda. (*Hint:* Specify two conditions in selecting records.)
9. Save the merged document file as Auto Letters to the Cases folder in the Tutorial.05 folder on your Student Disk.

10. Perform the merge again, this time sending the output directly to the printer, and at the same time printing envelopes on 8½ × 11-inch sheets of paper. (*Hint:* In the Perform Merge dialog box, click Envelope then use the Field button to insert field codes into the mailing addresses section of the dialog box.)
11. Close all the files saving any changes as needed.

4. Special Event Announcements Mailing List At some point, you might want to send announcements to your friends and family telling them about a special event—for example, a graduation, a marriage, or a move to a new city. You can do this easily with WordPerfect's Merge feature. Do the following:

1. Create a data file containing the names and addresses of at least five people. You can use real or fictitious names and addresses.
2. Save the data file as Special Event to the Cases folder in the Tutorial.05 folder on your Student Disk.
3. Write a brief form letter telling your friends and family about the special event. Include the following in the letter:
   a. WordPerfect DATE code for the current date
   b. merge codes for the inside address and salutation of the letter
   c. at least one merge code within the body of the letter
   d. information to your friends and family about the time, date, and location of your special event
4. Save the form file as Special Event Form Letter to the Cases folder in the Tutorial.05 folder on your Student Disk.
5. Sort the data file in ascending order by last name.
6. Merge the form file and data file. Save the merged document as Special Event Merge to the Cases folder in the Tutorial.05 folder on your Student Disk.
7. Print the first two pages (letters) of the merged document.
8. Create a labels form file. You can use any printer label type you like, as long as each name and address fits on one label and all the labels fit on one page.
9. Save the labels form file as Special Event Labels Form to the Cases folder in the Tutorial.05 folder on your Student Disk.
10. Merge the files, and save the merged document of labels as Special Event Labels to the Cases folder in the Tutorial.05 folder on your Student Disk.
11. Print the labels on an 8½ × 11-inch sheet of paper, then close all the files.

TUTORIAL 6

Desktop Publishing

Creating a Newsletter for FastFad Manufacturing Company

OBJECTIVES

In this tutorial you will:

- Identify design elements
- Create titles with TextArt
- Create newspaper-style columns
- Insert, resize, and move graphic images
- Incorporate drop caps and colored text
- Use typographic characters and other special typesetting features
- Hyphenate text
- Add a page border

CASE

FastFad Manufacturing Company

Gerrit Polansky works for FastFad Manufacturing Company, which designs and manufactures plastic figures (action figures, vehicles, and other toys) for promotional sales and giveaways in the fast-food and cereal industries. Gerrit's job consists of informing FastFad's sales staff about new products. He does this by producing and distributing a monthly newsletter that contains brief descriptions of these new items and ideas for marketing them. Recently, FastFad added MiniMovers, small plastic cars, trucks, and other vehicles to their line of plastic toys. Gerrit needs to get the information about these products to the sales staff quickly, so the company can market the toys to FastFad's clients while the toys are still the fad. He has asked you to help him create the newsletter.

In this tutorial, you'll review the text of Gerrit's newsletter and add desktop publishing elements. In Session 6.1, you'll learn the basic elements of desktop publishing, use TextArt to create the title for the newsletter that Gerrit wrote describing MiniMovers, and insert space before and after each heading. In Session 6.2, you'll create newspaper-style columns, and insert clip art, drop caps, and a pull quote into the text. In Session 6.3, you'll insert typographical characters and symbols, hyphenate the text, draw a border around the page, and draw a vertical line between the columns. Finally, you'll print the newsletter.

SESSION 6.1

In this session you will see how Gerrit planned his newsletter. Then you will create a title using TextArt, insert extra space before and after each heading, and insert the date before the text of the newsletter.

Planning the Document

A newsletter usually presents information in an entertaining and easy-to-read manner.

Content

In the business world, people who publish newsletters often use text written by others. This is the case with the *FastFad Update* newsletter. Gerrit and several others at FastFad have written the **copy**, or text, describing FastFad's new MiniMovers plastic toys for this month's newsletter. Gerrit combined all the copy into one WordPerfect file.

Organization

The newsletter will provide a brief overview of the new FastFad products, followed by a short explanation of what MiniMovers are and why children will like them.

Style

Newsletters and other promotional sales material often are written in an informal style that conveys information quickly. Because the FastFad newsletter is promotional material, Gerrit and the other employees used short sentences packed with detail.

Presentation

A newsletter must be eye-catching and easy to read. The text of the FastFad newsletter will be split into two columns to help readers quickly scan the information. Pull quotes, drop caps, and other special publishing elements will help draw a reader's attention to certain information and enhance the newsletter design.

Characteristics of Desktop Publishing

You can create professional-looking brochures, newsletters, advertisements, reports, or any other marketing, promotional, or printed documents with desktop publishing. **Desktop publishing** is the production of commercial-quality, printed material using a desktop computer system from which you can enter and edit text, create graphics, compose or lay out pages, and print documents. The following characteristics are commonly associated with desktop publishing:

- **High-quality printing.** A laser printer or high-resolution inkjet printer produces high-quality final output.
- **Multiple fonts.** Two or three font types and sizes provide visual interest, guide the reader through the text, and convey a mood.

- **Graphics**. Graphics, such as horizontal or vertical lines, boxes, electronic art, and digitized photographs help illustrate a concept or product, draw a reader's attention to the document, and make the text visually appealing.
- **Typographic characters and symbols**. Typographic characters and symbols make text more professional-looking and readable. Examples of typographic characters and symbols include long dashes, called **em dashes** (—), in place of double hyphens (--) to separate dependent clauses; typographic medium-width dashes, called **en dashes** (–), to replace hyphens (-) as minus signs and in ranges of numbers; and typographic bullets (●), to signal items in a list.
- **Columns and other formatting features**. Columns of text, pull quotes, borders, shading, and other special formatting features that you don't frequently see in letters and other documents distinguish desktop-published documents.

You'll incorporate most of these desktop-publishing features into the FastFad newsletter for Gerrit.

Elements of a Newsletter

Successful desktop publishing requires that you first know what elements professionals use to desktop publish a document. Figure 6-1 defines the desktop-publishing elements that you have not yet used.

Figure 6-1
Desktop publishing elements

Element	Description
Borders	Lines around a page(s) or paragraph(s)
Clip art	Prepared graphic images that are ready to be inserted into a document
Columns	Two or more vertical blocks of text that fit on one page
Drop cap	Oversized first letter of a word beginning a paragraph
Fill	Gray or colored backgrounds of pages or paragraphs
Graphics boxes	A box that contains a graphic image, such as a picture, TextArt, or graph
Pull quote	Phrase or quotation from text that is set in a larger size within borders
Rules	Vertical or horizontal lines
TextArt	Text modified with special effects, such as rotated, curved, bent, shadowed, or shaded letters
Typographic symbols	Special characters that are not part of the standard keyboard, such as em dashes (—), copyright symbol (©), or curly quotes (")

Gerrit wants you to incorporate these elements to produce the final copy of the newsletter, as shown in Figure 6-2. The newsletter includes some typical desktop-publishing elements that you can add to a document using WordPerfect.

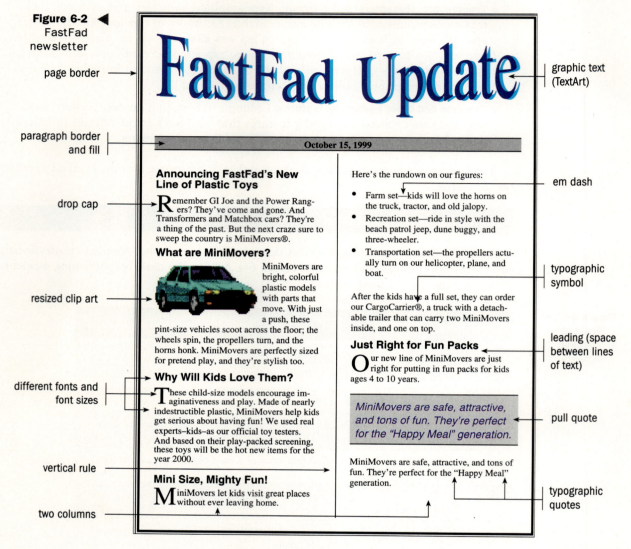

Figure 6-2 ◀ FastFad newsletter

Gerrit gives you the copy for the newsletter (a description of the new MiniMovers) on disk. You will begin by creating the title for the newsletter.

Using TextArt to Create a Title

Gerrit wants the title of the newsletter, *FastFad Update*, to be eye-catching and dramatic, as shown in Figure 6-2. WordPerfect's **TextArt feature** provides great flexibility in designing text with special effects that express the image or mood you want to convey in your printed documents. You can apply color and shading, as well as alter the shape and size of the text. You also can curve, angle, or rotate the text.

The TextArt feature creates a graphics box that contains the graphic image—in this case, text modified with special effects. A **graphics box** is a box that separates an image from other text and that you use to resize or reposition the image, add borders and fills, and set other options.

Creating a TextArt image is a two-part process. First, you type the text you want included in the image. Then, you add whatever special effects you want. You can perform this two-part process in any order and can change the text or the special effects at any time.

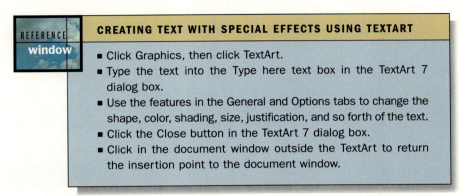

REFERENCE window

CREATING TEXT WITH SPECIAL EFFECTS USING TEXTART

- Click Graphics, then click TextArt.
- Type the text into the Type here text box in the TextArt 7 dialog box.
- Use the features in the General and Options tabs to change the shape, color, shading, size, justification, and so forth of the text.
- Click the Close button in the TextArt 7 dialog box.
- Click in the document window outside the TextArt to return the insertion point to the document window.

To begin, you'll open the file that contains the newsletter copy. Then, you'll use TextArt to create the title of Gerrit's newsletter. He wants the title in Times New Roman.

To create the title of the newsletter:

1. Start WordPerfect, if necessary, and conduct a quick screen check. For this tutorial, close the Ruler so you can see more text in the document window.

2. Open **MiniInfo** from the **Tutorial.06** folder on your Student Disk, then save it back to the same folder as **FastFad Newsletter**.

3. Press **Ctrl + Home** twice to move the insertion point to the very beginning of the document, before any format codes. This ensures that the blank line you're about to create is not in the Heading 2 style, the same style as the first heading.

4. Press the **Enter** key to insert a new, blank line, press the ↑ key to return the insertion point to the new, blank line.

5. Click Graphics then click TextArt to open the TextArt 7 dialog box; if necessary, click the **General** tab. See Figure 6-3.

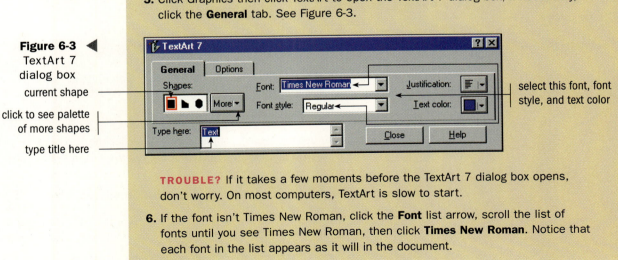

Figure 6-3
TextArt 7 dialog box
current shape
click to see palette of more shapes
type title here

select this font, font style, and text color

TROUBLE? If it takes a few moments before the TextArt 7 dialog box opens, don't worry. On most computers, TextArt is slow to start.

6. If the font isn't Times New Roman, click the **Font** list arrow, scroll the list of fonts until you see Times New Roman, then click **Times New Roman**. Notice that each font in the list appears as it will in the document.

7. Select the word **Text** in the Type here text box, then type **FastFad Update**. The word "Text" is replaced by the title of the newsletter.

   TROUBLE? If you typed "Fast Fad" (two words) instead of "FastFad" (one word), delete the space between the two words.

   TROUBLE? If you accidentally click in the document window and return to the document window, double-click the TextArt box to continue modifying the TextArt.

The newsletter title is already much larger than the text of the newsletter, so you won't change its font size. Later, if you wanted the text larger or smaller, you could resize the graphics box containing the TextArt, and the text would automatically increase or decrease in size accordingly. Instead, you'll apply special effects to the title that you created in TextArt.

Changing the Text Shape

You'll "pour" the title into a TextArt shape so it stands out from the newsletter text and draws attention. Gerrit asked you to change the shape of the text so it is straight across the bottom, rounded along the top, and has a drop shadow. A **drop shadow** is a three-dimensional effect created by adding a copy of a letter or shape in a different color slightly off center of the original letter or shape.

To change the shape and color of the TextArt text and add a drop shadow:

1. Click the **More** button next to the Shapes text box to open a palette of shapes. TextArt provides 57 shapes into which you can change your text. You'll use ⌣.

2. Click ⌣ in the top row, eight shapes from the right, as indicated in Figure 6-4. The shape appears in the Shapes box.

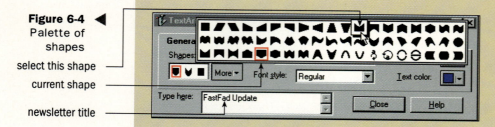

Figure 6-4 Palette of shapes
- select this shape
- current shape
- newsletter title

   TROUBLE? If your palette of shapes appears below the More button, don't worry. Just proceed to the next step.

3. Make sure the **Text color** button contains a blue tile.

   TROUBLE? If the Text color button doesn't contain a blue tile, click the Text color button, then select the blue tile near the middle of the top row of the Text color palette.

4. Click the **Options** tab to make it the frontmost tab, then click the **Shadow** button. A palette of shadow patterns opens.

5. Click the tile in the lower-right corner of the palette.

6. Click the **Shadow color** button, then click the light gray tile in the top row of colors, as shown in Figure 6-5.

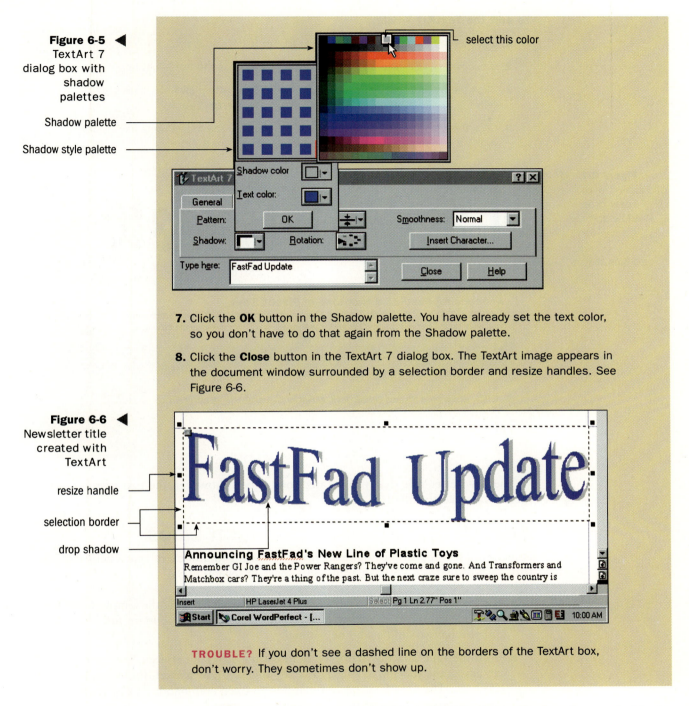

Figure 6-5
TextArt 7 dialog box with shadow palettes

Shadow palette

Shadow style palette

Figure 6-6
Newsletter title created with TextArt

resize handle

selection border

drop shadow

7. Click the **OK** button in the Shadow palette. You have already set the text color, so you don't have to do that again from the Shadow palette.

8. Click the **Close** button in the TextArt 7 dialog box. The TextArt image appears in the document window surrounded by a selection border and resize handles. See Figure 6-6.

TROUBLE? If you don't see a dashed line on the borders of the TextArt box, don't worry. They sometimes don't show up.

You have completed the design of the TextArt title. As you look at it, you decide the title would look better with more color.

Editing the TextArt Image

You can edit a TextArt image just as easily as you create an image. Just double-click anywhere in the graphics box to restart the TextArt program. After the TextArt 7 dialog box opens, you can change or remove any of the attributes already applied to the image or add new attributes.

Gerrit suggests you change the shadow color from gray to cyan (blue-green). To make this change, you need to reopen the TextArt 7 dialog box.

To edit the TextArt image:

1. Double-click the TextArt image to restart the TextArt program.

2. If necessary, click the **Options** tab to make sure it is the frontmost tab.

3. Click the **Shadow** button, click the **Shadow color** button, click the **cyan** tile, the fifth tile from the right in the top row, then click the **OK** button.

4. Click the **Close** button on the TextArt 7 dialog box. The image remains selected in the document with a cyan drop shadow. See Figure 6-7.

Figure 6-7
TextArt with new drop shadow color

cyan drop shadow

5. Click anywhere in the document window outside the graphics box to deselect the TextArt image.

6. Save the newsletter with the TextArt title.

The newsletter title that you created looks good; however, the text of the newsletter seems crammed together.

Adjusting the Space Between Lines

Sometimes, for appearance or readability, you want to add extra space between lines of text. In WordPerfect, you can adjust this space in several ways:

- Add an extra hard return between the paragraphs. This is the simplest but least efficient method of adding space. You can add only one or more *full* blank lines and you have to add each line manually.

- From the Line Spacing dialog box, adjust the spacing between lines of text. You can adjust the spacing to single (1.0), double (2.0), or partial (for example, 1.1 or 1.5) lines. The Line Spacing command is an open command; that is, it affects the entire document (or part of the document) at once.

- From the Paragraph Format dialog box, increase (or decrease) the space between paragraphs but not the space between lines within a paragraph. You can set the paragraph spacing to an even number of full lines (for example, 2.0) or to partial lines (for example, 1.2 or 1.4).

- Use the Advance typesetting command to insert any specified amount of space, vertically or horizontally, relative to the current location of the insertion point or relative to the top of the page. You'll see how the Advance command works in the steps below.

- Adjust the leading between lines of text. **Leading** (which rhymes with "wedding") is a typesetter's term for the space between the bottom of one line of text and the top of the next line of text. You'll also see how to adjust the leading in the steps below.

As you look at the newsletter, you can see that the headings (formatted in the Heading 2 style) are not sufficiently set apart from the rest of the text. The document would be more attractive and readable if more space appeared before and after each heading. You could manually insert a full blank line before and after each heading. However, this would be time-consuming, and you want only partial lines before and after the headings.

You'll use the Advance command to add 0.08" vertical space (about a half line) before each heading, and use the Leading command to add 0.03" of vertical space below each heading. You can change all Heading 2 paragraphs at once from the Styles Editor dialog box.

To adjust space with the Advance and Leading commands:

1. Click **Format**, then click **Styles** to open the Style List dialog box, click **Heading 2**, then click the **Edit** button. The Styles Editor dialog box opens.

2. Click **Format**, point to **Typesetting**, then click **Advance** on the dialog box menu bar. The Advance dialog box opens. See Figure 6-8.

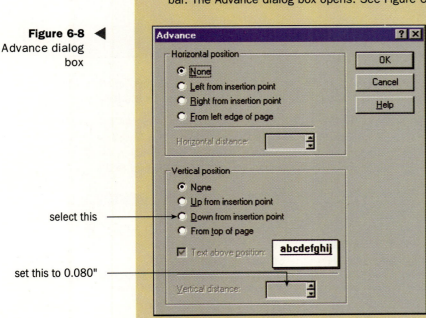

Figure 6-8
Advance dialog box

select this

set this to 0.080"

You want to increase the vertical distance from the insertion point to the location of the heading text.

3. In the Vertical position section of the dialog box, click the **Down from insertion point** radio button, then change the **Vertical distance** text box value from its current value (probably 0.001") to **0.080"**. This will insert 0.08" before each heading.

4. Click the **OK** button in the Advance dialog box to return to the Styles Editor dialog box.

Now you want to adjust the leading so more space appears after each heading.

5. Click **Format**, point to **Typesetting**, then click **Word/Letter Spacing** to open the Word/Letter Spacing dialog box. See Figure 6-9.

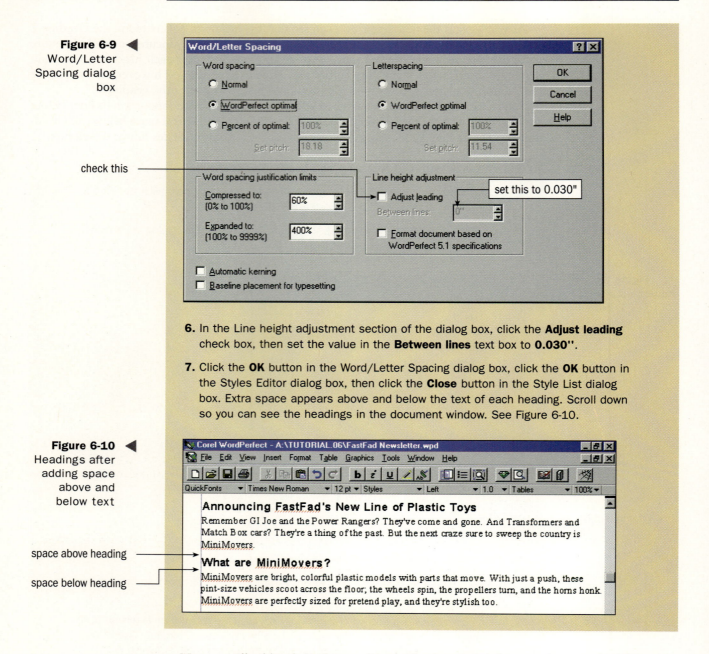

Figure 6-9
Word/Letter Spacing dialog box

check this

Figure 6-10
Headings after adding space above and below text

space above heading

space below heading

6. In the Line height adjustment section of the dialog box, click the **Adjust leading** check box, then set the value in the **Between lines** text box to **0.030"**.

7. Click the **OK** button in the Word/Letter Spacing dialog box, click the **OK** button in the Styles Editor dialog box, then click the **Close** button in the Style List dialog box. Extra space appears above and below the text of each heading. Scroll down so you can see the headings in the document window. See Figure 6-10.

Next, you'll add today's date to the newsletter, center it between lines, and add shading.

Inserting Rules and Fills

The design of the newsletter calls for the date to be centered between the margins, with lines above and below it, and with the background between the lines shaded gray. In desktop publishing, any vertical or horizontal line is called a **rule**. A shaded region (such as a paragraph or a graphics box) is called a **fill**.

To enter the centered date with rules and fill:

1. Position the insertion point in the blank line immediately below the TextArt title, press the **Enter** key to add another blank line, then press the ↑ key to return to the top blank line. This will leave a blank line below the date.

2. Press **Shift + F7** to center the insertion point between the left and right margins, then press **Ctrl + B** to turn on boldfacing.

3. Press **Ctrl** + **D** to insert the current date, which appears bold and centered between the margins. You're ready to add borders around the date and fill the borders with a 20% gray shading.

4. Click **Format**, point to **Border/Fill** then click **Paragraph**. The Paragraph Border/Fill dialog box opens. If necessary, click the **Border** tab.

5. Make sure the **Apply border to current paragraph only** check box is checked, then click the **Thin Top/Bottom** tile in the second row, third from the left in the Available border styles palette.

6. Click the **Fill** tab, click the **20% Fill** tile fourth from the left in the top row of the Available fill styles, then click the **OK** button.

7. Press the ↓ key to move down one line. See Figure 6-11.

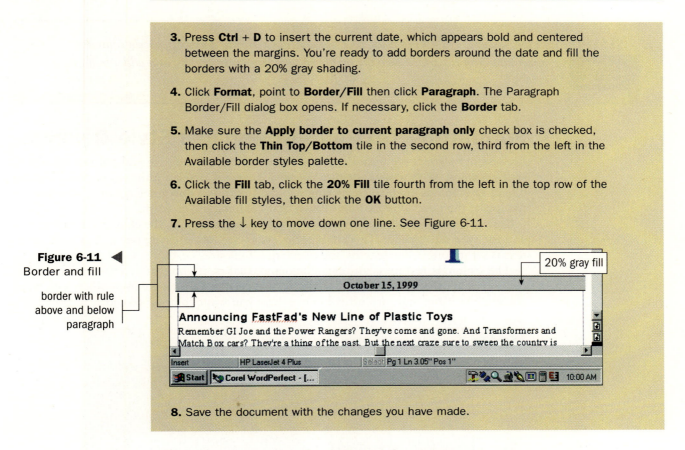

Figure 6-11
Border and fill

border with rule above and below paragraph

8. Save the document with the changes you have made.

You have set up the title of the newsletter and added the date. Next, you'll format the text of the newsletter, add clipart, and insert other desktop-publishing elements.

Quick Check

1. In your own words, explain three characteristics commonly associated with desktop publishing.

2. In your own words, define the following terms:
   a. graphics box
   b. resize handle
   c. leading

3. List the two steps for creating a TextArt image in a WordPerfect document.

4. Once you have created and deselected a TextArt image, how do you edit the image?

5. List four methods for adding extra space (but not full blank lines) between lines of text.

6. What is the advantage of adjusting the leading in a style rather than in the document window?

If you aren't going to work through Session 6.2 now, you should close the document and exit WordPerfect. When you're ready to begin Session 6.2, start WordPerfect, open FastFad Newsletter, then continue with the session.

SESSION 6.2

In this session, you'll format the text of the newsletter into newspaper-style columns, insert and crop clipart, change the text wrapping, create drop caps, and add a pull quote.

Formatting Text into Newspaper-Style Columns

Because newsletters are meant for quick reading, they usually are laid out in newspaper-style columns. With **newspaper-style columns**, a page is divided into two or more vertical blocks or columns of equal or varying widths. Text flows down one column, continues at the top of the next column, flows down that column, and so forth.

Newspaper-style columns are easier to read because usually the columns are narrower and the type size smaller. This enables the eye to see more text in one glance than when text is set in longer line lengths and in a larger font size.

The Columns feature is an open command; that is, if you want some of your text in columns and other text in full-line lengths, you need to turn on columns where you want columns to begin, and turn off columns where you want columns to end.

REFERENCE window

FORMATTING TEXT INTO NEWSPAPER-STYLE COLUMNS

- Move the insertion point to where you want columns to begin.
- Click the Columns button on the Power Bar, then click the number of columns you want.

or

- Click Format, point to Columns then click Define to open the Columns dialog box.
- Set the number of columns, type of columns, and other options.
- Click the OK button.

Gerrit wants the copy (text) of the newsletter below the title and date divided into two columns.

To apply newspaper columns to the body of the newsletter:

1. Move the insertion point to the left of "Announcing...," below the date line and before the first word in the title of the first news item. You want the newsletter divided into columns from here to the end.

2. Click **View** then click **Reveal Codes** to display the format codes, move the insertion point to the left of the Auto Heading 2 code, then turn off Reveal Codes. This ensures that the column definition begins prior to the heading style definition.

3. Click **Format**, point to **Columns**, then click **Define**. The Columns dialog box opens. See Figure 6-12.

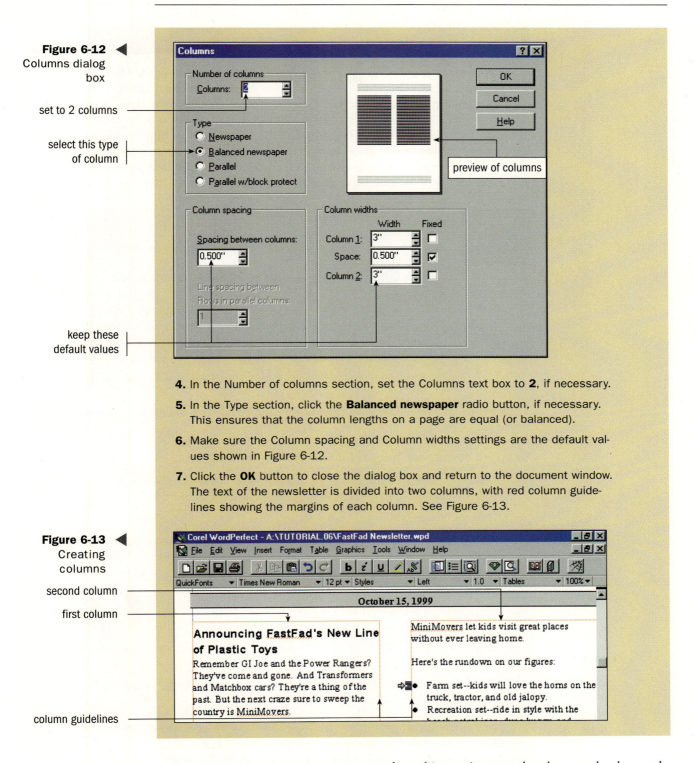

Figure 6-12 Columns dialog box

set to 2 columns

select this type of column

preview of columns

keep these default values

Figure 6-13 Creating columns

second column

first column

column guidelines

4. In the Number of columns section, set the Columns text box to **2**, if necessary.

5. In the Type section, click the **Balanced newspaper** radio button, if necessary. This ensures that the column lengths on a page are equal (or balanced).

6. Make sure the Column spacing and Column widths settings are the default values shown in Figure 6-12.

7. Click the **OK** button to close the dialog box and return to the document window. The text of the newsletter is divided into two columns, with red column guidelines showing the margins of each column. See Figure 6-13.

Most newsletters contain some sort of graphic or picture to break up and enhance the text. Gerrit thinks you should add a graphic to make the newsletter more eye-catching. Now that the copy is formatted into columns, you'll add a clip-art image to the newsletter.

Inserting WordPerfect Clipart

Graphics—which can include artwork, photographs, charts, diagrams, or even designed text like TextArt—add variety and are especially appropriate for newsletters. With WordPerfect, you can include many types of graphics in your documents. You can create a graphic in another Windows program, copy it to the Clipboard, and then paste the graphic into your WordPerfect document. Or you can insert an existing image into your document.

Inserting an Existing Image

In this newsletter, you'll insert a picture of a car that resembles one of the MiniMovers designs. The picture is a file in the WordPerfect collection of **clip-art images**, existing artwork that you can insert into your document. The Graphics folder contains two types of graphics files: bitmap images and WordPerfect graphics. **Bitmap images**, which use the filename extension .bmp, are pictures or drawings made up of little points (bits) of different colors or different shades of gray. **WordPerfect graphics**, which use the filename extension .wpg, is a special file format used in WordPerfect and related Corel products. You can insert either BMP images or WPG graphics, or a file with other graphic formats, into your WordPerfect document.

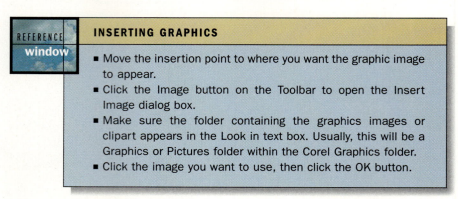

REFERENCE window

INSERTING GRAPHICS

- Move the insertion point to where you want the graphic image to appear.
- Click the Image button on the Toolbar to open the Insert Image dialog box.
- Make sure the folder containing the graphics images or clipart appears in the Look in text box. Usually, this will be a Graphics or Pictures folder within the Corel Graphics folder.
- Click the image you want to use, then click the OK button.

You'll insert the clipart with the car into the paragraph below the second main heading in the copy.

To insert the clip-art image of a car into the newsletter:

1. Move the insertion point to the left of the phrase "MiniMovers are bright, colorful plastic models..." in the second paragraph of the newsletter.
2. Click the **Image** button on the Toolbar. The Insert Image dialog box opens.
3. Make sure the Look in list box shows the **Graphics** folder. The path to this folder might be "c:\Corel\Office 7\Graphics. Double-click the **Pictures** folder, then double-click the **Commodit** folder. This folder contains a set of "commodity" clipart; that is, images of family and household products.

   TROUBLE? If your computer doesn't have the Commodit folder, click any clip-art image you choose from the Graphics folder, then skip to Step 5.

4. Click **Car** to select the image of a family car. This is a bitmap image, as indicated in the Insert Image dialog box.
5. Click the **Insert** button to insert the car image into the newsletter at the insertion point. See Figure 6-14.

Figure 6-14 ◀
Graphics image in newsletter

Edit Box QuickSpot

resize handle

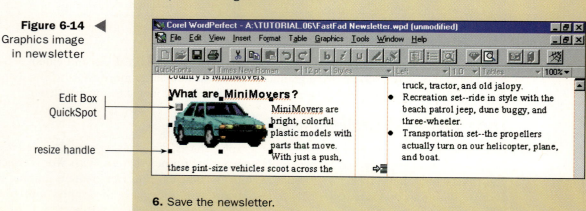

6. Save the newsletter.

Although the graphic fits nicely within the newsletter column, it would be more attractive if it were slightly larger.

Sizing an Image

Often, you need to change the size of a graphic so it fits into your document better. You might want to make it either larger and more dominant or smaller and less dominant.

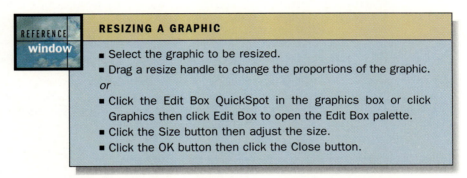

RESIZING A GRAPHIC

- Select the graphic to be resized.
- Drag a resize handle to change the proportions of the graphic.

or

- Click the Edit Box QuickSpot in the graphics box or click Graphics then click Edit Box to open the Edit Box palette.
- Click the Size button then adjust the size.
- Click the OK button then click the Close button.

You decide to enlarge the car image to attract more attention.

To resize the image of the car:

1. If necessary, click the car to select it. The resize handles appear around the graphics box.

2. Click the **Edit Box** QuickSpot (the little gray button in the upper-left corner of the graphics box) to open the Edit Box palette. See Figure 6-15.

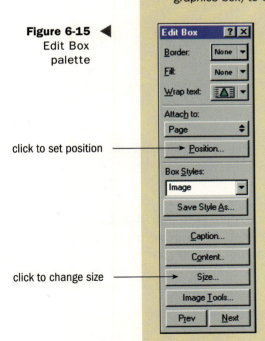

Figure 6-15 ◄
Edit Box palette

click to set position

click to change size

TROUBLE? If the QuickSpot doesn't appear on your graphics box, click Graphics then click Edit Box to open the Edit Box palette.

3. Click the **Size** button in the Edit Box palette. The Box Size dialog box opens.

4. If necessary, click the **Set** radio button in the Width section of the dialog box, then set the width to **1.85"**.

5. Make sure the **Maintain proportions** radio button is selected in the Height section of the dialog box, then click the **OK** button. This sets the height automatically to a value proportional to the width of 1.85 inches. If you tried to set a value on your own, you might make the picture too tall or too short.

   You want the graphics box positioned at the top of the current paragraph or relative to the current paragraph rather than relative to the page.

6. Click the **Position** button in the Edit Box palette to open the Box Position dialog box, click the **Attach box to** button, then click **Paragraph**.

   Now you need to specify how you want the graphic positioned within the paragraph. For the newsletter, you want the car to appear at the left margin.

7. Click the **Horizontal from** button, click **Left Margin**, then make sure the Horizontal distance from the left margin text box is set to **0"** and the Vertical distance from the top of the paragraph text box is set to **0"**. The Box Position dialog box should look like Figure 6-16.

Figure 6-16 ◀
Box Position dialog box

attach graphics box to current paragraph

position graphics box at left margin

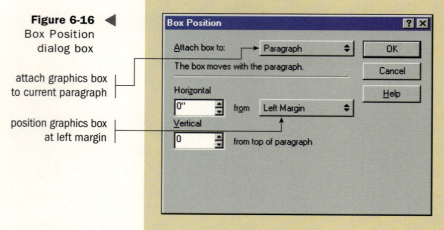

8. Click the **OK** button in the Box Position dialog box, click the **Close** button ⊠ in the Edit Box palette, then click anywhere outside the graphics box to deselect the graphic.

The car helps entice a reader to look at the beginning of the newsletter, but the rest of the text looks somewhat dull. Gerrit suggests adding a drop cap at the beginning of each section.

Inserting Drop Caps

A **drop cap** is a large, uppercase (capital) letter that highlights the beginning of the text of a newsletter, chapter, or some other document section. The drop cap usually extends from the top of the first line of the paragraph into two or more succeeding lines of the paragraph. The remaining text of the paragraph wraps around the drop cap. WordPerfect allows you to create a drop cap for the first letter, first several letters, or first word of a paragraph.

REFERENCE window	**INSERTING DROP CAPS**
	▪ Move the insertion point into the paragraph for which you want to create a drop cap.
	▪ Click Format then click Drop Cap to insert a drop cap and open the Drop Cap palette.
	▪ Using the Drop Cap palette, set the size, font, position, and other options.
	▪ Click the Close button.

Drop caps will help brighten the rest of the newsletter text. You will create a drop cap for the first paragraph following each heading in the newsletter (except for the second heading, where the clip-art image is located). The drop cap will extend two lines into the paragraph.

To insert drop caps in the newsletter:

1. Move the insertion point into the first paragraph of the document, following the heading, "Announcing FastFad's New Line of Plastic Toys."

2. Click **Format** then click **Drop Cap**. WordPerfect creates a drop cap for the first letter in the paragraph and opens the Drop Cap palette. You decide to extend the drop cap for two lines, not three, because most of the paragraphs are somewhat short and could be overwhelmed by a larger drop cap.

3. Click the **Size** button on the Drop Cap palette, then click **2 Lines High**. The drop cap becomes two lines high. See Figure 6-17.

Figure 6-17
Drop cap in first paragraph

two-line high drop cap

4. Place the insertion point in the first paragraph following the heading "Why Will Kids Love Them," then click the **Type** button (with the QuickTip "Select a pre-defined drop capital") on the Drop Cap palette, then click the two-line high drop cap icon, located in the lower-left corner of the palette.

5. Repeat Step 4 for the paragraphs after the other two headings.

A drop cap appears beneath each heading except the second heading, which would look too busy with both a drop cap and a graphic. The newsletter looks more lively with the drop caps, but the graphic at the top of the newsletter makes the columns seem unbalanced. Gerrit suggests adding a pull quote near the bottom of column two to balance the columns better.

Inserting a Pull Quote

Newsletters often contain pull quotes to draw attention to the text in one part of the article. A **pull quote** is a phrase or quotation taken from the text that summarizes a key point. It is set off from the rest of the text by special formatting, such as a larger point size, border, and fill. In WordPerfect, you set up a pull quote in a text box. A **text box**, similar to a graphics box, is a box that separates any text within the box from other text in the document and to which you can add borders, fills, and other options. You resize a text box for a pull quote just as you do a graphics box, by dragging the resize handles or specifying the exact width and height measurement on the Edit Box palette.

Gerrit thinks that the last paragraph in the newsletter really sums up the idea of MiniMovers and is perfect to emphasize in a pull quote. First, you'll copy the text from the article into the Clipboard, then you'll create an empty text box and paste the text into it.

To insert a text box for the pull quote:

1. Scroll down so you can see the last paragraph of the newsletter in column 2 ("MiniMovers are safe...generation."), then select that paragraph (including the period).

2. Click the **Copy** button on the Toolbar. A copy of the paragraph is saved to the Clipboard. Now, you're ready to insert the text box.

3. Move the insertion point to the beginning of that same paragraph, then click **Graphics** and click **Text Box**. WordPerfect inserts a text box with thick border lines at the top and bottom.

4. With the insertion point in the text box, click the **Paste** button on the Toolbar. A copy of the paragraph is inserted into the text box. See Figure 6-18.

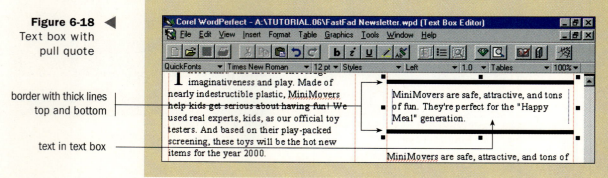

Figure 6-18
Text box with pull quote

border with thick lines top and bottom

text in text box

The text box containing the pull quote is positioned properly and appears prominently, but the text within the box doesn't stand out enough.

Formatting the Text in a Text Box

You can format text in a text box just as you would format any other text. You can select the text character by character to apply a format to just a portion of the contents of the text box. Or you can select the text box and apply a format to the entire contents of the box. For the newsletter, you'll format the entire pull quote in the text box at once.

You think that changing the font type, style, size, and color of the pull quote will more clearly distinguish it from the rest of the text in the newsletter.

To format the text in the text box:

1. If the insertion point is not in the text box, *right*-click anywhere in the text box, then click **Edit Text**.

2. Select all the text within the text box, click **Format** then click **Font** to open the Font dialog box.

3. Click **Arial** in the Font face list box, click **14** in the Font size list box, then click the **Italic** check box in the Appearance section.

4. Click the **Text color** button to open the Text color palette, then click the blue tile in the top row, seventh from the right.

5. Click the **OK** button to apply the font format to the pull quote.

6. Deselect the text and text box by clicking anywhere outside the text box in the document window. See Figure 6-19.

Figure 6-19
Formatted pull quote text

14-point, blue, italic Arial

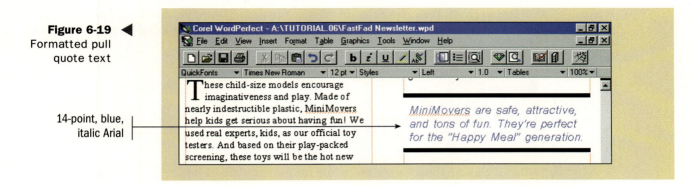

The text in the box becomes 14-point, blue, italic Arial. If you print the newsletter with a color printer, the pull quote and the TextArt title will be blue. On a black-and-white printer, the blue will print as dark gray or black.

Editing a Text Box

Once you have created a graphic or text box, you can easily edit it by clicking anywhere in the box. You decide to edit the text box because you want to change the top and bottom borders of the text box to thin lines and the fill to 10% gray.

To change the borders of the text box:

1. Click anywhere in the text box to select it. The pointer becomes ✥. You could drag the box to another location in the document, resize it, or make other changes. You'll change the border lines.

2. Click the **Edit Box** QuickSpot in the upper-left corner of the text box. The Edit Box palette opens.

    TROUBLE? If you don't see the QuickSpot, right-click the text box, then click Edit Box to open the Edit Box palette.

3. Click the **Border** button to open a palette of borders, then select the icon with the thin lines top and bottom, on the second row, fourth from the left.

4. Click the **Fill** button in the Edit Box palette, then click the **10%** tile, in the top row, third from the left.

5. Click the **Close** button ☒ in the Edit Box palette, then deselect the text box. See Figure 6-20.

Figure 6-20
Modified text box

thin border lines

10% gray fill

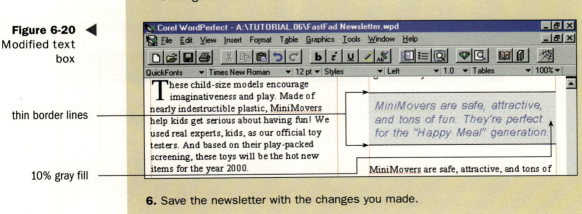

6. Save the newsletter with the changes you made.

You have put the text of the newsletter into newspaper-style columns, inserted clipart, created drop caps, and added a pull quote. Now, you're ready to make final changes to the newsletter and print it.

Quick Check

1. Define the following in your own words:
   a. newspaper-style columns
   b. text box

2. What is clipart? Describe the procedure for inserting clipart into a WordPerfect document.

3. What happens when you click the QuickSpot in a graphics box or a text box?

4. What are the two methods for changing the size of a graphics box or a text box?

5. Define drop cap in your own words, then describe the procedure for creating one.

6. What is a pull quote and what is its purpose?

7. Describe the procedure for changing the border or fill of a text box.

If you aren't going to work through Session 6.3 now, you should close the newsletter and exit WordPerfect. When you're ready to begin Session 6.3, start WordPerfect, open FastFad Newsletter, then continue with the session.

SESSION 6.3

In this session you will insert typographic symbols and special characters, hyphenate the text, place a border around the newsletter, draw a vertical line between the columns, and print the newsletter.

Inserting Symbols and Special Characters

Gerrit and the other FastFad employees who wrote copy for the newsletter used standard word-processing characters rather than typographic symbols. For example, they used two hyphens instead of em dashes and straight quotes instead of curly quotes, and they didn't insert the registered trademark symbol where appropriate. Typographic symbols and special characters make text read smoother and documents look more professional.

QuickCorrect will convert some standard word-processing characters into typographical characters automatically as you type them, such as quotation marks and em dashes. Figure 6-21 lists some of the characters that WordPerfect converts to symbols automatically.

Figure 6-21 ◀
Common symbols converted by QuickCorrect

To Insert This	Type	WordPerfect Converts It To
Em dash	- - (two hyphens)	—
Quotation marks	" "	" "
Copyright symbol	(c	©
Registered trademark	(r	®
Fraction	1/2	½

In addition, you can insert all the symbols, special characters, and picture symbols (called **Wingdings**) available in WordPerfect from the WordPerfect Characters dialog box.

To make the newsletter look professionally formatted, you'll insert special characters—namely, registered trademark symbols, typographic quotation marks, and em dashes—at the appropriate places.

REFERENCE window	INSERTING SYMBOLS AND SPECIAL CHARACTERS
	■ Move the insertion point to where you want a particular symbol or special character. ■ Click Insert then click Character to open the WordPerfect Characters dialog box. ■ Select the appropriate Character Set then click a symbol from the Characters list box. ■ Click the Insert and Close button.

FastFad protects the names of its products by registering the name as a trademark. You'll indicate that in the newsletter by inserting the registered trademark symbol (®) at the first occurrence of the trademark names "MiniMovers" and "CargoCarrier."

To insert the registered trademark symbol:

1. Move the insertion point after the word "MiniMovers" in the first paragraph, but before the period.

2. Click **Insert** then click **Character** to open the WordPerfect Characters dialog box.

3. Click the **Character Set** button, then click **Typographic Symbols**.

4. Scroll the Characters list box until you see the registered trademark symbol, then click (®). See Figure 6-22.

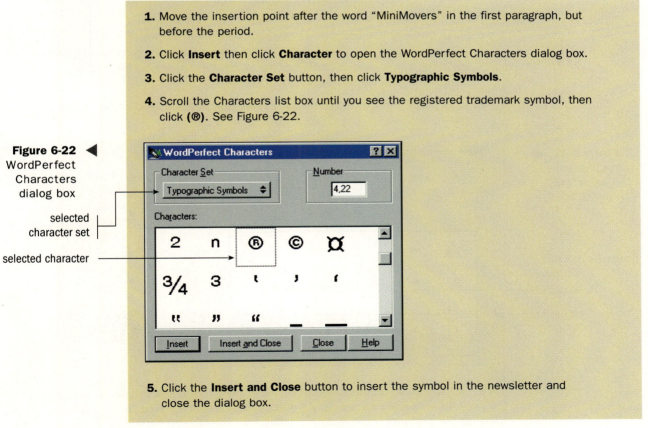

Figure 6-22
WordPerfect Characters dialog box

selected character set

selected character

5. Click the **Insert and Close** button to insert the symbol in the newsletter and close the dialog box.

You could insert the registered trademark symbol following the word CargoCarrier in the same way, but it is usually easier just to type a set of characters that WordPerfect will convert to the symbol than to open a dialog box.

To insert the registered trademark symbol by typing:

1. Move the insertion point after the word "CargoCarrier" in the paragraph just above the "Just Right for Fun Packs" heading in the second column.

2. Press the **spacebar**, type **(** (open parenthesis) then type **r**. You inserted a space because WordPerfect automatically replaces "(r" only if it is a separate word with spaces around it.

3. Press the **spacebar**. WordPerfect automatically converts the characters into (®).

4. Delete the spaces before and after the symbol.

As you look through the newsletter, you see that all the em dashes in the document actually appear as double hyphens (--). Instead of changing each set individually to typographic em dashes (—) using the WordPerfect Characters command, it's quicker to search the newsletter for each occurrence of double hyphens and then replace them with em dashes. You can do this with the Find and Replace command.

To replace hyphens with em dashes:

1. Move the insertion point to the beginning of the newsletter.

2. Click **Edit** then click **Find and Replace** to open the Find and Replace Text dialog box.

3. In the Find text box type -- (two hyphens), then press the **Tab** key to move to the Replace with text box.

4. Press **Ctrl + W** (the shortcut key combination to open the WordPerfect Characters dialog box). You cannot use the Insert Characters command to open the dialog box because WordPerfect would insert the character into your document rather than into the Replace with text box.

5. Make sure Character Set is still set to **Typographic Symbols**, then scroll until you see the em dash (—), and click—. See Figure 6-23.

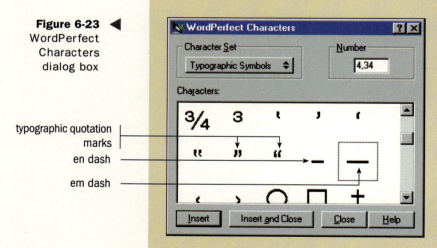

Figure 6-23
WordPerfect Characters dialog box

typographic quotation marks
en dash
em dash

6. Click the **Insert and Close** button in the WordPerfect Characters dialog box, then click the **Replace All** button. WordPerfect searches the newsletter and replaces all the double hyphens with em dashes.

7. Click the **Close** button in the Find and Replace Text dialog box to return to the newsletter.

As you read the newsletter again, you think the point that kids tested the product themselves should have more emphasis. Instead of separating the word "kids" with commas in the third section of the newsletter, you decide to separate the word with em dashes.

Like the registered trademark symbol, WordPerfect will convert text you type to the appropriate typographic symbol.

To type em dashes:

1. Scroll until you see the paragraph below the "Why Will Kids Love Them?" heading at the end of the first column.

2. Move the insertion point to the left of the word "kids" in the sentence, "We used real experts, kids, as our official toy testers."

3. Press the **Backspace** key twice to delete the space and the comma, type -- (double hyphen), then press the **spacebar**. The hyphens automatically convert to an em dash.

   TROUBLE? If the double hyphens don't change to an em dash after you press the spacebar, click Tools, click QuickCorrect, type two hyphens in the Replace text box, press the Tab key, and insert an em dash using the WordPerfect Characters dialog box into the With text box, click the Add Entry button, then click the Close button. Delete the space after the two hyphens in your document, and press the spacebar again.

4. Press the **Backspace** key to delete the extra space between the em dash and "kids."

5. Repeat Steps 3 and 4 to insert an em dash between "kids" and "as." Make sure only an em dash and no spaces appear between these words.

6. Save the newsletter with the typographic symbols.

As you look through the document, you notice that throughout the text the apostrophes and quotation marks are straight rather than "curly" typographic marks. Fortunately, WordPerfect provides a simple method for converting these characters to true typographic symbols: set QuickCorrect so single and double SmartQuotes are turned on, then perform a find and replace.

To convert the apostrophes and quotation marks to typographic symbols:

1. Move the insertion point to the beginning of the document. You want to make sure you don't miss any.

2. Click **Tools**, click **QuickCorrect**, then click the **Options** button in the QuickCorrect dialog box. If necessary, click the **turn on single quotes** check box and the **turn on double quotes** check box to check them.

3. Click the **OK** button to close the QuickCorrect Options dialog box, then click the **Close** button in the QuickCorrect dialog box. You're ready to perform the find and replace.

4. Click **Edit** then click **Find and Replace**, type ' (a straight apostrophe) in the Find text box, press the **Tab** key, type ' (another straight apostrophe) in the Replace with text box, then click the **Replace All** button. WordPerfect automatically replaces all the straight apostrophes with typographic ones. Then click the **Close** button.

5. Move the insertion point to the beginning of the document and repeat Step 4, using quotation marks ('') as the find and replace characters. All the quotation marks are true typographic symbols.

   TROUBLE? If the symbols in the pull quote didn't change, repeat Steps 4 and 5 again, except in Step 4 before you click the Replace All button, click Options, then click Include Headers, Footers, etc. in Find so WordPerfect will make the replacement in the text box.

You have changed all the standard word-processing characters in the document to typographic symbols and special characters. However, there seems to be excessively ragged text along the right margins of the newsletter.

Hyphenating a Document

Text in narrow columns often has one of two problems. If the text is full-justified, WordPerfect inserts extra space between words to stretch the lines of the text to align along the right margin, which causes unsightly **rivers**, or blank areas, in a column of text that distract the reader. If the text is left-justified, an extremely ragged right edge might occur. Figure 6-24 shows both problems.

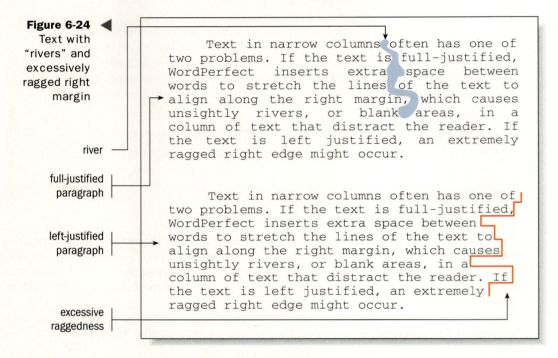

Figure 6-24
Text with "rivers" and excessively ragged right margin

river

full-justified paragraph

left-justified paragraph

excessive raggedness

Hyphenating the text sometimes eliminates these rivers or ragged edges. WordPerfect's Hyphenation feature allows you to hyphenate a document semi-automatically. WordPerfect usually decides where to divide a word, but if the hyphenation location is not in its dictionary, WordPerfect opens a dialog box from which you can accept, reject, or change the suggested hyphenation.

Before you hyphenate a document, you must specify the **hyphenation zone**, the amount of space at the right margin within which a word will be hyphenated. As shown in Figure 6-25, whenever a word in the document window begins before the left hyphenation zone and extends past the right hyphenation zone, WordPerfect tries to hyphenate the word. If a word begins after the left hyphenation zone or ends before the right hyphenation zone, WordPerfect wraps the word to the next line. The hyphenation zone is expressed in terms of a percentage of the line's width. To reduce the amount of white space inserted between words in justified text or reduce the amount of raggedness in left-aligned text, you would increase the number of hyphenated words by decreasing the size of the hyphenation zone.

HYPHENATING A DOCUMENT WP 227

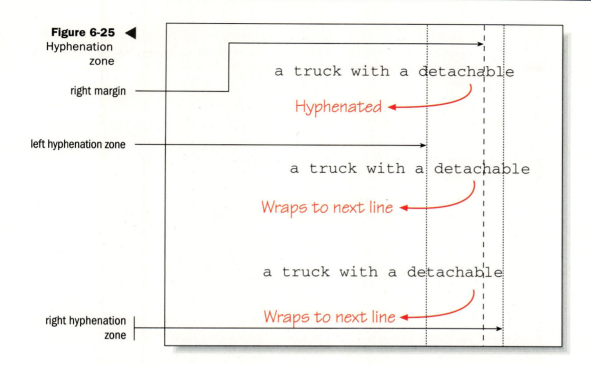

Figure 6-25
Hyphenation zone

right margin

left hyphenation zone

right hyphenation zone

Gerrit asks you to hyphenate the newsletter to eliminate the excessive raggedness on the right edge of the columns.

To hyphenate the newsletter:

1. Move the insertion point to the beginning of the document.

2. Click **Format**, point to **Line** then click **Hyphenation**. The Line Hyphenation dialog box opens.

3. In the Hyphenation zone section, set the Percent left to **8%** and the Percent right to **3%**. See Figure 6-26.

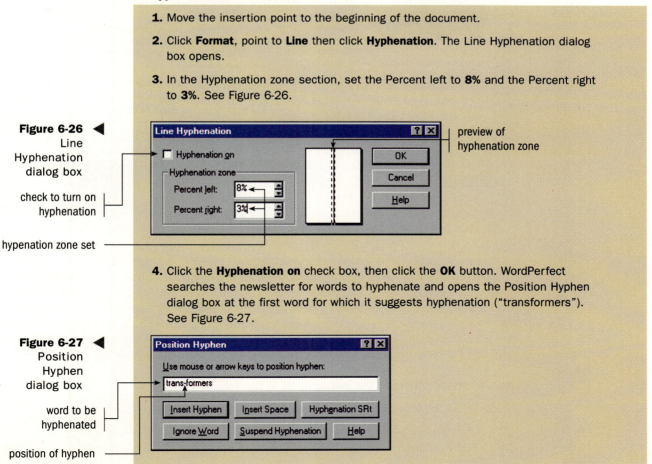

Figure 6-26
Line Hyphenation dialog box

check to turn on hyphenation

hypenation zone set

preview of hyphenation zone

4. Click the **Hyphenation on** check box, then click the **OK** button. WordPerfect searches the newsletter for words to hyphenate and opens the Position Hyphen dialog box at the first word for which it suggests hyphenation ("transformers"). See Figure 6-27.

Figure 6-27
Position Hyphen dialog box

word to be hyphenated

position of hyphen

TROUBLE? If the word in your Position Hyphen dialog box is different, don't be concerned. Because character spacing can vary slightly with different printers, the text that can fit on each line might be somewhat different. Continue with Step 6; just make the best decision you can with each word.

You can either accept WordPerfect's suggested hyphenation, move the hyphenation point to another place in the word, or choose not to hyphenate the word.

5. Click the **Insert Hyphen** button to accept the suggested hyphenation because it will improve readability. The next word with a suggested hyphen is "MiniMovers" or "three-wheeler" (or some other word).

6. If the word in the Position Hyphen dialog box is "minimovers," press the ← key until the hyphen appears after "mini," as in "mini-movers," then click the **Insert Hyphen** button. If the word is "three-wheeler," click the **Ignore Word** button to tell WordPerfect not to hyphenate the word.

TROUBLE? If WordPerfect suggests hyphenating any other word, position the hyphen where you think it should go, then click the Insert Hyphen button, or if you don't think the word should be hyphenated (for example, a short word), click the Ignore Word button.

When WordPerfect completes the hyphenation, the dialog box automatically closes.

7. Scroll through the newsletter to see the hyphens that WordPerfect inserted into words at the ends of lines. See Figure 6-28.

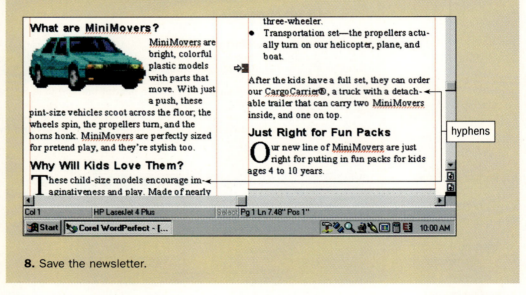

Figure 6-28 ◄
Hyphenated text

8. Save the newsletter.

The hyphenation removed the excessive raggedness along the right edges of the columns.

As you look through your newsletter, you notice a widow (isolated last line of a paragraph) that appears at the top of the second column. To fix this problem and still keep balanced newspaper-style columns, you need to add more text or space below the widow to increase the length of the second column so WordPerfect will pull the first line of the right column back to the bottom of the first column. You can solve that problem and make the bulleted list more readable by adding space between the paragraphs of the bulleted list.

To add space between the paragraphs of the bulleted list:

1. Select the text of the three paragraphs in the bulleted list in the right column.

2. Click **Format**, point to **Paragraph**, then click **Format** to open the Paragraph Format dialog box.

3. Change the Spacing between paragraphs to **1.2"** then click the **OK** button. Additional space appears between the paragraphs and the top line of the second column moves to the bottom of the first column.

    TROUBLE? If this step causes the last word of the document ("Generation") to appear on the next page, repeat steps 1 through 3, but set the spacing between paragraphs to 1.1".

The text of your newsletter is completely formatted how you want it. Now you'll add a border around the page.

Adding a Border Around the Page

Gerrit wants to give the newsletter some additional pizzazz. He suggests you add a border around the newsletter. WordPerfect has two types of borders: line borders and fancy borders. You'll use the simpler line border instead of the more decorative and graphic fancy border.

To add a border around the newsletter:

1. Move the insertion point to the beginning of the document.

2. Click **Format**, point to **Border/Fill**, then click **Page** to open the Page Border/Fill dialog box; if necessary, click the **Border** tab.

3. If necessary, click the **Border type** button, then click **Line**. You don't want a fancy graphic border but rather a simpler line border.

4. Click the **Available border styles** down scroll arrow to display the third row of styles, then click **Thin/Thick 2**, the fourth border from the left. See Figure 6-29. This is a simple but attractive border.

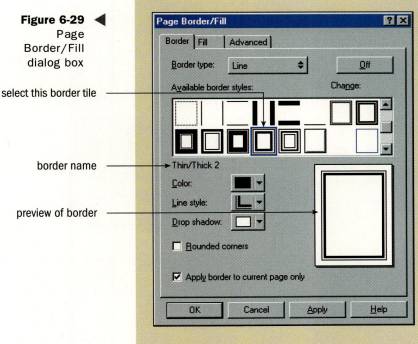

Figure 6-29 ◀ Page Border/Fill dialog box

select this border tile

border name

preview of border

5. Click the **OK** button. A border appears around the page.

The newsletter looks sharp with the line border. You'll make one more formatting change to finish the newsletter.

Inserting a Vertical Line Between Columns

As a final touch, Gerrit wants you to draw a vertical line between the columns of the newsletter. You don't want to use the Vertical Line command on the Graphics menu, because WordPerfect would insert a vertical line at the location of the insertion point. Instead, you'll create a custom line.

To insert a vertical line between columns:

1. Move the insertion point anywhere within the columns, for example, at the beginning of the paragraph below the first heading.

2. Click **Graphics** then click **Custom Line**. The Create Graphics Line dialog box opens.

3. In the Line type section, make sure the **Vertical** radio button is selected.

4. In the Position section of the dialog box, click the **Horizontal** button, then click **Column Aligned**, and make sure the After Column text box is set to **1**. This tells WordPerfect to draw a line after column 1 and before column 2.

5. Click the **Vertical** button then click **Bottom** so the line is positioned at the bottom margin.

6. In the Line options section, set the Length text box to **6.75"**. This is the approximate length of the two columns.

7. Click the **OK** button. A vertical line appears centered between the two columns.

8. Save the final version of the document, click the **Page/Zoom Full** button on the Toolbar so you can see the entire newsletter. See Figure 6-30.

Figure 6-30 ◀
Completed newsletter

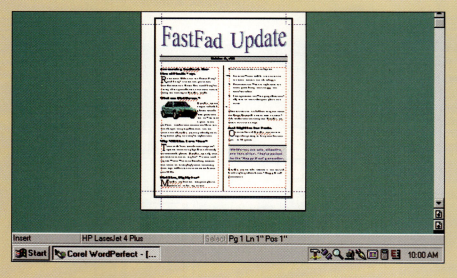

9. Click again to return to Page view, print the document, close it, then exit WordPerfect.

You give the completed newsletter to Gerrit. He thinks it looks great and thanks you for your help. He duplicates and distributes the newsletter to FastFad's marketing staff.

Quick Check

1. Describe the following in your own words:
   a. em dash
   b. rivers
   c. ragged right edge
2. What are two methods for inserting the registered trademark symbol in a document?
3. If you use text typed by someone else and it has straight quotation marks and apostrophes, what is a simple way to change them to typographic quotation marks and apostrophes?
4. What is hyphenation and when would you use it?
5. Describe the process for adding a border around a page.
6. How do you insert a vertical line between columns of text?

Tutorial Assignments

Start WordPerfect and, if necessary, conduct a screen check. Open the file FigSpecs from the TAssign folder in the Tutorial.06 folder on your Student Disk, save it as Figures Specifications, then do the following:

1. Insert a new, blank line at the top of the document, make sure the blank line has no applied style, then start TextArt.
2. Make "FastFad Figures" the TextArt text.
3. Format the TextArt with the shape second from the left in the third row, then set the font to Book Antiqua. Change the text color to red.
4. Create a gray shadow to the left and above the main text and as far from the text as possible.
5. In the Heading 2 style, which has been applied to two headings in the document, insert 0.1 inches of space above and 0.05 inches below the heading text.
6. Below the TextArt and above the heading, type "FastFad Manufacturing Company" at the left margin and insert the date at the right margin.
7. Around the paragraph with the company name and date, draw a border with thin lines on all four sides, and fill the border with 10% gray scale.
8. Format the text from the first heading ("Product Overview") to the end of the document in two "Newspaper" columns. Do *not* use "Balanced newspaper" columns.
9. Move the insertion point immediately after the second paragraph, then insert the graphic file "Winrace" from the WordPerfect clipart in the Graphics folder. Resize the image so it is one-inch wide with the proportions maintained.

10. Using the Edit Box palette, set the Position to 0 inches from the right margin and 0 inches from the top of the paragraph. If necessary, attach the graphics box to the current paragraph rather than the page.

11. Again using the Edit Box palette, draw a thin-line border around all four sides of the graphics box.
12. Format a drop cap for the first paragraph following each heading. Make the drop cap span four lines of text.
13. Cut the phrase "FastFad: We take play seriously" from the end of the document and paste it into a text box to create a pull quote.

14. Set the border for the text box to a thin red line on all four sides. Add a 10% fill to the pull quote.
15. Center, bold, and italicize the text in the pull quote.
16. Replace the double hyphens (--) with em dashes (—), and replace all straight apostrophes and quotation marks with typographic ones.
17. Insert the registered trademark symbol after the first occurrence of FastFad Sports figures.
18. Change the justification of the text in the columns to full.
19. Apply hyphenation to the appropriate words in the document using the default hyphenation zone.

20. If necessary, insert a column break to force the heading "Six Sets of Figures" to the top of the second column. (*Hint*: Move the insertion point where you want the column break and press Ctrl + Enter. Column breaks don't work the same with Balanced newspaper columns.)
21. Add the fancy border "bord12p.wpg" located in the seventh row, second from the right in the Available border styles list box.
22. Save and print the document, then close it.

Case Problems

1. City of San Antonio, Texas Blas Rodriguez is the manager of information systems for the city of San Antonio. He and his staff, along with the city manager, have decided to convert all city computers from the DOS/Windows 3.1 operating system to Windows 95 and to standardize software to Corel Office 7. Blas writes a monthly newsletter on computer operations and training, so this month he decides to devote the newsletter to the conversion to Windows 95 and Corel Office 7.

Open the document CityComp from the Cases folder in the Tutorial.06 folder on your Student Disk, save the file as Computer Newsletter and then do the following:

1. Cut the newsletter title, "Focus on Computers," and paste it into the TextArt dialog box. (*Hint*: Use the shortcut keys to paste the text.)
2. In TextArt, set the foreground text color to cyan (blue-green); include a text shadow of your choice and set its color to black; set the font to Arial bold; then set the shape of the text to the stop sign shape.

3. Set the border of the TextArt graphics box to a thin black line on all four sides. (*Hint*: Use the Edit Box palette.)
4. Below the title, center and italicize the subtitle of the newsletter.
5. Insert a rule on all four sides of the paragraph with the city name, add a 20% gray fill, then center the text.
6. Format the body of the newsletter into two balanced newspaper columns. Insert a vertical rule whose length equals the height of the columns, between the columns.

7. Using a style, format all the headings ("The Big Switch," "Training on Corel Office for Win95," and so forth, which all have a blank line above them) into 16-point Arial.
8. In the heading style, add 0.08-inch leading below the heading text, and set the heading justification to Left.
9. Insert the "Computer" clip-art image from the Graphics\Pictures\Comodit folder to the beginning of the first paragraph below the heading "Training on Corel Office for Win95."
10. Reduce the size of the graphic to one half its default size.

11. Draw a thin, single-line border around the graphics box. (*Hint*: Use the Edit Box palette.)
12. Replace all the straight double quotation marks (") and single quotation marks (') with typographic characters.
13. Replace any double hyphens with typographic em dashes.
14. Replace any hyphen in a range of numbers (that is, the meeting times for training sessions) with typographic en dashes.

15. Hyphenate the newsletter to help alleviate the rivers; use hyphenation zones of 8% left and 3% right. Don't allow hyphenation of words in headings. (*Hint*: If WordPerfect hyphenates a word in a heading, move the insertion point to the beginning of the word, click Format, click Line, click Other Codes, click the Cancel hyphenation of word radio button, then click the Insert button.)

16. Decrease the height of the TextArt title to make the newsletter fit on one page, if necessary.
17. Add a rectangular double-line border around the newsletter.
18. Save and print the newsletter, then close the file.

2. Federal Van Lines Corporation Martin Lott is the executive secretary to Whitney Kremer, director of personnel for Federal Van Lines (FVL) Corporation, a national moving company with headquarters in Minneapolis, Minnesota. Whitney assigned Martin the task of preparing the monthly newsletter *People on the Move*, which provides news about FVL employees. Although Martin and others before him have been preparing the newsletter for several years, Martin decides it's time to change the layout and wants to use WordPerfect's desktop-publishing capabilities to design the newsletter. You will use text assembled by other FVL employees for the body of the newsletter. Open the file FVLNews from the Cases folder in the Tutorial.06 folder on your Student Disk, save the file as FVL Newsletter, then do the following:

1. Change the margins to 0.75 inch on the top and bottom, 1.25 inches on the right and the left, set the Initial Font to 10-point Times New Roman, then insert a blank line at the beginning of the newsletter.
2. Create a TextArt title for the newsletter "People on the Move"; set the foreground text color to red; include a drop shadow of your choice and set its color to any shade of gray; set the font to Arial bold; and use the shape fourth from the left in the top row, on the shape palette.

3. Resize the TextArt graphics box so that it is 5 inches wide and 2 inches high.
4. Change the Wrap text of the TextArt graphics box so text appears on neither side of the graphics box, then set the graphics box position to centered between the left and right margin. (*Hint*: Use the Edit Box palette.)
5. Add two extra blank lines below the graphics box, move the insertion point up one line, then type "Volume 5 Number 11" at the left margin and "November 1999" at the right margin.
6. Insert a rule above and below the text of the issue volume and number, and set the fill to 20% gray.
7. Format the body of the newsletter into three newspaper-style columns of equal width and place a vertical rule between the columns.
8. Insert the Knight bitmap image from the Cases folder in the Tutorial.06 folder on your Student Disk at the beginning of the paragraph below the "FLV Chess Team Takes Third" heading. (*Hint*: Change the Look in text box in the Insert Image dialog box to the appropriate folder on your Student Disk.)
9. Set the width of the image to 1 inch, keeping its dimensions proportional.

10. Crop (cut off one or more edges) the chess board around the chess knight so the knight just barely fits inside the graphics box. (*Hint*: Right-click the image, open the Image Tools palette, click the Zoom button, drag the pointer over the image region you want to remain after the crop.)

11. Drag the clipart to the right side of the center column just below the heading until it overlaps into the third column. (*Hint*: Select the clipart, then drag it from the center.)
12. Copy the phrase from the first paragraph of the newsletter, "Powell was cited ... her community service," to the Clipboard.
13. Paste the text from the Clipboard into a text box between the first and second paragraph that spans the entire left column.
14. Set the pull quote font to 11-point, blue Arial, then center the text.
15. Set the fill of the pull quote to 20% gray and change the border to thick vertical lines on the left and right but no lines on the top and bottom.
16. Replace any double hyphens with typographic em dashes, and replace any apostrophes and quotation marks with the appropriate typographic symbol.

17. Full-justify the text then hyphenate the body of the newsletter with a 9% left and 4% right hyphenation zone to help alleviate rivers. Don't hyphenate any words in the headings or pull quote. (*Hint*: If WordPerfect hyphenates a word in a heading, move the insertion point to the beginning of the word, click Format, click Line, click Other Codes, click the Cancel hyphenation of word radio button, then click the Insert button.)

18. Format three-line high drop caps in red, bold, Arial in the first paragraph after each heading.
19. Decrease the height of the TextArt title until the entire newsletter fits onto one page.
20. Add a single-line border around the entire page of the newsletter, and set the fill to 20% gray.
21. Save and print the newsletter, then close the file.

3. Riverside Wellness Clinic The Riverside Wellness Clinic, located in Vicksburg, Mississippi, is a private company that contracts with small and large businesses to promote health and fitness among their employees. MaryAnne Logan, an exercise physiologist, is director of health and fitness at the clinic. As part of her job, she writes and desktop publishes a newsletter for the employees of the companies with which the clinic contracts. She's ready to prepare the newsletter for the October 1999 issue. Open Wellness from the Cases folder in the Tutorial.06 folder on your Student Disk, save the file as Wellness Newsletter, and then do the following:

1. Change the margins to 0.5 inch on the top and bottom and 0.75 inch on the left and right. Set the Initial Font to 10-point Times New Roman.
2. Create a TextArt title "To Your Health" at the beginning of the newsletter.
3. In TextArt, set the text color to green; choose any drop shadow and set its color to gray; set the font to Arial bold; set the shape to a rectangle (the first shape in the first row of the shape palette).

4. Rotate the TextArt 90 degrees counter clockwise. (*Hint*: Click the Options tab in the TextArt dialog box, then double-click the Rotations button.)
5. Resize the TextArt graphics box so its height is 5.0 inches and its width is 1.25 inches, then position it at the left and top margins. Set the Wrap text to Square/Largest Side. (*Hint*: Use the Edit Box palette to set the size, position, and wrap style.)
6. At the top of the page to the right of the title, italicize the subtitle and the line that contains the issue volume and number of the newsletter.
7. Format the body of the newsletter into two balanced newspaper-style columns with a vertical rule between the columns. (*Hint*: The columns will be uneven because the TextArt title takes up part of the first column space.)

8. Change all the headings to blue Arial, with a leading of 0.05 inch below the text. (*Hint*: Modify the Heading 2 style.)
9. Move the insertion point to the left of the first heading, then change the paragraph format so that the spacing between paragraphs is 1.2. (*Hint*: Make sure the insertion point is not within the Heading 2 style but to the left of the style code, then use the Format Paragraph dialog box to adjust the spacing.)
10. Change all the straight double quotation marks and single quotation marks to typographic symbols.
11. Change any double hyphens to typographic em dashes.

12. To help alleviate the problem of excessive raggedness along the right margin, apply hyphenation to the body of the newsletter with a hyphenation zone of 8% right and 3% left. (*Hint*: If WordPerfect hyphenates a word in a heading, move the insertion point to the beginning of the word, click Format, click Line, click Other Codes, click the Cancel hyphenation of word radio button, then click the Insert button.)
13. To the right of "NordicTrack" and "HealthRider," insert a registered trademark symbol, then change the font size of the symbol to 8 point.
14. Drag a resize handle to decrease the width of the TextArt graphics box to about 1 inch. (*Hint*: Open the Ruler.)

15. Use the Make It Fit command to fit the newsletter onto one page. Allow Make It Fit to change the top and bottom margins but not the line spacing, font size, or other margins.
16. Save and print the newsletter, then close the file.

4. Holiday Greetings Newsletter As a way of keeping in touch with family and friends, a relative suggests that you send out a holiday greetings newsletter. In the one-page newsletter, you'll include articles about you and your family or friends, recent activities, favorite hobbies, movies, books, and future plans. You'll desktop publish the copy into a professional-looking newsletter.

Open a new, blank document, then complete the following:
1. Write at least two articles to include in the newsletter; save each article in a separate file, and close the files.
2. Plan the general layout of your newsletter, then open a new document window for the newsletter.
3. Create a colorful and attractive title ("Holiday News" or some other title of your choosing) for your newsletter using WordPerfect TextArt.
4. Save the document as Holiday News, in the Cases folder in the Tutorial.05 folder on your Student Disk.
5. Insert the current date and your name as editor below the title.
6. Insert the articles you wrote into your newsletter.
7. Create (or modify an existing) style for the titles of the articles. Add spacing above the text and leading below the text of the headings.
8. Format your newsletter with multiple (2 or 3) columns.

9. Insert at least one clip-art image into your newsletter, sized and positioned appropriately.
10. Format at least two drop caps in the newsletter.
11. Create a pull quote, insert text, modify the borders, and add a fill.

12. Add a fancy border around the newsletter.
13. Set the justification to Full, then hyphenate the text to avoid rivers.
14. Save and print the newsletter, then close the file.

TUTORIAL 7

Integrating WordPerfect with Other Windows Programs

Writing a Proposal to Open a New Branch of Family Style, Inc.

OBJECTIVES

In this tutorial you will:

- Import a Microsoft Word document
- Import a WordPerfect document
- Import a scanned photograph
- Embed a spreadsheet from Corel Quattro Pro
- Embed a Chart
- Modify an embedded file
- Link a graphic image from Microsoft Paint
- Modify a linked file

CASE

Family Style, Inc.

Nalani Tui is one of the founders and owners of Family Style, Inc., a retail company with six outlets in the central and southern regions of Indiana. When she and her partners founded Family Style in 1988, their concept was simple: They would buy high-quality used home merchandise—clothing, sports equipment, appliances, furniture, televisions, personal computers, and so forth—for about 25 percent of its retail value and sell it for 80–90 percent of its current value, which still would be less than half the retail price of similar new merchandise. In each store, the sales representatives, who also were trained as purchasers, would appraise items brought to the store and, if the items were functional and in good condition, offer cash for the items.

The concept was immediately popular. Customers who have items for sale can receive immediate cash, and those who want to buy items can purchase them at very low prices. Family Style is successful because the outlets readily attract sellers and buyers, and management has kept administrative, marketing, and overhead expenses low.

Nalani thinks that Family Style is ready to expand to cities in northern Indiana. She is preparing a written proposal for the other owners and investors of Family Style on the advantages and disadvantages of opening new outlet stores. The proposal will include an overview of the company's current financial picture, the rationale for expanding, possible sites for new outlets, and Nalani's recommendations for the new branch site and manager. Nalani asks you to help prepare the proposal.

In this tutorial, you'll combine the text that Nalani has already written in WordPerfect with text, graphics, and spreadsheet files other Family Style employees prepared using different software.

In Session 7.1, you'll import both WordPerfect and Microsoft Word text into a WordPerfect document, then you'll import and position a scanned photograph into the document. In Session 7.2, you'll embed a Quattro Pro file and create a chart in Corel Presentations 7 Chart (or in WP Draw 7 Chart). Then, you'll modify the embedded graph. In Session 7.3, you'll link a Microsoft Paint file to the WordPerfect document, modify the file, and then print the proposal.

SESSION 7.1

In this session you'll see how Nalani planned the proposal, then you'll import a Microsoft Word document, import a WordPerfect document, and import and position a scanned photograph.

Planning the Document

Nalani assigned employees of Family Style to prepare different parts of the proposal. Each person gathered information and wrote a section of the proposal. Now Nalani needs to combine these sections of the proposal with the sections she has already written. Before Nalani asked you to prepare the proposal, she planned the document carefully for content, organization, style, and presentation.

Content

The main content for the proposal is text, data, and graphs showing the company's current financial state, the possible sites for new branches (retail outlets), and Nalani's recommendations for a new site and branch manager. Nalani gives you several files to combine as the proposal content: a document from a Family Style employee who uses Microsoft Word, a scanned photograph of a potential branch manager, a graphic image from an employee who uses Microsoft Paint, a Quattro Pro spreadsheet of financial data from the accounting office, and data that you'll use with Presentations 7 Chart to create a chart. Figure 7-1 shows how Nalani wants to combine these segments into a complete proposal.

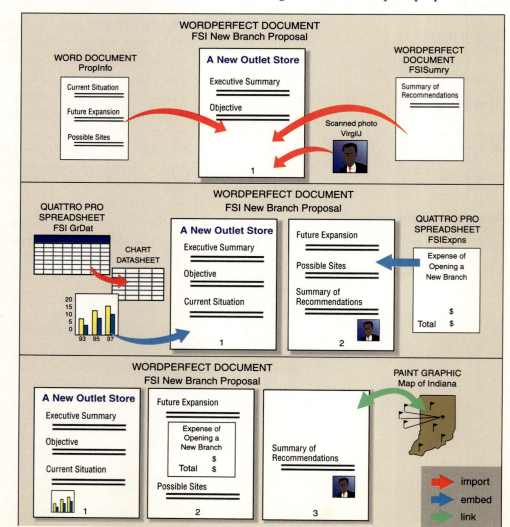

Figure 7-1 ◄
Nalani's plan for the proposal

Organization

The proposal begins with an executive summary, then reviews the company objective, explains the current situation, suggests some location options, and gives a final recommendation.

Style

The report follows established standards of business writing style, emphasizing clarity, simplicity, and directness.

Presentation

Nalani wants the format of the proposal to be simple and easy-to-read. The document will use WordPerfect's default format and system styles. Each page will include a footer with the document title and page number.

Integrating Files from Other Programs

Every software program is designed to accomplish a specific task. As you've seen with WordPerfect, with a word-processing program you can create, edit, and format documents such as letters, reports, newsletters, and proposals. For Nalani's proposal, you'll need to integrate text files from WordPerfect and Microsoft Word (another word-processing program) into Nalani's WordPerfect document.

A **spreadsheet** program calculates and analyzes numerical data using a formula. For example, Quattro Pro is a spreadsheet program that the Family Style accounting department used to prepare a breakdown of expenses involved in opening a new branch. You'll also need to create a graph for the proposal that provides a visual representation of income and profit from the Quattro Pro spreadsheet.

With a **graphics** program, you can draw or create a wide variety of graphic images, such as logos and line drawings. A Family Style employee drew a map of Indiana in Microsoft Paint—a graphics program that comes with Windows 95. You'll add this map to Nalani's proposal.

In each of these instances, you'll need to integrate an object into Nalani's document. An **object**, in WordPerfect and other Windows 95 programs, is text or graphics created in one software program and used in another. An object, for example, can be a word-processing file, a spreadsheet, a graphic image, or a chart. The program used to create the original version of the object is called the **source application** (in this case, Microsoft Word, Corel Presentations Chart, Quattro Pro, and Microsoft Paint). The program into which the object is integrated is called the **destination application** (in this case, WordPerfect). Similarly, the original file is called the **source file** and the file into which you insert it is called the **destination file**.

WordPerfect supports three methods for inserting an object from a source application into a destination application: importing, embedding, and linking. Figure 7-2 shows the differences among the three methods.

Figure 7-2
Integration techniques

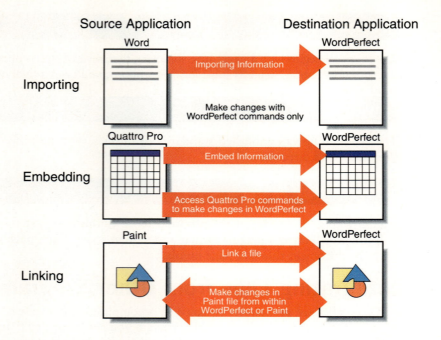

You'll need to use all three methods to complete Nalani's proposal.

Importing

Importing an object means inserting a file that you created using one program (the source application) into another program (the destination application). When you import a file, the source application and the destination application don't communicate with each other in any way. Information from the source file becomes part of the document in the destination application. If you want to edit the imported file, you use the destination application's editing tools, not those in the source application. Any changes to the imported file don't affect the original file, and vice versa.

For example, you'll import a word-processing document created in Microsoft Word into Nalani's WordPerfect document proposal. When you insert a Word document into a WordPerfect document, WordPerfect automatically reformats the text so it becomes part of the WordPerfect document. The imported text no longer retains a connection to Word. If you want to modify the text after importing it into WordPerfect, you edit it in WordPerfect, using WordPerfect commands, not Word commands. After you import the file, any changes you make to the original Word file don't appear in the imported text, and any changes you make to the imported file don't appear in the original Word file.

Embedding

Embedding is similar to importing, except that the object maintains a one-way connection from the destination application to the source application. As long as both programs are installed on your computer, you can edit the embedded object using the source application's editing tools rather than the destination application's tools. However, any changes you make to the embedded object are not made in the original file, and vice versa.

For example, you'll embed a spreadsheet file created as a Quattro Pro spreadsheet into Nalani's WordPerfect document proposal; you can double-click the spreadsheet to place the object in a Quattro Pro window and use Quattro Pro commands to edit the spreadsheet while you're still in WordPerfect. (Note that Quattro Pro must be installed on the computer you're using if you want to edit the embedded Quattro Pro spreadsheet.) Any edits you make to the embedded spreadsheet, however, appear only in WordPerfect, not in the original Quattro Pro spreadsheet file. Similarly, after you embed the file, any changes you make to the original Quattro Pro spreadsheet don't appear in the embedded spreadsheet in WordPerfect.

Linking

Linking is similar to embedding, except that the linked object maintains a two-way connection between the source application and destination application. As long as the source application is installed on your computer, you can edit a linked file. If you want to edit the linked object, you can open the source application from within the destination application and make changes that also will appear in the original file. Likewise, if you edit the original file in the source application, the changes will appear in the linked object the next time you open that file in the destination application.

For example, you'll link a map of India created as a graphic in Microsoft Paint into Nalani's WordPerfect document proposal. You can double-click the graphic in WordPerfect to open the source application (Microsoft Paint), edit the graphic in Paint, then return to WordPerfect. The changes you make to the graphic appear in both the Paint and WordPerfect files. You also can edit the graphic directly in the Paint file, and the next time you open the WordPerfect document to which the graphic is linked, the updated version of the graphic appears automatically.

Not all software programs allow you to embed or link objects. Only those programs that support **object linking and embedding** (OLE, pronounced oh-LAY) let you embed or link objects from one program to another. Fortunately, Windows 95 programs like WordPerfect, Quattro Pro, and Presentations all are OLE-enabled programs and fully support object linking and embedding. To link a file created in an OLE program, the program must be installed on your computer.

Choosing Among Importing, Embedding, and Linking

When you want to integrate information created in WordPerfect or another program (the source application) into WordPerfect (the destination application), which method should you choose—importing, embedding, or linking?

Import a file whenever you want to integrate information into WordPerfect but don't need (or don't have) access to the source application commands. For example, if you want to integrate text from another file into your WordPerfect document, you should import it because WordPerfect has all the necessary commands to edit text (you don't need the source application commands). That's why you'll import text from Microsoft Word and WordPerfect files into the proposal.

Another example is if you want to integrate a Quattro Pro spreadsheet into your WordPerfect document but Quattro Pro isn't installed on your computer. You should import the Quattro Pro file and WordPerfect will format the data as a WordPerfect table. You no longer can access Quattro Pro's sophisticated formulas, but you can change the data and formatting using WordPerfect's Table commands.

Embed a file whenever you want to maintain access to the source application commands but don't want to modify the source file. For example, if you want to integrate a Quattro Pro spreadsheet into your WordPerfect document and Quattro Pro is installed on your computer, you should embed the spreadsheet so you can access Quattro Pro commands if you ever need to modify formulas or data. The original Quattro Pro spreadsheet (the source file) remains unchanged, and you can delete it without affecting the copy embedded in your WordPerfect document.

Link a file whenever you want to maintain access to the source application commands and want to update both the source and destination files from within either WordPerfect or the source application. For example, if you want to integrate a Quattro Pro spreadsheet into your WordPerfect document and Quattro Pro is installed on your computer, you should link the spreadsheet file so you can update both the original spreadsheet and the copy in your WordPerfect document from either WordPerfect or Quattro Pro.

The advantage to linking is that the data in both the Quattro Pro spreadsheet and the WordPerfect document always reflect the latest revisions. The disadvantages to linking are that you must have access to both Quattro Pro and the linked file on your computer. If you don't want to modify the original Quattro Pro spreadsheet because it contains information and formatting you'll need later, you should embed the spreadsheet rather than link it.

Importing Files into WordPerfect

Sometimes you'll want to integrate information into your WordPerfect document from other programs, such as a document file from Microsoft Word. You also can import other WordPerfect files. The need for importing files might occur when you're working with other people on a project and need to combine everyone's files into one document. When you import a file, you import the entire file, not selected sections.

Nalani prepared the executive summary and objectives for the proposal using WordPerfect, but another Family Style employee prepared the "Current Situation," "Future Expansion," and "Possible Sites" sections using Microsoft Word. Nalani asks you to import the Word file into her original WordPerfect document. You'll begin by opening Nalani's WordPerfect document (the destination file).

To open the destination file:

1. Start WordPerfect and, if necessary, conduct a quick screen check. For this tutorial, you don't need to display the Ruler.
2. Open the file **FSIProp** from the **Tutorial.07** folder on your Student Disk.
3. Save the file to the same folder as **FSI New Branch Proposal**.
4. Read the document to get an idea of its content. The document includes only the beginning sections of the proposal.

With the WordPerfect file open, you can import the Word document.

Importing a Microsoft Word Document

Importing a Microsoft Word file into a WordPerfect document is as easy as importing a WordPerfect file into the document. This is because WordPerfect recognizes the Word file format and can quickly convert the Word codes. In fact, WordPerfect recognizes a wide variety of file formats, so you can import information from other word-processing, spreadsheet, database, and graphics programs, among other types.

In general, if you want to import information from any type of file, try using WordPerfect's Insert File command. If WordPerfect doesn't recognize the file format, you'll see an error message, and your WordPerfect document will usually be unaffected. (To be on the safe side, however, you should always save your WordPerfect document before trying to import a file.) If WordPerfect recognizes the file format, the information from the imported file will appear in WordPerfect ready either to use as is, or to edit and format as needed.

IMPORTING A FILE INTO WORDPERFECT

- Move the insertion point to the location in your destination document where you want the imported file to appear.
- Click Insert then click File to open the Insert File dialog box.
- Select the file that you want to import, click the Insert button, then click the OK button.

Having opened and saved Nalani's document, you're ready to import the Microsoft Word file.

IMPORTING FILES INTO WORDPERFECT   WP 243

To import a file from a different program:

1. Move the insertion point to the blank line at the end of the document. This is the location where you want to insert the text of the Word document.

    TROUBLE? If the document doesn't have a blank line at the end, move the insertion point to the end of the last paragraph and press the Enter key.

2. Click **Insert** then click **File** to open the Insert File dialog box.

3. Make sure the **Tutorial.07** folder is still open, then if necessary, click the **For type** list arrow, then click **All Files (*.*)** to make sure the Insert File dialog box displays all files in the folder regardless of what program they were created in. See Figure 7-3.

Figure 7-3 ◀
Insert File dialog box

all files displayed

Word file to be inserted

4. Click **PropInfo** (the Word filename, which is short for Proposal Information) in the list of files, then click the **Insert** button. WordPerfect recognizes the file that you're importing as a Word document, so it opens the Convert File Format dialog box with "MS Word for Windows 6.0/7.0" in the Convert file format from list box.

5. Click the **OK** button. WordPerfect inserts the text into the WordPerfect document, and converts the text into WordPerfect format.

    TROUBLE? If you can't find the filename PropInfo, use the file that appears with the filename propinfo or propinfo.doc.

The text from the Word file is integrated into the WordPerfect document as if you had typed it into WordPerfect instead of importing it from Word. The original Word file remains unchanged on the disk.

As you scroll through the imported text, you notice that the headings don't have the same spacing and that bullets would help distinguish the three possible sites for the new branch.

Formatting the Imported Text

You can format imported text exactly the same way as text entered directly into WordPerfect. You can use all WordPerfect's editing and formatting tools, including system styles, to make the imported text read and look exactly like you want it to.

In Nalani's proposal, the imported text needs some minor formatting. You will format a group of short paragraphs describing the three potential sites as a bulleted list and then you'll reformat the headings using WordPerfect's system styles.

To format the imported text:

1. Just above the final paragraph of the document, select the three short lines of text that begin "State Fair Shopping Center in Kokomo" and end with "Boilermaker Shopping Center in West Lafayette." See Figure 7-4.

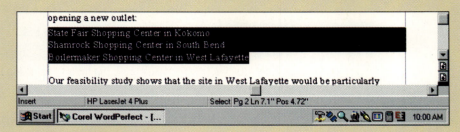

Figure 7-4
Selected text for bulleted list

TROUBLE? If you haven't selected text exactly as shown in Figure 7-4 but have selected at least one character in each line, then continue with Step 2. If you haven't selected at least one character in each line of text, click outside the selected area and try again.

2. Click the **Insert Bullets** button 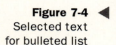 on the Formatting Toolbar to create a bulleted list. A bullet appears before each of the three lines, and the text in the list indents.

TROUBLE? If numbers appear rather than bullets, or if small dots appear for the bullets, make sure the text is still selected, click Insert, click Bullets & Numbers, click Large Circle, then click the OK button.

The headings you imported from Word appear in the same font as the current Heading 2 style (bold, 14-point Arial), but they lack some of the formatting features, such as the space before the heading. You'll format the three Word headings using the Heading 2 style to match the other headings in the proposal.

3. If necessary, scroll up until you see the heading "Possible Sites," then move the insertion point to the left of that heading.

4. Turn on Reveal Codes and delete *all* the formatting codes (there are many), except HRt and SRt, on the same line as the heading and on the next line, then delete the blank line above the heading. The heading should now appear in normal, 12-point Times New Roman font, without spacing above or below.

5. With the insertion point in the same line as the now unformatted heading, click the **Styles** button [Styles] on the Power Bar, then click **Heading 2** to apply the Heading 2 style to "Possible Sites." The heading is reformatted.

6. Repeat Steps 4 and 5 for the headings "Future Expansion" and "Current Situation" located near the beginning of the proposal.

7. Turn off Reveal Codes.

The imported text is formatted appropriately. As you scan the proposal, you realize that Nalani didn't include the summary in the file.

Importing One WordPerfect Document into Another

Nalani explains that she was writing the summary as you were integrating the Word file into the proposal and formatting it. She has written the summary as another WordPerfect file. You could just open the new file and cut and paste the text between the open document windows, but it is easier to import the WordPerfect file into the proposal document. You import WordPerfect files just as you do any other file type.

To import one WordPerfect document into another:

1. Move the insertion point to the blank line at the end of the proposal. This is the location where you want to import the new WordPerfect text.

2. Click **Insert** then click **File** to open the Insert File dialog box.

3. Click **FSISumry** from the filename list of the **Tutorial.07** folder in the dialog box, then click the **Insert** button. The summary heading and paragraph appear in the proposal. See Figure 7-5.

Figure 7-5
Document window with imported text

imported text

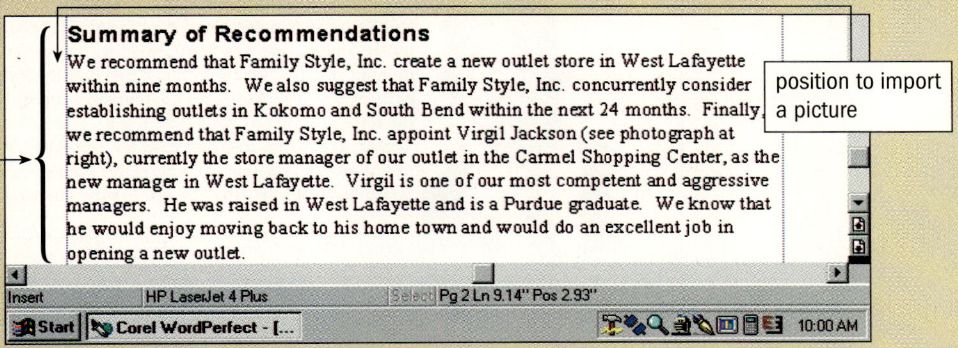

position to import a picture

4. Save the proposal with the imported text.

All the sections of the proposal are now in one WordPerfect file. The imported WordPerfect file is already formatted in the same style as the earlier sections, so you don't have to reformat it. Sometimes, two or more people working on different parts of a document will format the headings and other text differently. When they combine the files into one document, sections of the imported text need to be reformatted to ensure consistentency throughout the document, even though the entire document was created using the same word-processing program.

Importing a Picture into WordPerfect

As you read the final paragraph of the proposal, you learn that Nalani is recommending that Virgil Jackson be appointed manager of the new branch in West Lafayette. You also notice a reference to a photograph of Virgil. Nalani put the file containing the picture on the same disk as her summary. She asks you to import the scanned photograph into the proposal. A **scanned** image is a picture that was digitized using an electronic device (called a **scanner**) and saved in an electronic form as a file. In WordPerfect, a **graphic** is any type of image: a clip-art image, a drawing, or a scanned photograph. After you have a picture in a disk file, you can import and manipulate the picture in WordPerfect.

The procedure for importing a picture is always the same regardless of the type of graphic. You'll use WordPerfect's Insert Picture command to import the scanned photograph of Virgil into Nalani's proposal.

To import a picture into WordPerfect:

1. Move the insertion point to the beginning of the final paragraph in the document, just to the left of "We recommend that... ."

2. Click the **Image** button on the Toolbar to open the Insert Image dialog box. Usually, the folder that appears in the dialog box is the default Graphics folder. Because you'll insert a picture from your Student Disk, you'll change to a different folder.

3. Change the Look in list box to the **Tutorial.07** folder on your Student Disk. The dialog box displays a list of the pictures and other files in that directory.

4. Click **VirgilJ**, the file with the scanned photograph of Virgil Jackson, then click the **Insert** button. Virgil's picture is inserted at the beginning of the paragraph. See Figure 7-6.

Figure 7-6 ◀
Imported scanned image

Nalani thinks the picture would look better at the right margin (therefore, she refers to the "photograph at right" in her summary paragraph), and that its size should be reduced so it doesn't extend below the last line of the document.

Moving the Picture

When you insert a picture into WordPerfect, the picture is in a graphics box that you can reposition or resize as you want. When you insert a graphics box into a document, the text wraps around the box; although you can format the box so text doesn't wrap around it. You can also **attach** the graphics box to a page, paragraph, or characters, and then specify the box location relative to where it's attached. For example, if you want a graphics box always to appear at a particular location on a page regardless of how the text on that page changes, then attach the graphics box to the page. On the other hand, if you want a graphics box associated with a particular paragraph, attach the graphics box to that paragraph. Then, if you move that paragraph within the document, the graphics box automatically moves with it. In this case, you want to attach Virgil Jackson's picture to the paragraph that includes his name and refers to the picture. You decide to resize the picture so it is one-inch wide.

To set the attachment, position, and size of the picture:

1. Click the **Edit Box** QuickSpot in the upper-left corner of the graphics box to open the Edit Box palette.

    TROUBLE? If you can't see the QuickSpot button, right-click the picture, then click Edit Box.

2. Click the **Attach to** button, then click **Paragraph** to attach the picture to the paragraph.

3. Click the **Position** button to open the Box Position dialog box, then set the Horizontal position to **0"** from the **Right Margin**, and set the Vertical position to **0"** from the top of the paragraph. See Figure 7-7.

Figure 7-7
Box Position dialog box

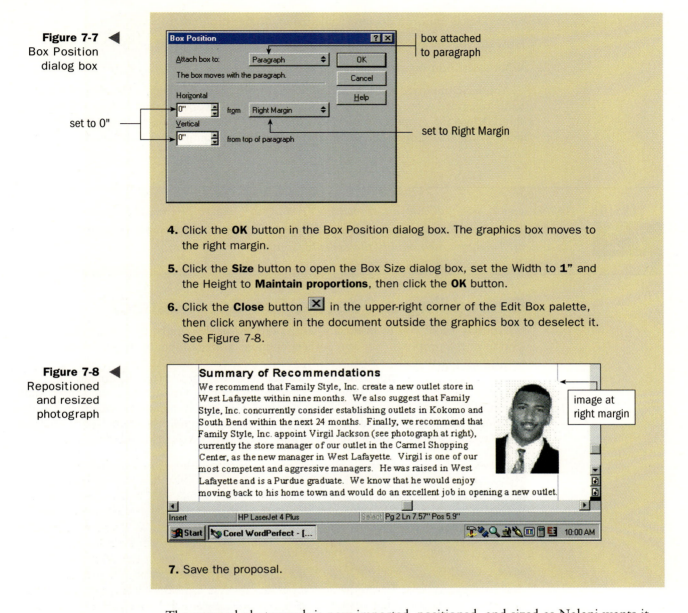

set to 0"

box attached to paragraph

set to Right Margin

4. Click the **OK** button in the Box Position dialog box. The graphics box moves to the right margin.

5. Click the **Size** button to open the Box Size dialog box, set the Width to **1"** and the Height to **Maintain proportions**, then click the **OK** button.

6. Click the **Close** button ⊠ in the upper-right corner of the Edit Box palette, then click anywhere in the document outside the graphics box to deselect it. See Figure 7-8.

Figure 7-8
Repositioned and resized photograph

image at right margin

7. Save the proposal.

The scanned photograph is now imported, positioned, and sized as Nalani wants it.

1. Define the following in your own words:
   a. object
   b. source application
   c. destination application

2. What is importing?

3. What is embedding?

4. What is linking?

5. What does OLE stand for? What does OLE-enabled program mean?

6. How do you import a document file from another program into WordPerfect?

7. How do you import a scanned picture file into WordPerfect?

8. What is the Edit Box palette?

You have imported the text and photograph that Nalani wants in the proposal and are ready to embed some other files. If you aren't going to work through Session 7.2 now, you should close the proposal and exit WordPerfect. When you're ready to begin Session 7.2, start WordPerfect, open FSI New Branch Proposal, then continue with the session.

SESSION 7.2

In this session, you will embed a spreadsheet created in Quattro Pro and a chart created in Corel Presentations 7 Chart (or in WP Draw 7 Chart) into Nalani's proposal document. Then, you will modify the embedded graph.

Embedding a Quattro Pro Spreadsheet

Nalani has asked you to insert a Quattro Pro spreadsheet into the "Future Expansion" section of the proposal. The spreadsheet contains a breakdown of the expenses incurred in opening a new outlet store.

You could simply import the spreadsheet into the WordPerfect document, but if you import a spreadsheet, it no longer has any connection to Quattro Pro, the source application. If you embed the spreadsheet, a one-way connection remains between Quattro Pro and the spreadsheet in WordPerfect. Then, if you want to edit the spreadsheet, you have access to the Quattro Pro commands as long as Quattro Pro is installed on your computer.

REFERENCE window | EMBEDDING AN EXISTING FILE

- Move the insertion point to the location in your document where you want the file to appear.
- Click Insert then click Object to open the Object dialog box.
- Click the Create from File radio button.
- Type the path of the filename or click the File folder button and select the file you want to embed, then click the OK button.

You'll embed the Quattro Pro spreadsheet into the proposal.

To embed a Quattro Pro spreadsheet:

1. Scroll up until you see the bracketed phrase "[insert spreadsheet]" a few lines above the "Possible Sites" heading.

2. Delete the phrase **[insert spreadsheet]** and the line on which it was located. The insertion point should appear on the blank line between the two paragraphs. This is where you want to embed the Quattro Pro spreadsheet.

    TROUBLE? If the insertion point is not on a blank line, or if two blank lines appear between the paragraphs, edit the proposal so only one blank line appears between the paragraphs and the insertion point is on that line.

3. Click **Insert** then click **Object** to open the Insert Object dialog box.

4. Click the **Create from File** radio button. See Figure 7-9. You need to find the Quattro Pro spreadsheet file on your Student Disk.

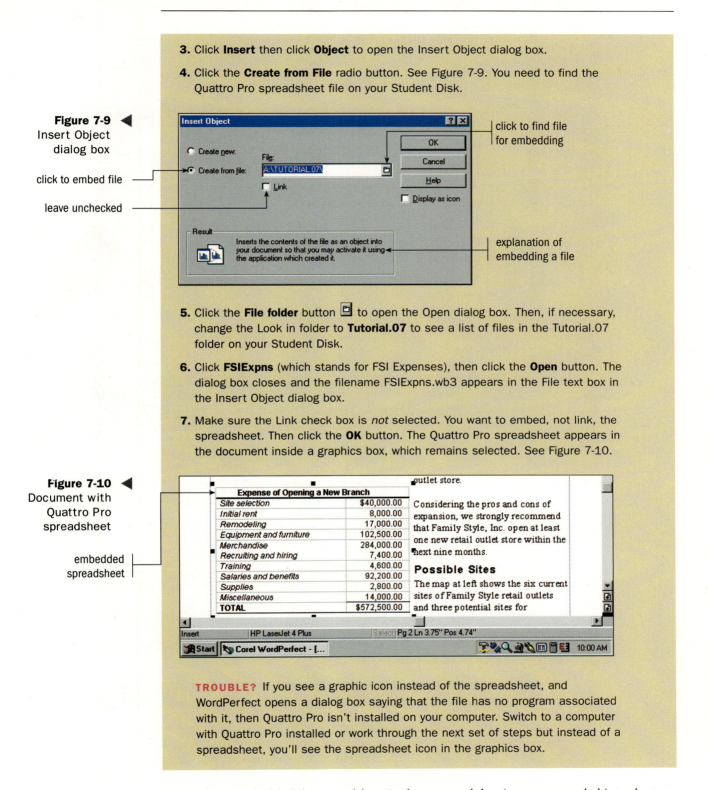

Figure 7-9 ◀ Insert Object dialog box

click to embed file

leave unchecked

click to find file for embedding

explanation of embedding a file

5. Click the **File folder** button to open the Open dialog box. Then, if necessary, change the Look in folder to **Tutorial.07** to see a list of files in the Tutorial.07 folder on your Student Disk.

6. Click **FSIExpns** (which stands for FSI Expenses), then click the **Open** button. The dialog box closes and the filename FSIExpns.wb3 appears in the File text box in the Insert Object dialog box.

7. Make sure the Link check box is *not* selected. You want to embed, not link, the spreadsheet. Then click the **OK** button. The Quattro Pro spreadsheet appears in the document inside a graphics box, which remains selected. See Figure 7-10.

Figure 7-10 ◀ Document with Quattro Pro spreadsheet

embedded spreadsheet

TROUBLE? If you see a graphic icon instead of the spreadsheet, and WordPerfect opens a dialog box saying that the file has no program associated with it, then Quattro Pro isn't installed on your computer. Switch to a computer with Quattro Pro installed or work through the next set of steps but instead of a spreadsheet, you'll see the spreadsheet icon in the graphics box.

You have embedded the spreadsheet in the proposal, but it seems crowded into the text.

Centering the Embedded Spreadsheet

You think the spreadsheet would look better centered between the left and right margins without text wrapped around either side.

To center the spreadsheet and turn off text wrap:

1. Make sure the Quattro Pro spreadsheet is still selected.

2. Click the **Edit Box** QuickSpot to open the Edit Box palette.

   TROUBLE? If the QuickSpot doesn't appear in the spreadsheet box, right-click anywhere in the spreadsheet, then click Edit Box.

   You'll change the text wrap option so no text appears on either side of the spreadsheet.

3. Click the **Wrap Text** button, then click **Neither Side**. The text moves away from the right side of the spreadsheet.

4. Click the **Position** button to open the Box Position dialog box, set the Attach box to button to **Paragraph**, set the Horizontal position to **0"** from **Center of Paragraph** and **0"** from top of paragraph.

5. Click the **OK** button, then close the Edit Box palette. The box with the spreadsheet centers between the margins and no text wraps around it.

6. Click anywhere outside the spreadsheet to deselect the box. The Quattro Pro spreadsheet is embedded and formatted in Nalani's proposal document. See Figure 7-11.

Figure 7-11 ◄
Embedded Quattro Pro worksheet centered horizontally

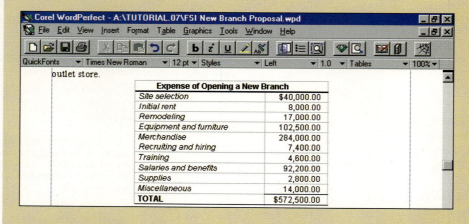

7. Save the proposal.

Nalani stops in to verify the figures in the spreadsheet. She thinks some of the numbers might need to be modified.

Modifying an Embedded Quattro Pro Spreadsheet

Because the spreadsheet is embedded, and as long as the source application (Quattro Pro) is installed on your computer, you can edit the spreadsheet by double-clicking it and using the available Quattro Pro commands. For example, if you discovered that a number is wrong in the embedded spreadsheet or if you wanted the monetary values expressed as whole dollar increments rather than as partial increments (with the two zeros to the right of the decimal place), you would edit the embedded spreadsheet. In either case, you could easily modify the spreadsheet by double-clicking it and then using the Quattro Pro commands to modify the number format. After you modify the spreadsheet, you can click anywhere else in the WordPerfect document to deselect the spreadsheet and return to the usual WordPerfect editing commands. Any changes you make in the embedded spreadsheet will affect only the copy in WordPerfect and not the original file, FSIExpns.

Nalani doesn't see any changes that need to be made to the current version of the spreadsheet, so you won't have to modify it.

Embedding a Graph Created with Chart

Nalani wants to include figures for the gross income and net profit of Family Styles for the previous five years in the proposal. The figures look good and she thinks they will help convince the other owners and investors of Family Style that they should open a new branch outlet. She thinks the data will be even more dramatic as a chart than as a spreadsheet. You need to embed a graph that shows the gross income and net profit for each of the previous five years.

The accounting department has supplied data about the company's income and profits in a Quattro Pro spreadsheet. You'll create the graph from this spreadsheet with Presentations 7 Chart, a program that comes with WordPerfect in the Corel WordPerfect Suite and in the Corel Office Professional. Chart is not a stand-alone program. That is, you can run it only from within another program, and you can't save a separate Chart file to your disk.

To embed a graph using Chart:

1. Scroll up to the middle of page 1, until you see the "Current Situation" heading and the phrase "[insert graph]" at the beginning of the second paragraph under "Current Situation."

2. Delete the phrase **[insert graph]** and the space after it. The insertion point blinks just to the left of the word "These," the place where you want to create the graph.

3. Click **Graphics** then click **Chart** to run Corel Presentations 7 Chart.

   After a few moments, a sample graph is inserted into a graphics box in the proposal, the Chart menu bar and toolbar open, and a Datasheet with sample data appears on the screen. A **Datasheet** is similar to a Quattro Pro spreadsheet in that it analyzes numerical data from which it creates graphs. See Figure 7-12.

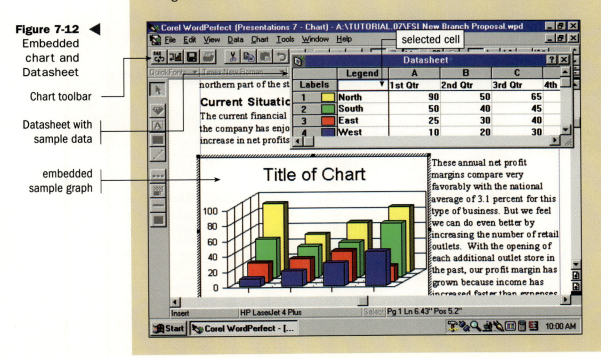

Figure 7-12 ◀ Embedded chart and Datasheet

Chart toolbar

Datasheet with sample data

embedded sample graph

You will replace the sample data in the Datasheet with new labels and numbers to create the graph that shows gross income and net profit. Rather than typing the labels and numbers, Nalani had an employee in the accounting department create a Quattro Pro spreadsheet with the necessary information. You will import that spreadsheet into the Chart Datasheet.

To import a Quattro Pro spreadsheet into a Chart Datasheet and create a graph:

1. Make sure the cell in the upper-left corner of the Datasheet is selected, as shown in Figure 7-12, click **Data** on the Chart menu bar, then click **Import**. The Import Data dialog box opens.

2. Make sure the Data type button is set to **Spreadsheet**, click the **Clear current data** check box (if necessary) to select it, then set the filename to **A:\TUTORIAL.07\FSIGrDat.wb2**. See Figure 7-13.

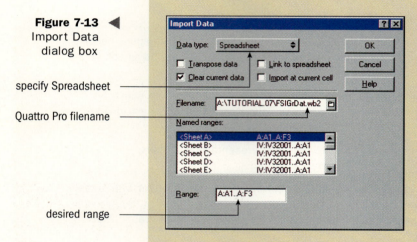

Figure 7-13
Import Data dialog box

specify Spreadsheet

Quattro Pro filename

desired range

3. Click the **OK** button to import the data from the spreadsheet. The data appear in the Datasheet and the corresponding graph appears in the graphics box. See Figure 7-14.

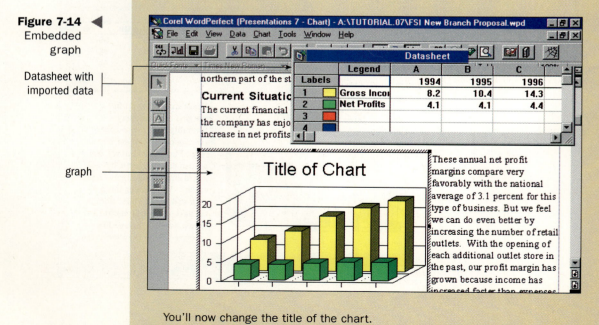

Figure 7-14
Embedded graph

Datasheet with imported data

graph

You'll now change the title of the chart.

4. Click **Title of Chart** in the chart, click **Chart**, click **Title**, type **Company Growth** in the Title Properties dialog box, then click the **OK** button.

5. Click anywhere in the document window but outside the Datasheet to close Chart.

6. Open the Edit Box palette, attach the chart to the paragraph, position the chart at the left and top of the paragraph, set the width to 3.5" (keeping the height proportional), then close the Edit Box palette.

7. Click outside the chart to deselect it. The completed chart appears in the proposal. See Figure 7-15.

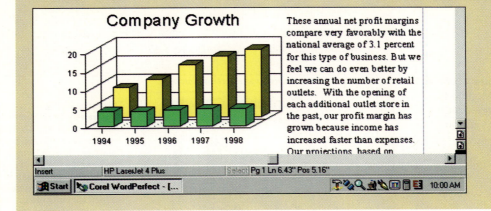

Figure 7-15 ◀
Completed chart embedded in document

The graph is embedded, positioned, and sized in Nalani's proposal.

Modifying the Chart

As mentioned earlier, you can easily edit an embedded object. When you double-click the embedded object (in this case a graph), the Chart menu bar and toolbar and the Datasheet reappear on the screen and you can make any changes you want. Remember that with an embedded object, any changes will appear only in the destination file and not in the source file.

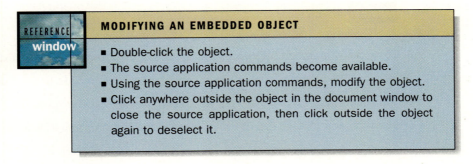

REFERENCE window

MODIFYING AN EMBEDDED OBJECT

- Double-click the object.
- The source application commands become available.
- Using the source application commands, modify the object.
- Click anywhere outside the object in the document window to close the source application, then click outside the object again to deselect it.

After you create the graph, Nalani realizes the 1998 gross income number is wrong. It should be $19.8 million, not $18.4 million. You can easily modify the embedded graph.

To modify an embedded graph:

1. Double-click anywhere within the graph. The graphics box becomes selected, and the Chart menu bar and toolbar and the Datasheet open.

   TROUBLE? If the Datasheet doesn't open, click View, then click Datasheet.

2. Click the right horizontal scroll arrow on the Datasheet until you can see the 1998 data, then click ✥ in cell E1, just below the label "1998," to select that cell.

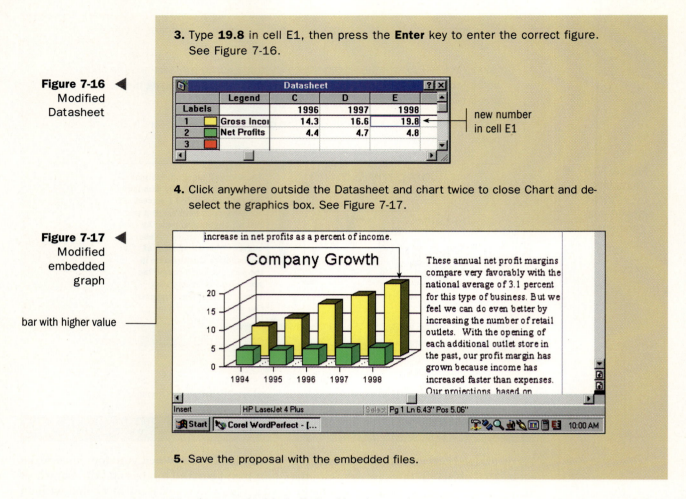

Figure 7-16
Modified Datasheet

3. Type **19.8** in cell E1, then press the **Enter** key to enter the correct figure. See Figure 7-16.

4. Click anywhere outside the Datasheet and chart twice to close Chart and de-select the graphics box. See Figure 7-17.

Figure 7-17
Modified embedded graph

bar with higher value

5. Save the proposal with the embedded files.

You have embedded all the files that Nalani wants in the proposal and corrected the graph. You're ready to link some files in the proposal.

Quick Check

1. How do you embed a Quattro Pro spreadsheet into a WordPerfect document?
2. What is the effect of setting the Wrap Text to Neither Side in the Edit Box palette?
3. How do you create a graph in WordPerfect using Presentations 7 Chart?
4. How do you change the title of a chart using Presentations 7 Chart?
5. What is one advantage of embedding a file over importing it?
6. True or False: You can import data from a Quattro Pro spreadsheet into a Chart Datasheet to create an embedded graph.

If you aren't going to work through Session 7.3 now, you should close the proposal and exit WordPerfect. When you're ready to begin Session 7.3, start WordPerfect, open FSI New Branch Proposal, then continue with the session.

SESSION 7.3

In this session you will link a Paint file to your WordPerfect document then modify the file from within Paint and from within WordPerfect. Then, you will print the proposal.

Linking and Modifying an Object

The advantage of linking a file over importing or embedding it is that the file is updated whenever you modify either the original file from within the source application or the linked file from within the destination application. That way, you can use the object not only in your current document but also in future documents, and you'll always have the latest version of the object available on a disk file.

Linking a Paint File

As part of the proposal, Nalani wants to include a map of the state of Indiana that shows the current sites of Family Style outlets and the proposed sites for the new branch. This will help the board quickly see how Family Style is expanding within the state.

> **REFERENCE window**
>
> **LINKING AN OBJECT**
>
> - Move the insertion point to the location in your document where you want the file to appear.
> - Click Insert then click Object to open the Object dialog box.
> - Click the Create from file radio button.
> - Type the path of the filename or click the Browse button and select the file you want to link.
> - Click the Link to file check box, then click the OK button.

You need to link the map, which was created in the Microsoft Paint graphics program, to the WordPerfect document.

To begin linking a Paint file to WordPerfect and copy a file in a dialog box:

1. Move the insertion point to the beginning of page 3. Because the map won't fit well on the bottom of page 2 where the section on "Possible Sites" begins, you'll put it at the beginning of page 3. The insertion point is probably next to the bulleted item "Boilermaker Shopping Center...," but the location might be different in your document.

2. Click **Insert**, click **Object** to open the Insert Object dialog box, then click the **Create from file** radio button.

3. Click the **File folder** button , and make sure you're looking in the **Tutorial.07** folder on your Student Disk in the Open dialog box.

   Because you'll modify the linked file but don't want to modify the original Paint file, you'll make a copy of the Indiana file.

4. Click the filename **Indiana** in the Open dialog box to select it, click the **Copy** button on the dialog box Toolbar, click anywhere in the file list box except on a filename so no filename is selected, then click the **Paste** button on the dialog box Toolbar. WordPerfect creates a copy of the file with the filename "Copy of INDIANA."

   TROUBLE? If you don't see the figure, click View then Refresh.

5. Right-click **Copy of INDIANA** to select it and to open the shortcut menu, click **Rename**, then type **Map of Indiana** as the new filename. If your dialog box shows filename extensions, make sure you type "Map of Indiana.bmp" as the complete, new filename.

6. Press the **Enter** key to accept the new filename. WordPerfect reorders the list so the new filename appears in alphabetical order.

Now that you have a copy of the original file to work with, you're ready to finish linking the file and then place it to the left of the text.

To finish linking a Paint file and position it in WordPerfect:

1. Double-click the filename **Map of Indiana** in the file list box to select and open it. (Notice double-clicking performs the same action as selecting the filename and then clicking the Open button.) The path and filename "Map of Indiana.bmp" appears in the File text box in the Insert Object dialog box.

   TROUBLE? If you can't see the complete filename "Map of Indiana.bmp," don't worry. The path might take up more room than is visible in the text box.

2. Click the **Link** check box in the Insert Object dialog box to select it. The Result section at the bottom of the dialog box explains the results of linking the graphics file to your WordPerfect document.

3. Click the **OK** button in the Insert Object dialog box. The Paint graphic, a large map of Indiana, appears in your document. See Figure 7-18.

Figure 7-18 ◄
Linked object (map)

graphics box

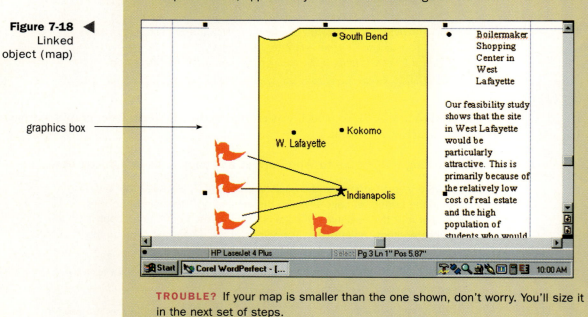

TROUBLE? If your map is smaller than the one shown, don't worry. You'll size it in the next set of steps.

The map of Indiana is much too large in the proposal. The graphics box with the map needs to be attached, sized, and positioned.

To attach, size, and position the map:

1. Make sure the graphics box with the map is still selected.

2. Right-click the map, click **Edit Box** to open the Edit Box palette, then attach the box to **Page** (if necessary) and position the graphics box to **0"** from the **Left Margin** and **0"** from the **Top Margin**, then click the **OK** button.

3. Click the **Size** button, set the Width of the graphics box to **2.5"**, set the Height to **Maintain proportions**, then click the **OK** button.

4. Close the Edit Box palette, then click anywhere in the document window outside the map to deselect it. See Figure 7-19.

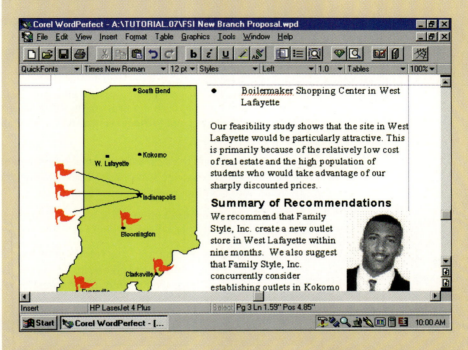

Figure 7-19 ◀
Graphics box of map repositioned and resized

5. Move the insertion point to the beginning of the first paragraph below the heading "Possible Sites," then fix the reference to the map. For example, if the insertion point is near the bottom of page 2 rather than the top of page 3, change the phrase "The map at left" to "The map below." If the insertion point and the map are on the same page, then the map actually is at left, so leave the phrase unchanged.

6. Save the proposal with the linked map.

You have linked the Paint file to the proposal document. Red flags point out the sites of all the current Family Style branches. Sites without flags are proposals for new branches. Nalani asks you to copy one of the flags already on the map to West Lafayette, the proposed site to which she is recommending Family Style expand.

Modifying the Linked File in Paint

You can modify the file by double-clicking the object in the WordPerfect document, which would start the Paint program, and then using the Paint commands to make changes. Any changes appear in the WordPerfect document immediately. Or, you can start Paint using the Windows 95 Start button on the taskbar, open the Map of Indiana file, make any changes, and save the file. These changes will appear in the WordPerfect document when you update the link. Remember that when you modify a linked file, either from the source application (Paint) or from the destination application (WordPerfect), both the original file and the linked copy change.

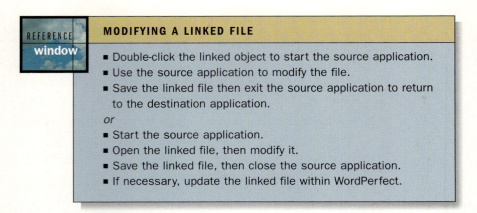

REFERENCE window

MODIFYING A LINKED FILE

- Double-click the linked object to start the source application.
- Use the source application to modify the file.
- Save the linked file then exit the source application to return to the destination application.

or

- Start the source application.
- Open the linked file, then modify it.
- Save the linked file, then close the source application.
- If necessary, update the linked file within WordPerfect.

You'll open the Paint program and copy the flag to West Lafayette on the original file.

To modify the graphics file in Paint:

1. With WordPerfect still running, click the **Start** button [Start] on the Windows 95 taskbar, point to **Programs**, point to **Accessories**, then click **Paint** to launch the Paint program.

   TROUBLE? If you can't find the Accessories folder on the Programs menu or you can't find Paint in the Accessories folder, ask your instructor or technical support person to make sure Paint is installed on your computer.

2. If necessary, click the **Maximize** button □ in the upper-right corner of the Paint window to maximize it.

3. Open the Paint file **Map of Indiana** from the **Tutorial.07** folder on your Student Disk. Then scroll down until you see both Bloomington and W. Lafayette on the map, if necessary. You will copy the flag from Bloomington to W. Lafayette. See Figure 7-20.

Figure 7-20
Editing the graphic in Paint

Select button

scroll to see this flag

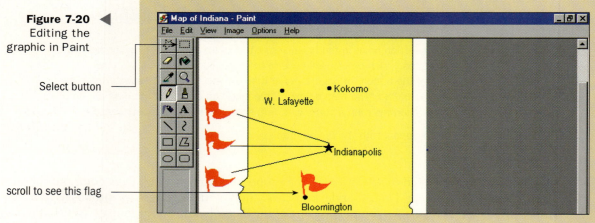

4. Click the **Select** button □ on the Paint Toolbar. The pointer changes to ✢.

5. Drag the pointer from the upper-left corner of the red flag of Bloomington to the lower-right corner of the flag; make sure you include the black dot that marks the city location and that you don't select any text, then release the mouse button. See Figure 7-21.

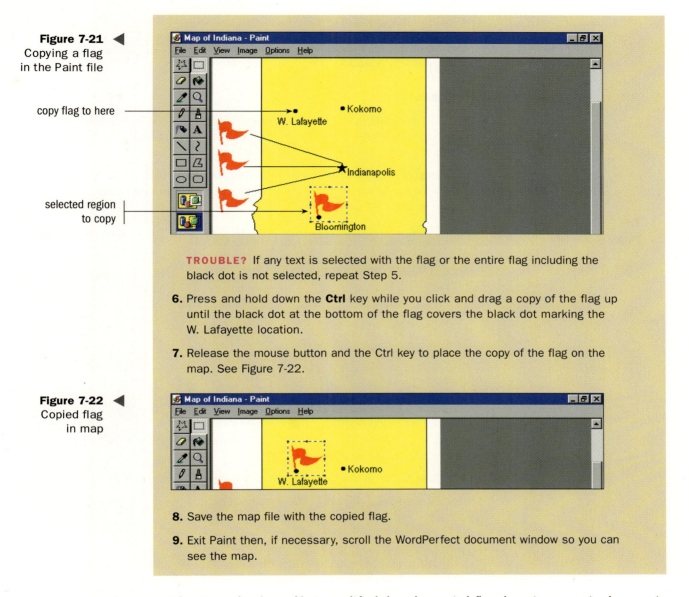

Figure 7-21 ◀ Copying a flag in the Paint file

copy flag to here

selected region to copy

TROUBLE? If any text is selected with the flag or the entire flag including the black dot is not selected, repeat Step 5.

6. Press and hold down the **Ctrl** key while you click and drag a copy of the flag up until the black dot at the bottom of the flag covers the black dot marking the W. Lafayette location.

7. Release the mouse button and the Ctrl key to place the copy of the flag on the map. See Figure 7-22.

Figure 7-22 ◀ Copied flag in map

8. Save the map file with the copied flag.

9. Exit Paint then, if necessary, scroll the WordPerfect document window so you can see the map.

The Map of Indiana file is modified, but the copied flag doesn't appear in the map in the current WordPerfect document. Before the change will be reflected in the WordPerfect document, you have to update the link.

Updating a Link

To **update** a link means to make sure the linked object in the destination file reflects the latest version of the source file. If you modify a linked object in the source application and the WordPerfect document to which it's linked is closed, the next time you open the file, in this case the proposal, WordPerfect will automatically update the link. But if you modify a linked object in the source application and the WordPerfect document is still open, such as you did with the Map of Indiana, you might have to tell WordPerfect to update the link.

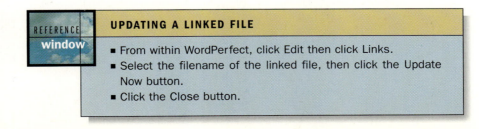

UPDATING A LINKED FILE

- From within WordPerfect, click Edit then click Links.
- Select the filename of the linked file, then click the Update Now button.
- Click the Close button.

The Map of Indiana linked to your WordPerfect document doesn't reflect the change you just made. The modified version of the file is saved to disk while the unmodified version still appears in the WordPerfect document window. You need to have WordPerfect update the linked file in the proposal.

To update a linked file:

1. Make sure WordPerfect is the active program in Windows 95 and that you still see Map of Indiana in the document window. You should be looking at the original version of the file, not the one with the flag at W. Lafayette.

2. Click **Edit** then click **Links** to open the Links dialog box. See Figure 7-23. The only source file involved in a link in this document is Map of Indiana, which appears in the Links list box.

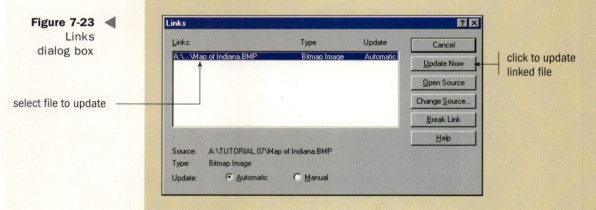

Figure 7-23
Links dialog box

select file to update

click to update linked file

3. With the source file selected, click the **Update Now** button. WordPerfect retrieves the latest version of the linked file.

4. Click the **Close** button in the Links dialog box.

5. If necessary, deselect the graphic. The updated version of the map appears in WordPerfect.

As you look at the map, you see it's difficult to tell that W. Lafayette is a proposed site for a Family Style branch, not an established site like Indianapolis, Bloomington, Clarksville, or Evansville.

Modifying the Linked File in WordPerfect

You decide to change the color of the flag at W. Lafayette from red to blue to help make it stand out from the flags at the established sites. Rather than clicking the Start button on the Windows 95 taskbar again to open the Paint program, you'll launch the Paint program from within WordPerfect. WordPerfect will update your change in the Paint file automatically. As long as the WordPerfect document is open, it is usually easier to modify a linked object by double-clicking it to start the source application rather than using the Start button and updating the link.

To modify a linked object from within WordPerfect:

1. Double-click the map to open the Paint program. The map appears in the Paint document window.

2. If necessary, click the **Maximize** button in the upper-right corner of the Paint window to maximize it.

3. Scroll the map until you see the flag at W. Lafayette.

4. Click the **Fill With Color** button on the Paint toolbar, then click the **bright blue** tile on the bottom row of the color palette at the bottom of the window to set the fill color to blue.

5. Click anywhere in the red flag at W. Lafayette. The red flag turns blue. See Figure 7-24.

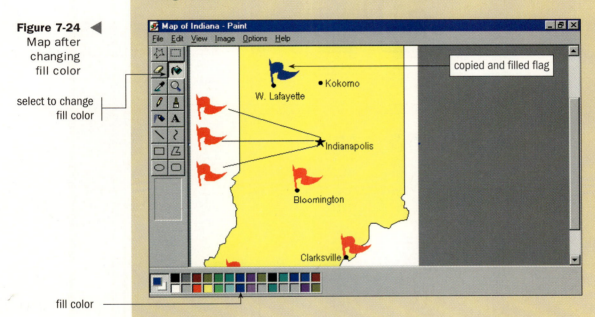

Figure 7-24 Map after changing fill color

select to change fill color

fill color

copied and filled flag

TROUBLE? If anything else changes to blue, then press Ctrl + V to undo the color change and try again making sure you click within the flag.

6. Save the changes to the map, then exit Paint. The change you made appears in both the original source file (Map of Indiana) and in the linked copy in WordPerfect.

You have completed the proposal for Nalani, and are ready to save and print it.

7. Deselect the map then save the final version of the proposal.

8. Preview then print the document. Your three-page document should look like Figure 7-25.

Figure 7-25
Final version of the proposal

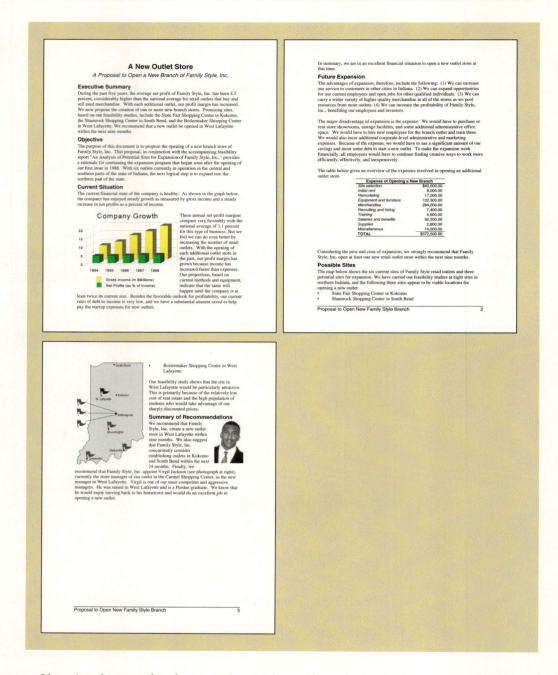

You give the completed proposal to Nalani, who is pleased with your work. She distributes the proposal to the other owners and investors involved in deciding on the expansion of Family Style, Inc. At the next board of director's meeting, the board votes unanimously to accept Nalani's proposal.

Quick Check

1. How do you link a Paint file to a WordPerfect file?
2. What is one advantage of linking an object rather than embedding the object?
3. From within the Open dialog box, how do you copy a file into the same folder?
4. What are the two methods for modifying a linked object?
5. What does it mean to update a linked object?

6. True or False: When you open a WordPerfect document that contains a linked file, the file is automatically updated to the latest version of the file.

Tutorial Assignments

Start WordPerfect, open the file SalesRep from the TAssign folder in the Tutorial.07 folder on your Student Disk. Save the document as Family Style Sales Report, then complete the following:

1. Move the insertion point to the phrase "[insert graph here]," delete the line, then start Chart so you can create the graph.
2. Import the data from the Quattro Pro spreadsheet 2QSales (located in the TAssign folder in the Tutorial.07 folder on your Student Disk) into the Chart Datasheet.
3. Center the chart between the left and right margins. Make sure no text appears on either side of the graphics box.
4. Locate and then delete the phrase "[link figure here]" from the WordPerfect document.
5. At the current location of the insertion point, open the Insert Object dialog box from which you'll select an existing file to link.
6. Click the File folder button in the Insert Object dialog box, make a copy of the graphic file BrnchSls, then rename the copy as Branch Sales.
7. Select the Branch Sales file and link it to the WordPerfect document.
8. Attach the Branch Sales graphic to the current paragraph, position it at the right margin, allow text wrapping on its left side and resize it to a width of 2.5", with a height to maintain proportion.
9. Locate the phrase "[insert policy here]" and delete it.
10. At the location of the insertion point, import the Microsoft Word document PurPolcy that explains the new purchase policy.
11. Save then print the current version of the report.
12. Marina Leavitt, director of sales for Family Style, Inc., finds an error in the profit figure for the Clarksville branch. The figure is currently 6.2% but should be 6.8%. Start Paint from the Windows 95 taskbar and open Branch Sales. Click the Eraser button, click the white tile on the color palette, drag over 6.2% to erase it, copy and paste 6.8% from Indianapolis, then update the linked file in the WordPerfect document.
13. Save this version of the report as Family Style Sales Report 2.
14. Preview and print the updated report, then close the document.

Case Problems

1. Office Location for Workman Insurance Company John Rowley works for the Workman Insurance Company, a new insurance company that is growing rapidly. Arlene Herlevi, vice president of operations for the company, has proposed that Workman open a new downtown office and has assigned John the responsibility of finding a good location. John contacted local real estate agencies through the World Wide Web and located an available office building that seems satisfactory. He downloaded an image of the office building that he will use to prepare a memo to Arlene describing the office.

Open the file NewOffic from the Cases folder in the Tutorial.07 folder on your Student Disk, save the document as New Office Memo, then do the following:

1. At the end of the memo, import from the text file OfficDes (which was prepared using WordPad—a text editor that ships with Windows 95—and saved as a text file with no formatting).
2. Import the scanned image file NewOffic at the end of the second paragraph, which begins "The photograph below... ." Attach it to the paragraph, center it horizontally, position it 0.3" from the top of the paragraph, with no text wrapping on either side, and resize it to a width of 2.5", with the height to maintain proportions.

3. At the beginning of the third paragraph, begin to embed a graph (using Chart). You will create a graph to show the increase in average monthly rent over the past four years.

4. In the Datasheet, delete all the current labels and data. (*Hint*: To select the entire Datasheet, click the blank, gray cell in the upper-left corner of the Datasheet.)

5. Type the following labels along the top row (above row 1) beginning in column A: "1995," "1996," "1997," and "1998." (*Hint*: Click in the first cell, then press the Right Arrow key to move to the next cell.)
6. Type the following label for row 1 in the first cell in row 1 to the left of column A: "Average Monthly Rent (in $)."
7. Type the following data in cells A1 through D1: "2875," "2995," "3100," and "3250."
8. Attach the graph to the current paragraph, then position it at the left margin and top of the paragraph, with text wrapping on the right.
9. Save the updated version of the file.
10. Preview the document. If it doesn't fit on one page, use the resize handles to resize the chart until it does.
11. Print and close the document.

2. Wasatch Tours Brochure Alisha McClure is a sales representative for Wasatch Tours, a company that offers guided tours to many of the popular tourist sites in the western United States. She is preparing a flyer describing upcoming tours to the National Parks in the Intermountain West.

Open the document NatBroch from the Cases folder in the Tutorial.07 folder on your Student Disk, save the document as National Parks Tours, then do the following:

1. Import the text file Wasatch at the end of the document.
2. Import the scanned photograph with the filename Arch at the beginning of the first paragraph.
3. Attach the image to the current paragraph, then position it at the right margin and top of the paragraph, with text wrapping turned on.

4. Increase the size of the image to about 2-by-2-inches. (*Hint*: Drag the resize handle in the lower-right corner up and to the left while watching the Ruler to see the size of the image and keeping the image approximately square.)
5. Double space at the end of the document, then import (don't embed) Spreadsheet A of the Quattro Pro spreadsheet WasTours. When you import a Quattro Pro spreadsheet into WordPerfect it becomes a WordPerfect table. (*Hint*: Click Insert, point to Spreadsheet/Database, and click Import. In the Import Data dialog box, change Named ranges to Spreadsheet A A:A1..A:D7.)
6. Center the table between the left and right margins.
7. Adjust column widths in the table, if necessary, to make sure the table fits between the left and right margins.
8. Save the flyer, then preview it.
9. Print then close the document.

3. Zeke's Sales Organization Report Charles Turner is vice president of marketing for Zeke's Sports Equipment, a national distributor of sporting goods headquartered in Birmingham, Alabama. Because of the enormous volume of sales in California, Charles has decided to reorganize the sales regions. To lessen the load on the western region, he has decided to enlarge the southeast region to include Texas. He will explain this change in a report to all regional sales representatives.

Open the file ZekesRep from the Cases folder in the Tutorial.07 folder on your Student Disk, save the document as Zeke's Sales Org, then do the following:

1. Embed the Quattro Pro chart in the file Zekes98 at the blank line after the first paragraph. (*Hint*: The chart was created in Quattro Pro on a Chart tab. You embed it the same way you embed any Quattro Pro spreadsheet.)
2. Attach the chart to the current paragraph, center the chart between the left and right margins and position it at the top of the paragraph, with no text wrapping.

3. Set the width of the chart to 4 inches and the height to 2.5 inches.
4. Move the insertion point to the end of the document, then open the Object dialog box and look in the Cases folder in the Tutorial.07 folder on your Student Disk.
5. Copy the Paint image file ZekesReg, then rename the copy Zekes Regions Map.
6. Link Zekes Regions Map to the WordPerfect document.
7. Center the image between the left and right margins, with no text wrapping.
8. Double-click the image to edit it using Paint.
9. Select the fill color blue from the color palette.
10. Change Texas to blue.
11. Save the image and close Paint.
12. Save the document then preview it.
13. Print then close the document.

4. Your Educational Expenses As a student, you have many expenses—tuition, books, meals, etc. Write a report or memo about your educational expenses during the past six months. Open a new, blank document in WordPerfect, then do the following:
1. Explain your educational pursuits and goals in at least one paragraph.
2. In a paragraph, summarize your monthly expenses for the previous six months.
3. Create a graph using Chart that shows your expenses by month for the previous six months. You can use real or fictitious expense data.
4. Embed or link a picture, diagram, or spreadsheet. For example, if you have access to a scanner, you could scan a picture of one of the buildings on campus or your own picture. You can use Paint to modify the map of the United States in the graphics file ZekesReg, showing the location of your hometown or your educational institution. If you have access to Quattro Pro, you could create a spreadsheet comparing your income and expenses for the last six months.
5. Save the WordPerfect document as My School Expenses to the Cases folder in the Tutorial.07 folder on your Student Disk.
6. Preview and print the document.
7. Close the document.

Answers to Quick Check Questions

SESSION 1.1

1. Determine what you want to write about; organize ideas logically; determine how you'll say what you want to say; produce your document with WordPerfect.

2. a. ribbon of icons providing menu shortcuts; b. bar displaying grid marks every 1/8 inch; c. bar indicating where insertion point is and other information; d. keystrokes providing quick access to WordPerfect commands; e. set of standard format settings.

3. Insertion point is located 3.3 inches from top of page.

4. Click Insert, point to Date, click Date Text; press Ctrl + D.

5. A set of characters with certain style and appearance; click Font Size button on Power Bar, then click a font size.

6. Click View, click Toolbars/Ruler, click check box for Ruler, then click OK button.

7. WordPerfect's automatic spelling checker; red line beneath potential spelling error; right-click word then click correct spelling in shortcut menu.

8. Automatically replaces commonly misspelled or mistyped words with the correct spelling as you type.

SESSION 1.2

1. So you won't lose work if you exit WordPerfect, turn off computer, or experience accidental power failure.

2. Save command saves document with current filename; Save As allows you to save document with a different filename.

3. Click the Scroll up or down button on the vertical scroll bar.

4. Shows full page in document window; use to preview document before you print it.

5. Scrolling shifts or moves the text in the document window so you can see different sections of entire document; word wrap automatically breaks a line of text to ensure text fits between left and right margins.

6. At least every 15 minutes.

7. Place envelope in envelope feeder of printer. Click Format, click Envelope, type return or mailing addresses as needed, click Print Envelope button.

8. Click File, then click Exit. If prompted to save changes to document, click Yes button. If necessary, type filename, then click OK button.

SESSION 1.3

1. Click Open button; click File, then click Open; or click name of document at bottom of File menu.

2. Position mouse pointer at new location and click mouse button.

3. Insertion point: blinking vertical bar where typed character will appear; Shadow pointer: gray insertion point that follows mouse pointer and where insertion point would move if you clicked mouse button.

4. Typing mode that replaces existing text as you type; if you wanted to replace existing text with new text.

5. Backspace deletes space or character to left of insertion point; Delete deletes space or character to right of insertion point.

6 Click File, then click Save As. Type new filename, then click Save button.

7 Information about commands, features, and screen elements as you are working with them; press Shift + F1, then click any item on the screen.

8 Click Help then click Help Topics. Click Index tab, type "print," click appropriate entry, then click Display button.

SESSION 2.1

1 Ctrl + End; Ctrl + Home; Alt + PgDn; Alt + PgUp.

2 To the left of the first character in the next line.

3 D

4 Undo reverses your last edit; Redo reverses the action of an Undo command.

5 Move insertion point to target location, click Edit, click Undelete, click Restore button.

6 Location of shadow pointer indicates to where text will move.

7 Cut and paste removes text and places it in new location; copy and paste transfers copy of text to new location.

SESSION 2.2

1 Document layout; open; line and paragraph.

2 Portrait.

3 Left justification aligns text along left margin with a ragged right margin; right justification aligns text along right margin with a ragged left margin; center alignment aligns text an equal distance from left and right margins; full justification aligns text along both left and right margins; all justification is same as full except partial lines are spaced to also align at both margins.

4 Positions numbers so decimal points are aligned at tab stop.

5 The F7 key.

6 Tab stop: location where text moves when you press Tab or Indent key; Tab icon: icon in left margin indicating location of change in tab stops; tab bar appears at that location.

7 Insert a Conditional End of Page command at the beginning of the heading.

8 They decrease attractiveness and readability.

SESSION 2.3

1 a. letter, digit, punctuation mark, or typographical symbol; b. text appearance (font, size, and color) of character.

2 False.

3 Serif font has embellishment at tips of characters; sans serif font has no embellishments.

4 Select items in list, then click Insert, click Bullets & Numbers, click Numbers style, click OK button.

5 Key or command that alternates between on and off; Italic, Bold, and Underline buttons.

6 Title of a book or emphasized phrase.

7   Displays format codes in window below document window; to find, view, edit, move, or delete formatting.

8   Click File, point to Document, click Properties, click Information tab.

SESSION 3.1

1   Click Edit, then click Find and Replace, type search string, then click Find Next button.

2   A character, word, phrase, or format code (or combination of these) that you want to find in your document; a character, word, phrase, or format code (or combination of these) that you want to replace the search string.

3   Spell-As-You-Go sometimes fails to find duplicate words and other problems.

4   Click Edit, click Find and Replace, type IRS as search string and Internal Revenue Service as replacement string, click Replace All button; click Match then click Whole Word.

5   Arrange, assign, attribute, camp (and others).

6   Highlights possible problem and provides suggestions for improving grammar of marked text; click Skip Once button; click appropriate replacement then click Replace button.

7   Formal writing flags contractions and colloquial language; informal writing ignores these same constructions.

SESSION 3.2

1   Moves subsequent text to a new page even if the current page isn't filled.

2   A command that centers the text of a page between the top and bottom margins.

3   Header is printed at top of page; footer is printed at bottom of page.

4   Press Alt + F7 to move insertion point to right margin, click Number button, click Page Number.

5   Move insertion point to end of header text, press the Enter key, click Insert Line button.

6   Footnote prints at bottom of page where reference appears; endnote prints at end of document.

7   Notes are numbered automatically and renumbered if you add, delete, or move a note; WordPerfect automatically formats note text; can edit a note at any time.

SESSION 3.3

1   a. set of character- and paragraph-level formatting commands you save with a specific name; b. character-level formats you save and reapply to words, phrases, and other text; c. character- and paragraph-level formats you save and reapply to other paragraphs; d. character- and paragraph-level formats you save and reapply to other paragraphs, and which, if you change in one paragraph to which style is applied with change in all other paragraphs to which style is applied.

2   To make document formatting more consistent; to apply formatting to similar elements of document automatically; to make formatting changes quickly and efficiently.

3   Select text, click Styles button on Power Bar, click style name.

4   Modify any one of the paragraphs to which the style is applied.

5   Click Format, click Styles, click Create, insert codes for justification, margins, and line spacing in the Contents box.

6   File containing set of styles. To be able to use styles from one document in another document.

SESSION 4.1

1. To keep page numbering, headers, footers, and so forth from appearing on a particular page or range of pages.

2. Click Tools, click Outline, click Outline Definition list arrow, click Outline.

3. Promote changes an outline item from lower-level to higher-level paragraph (e.g., level-2 to level-1); demote changes item from higher-level to lower-level paragraph.

4. Table is information arranged in horizontal rows and vertical columns; table guidelines mark the structure of the table by outlining rows and columns on the screen.

5. Press the Tab key; click in cell A2; click Up Arrow key; click in cell B6.

6. Move insertion point where you want new row, click Table, click Insert, click Rows radio button, click OK button

7. B

8. Click Numeric Format button, click Percent radio button, click OK button.

SESSION 4.2

1. Click Tables button on Power Bar, drag pointer to select table size; click Table, click Create, set size of table, click OK button.

2. Active window has highlighted title bar and scroll bars.

3. Drag one or more vertical guideline.

4. WordPerfect displays the width in a QuickTip.

5. D

6. A shaded box, usually behind, slightly below, and to the right of the border, that looks like a shadow of the box.

SESSION 4.3

1. You can apply a predefined format automatically.

2. False.

3. Automatically changes the column widths to fit the information in the table.

4. False.

5. Apply Heading 1, Heading 2, Heading 3, etc., styles to document headings, move insertion point to where you want table of contents, define and then generate table of contents.

6. Use same number as you used heading levels in document or the number of headings you want to appear in the table of contents.

SESSION 5.1

1. a. letters containing similar content but with personal information in specific locations; b. document containing merge codes where personal information will be inserted; c. document containing personal information; d. instructions for retrieving specific information from data source.

2. Data text file has records and fields arranged consecutively, one after another, on separate lines or paragraphs; data table file has records and fields arranged with one record per row and one field per cell.

3 Record.

4 True.

5 To make it easier to enter, edit, or delete data records.

6 Click First, Previous, Next, or Last buttons, or scroll through records.

SESSION 5.2

1 Inserts the current date when document is printed.

2 Click Insert Merge Code on Merge feature bar, then click code name.

3 Merge code is in red text.

4 a. document created after merging form file and data source; b. rearrange order of records; c. specification of which records are selected from data source during a merge.

5 In the Select Records dialog box, set Field to Salary, and type "<15000" in the Conditions text box.

6 23

SESSION 5.3

1 True.

2 Format the document using the Format Labels command and specifying the labels type, make the document a form file, insert appropriate merge codes, merge labels form file with data source.

3 True.

4 Dotted line extending from text on left margin to text at tab stop or at flush right.

5 Display data table, click Options, click Sort, click Edit or New to set the conditions of the sort, specify for Key 1 the field number for Last Name, set Type to Alpha, set sort order to Descending, click OK button, click Sort button.

SESSION 6.1

1 High quality printing; multiple fonts; graphics, typographic characters, columns and other formatting features.

2 a. Box containing image or text; b. small squares used to change size of image; c. space between lines of text.

3 Click Graphics then click TextArt, type the text, click the Close button.

4 Double-click it.

5 Adjust spacing in Line Spacing dialog box; change space between paragraphs in the Paragraph Format dialog box; use the Advance typesetting command; adjust the leading between lines.

6 All paragraphs to which that style has been applied will automatically have the leading adjusted.

SESSION 6.2

1. a. two or more vertical blocks or columns of equal or varying widths on a page; b. a box containing text (you can move, edit, resize, border, and fill the box).
2. Disk files containing pictures; click the Image button, change directory to location of clip-art files, click image filename, click OK button.
3. WordPerfect opens a palette of frequently used options for editing the box.
4. Use the Size command on the Edit Box palette or drag the resize handles.
5. An oversized letter at the beginning of a paragraph; click within a paragraph, click Format then click Drop Cap, set options in feature bar, click Close button.
6. Part of text set off by special formatting; draws attention to key point in text.
7. Click QuickSpot, click Border button, click border style, click Fill button, click fill style.

SESSION 6.3

1. a. special typographic character for double hyphen; b. distracting blank areas in column of text caused by full-justifying paragraphs; c. distracting uneven right edge of text in left-justified paragraphs.
2. Click Insert, click Character, select the character set and character number for the symbol, click Insert and Close; type "(r" (QuickCorrect must be on).
3. Make sure the QuickCorrect options are set to insert typographic quotation marks, then do a find and replace of all straight quotes, replacing with straight quotes; repeat with straight apostrophes.
4. Divides a word to force part of it to next line of text; to reduce spacing between words in columns, preventing rivers and excessive ragged right edges.
5. Click Format, point to Border/Fill, click Page, select border type and border style, click OK button.
6. Click Graphics, click Custom Line, click Vertical radio button, set Horizontal Position to Column Aligned, specify any other options, click OK button.

SESSION 7.1

1. a. text or graphics you create in one program and use in another; b. program you use to create original version of object; c. program into which object is imported.
2. Inserting an object from source application into destination application without any connection between the two.
3. Inserting an object from source application into destination application that allows changes to embedded object using commands from source application.
4. Inserting an object from source application into destination application that allows changes in linked file using either source or destination application.
5. Object linking and embedding; program enables you to embed or link objects from one program to another.
6. With insertion point at desired location, click Insert and File, select file you want to import, then click OK button.
7. With insertion point at desired location, click Image button, select picture file you want to import, then click Insert button.
8. A box of frequently used options for editing a graphics or text box.

SESSION 7.2

1. With insertion point at desired location, click Insert then click Object, click Create from File radio button, select file you want to embed, click OK button.

2. Ensures text doesn't appear on either side of object.

3. Click Graphics, click Chart, modify information in Datasheet.

4. If necessary, double-click chart to select it, double-click current title, type new title, click OK button.

5. You can edit an embedded file.

6. True.

SESSION 7.3

1. With insertion point at desired location, click Insert then click Object. Click Create from file radio button, select the file, click Link check box, click OK button.

2. Linking keeps file updated for use by either source or destination application.

3. Right-click filename, click Copy, press Ctrl + V.

4. Double-click object from within destination application then edit it; edit file from within source application without running destination application.

5. To make sure linked object in destination file reflects latest version of source file.

6. True (if you click Yes, you want it updated).

Index

A

Accessories folder, launching Paint program from, WP 258
active document, WP 86, WP 151
active voice, WP 106
adding
  border around newsletter, WP 229
  bullets, WP 76-77
  captions to table, WP 159-160
  endnotes, WP 112–113
  field names, WP 175–176
  footers, WP 109–111
  footnotes, WP 112–114
  headers, WP 109–111
  records to data file, WP 179
address
  data source, WP 171
  envelope, WP 31
  inside, WP 23–24
  mailing labels, WP 191–194
  return, WP 31
Adjust leading check box (Word/Letter Spacing dialog box), WP 212
Advance command, adjusting spacing between lines of text using, WP 211
alignment
  dot leader and, WP 195
  justification and, WP 62, WP 63
  ragged, WP 63, WP 226
  tables and, WP 154
  tab settings and, WP 67, WP 68–69
  vertical columns, WP 68–69
Align Text button, WP 63
  tables and, WP 154
all justification, WP 63
alphabetical sort, for telephone list, WP 195–196
Alt key, WP 13
Annuity document
  editing, WP 48–59
  font appearance, WP 78–81
  formatting, WP 60–85
  opening, WP 46–48
  printing, WP 87
antonyms, WP 103
apostrophe, converting to typographic symbol, WP 225
appearance
  of character, WP 74–76
  font, WP 78–81
  tables, WP 153–155
application
  destination, WP 239, WP 240, WP 241
  source, WP 239, WP 240, WP 241
application Control menu buttons, WP 8, WP 9
application programs, integrating, WP 237–262
application window, WP 8
applying
  border to paragraph in newsletter, WP 213
  border to paragraph in table, WP 156
  formatting with QuickFormat, WP 81–82
  newspaper–style columns to newsletter, WP 214–215
  numbers to list of items, WP 78
  styles, WP 116–117, WP 122
  table formats, WP 157–158
Arial font, WP 9, WP 76
arrow keys
  moving insertion point in text using, WP 49
  moving to cell in table using, WP 141
ascending order sort, WP 186–187, WP 195–196
Ask the PerfectExpert, WP 39
Associate a data file radio button (Create Form File dialog box), WP 180, WP 181
associating data file, WP 180, WP 181
  for mailing labels, WP 193
  for telephone list, WP 195
attaching
  graphics box, WP 246
  linked object, WP 257
automatic page numbering, header and, WP 110
Avery labels, WP 192

B

background, newsletter date, WP 212–213
Backspace key, erasing characters using, WP 19, WP 52
Balanced newspaper radio button (Columns dialog box), WP 215
Between lines text box (Word/Letter Spacing dialog box), WP 212
bitmap images, WP 216, WP 256
blank lines, inserting, WP 22–23
block of text
  cutting and pasting, WP 56–57
  keeping together, WP 70–71
  restoring deleting, WP 54
  selecting and modifying, WP 50–53
bmp (bitmap) filename extension, WP 216, WP 256
Bold button
  existing text and, WP 81
  new text and, WP 79
boldface text, WP 76, WP 79, WP 81
bold font, WP 76
border(s), WP 155
  newsletter, WP 205, WP 206
  newsletter date, WP 213
  newsletter page, WP 229
  newsletter pull quote, WP 220, WP 221
  paragraph in table, WP 156
  text box, WP 220, WP 221
Border/Fill, Paragraph command (Format menu)
  newsletter and, WP 213
  table and, WP 155
bottom margin, changing, WP 62
boxes
  graphics, see graphics boxes
  text, see text boxes
Box Position dialog box, WP 218
Browse tab (Save As dialog box), WP 24, WP 25
bullet(s), WP 76–77
bulleted lists
  adding space between paragraphs of, WP 228–229
  creating in imported text, WP 244
  desktop publishing and, WP 205
  styles for, WP 116
Bullets & Numbers command (Insert menu), WP 76, WP 77, WP 78
business letter
  editing, WP 35–37
  moving insertion point in, WP 35
  opening existing, WP 33–35
  organization of, WP 6
  previewing, WP 29–30
  printing, WP 30
  printing envelope for, WP 31
  typing, WP 22–24
business plan, WP 131–163

C

Calculate command (Tables menu), WP 146
cap, drop, see drop cap
capitalization, finding and replacing text and, WP 99
captions, adding to table, WP 159–160
case, finding and replacing text and, WP 99
cell, table, WP 139
  justifying text within, WP 153–155
  selecting, WP 142
  typing text in, WP 141
centering
  date in newsletter, WP 212–213
  embedded spreadsheet, WP 249–250
  headings in columns, WP 153
  line of text, WP 64–65
  page vertically, WP 107–108
  table, WP 158–159
  text between left and right margins, WP 118
center justification, WP 63, WP 118, WP 121, WP 158
Center Justify command, WP 118, WP 158
Center Line command, WP 64–65, WP 118
center tab stop, WP 68
changing
  font, WP 74–76
  font size from Power Bar, WP 12–13
  format codes, WP 82
  margins, WP 61–62
  page size and orientation, WP 60–61
  styles, WP 117–120
character(s)
  appearance of, WP 74–76
  deleting, WP 19, WP 36–37
  drop cap, see drop cap
  font changes, WP 74–76
  moving insertion point one at a time, WP 49
  selecting, WP 50
  spacing between, WP 62
  special, see special characters
  typographic, WP 205, WP 206, WP 222–225
character (paired) style, WP 115
Character command (Insert menu), WP 223
Chart, embedding graph created with, WP 251–254
Chart command (Graphics menu), WP 251
Chart menu, Title command, WP 252
Chart menu bar, WP 251
Chart toolbar, WP 251
Checking Styles dialog box, WP 105
choosing commands, WP 11–14
clipart, newsletter and, WP 205, WP 206
  editing, WP 217–218
  inserting existing into newsletter, WP 216–217
  resizing, WP 217–218
Clipboard, WP 56–57, WP 58
clock/calendar, WP 12
Close button, WP 32
Close command (File menu), WP 21

closing
    document window, WP 21
    WordPerfect, WP 32
codes
    format, see format codes
    merge, see merge codes
color
    font, see font color
    linked object, WP 261
    newsletter background, WP 205
    shadow, for TextArt, WP 208–210
column(s), newspaper–style, see newspaper–style columns
column(s), table, WP 139
    creating, WP 140, WP 148
    deleting, WP 145
    indicators, WP 140
    inserting, WP 145
    selecting, WP 142
    width of, WP 153
Columns, Define command (Format menu), WP 214
Columns button, newspaper–style columns and, WP 214
Columns dialog box, WP 214–215
columns of text
    aligning with tabs, WP 67, WP 68–69
    newspaper–style, see newspaper–style columns
    vertical, WP 68–69
commands
    choosing, WP 11–14
    toggle switch and, WP 79
command shortcuts, WP 9
condition(s), selecting records to merge based on, WP 172, WP 188–190
Conditional end of page check box (Keep Text Together dialog box), WP 72
Conditional End of Page command, WP 71
content of documents, WP 5–6
context–sensitive help, WP 39
Control menu (application) buttons, WP 8, WP 9
Control menu (document) buttons, WP 8, WP 9
copies, printing number of, WP 30, WP 87
copy and paste text
    between documents, WP 149–150
    for pull quote, WP 220
    within document, WP 57–59
Copy button
    copying text in document using, WP 58
    transferring data between documents using, WP 149
Copy command (Edit menu), WP 58
copying
    linked graphic, WP 258–259
    text for pull quote, WP 220
    text from one document to another, WP 149–152
    text in document, WP 57–59
copyright symbol, WP 222
Corel DAD (Desktop Application Director), WP 7, WP 9
Corel WordPerfect 7, WP 7
correcting errors, WP 6
    data files and, WP 175
    finding and replacing text, WP 98–100
    format codes and, WP 82
    Grammatik and, WP 104–106
    spelling check, WP 19–21, WP 101–103
    Thesaurus and, WP 103–104
Courier font, WP 9
Create command (Table menu), WP 147–148

Create Data File dialog box, WP 174, WP 175–176
Create Form File dialog box, WP 180, WP 181
Create from File radio button (Insert Object dialog box), WP 249, WP 255
Create Merge File dialog box, WP 174
Create Table dialog box, WP 147–148
creating
    data file, WP 173–176
    documents, WP 5–6, WP 15–32
    footer, WP 112
    footnotes, WP 113
    form file for letter, WP 180–181
    form file for mailing labels, WP 192–193
    headers, WP 109
    mailing labels, WP 191–194
    multiple–page report, WP 93–126
    outline, WP 132–136
    paragraph style, WP 115–117
    records in data file, WP 178
    styles, WP 120–122
    table using Table button, WP 139–140
    table using Table Create command, WP 147–148
    telephone list from merge, WP 194–197
    text file, WP 175–176
    title for newsletter using TextArt, WP 206–209
Ctrl key, WP 13
curly quotes, WP 205, WP 206, WP 222, WP 225
Custom Line command (Graphics menu), WP 230
cut–and–paste method, moving footnote or endnote using, WP 114
Cut button
    moving data in document using, WP 57
    transferring data between documents using, WP 149
cutting text
    between documents, WP 149
    within document, WP 56–57

D

dashes, desktop publishing use of, WP 205
dat (data file) filename extension, WP 179
data
    entering into data file, WP 176–179
    importing from another application, WP 251–254
    transferring between documents, WP 148–152
data file, WP 171
    adding new records to, WP 179
    associating for mailing labels, WP 193
    associating for telephone list, WP 195
    creating, WP 173–176
    entering data into, WP 176–179
    linking to form file, WP 180, WP 181
    mailing labels and, WP 192
    merging form file with, WP 185–191
    saving, WP 179
    sorting for form letters, WP 186–188
Data File button (Merge dialog box), WP 174, WP 175
Datasheet, WP 251–252, WP 253
Datasheet command (View menu), WP 253

data source, WP 171
    combined with form file, WP 171–172, WP 185–186
    selecting in Merge dialog box, WP 174, WP 175
data table file, creating, WP 174
date, WP 11–13, WP 23
    current, in merge document, WP 172, WP 181–182
    font size of, WP 12–13
    newsletter, WP 212–213
    in report, WP 112
    status bar display and, WP 10
Date button (Merge feature bar), WP 182
Date command (Insert menu), WP 11, WP 12, WP 112
Date menu, Date Text command, WP 11–12
DATE merge code, WP 172, WP 181–182
Date Text command, WP 11–12
decimal tab stop, WP 68
default format codes, WP 119
default settings, WP 15
defining table of contents, WP 160–161
Delete key, deleting text using, WP 36, WP 52
deleting
    characters, WP 19, WP 36–37
    columns, WP 145
    endnote, WP 114
    to end of line, WP 37
    entire word, WP 36
    footnote, WP 114
    format codes, WP 84–85
    rows, WP 145
    selecting text and, WP 51–53
    text in document, WP 36–37, WP 52
    undoing, WP 53–54
demote an outline paragraph, WP 134–135
descending order sort, WP 143–144, WP 186
desktop publishing, WP 203–231
destination application, WP 239, WP 240, WP 241
destination file, WP 239
dictionary, WordPerfect, WP 101
displaying
    end–of–paragraph symbol, WP 18
    formatting codes, WP 82–84
    margin guidelines, WP 11
    nonprinting symbols, WP 18
    Power Bar, WP 10, WP 16
    Ruler, WP 10, WP 16
    status bar, WP 10
    Toolbar, WP 10, WP 16
document(s)
    active, WP 86, WP 151
    closing without saving changes, WP 21
    content of, WP 5–6, WP 46
    copying and pasting between, WP 149–150
    desktop publishing, WP 203–231
    editing, see editing
    finding and replacing text in, WP 98–100
    finding text in, WP 96–97
    font setting, WP 16–17
    formatting, see formatting
    form file, see form file
    hyphenating, WP 226–228
    inactive, WP 151
    inserting objects in, see inserting objects
    merged, WP 171–172, WP 185–186
    moving insertion point in, WP 35, WP 49–50
    moving text within, WP 54–59

multiple, *see* multiple documents
multiple–page report, WP 93–126
newsletter, WP 203–231
open, *see* open documents
opening existing, WP 33–35,
   WP 46–48
opening multiple, WP 86
organization of, WP 6
outline for, WP 132–137
page size or orientation, WP 60–61
planning, WP 5–6
presentation, WP 6, WP 46
previewing, WP 29–30
printing, WP 6, WP 30
producing, WP 5–6, WP 15–32
renaming, WP 48
retrieving styles file into,
   WP 123–124
saving for first time, WP 24
saving while working, WP 29
saving with new filename, WP 38,
   WP 48
scrolling through, WP 27–29
selecting text in, *see* selecting text
sizing, WP 15
spell checking, WP 19–21,
   WP 101–103
style, WP 6, WP 114–124
switching between, WP 86–87
tab settings, WP 67–70
transferring data between,
   WP 148–152
word wrap and, WP 26–27
Document, Initial Codes Style
   command (Format menu), WP 119
Document, Properties command
   (File menu), WP 85
document Control menu buttons,
   WP 8, WP 9
document file, WP 5
Document Initial Font dialog box,
   WP 17
document–layout commands, WP 60
document name, WP 8
   header and, WP 110, WP 111
document (open) style, WP 115
Document Properties feature, WP 85
document views, WP 16
document window(s), WP 9
   closing, WP 21
   maximizing, WP 8
   scrolling, WP 27–29
   tiling, WP 150
   viewing two, WP 150–151
   views, WP 16
dot leader, WP 68, WP 195
double–indent paragraph, WP 65
double line spacing, WP 210
desktop publishing characteristics
   of, WP 204–206
Draft command (View menu), WP 16
draft of report, opening, WP 94–96
Draft view, WP 16
drag–and–drop
   copying between documents
      using, WP 151–152
   moving text using, WP 54–56
   outline family, WP 137
dragging
   changing column width by,
      WP 153
   changing margins by, WP 61
   copying linked graphic by,
      WP 258–259
   moving outline paragraphs by,
      WP 136
   moving tab stop by, WP 70
   removing tab stop from Ruler by,
      WP 69
   selecting paragraph by, WP 53
   table grid, WP 140
drive
   opening document and, WP 34,
      WP 46, WP 48
   saving files and, WP 24, WP 25

drop cap, newsletter and, WP 205,
   WP 206, WP 218–219
Drop Cap command (Format
   menu), WP 218, WP 219
drop shadow
   around chapter title, WP 155
   color, WP 208, WP 209–210
   TextArt in newsletter and,
      WP 208, WP 209–210
duplicated words, WP 101

Edit Box command (Graphics
   menu), WP 217
Edit Box palette
   chart and, WP 253
   graphic in newsletter and, WP 217
Edit Box QuickSpot
   centering embedded spreadsheet
      using, WP 250
   sizing clipart and, WP 216,
      WP 217
editing, WP 6
   annuity document, WP 48–59
   business letter, WP 35–37
   clipart, WP 217–218
   embedded object, WP 240,
      WP 250, WP 253
   endnotes, WP 113
   footnotes, WP 113
   form letter, WP 189
   Grammatik and, WP 104–106
   header, WP 124–125
   imported object, WP 240
   imported text, WP 243–244
   linked object, WP 241,
      WP 257–259, WP 261
   moving text and, WP 54–59
   outlines, WP 133
   report, WP 98–114
   Reveal Codes window and, WP 84
   Spell Checker and, WP 101–103
   styles, WP 117–120
   table, WP 142–144
   TextArt image, WP 209–210
   text box, WP 221–222
   Thesaurus and, WP 103–104
   undoing, WP 53–54
Edit menu
   Copy command, WP 58
   Find and Replace command,
      WP 96–100
   Links command, WP 259–260
   Paste command, WP 58
Edit Text shortcut menu, text box
   and, WP 220
embedding objects, WP 238, WP 240,
   WP 248–254
   centering, WP 249–250
   graph created with Chart,
      WP 251–254
   modifying, WP 250
   Quattro Pro spreadsheet,
      WP 248–250
em dashes (—), WP 205, WP 222,
   WP 224–225
en dashes (–), WP 205
ENDFIELD merge code, WP 174
End key, moving insertion point
   using, WP 49
endnotes
   adding, WP 112–113
   deleting or moving, WP 114
end of line, deleting to, WP 37
end-of-paragraph symbol, displaying,
   WP 18
ENDRECORD merge code, WP 174
entering
   data into data file, WP 176–179
   text in business letter, WP 23–24
   text in table, WP 141
Enter key
   data entry for data file and,
      WP 177
   hard return and, WP 83

outline levels and, WP 133,
   WP 134
envelope(s)
   mailing labels for, WP 191–194
   printing, WP 31–32
Envelope command (Format menu),
   WP 31
Envelope dialog box, WP 31
erasing characters, WP 19
error correction, *see* correcting
   errors
example, modifying style by,
   WP 117–119
existing document, opening,
   WP 33–35, WP 46–48
Exit command (File menu), WP 32
exiting WordPerfect, WP 32

F2 (find and replace), WP 96, WP 98,
   WP 99
F7 (align paragraphs), WP 69
F7 (indent), WP 66
family, outline, WP 137
field(s)
   conditions for, in selecting
      records to merge, WP 188–190
   entering information into, WP 174,
      WP 176–179
field codes, inserting for mailing
   labels, WP 193
FIELD merge codes, WP 172
   inserting for form letter, WP 182
   inserting for mailing labels,
      WP 193
field name(s)
   adding, WP 175–176
   inserting in form file, WP 183–184
   order of, WP 174
   specifying, WP 173–176
Field name list (Create Data File dialog box), WP 175–176
FIELDNAMES merge code,
   WP 173–176
file(s), WP 5
   bitmap images, WP 216
   Chart, WP 251
   data, *see* data file
   destination, WP 239
   form, *see* form file
   importing, WP 240
   integrating from other programs,
      WP 237–262
   opening existing, WP 46–48
   Paint, WP 255–257
   saving styles in separate,
      WP 122–123
   source, WP 239
   styles, WP 122–124
   table, WP 171
   text, WP 171, WP 175–176
   WordPerfect graphics, WP 216
File command (Insert menu)
   adding records to data file and,
      WP 179
   importing files and, WP 242,
      WP 243, WP 245
File menu
   Close command, WP 21
   Document, Properties command,
      WP 85
   Exit command, WP 32
   Print command, WP 38
   Save As command, WP 38, WP 48
   Save command, WP 24
filename, WP 24–25
   saving document with new, WP 38,
      WP 48
filename extensions, WP 25
fill
   newsletter and, WP 205,
      WP 212–213
   text box, WP 221

fill, border
  in newsletter, WP 213
  in table, WP 155–156
Find and Replace command (Edit menu), WP 96–100
Find and Replace Text dialog box, WP 97, WP 98–100
Find Next button (Find and Replace Text dialog box), WP 97, WP 100
find and replace text, WP 98–100
find text, WP 96–97
first–line tab command, WP 67
first record, moving to, WP 178, WP 179
floppy disk, WP 5
flush right, page number at, WP 110
Flush Right with Dot Leaders command, WP 195
folder
  clipart, WP 216
  embedding object and, WP 249
  importing object and, WP 242
  opening document and, WP 34, WP 48
  saving files and, WP 24, WP 25
font
  changing, WP 74–76
  default settings, WP 15
  desktop publishing and, WP 204
  Power Bar display, WP 9
  sans serif, WP 74
  serif, WP 74
  setting from Format menu, WP 16–17
  TextArt and, WP 207
font appearance, changing, WP 78–81
font color, text box and, WP 220
Font command (Format menu)
  changing font and, WP 75
  setting initial font and, WP 17
  text box and, WP 220
Font dialog box
  changing font and, WP 75
  setting initial font and, WP 17
Font face list box (Document Initial Font dialog box), WP 17
Font face scroll box, WP 76
Font list arrow (TextArt 7 dialog box), WP 207
font size
  changing from Font dialog box, WP 74, WP 76
  changing from Power Bar, WP 12–13
  date, WP 12–13
  default settings, WP 15
  desktop publishing and, WP 204
  newsletter, WP 206
  newspaper–style columns, WP 214
  Power Bar display, WP 9
  setting from Format menu, WP 16–17
  text box, WP 220
  very large, WP 116
Font Size button (Power Bar), WP 12–13
font style
  changing, WP 74, WP 76
  newsletter, WP 206
  text box, WP 220
Font style list box (Document Initial Font dialog box), WP 17
footers, WP 109–111, WP 112
footnote(s)
  adding, WP 112–114
  deleting or moving, WP 114
Footnote, Create command (Insert menu), WP 113
footnote separator line, WP 113
Formal Memo or Letter style, WP 105
format codes
  deleting, WP 84–85
  initial (default), WP 119
  modifying initial, WP 119
  revealing, WP 82–84

Format menu
  Border/Fill, Page command, WP 229
  Border/Fill, Paragraph command, newsletter and, WP 213
  Border/Fill, Paragraph command, table and, WP 155
  Columns, Define command, WP 214
  Document, Initial Codes Style command, WP 119
  Drop Cap command, WP 218, WP 219
  Envelope command, WP 31
  Font command, changing font and, WP 75
  Font command, setting initial font and, WP 17
  Font command, text box and, WP 220
  Header/Footer command, WP 109, WP 112, WP 124
  Justification command, WP 63
  Justification, Center command, WP 121
  Justification, Full command, WP 119
  Labels command, WP 192
  Line, Center command, WP 65
  Line, Flush Right command, WP 110
  Line, Flush Right with Dot Leaders command, WP 195
  Line, Hyphenation command, WP 227
  Line, Spacing command, WP 119
  Margins command, WP 62
  Page, Center command, WP 107–108
  Page, Keep Text Together command, WP 71, WP 72, WP 73, WP 120
  Page, Suppress command, WP 138
  Page Numbering, Value/Adjust command, WP 111
  Paragraph, Format command, WP 228–229
  Paragraph, Indent command, WP 66
  Styles command, WP 121, WP 123, WP 211
  Typesetting, Advance command, WP 211
  Typesetting, Word/Letter Spacing command, WP 211
formatting, WP 6, WP 60–85
  bullets, WP 76–77
  centering page vertically, WP 107–108
  default settings, WP 15
  endnotes, WP 112–113
  finding text with, WP 96
  font, WP 16–17, WP 74–76
  font appearance, WP 78–81
  font size, WP 16–17
  footers, WP 109–111
  footnotes, WP 112–114
  headers, WP 109–111
  imported text, WP 243–244
  indenting paragraphs, WP 65–67
  justifying text, WP 62–64
  keeping lines of text together, WP 70–73, WP 120
  lines, WP 64–65
  line spacing in newsletter, WP 210–212
  margins, WP 61–62
  modifying table, WP 159
  newspaper–style columns, WP 214
  numbered lists, WP 78
  orientation, WP 60–61
  page size, WP 60–61
  pull quote, WP 219, WP 220–221
  QuickFormat and, WP 81–82
  QuickStyle and, WP 120–121
  revealing codes, WP 82–84
  with styles, WP 114–124
  tables, WP 139–140, WP 143, WP 153–155, WP 157–158
  tab settings, WP 67–70
  telephone list, WP 195
  text in text box, WP 220–221
  widow/orphan protection, WP 72–73
formatting commands, categories of, WP 60
form file, WP 170
  creating for letter, WP 180–181
  creating for mailing labels, WP 192–193
  data source combined with, WP 171–172, WP 185–186
  editing, WP 181–185
  inserting merge codes in, WP 172, WP 181–184, WP 193
  linking data file to, WP 180, WP 181
  merging with data file, WP 185–191
  saving, WP 181
  telephone list and, WP 195, WP 196
form letters, WP 169
  creating data file for, WP 173–176
  editing, WP 189
  entering data into data file for, WP 176–179
  form file for, WP 170, WP 180–186
  mailing labels for, WP 191–194
  merging data file and form file for, WP 185–186
  selecting records to merge for, WP 188–191
  sorting records for, WP 186–188
  See also merge
formulas, table, WP 146
fraction symbol, WP 222
frm (form file) filename extension, WP 181
From text box (Envelope dialog box), WP 31
full justification, WP 63, WP 64, WP 119, WP 226
Full Page view, WP 29, WP 108
function keys, WP 13

G

General tab (TextArt 7 dialog box), WP 207
Generate, Table of Contents command (Tools menu), WP 160, WP 161
Go to Data button (Merge feature bar), WP 187, WP 195
Go to Form button (Merge feature bar), WP 188
grammar checker, WP 104–106
Grammatik, WP 104–106
Grammatik command (Tools menu), WP 105
graph created with Chart, embedding, WP 251–254
graphics
  desktop publishing and, WP 205
  importing, WP 245–247
  newsletter and, WP 205, WP 206, WP 215–218
  positioning, WP 218
  sizing, WP 217–218
graphics boxes
  attaching, WP 246
  imported picture in, WP 246
  linked map and, WP 256–257
  newsletter and, WP 205
  TextArt and, WP 206–207
Graphics menu
  Chart command, WP 251
  Custom Line command, WP 230
  Edit Box command, WP 217

TextArt command, WP 207
Text Box command, WP 220
graphics program, WP 239
grid, table, WP 140
grid marks, Ruler and, WP 10
guidelines
   margin, see margin guidelines
   newspaper–style columns, WP 215
   table, see table guidelines
Guidelines command (View menu), WP 11
Guidelines dialog box, WP 11

H

hanging indent paragraph, WP 65
hard disk, WP 5
hard page break, WP 107–108
hard return
   adding space between lines of text using, WP 210
   code for, WP 83
   ending paragraph with, WP 115
Has Types word, Thesaurus and, WP 103
header
   adding, WP 109–111
   editing, WP 124–125
   inserting horizontal line in, WP 110
   suppressing, WP 138
Header/Footer command (Format menu), WP 109, WP 112, WP 124
Header/Footer feature bar, WP 109
header row, specifying in table, WP 143
heading, WP 6
   centering in table, WP 153
   modifying styles, WP 118
   space before and after in newsletter, WP 211
   styles for, WP 116
Heading 1 style, WP 116
   modifying, WP 118–119
Heading 2 style, WP 116
   modifying, WP 118
   newsletter and, WP 211
Heading 3 style, WP 117
   modifying, WP 119
heading styles, WP 116–119
   newsletter, WP 211
   table of contents, WP 161
help, context-sensitive, WP 39
Help feature, WP 38–41
Help menu, Help Topics command, WP 39
Help Topics command, WP 39
Help Topics dialog box, WP 39–40
Help Topics window, WP 39–40
hidden format codes, revealing, WP 82–84
Hide Ruler Bar command (Ruler shortcut menu), WP 14
hiding
   nonprinting symbols, WP 18
   Ruler, WP 14
highlighting block of text, WP 50–53
Home key, moving insertion point using, WP 49
homonym, WP 105
horizontal line, inserting in header, WP 110
horizontal scroll bar, WP 9
hyphenating text, WP 226–228
hyphenation zone, WP 226–227
hyphens, replacing with em dashes, WP 224–225

I

IF merge code, WP 172
image
   clipart, see clipart
   TextArt, see TextArt
Image button
   inserting clipart using, WP 216
   inserting picture using, WP 245

Import Data dialog box, WP 252
importing objects, WP 238, WP 240, WP 241, WP 242–247
   formatting text, WP 243–244
   one WordPerfect document into another, WP 244–245
   pictures, WP 245–247
inactive document, WP 151
inches
   size of graphic image in, WP 217
   sizing linked object in, WP 257
   spacing between lines of text in, WP 211
   spacing between paragraphs in bulleted list in, WP 228–229
   tab stops in, WP 69, WP 70
indent paragraph, WP 65–67
Index tab (Help Topics dialog box), WP 39
Information tab (Properties dialog box), WP 85
Initial Codes Style, WP 119
Initial Font button (Font dialog box), WP 17
inkjet printer, desktop publishing and, WP 204
Insert Bullet button, WP 77, WP 78
Insert Bullets button, WP 244
Insert Field button (Merge feature bar), WP 180, WP 182, WP 193
Insert File dialog box
   adding records to data file and, WP 179
   importing files and, WP 243, WP 245
Insert Image dialog box, WP 216, WP 245–246
inserting
   blank lines, WP 22–23
   columns, WP 145
   current date, WP 11–13, WP 23, WP 112
   drop cap in newsletter, WP 218–219
   endnotes, WP 113
   existing clipart image, WP 216–217
   field codes for mailing labels, WP 193
   footer, WP 109, WP 112
   footnotes, WP 113
   header, WP 109
   hyphenation, WP 228
   information in form file by linking to data file, WP 180, WP 181
   merge codes in form file, WP 181–184, WP 193
   new text into existing text, WP 35–36
   objects, see inserting objects
   page break, WP 71, WP 108
   pull quote in newsletter, WP 219–222
   rows, WP 145
   special characters in newsletter, WP 222–225
   symbols in newsletter, WP 222–225
   tables, WP 139–140, WP 148
   text in document, WP 35–36
   vertical line between newsletter columns, WP 230
   WordPerfect clipart into newsletter, WP 215–218
inserting objects, WP 237–239
   choosing method of, WP 241
   embedding, WP 240, WP 241, WP 248–254
   importing, WP 240, WP 241, WP 242–247
   linking, WP 241, WP 255–261
insertion point, WP 8, WP 10
   applying styles and, WP 116
   clipart and, WP 216
   drop cap and, WP 218, WP 219

importing files and, WP 243
linking object and, WP 255
margin changes from, WP 61
moving to text using Find and Replace command and, WP 97
moving with keystrokes, WP 49–50
moving with mouse pointer, WP 35
newspaper–style columns, WP 214
table and, WP 140, WP 141
TextArt and, WP 207
Insert key, switching to Typeover mode using, WP 37
Insert menu
   Bullets & Numbers command, WP 76, WP 77, WP 78
   Character command, WP 223
   Date command, WP 11
   Date, Date Code command, WP 112
   File command, adding records to data file and, WP 179
   File command, importing files and, WP 242, WP 243, WP 245
   Footnote, Create command, WP 113
   Object command, WP 249, WP 255
Insert mode, WP 35
Insert Object dialog box, WP 249, WP 255
inside address, entering, WP 23–24
integrating WordPerfect with other Windows programs, WP 237–262
Interactive Labs, WP 4
Is a Type of word, Thesaurus and, WP 103
Italic button
   existing text and, WP 81
   new text and, WP 80
italicizing text, WP 80–81
   removing format code for, WP 84–85

J

justification, WP 62–64
   center, WP 63, WP 118, WP 121, WP 158
   default settings, WP 15
   full, WP 63, WP 64, WP 119, WP 226
   left, WP 63
   narrow columns and, WP 226
   right, see right justification
   numbers within cells, WP 153–154
   text within cells, WP 153–155
Justification command (Format menu), WP 63
   Center option, WP 121
   Full option, WP 119

K

Keep Text Together dialog box, WP 71, WP 72, WP 73, WP 120
KEYBOARD merge code, WP 172
keyboard shortcuts
   copying and pasting text, WP 58
   cutting and pasting text, WP 57
   finding and replacing text, WP 98
   justifying text, WP 63
Key definitions (New Sort dialog box), WP 187, WP 196
keystrokes, moving insertion point with, WP 49–50

L

label, column and row, WP 139
Labels command (Format menu), WP 192
landscape orientation, WP 60–61
laser printer, desktop publishing and, WP 204
last record, moving to, WP 178
leading, between lines of text, WP 210, WP 211–212
left–aligned tab stop, WP 69

left hyphenation zone, WP 226
left justification, WP 63
left margin
 changing, WP 61–62
 graphic image positioned at, WP 218
 guideline, WP 8
 location of on Ruler, WP 61
left tab stop, WP 68
letter
 drop cap, *see* drop cap
 table column labeled with, WP 139
 See also character(s)
letterhead, space for, WP 22
letters
 business, *see* business letter
 form, *see* form letters
levels
 outline, WP 132–136
 table of contents, WP 160, WP 161
line
 dotted (dot leader), WP 195
 horizontal, inserting in header, WP 110
 inserting blank, WP 22–23
 vertical, *see* vertical line
 See also rules
line, border
 around newsletter page, WP 229
 pull quote and, WP 220, WP 221
Line command (Format menu)
 Center option, WP 65
 Flush Right option, WP 110
 Flush Right with Dot Leaders option, WP 195
 Hyphenation option, WP 227
 Spacing option, WP 119
line formatting commands, WP 60, WP 64
Line Hyphenation dialog box, WP 227
line number (vertical position), WP 10
Lines/Fill Button, tables and, WP 159
lines of text
 centering, WP 64–65, WP 118
 codes marking end of, WP 83
 formatting, WP 64–65
 keeping together, WP 70–73, WP 120
 leading between, WP 210, WP 211–212
 moving insertion point one at a time, WP 49
 selecting, WP 50
 space between in newsletter, WP 206, WP 210–212
line spacing, WP 6
 default settings, WP 15
 header, WP 124
 methods for changing, WP 210
 modifying style and, WP 119
Line Spacing command, WP 119, WP 210
linking data file to form file, WP 180, WP 181
linking objects, WP 238, WP 241, WP 255–261
 modifying in Paint, WP 257–259
 modifying in WordPerfect, WP 260–261
 updating and, WP 259–260
Links command (Edit menu), WP 259–260
list of items
 applying bullets to, WP 76–77
 applying numbers to, WP 78
 styles for, WP 116
Look In list arrow (Open dialog box), WP 34, WP 46

M

mailing labels, WP 191–194
margin(s)
 changing, WP 61–62
 default settings, WP 15, WP 61
 narrow columns of text and, WP 226
 orientation and, WP 60
 telephone list, WP 195
 See also bottom margin; left margin; right margin; top margin
margin guidelines, WP 10
 changing by dragging, WP 61
 displaying, WP 11
Margins command (Format menu), WP 62
Margins dialog box, WP 61, WP 62
Match menu, finding and replacing text and, WP 99
mathematical calculations, performing in tables, WP 146–147
Maximize button, WP 7
maximizing
 document window, WP 8
 WordPerfect screen, WP 7
menu(s), shortcut, *see* shortcut menus
menu bar, WP 8, WP 9
 choosing commands using, WP 11–12
 opening document from, WP 34
merge, WP 170–197
 creating data file for, WP 173–176
 data source and, WP 171
 entering data into data file, WP 176–179
 form file and, WP 170, WP 180–186
 form file and data file, WP 185–191
 mailing labels, WP 191–194
 process, WP 170–173
 selecting records to, WP 188–191
 sorting records for form letter, WP 186–188
 sorting records for telephone list, WP 195–196
 table file and, WP 171
 telephone list, WP 194–197
 text file and, WP 171
Merge button (Merge feature bar), WP 185, WP 188
merge codes, WP 170, WP 172
 form file and, WP 180, WP 181–184, WP 193
 inserting for mailing labels, WP 193
 inserting for telephone list, WP 195
Merge Codes button (Merge feature bar), WP 180
Merge command (Tools menu)
 creating data file and, WP 174
 creating form file and, WP 180, WP 181
merged document, WP 171–172, WP 185–186
Merge dialog box
 creating data file and, WP 174–175
 creating form file and, WP 180–181
 mailing labels and, WP 193
Merge feature bar
 adding merge codes to form file and, WP 180, WP 182, WP 193
 field codes for mailing labels and, WP 193
 merging data file and form file, WP 185, WP 188
 sorting data file and, WP 187
Merge feature button, sorting data file and, WP 195
Microsoft Word document, *see* Word document

modifier keys, WP 13
modifying
 embedded graph, WP 253–254
 embedded spreadsheet, WP 250
 initial format codes, WP 119
 linked object in Paint, WP 257–259
 linked object in WordPerfect, WP 260–261
 outline, WP 136–137
 styles, WP 117–120
 table format, WP 159
 table structure, WP 145–146
 text, WP 50–53
mouse
 dragging and dropping text using, WP 54–55
 selecting text using, WP 50–51
mouse pointer, WP 9
 dragging and dropping text and, WP 54–55
 moving insertion point using, WP 35
 shadow pointer and, WP 20
Move Down button, outline and, WP 133
Move Up button, outline and, WP 133
moving
 endnote, WP 114
 footnote, WP 114
 imported picture, WP 246–247
 insertion point with keystrokes, WP 49–50
 insertion point with mouse pointer, WP 35
 outline paragraphs up and down, WP 136–137
 to records in data file, WP 178
 in table, WP 141
 tab stops, WP 70
 to text using Find, WP 96
moving text, WP 54–59
 using copy and paste, WP 57–59
 using cut and paste, WP 56–57
 using drag and drop, WP 54–56
multiple documents, switching between, WP 86–87
multiple-page report, WP 93–126
multiple paragraphs
 indenting, WP 67
 selecting, WP 51

N

name, file, *see* filename
Name a field text box (Create Data File dialog box), WP 175
New Document Window button, creating form file and, WP 180
New Record button (Quick Data Entry dialog box), WP 178
newsletter, WP 203–231
 border around page of, WP 229
 columns of text in, WP 205, WP 206, WP 214–215
 date centered in, WP 212–213
 drop cap and, WP 205, WP 206, WP 218–219
 elements of, WP 205–206
 fill and, WP 205, WP 212–213
 graphics in, WP 205, WP 206, WP 215–218
 hyphenating text in, WP 226–228
 positioning graphic in, WP 218
 pull quote in, WP 205, WP 206, WP 219–222
 rules and, WP 205, WP 206, WP 212–213
 space between lines of text in, WP 206, WP 210–212
 space between paragraphs of bulleted list in, WP 228–229
 special characters in, WP 206, WP 222–225

symbols in, WP 206, WP 222–225
title for, WP 206–210
vertical line between columns, WP 230
New Sort dialog box, WP 187, WP 196
newspaper–style columns, WP 205, WP 206, WP 214–215
   hyphenating text in, WP 226–228
   spacing and, WP 215
   vertical line between, WP 230
   width of, WP 215
Next Page button, WP 8
next record, moving to, WP 178, WP 179
No Lines Totals format, table and, WP 159
nonprinting symbols, displaying, WP 18
notes, *see* endnotes; footnote(s)
number(s)
   applying to list of items, WP 78
   in cells, right–justifying, WP 153–154
   footnote, WP 113
   page, *see* page number/numbering
   paragraph outline, WP 132–133
   table row labeled with, WP 139
numbered lists, styles for, WP 116
numbered notes, WP 112
number of copies, printing, WP 30, WP 87
numerical order sort, table and, WP 143–144
Numeric Format button (Tables toolbar), WP 146

O

object(s), WP 239. *See also* inserting objects
Object command (Insert menu), WP 249, WP 255
object linking and embedding (OLE), WP 241
OLE, *see* object linking and embedding
online Help, WP 38–41
Open button (Open dialog box), WP 34
Open button (Toolbar)
   opening document using, WP 34, WP 46
   opening multiple documents using, WP 86
Open dialog box
   opening document and, WP 34, WP 46
   opening multiple documents and, WP 86
open documents
   switching between, WP 86–87
   viewing two, WP 150–151
open formatting commands, WP 60, WP 61
opening
   draft of report, WP 94–96
   existing document, WP 33–35, WP 46–48
   multiple documents, WP 86
Options tab (TextArt 7 dialog box), WP 208
organization of document, WP 6
orientation
   changing, WP 60–61
   default settings, WP 15
orphan, WP 72–73
outline(s)
   creating, WP 132–136
   editing, WP 133
   levels, WP 132–136
   modifying, WP 136–137
   types of, WP 134
Outline command (Tools menu), WP 133, WP 134

outline family, WP 137
Output button (Merge feature bar), WP 185

P

page
   border around, in newsletter, WP 229
   centering vertically, WP 107–108
   keeping lines of text together on same, WP 71–72, WP 120
   moving insertion point to beginning of previous or next, WP 49
   moving insertion point to top or bottom of current, WP 49
   orphan alone at bottom of, WP 72
   selecting, WP 50
   size of, WP 60–61
   widow alone at top of, WP 72
page border, newsletter and, WP 206
page break
   automatic, WP 71
   hard, WP 107–108
   inserting, WP 71, WP 108
Page command (Format menu)
   Center option, WP 107–108
   Keep Text Together option, WP 71, WP 72, WP 73, WP 120
   Suppress option, WP 138
Page command (View menu), WP 16
PageDown key, WP 49
Page Margins button, WP 61
page number/numbering
   default settings, WP 15
   header and, WP 109–111
   status bar display of current, WP 10
   table of contents, WP 160
Page Numbering, Value/Adjust command (Format menu), WP 111
PageUp key, WP 49
Page view
   business plan in, WP 138
   returning to, WP 30
   setting document view to, WP 16
Page/Zoom Full button, WP 29, WP 108
Paint program
   linking file from, WP 255–257
   modifying linked object in, WP 257–259
paper size, default settings, WP 15
paragraph(s)
   adding spacing between, in bulleted list, WP 228–229
   aligning vertically, WP 68–69
   attaching picture to, WP 246–247
   bulleted list, adding space between, WP 228–229
   defined, WP 115
   deleting, WP 52
   double–indent, WP 65
   formatting commands, WP 60, WP 65
   hanging indent, WP 65
   indenting, WP 65–67
   indenting first line of, WP 67
   indenting multiple, WP 67
   moving insertion point down one at a time, WP 49
   numbered in outline, WP 132–133
   outline, WP 132–136
   orphan and, WP 72
   positioning graphic in, WP 218
   QuickFormat and, WP 81–82
   selecting, WP 50, WP 51, WP52
   selecting multiple, , WP 51
   spacing between, WP 210
   style of current, WP 116
   widow and, WP 72
paragraph (paired) style, WP 115, WP 121
paragraph (paired–auto) style, WP 115

modifying by example, WP 117–118
paragraph border
   newsletter and, WP 206, WP 213
   table and, WP 156
Paragraph Border/Fill dialog box
   newsletter and, WP 213
   table and, WP 155–156
Paragraph command (Format menu)
   Format option, WP 228–229
   Indent option, WP 66
Paragraph Edit QuickSpot, WP 20, WP 50
Paragraph Format dialog box
   adding space between paragraphs of bulleted list and, WP 228–229
   spacing between paragraphs and, WP 210
paragraph symbol, displaying, WP 18
partial line spacing, WP 210
passive voice, WP 106
paste
   copying data in document and, WP 57–59
   cutting and, WP 56–57
   transferring data between documents and, WP 149, WP 150
Paste button
   transferring data in document using, WP 57, WP 58
   transferring data between documents using, WP 149, WP 150
Paste command (Edit menu), WP 58
percentage, hyphenation zone in, WP 227
Perform Merge dialog box, WP 185, WP 188, WP 189
photograph, importing scanned, WP 245–247
phrase
   deleting, WP 53
   finding, WP 96
   selecting, WP 50, WP 53
   See also pull quote
picture
   importing into WordPerfect, WP 245–247
   moving, WP 246–247
   See also clipart
picture symbols, WP 223
placeholder text, merges and, WP 170, WP 172
Place records in a table check box (Merge dialog box), WP 174, WP 175
planning documents, WP 5–6
point–and–click, moving insertion point using, WP 49
points, WP 9, WP 74
portrait orientation, WP 60–61
Position Hyphen dialog box, WP 227–228
positioning
   embedded chart, WP 253
   embedded spreadsheet, WP 249–250
   graphic image, WP 218
   hyphens, WP 227–228
   imported picture, WP 246
   linked map, WP 257
   linked Paint object, WP 256
position number (horizontal position), WP 10
Power Bar, WP 8, WP 9
   changing font size from, WP 12–13
   choosing commands from, WP 12–13
   displaying, WP 10, WP 16
presentation of document, WP 6
Presentations 7 Chart, embedding graph created with, WP 251–254
previewing document, WP 29–30
Previous Page button, WP 8
previous record, moving to, WP 178

Print button (Print dialog box), WP 30
Print button (Toolbar), WP 30
Print command (File menu), WP 38
Print dialog box, WP 30
   number of copies and, WP 87
Print Envelope button (Envelope dialog box), WP 31
printer
   current, WP 30
   name of on status bar, WP 10
printing, WP 6
   Annuity document, WP 87
   business letter, WP 30
   desktop publishing and, WP 204
   envelope, WP 31–32
   number of copies, WP 30, WP 87
   orientation and, WP 60–61
producing documents, WP 5–6, WP 15–32
promote an outline paragraph, WP 134, WP 135–136
prompt, displaying during merge, WP 172
properties
   document, WP 85
   table, WP 143
Properties dialog box, WP 85
proportions
   graphic image, WP 217–218
   imported picture, WP 247
pull quote, newsletter and, WP 205, WP 206, WP 219–222

Q

Quattro Pro spreadsheet, embedding, WP 248–250
Quick Check questions, WP 4
QuickCorrect
   converting apostrophes and quotations marks to typographic symbols using, WP 225
   correcting spelling using, WP 20–21
QuickCorrect command (Tools menu), WP 20
Quick Data Entry dialog box, WP 177–179
QuickFormat, WP 81–82
QuickSpot button, WP 50
QuickStyle, WP 120–121
QuickSum command, tables and, WP 146
QuickTip
   display of on Toolbar, WP 9
   margins and, WP 61–62
quote, pull, *see* pull quote
quotes, curly, WP 205, WP 206, WP 222, WP 225

R

ragged edges, narrow columns of text and, WP 226
records
   adding new, WP 179
   creating additional, WP 178
   entering information into, WP 176–179
   merging, WP 185–191
   moving to, WP 178
   selecting to merge, WP 188–191
   sorting for form letters, WP 186–188
   sorting for telephone list, WP 195–196
   specifying names of fields in, WP 173
Redo button, WP 54
Redo command, WP 53
references, footnotes/endnotes and, WP 112
Reference Windows, WP 4
registered trademark symbol (®), WP 222, WP 223–224
related words, WP 103
renaming document, WP 48

Replace button (Find and Replace Text dialog box), WP 100
Replace button (Grammatik dialog box), WP 105
Replace button (Spell Checker dialog box), WP 102
Replace button (Thesaurus dialog box), WP 103, WP 104
replacement string, WP 98–100
replacing text, WP 98–100
report
   centering page vertically in, WP 107–108
   editing, WP 98–114
   editing header, WP 124–125
   endnotes in, WP 112–113
   footnotes in, WP 112–114
   formatting with styles, WP 114–124
   headers and footers in, WP 109–111
   multiple–page, WP 93–126
   opening draft of, WP 94–96
   spell checking, WP 101–103
   table of contents, WP 160–162
   Thesaurus and, WP 103–104
resize handle
   clipart and, WP 216, WP 217
   TextArt image and, WP 209
resizing
   graphic image, WP 217
   text box, WP 219
restoring deleted text, WP 53–54
return
   hard, WP 83, WP 115
   soft, WP 83
return address, printing, WP 31
Reveal Codes, WP 82–84
Reveal Codes command (View menu), WP 82
Reveal Codes window, WP 82–84
reversing edits, WP 53–54
right–aligned tab stop, WP 69
right hyphenation zone, WP 226
right justification
   numbers within cells, WP 153–154
   paragraph, WP 63
right margin
   automatic page numbering at, WP 110
   changing, WP 61
   hyphenation zone and, WP 226
   justification and, WP 63, WP 226
   location of on Ruler, WP 61
   narrow columns and, WP 226
right tab stop, WP 68
rivers, narrow columns and, WP 226
row(s), table, WP 139
   creating, WP 140, WP 148
   deleting, WP 145
   indicators, WP 140
   inserting, WP 145
   selecting, WP 142
   sorting, WP 142–144
Row/Column Indicators button (Tables toolbar), WP 140
Ruler, WP 8
   displaying, WP 10, WP 16
   hiding/showing using shortcut menu, WP 14
   indenting paragraphs and, WP 66
   margin location on, WP 61
   tab stops on, WP 67, WP 69
Ruler Bar, *see* Ruler
Ruler shortcut menu
   Hide Ruler Bar command, WP 14
   right–aligned tab stop and, WP 69
rules
   newsletter and, WP 205, WP 206, WP 212–213
   table borders and, WP 155

S

salutation, WP 24
sans serif font, WP 74
Save As command (File menu), WP 38, WP 48
Save As dialog box, WP 24, WP 25–26, WP 38, WP 48
Save button (Save As dialog box), WP 26, WP 38, WP 48
Save button (Toolbar), WP 24, WP 25, WP 29
Save command (File menu), WP 24
saving
   before exiting WordPerfect, WP 32
   data file, WP 174, WP 179
   document for first time, WP 24
   document with new filename, WP 38, WP 48
   form file, WP 181
   merged document, WP 185
   styles in separate file, WP 122–123
   while working, WP 29
Save In list arrow (Save As dialog box), WP 25
scanned image, WP 245
scanner, WP 245
screen, moving insertion point to previous or next, WP 49
scroll bar, WP 8, WP 9, WP 28
scroll buttons, WP 8, WP 28
Scroll Down button, WP 28
scrolling, WP 27–29
Scroll Up button, WP 28
search string, WP 96–100
selecting records, to merge, WP 188–191
selecting text, WP 50–53
   aligning in vertical columns and, WP 68
   applying styles and, WP 116
   copying and pasting and, WP 57–58
   copying from one document to another, WP 149, WP 151
   cutting and pasting and, WP 56
   deleting and, WP 51–53
   drag and drop and, WP 54
   font changes and, WP 75
   formatting imported, WP 244
   formatting text box and, WP 220
   and moving using drag and drop, WP 54–56
   paragraphs for indentation, WP 66
   in table, WP 142
selection border, TextArt image, WP 209
sentence
   deleting, WP 51–52
   selecting, WP 50, WP 51
serif font, WP 74
Set as printer initial font check box (Document Initial Font dialog box), WP 17
setting tabs, WP 67–70
shading
   newsletter date background, WP 212–213
   table, WP 155
Shadow button (TextArt 7 dialog box), WP 208, WP 210
shadow color, TextArt, WP 208–210
Shadow color button (TextArt 7 dialog box), WP 208, WP 210
shadow palette, WP 208–209
shadow pointer, WP 20, WP 35
   cutting and pasting text and, WP 57
   moving text by dragging and dropping and, WP 55
shadow style palette, WP 209
shape of text, in newsletter title, WP 208
Shapes box (TextArt 7 dialog box), WP 208
Shift key, WP 13

Shift+F1 (context-sensitive help), WP 39
shortcut keys
    centering line of text using, WP 65
    choosing commands using, WP 13
    inserting date using, WP 13
    paragraph indents and, WP 66
    switching between open documents using, WP 86
shortcut menus
    choosing commands using, WP 14
    hide/show Ruler Bar using, WP 14
Show command (View menu), paragraph symbol and, WP 18
showing nonprinting symbols, WP 18
single line spacing, WP 210
sizing
    document, WP 15
    drop cap, WP 219
    graphic image, WP 217–218
    imported picture, WP 247
    linked map, WP 257
    See also resizing
Skip Always button (Spell Checker dialog box), WP 102
soft return, WP 83
Sort command (Tools menu), WP 143
Sort dialog box, WP 187, WP 195
sorting records
    for form letter merge, WP 186–188
    for telephone list merge, WP 195–196
sorting rows, in table, WP 142–144
sort key, WP 143
source application, WP 239, WP 240, WP 241
source document, information extracted from, WP 172
source file, WP 239
space
    adding between paragraphs of bulleted list, WP 228–229
    between lines of text, in newsletter, WP 206, WP 210–212
    between words, symbol marking, WP 18
    narrow columns of text and, WP 226
    white, WP 6
spaces, merged data and, WP 184
spacing
    between paragraphs, WP 210
    justification and, WP 62
    line, see line spacing
special characters
    adding to list, WP 76
    in newsletter, WP 206, WP 222–225
special effects, creating using TextArt, WP 207, WP 208
SpeedFormat, tables and, WP 157–158
Spell-As-You-Go feature, WP 19–20, WP 101
Spell-As-You-Go shortcut menu, WP 20
Spell Check button, WP 101
Spell Check command (Tools menu), WP 101
Spell Checker, WP 101–103
Spell Checker dialog box, WP 101
Speller, see Spell Checker
spelling
    QuickCorrect feature, WP 20–21
    Spell-As-You-Go feature, WP 19–20, WP 101
    Spell Check command and, WP 101
    Spell Checker and, WP 101–103
spreadsheet, WP 239
    embedding Quattro Pro, WP 248–250

Start button (Windows 95 taskbar)
    launching Paint program from, WP 258
    launching WordPerfect from, WP 7, WP 9
starting
    Paint program, WP 258
    WordPerfect, WP 7–8
Start menu (Windows 95), WP 7
status bar, WP 8
    displaying, WP 10
storage, WP 5
string
    replacement, WP 98–100
    search, WP 96–100
structure, table, see table structure
style(s), WP 6, WP 46, WP 114–124
    applying, WP 116–117, WP 122
    changing, WP 117–120
    creating, WP 120–122
    modifying, WP 117–120
    QuickStyle and, WP 120–121
    saving in separate file, WP 122–123
    system, WP 116
    table of contents, WP 160
    types of, WP 115
    user, WP 116
style errors, Grammatik and, WP 104
Styles button, WP 116
Styles command (Format menu), WP 121, WP 123, WP 211
Styles Editor, WP 117
    creating styles with, WP 121
    modifying style with, WP 119–120
styles file
    retrieving, WP 123–124
    saving styles in, WP 122–123
subject-verb agreement, WP 106
suppressing headers, WP 138
switching between documents, WP 86–87
symbols
    bullet, WP 76–77
    newsletter and, WP 206, WP 222–225
    nonprinting, see nonprinting symbols
    typographic, using in desktop publishing, WP 205, WP 206, WP 222–225
synonyms, WP 103–104
system styles, WP 116

T

tab(s), WP 67
    default settings, WP 15
    symbol marking location of, WP 18
    See also tab stops
tab bar, WP 70
Tab icon, WP 70
Tab key
    creating tab stop with, WP 67–68
    data entry for data file and, WP 177
    indenting first line of paragraph with, WP 67
    moving to cell in table using, WP 141
table(s)
    captions added to, WP 159–160
    centering, WP 158–159
    column width, WP 153
    creating using Table button, WP 139–140
    creating using Table Create command, WP 147–148
    editing, WP 142–144
    entering text in, WP 141
    formatting, WP 139–140, WP 143, WP 153–155
    formatting automatically using SpeedFormat, WP 157–158
    inserting, WP 139–140

justifying text within cells, WP 153–155
    mathematical calculations in, WP 146–147
    modifying format, WP 159
    selecting text in, WP 142
    sorting rows in, WP 142–144
    specifying header row in, WP 143
Table button, creating table using, WP 139–140
Table Create command, WP 147–148
Table feature, WP 139
table file, WP 171
Table Format button (Tables toolbar), WP 143
    centering table and, WP 158
    column widths and, WP 153
    justifying text in cells and, WP 154
Table Formula command, WP 146
table guidelines, WP 139
    changing column width by dragging, WP 153
Table menu
    Calculate command, WP 146
    Create command, WP 147–148
    QuickSum command, WP 146
    SpeedFormat command, WP 157
table of contents, generating, WP 160–162
Table shortcut menu, deleting row using, WP 145
Table SpeedFormat button, WP 157
Tables toolbar, WP 140, WP 143, WP 146
table structure, WP 139
    modifying, WP 145–146
tab stops, WP 67
    default, WP 66
    moving, WP 70
    outline paragraphs and, WP 135
    Ruler and, WP 10, WP 69
    removing from Ruler, WP 69
    types of, WP 68
taskbar, Windows 95, WP 7, WP 9
Task Reference, WP 4
telephone list, creating merge for, WP 194–197
text
    applying system styles to, WP 116
    bolding, WP 79, WP 81
    borders around, WP 155–156
    in cells, justifying, WP 153–155
    centering, WP 107–108, WP 118, WP 121
    columns of, see columns of text
    copying and pasting, WP 57–59
    copying from one document to another, WP 149, WP 151
    cutting and pasting, WP 56–57
    deleting in document, WP 36–37
    drop cap, see drop cap
    endnote, WP 113
    entering for business letter, WP 23–24
    entering into data file, WP 176–179
    finding, WP 96–97
    finding and replacing, WP 98–100
    font appearance, WP 78–81
    footnote, WP 113
    footnote number in, WP 113
    form file, WP 180–181
    header, WP 110
    hyphenating, WP 226–228
    imported, WP 242–247
    inserting in document, WP 35–36
    italicizing, WP 80–81
    justifying, WP 62–64
    keeping lines of together, WP 70–73, WP 120
    lines of, see lines of text
    moving to using Find, WP 96
    moving within document, WP 54–59

newspaper-style columns,
  WP 206, WP 214–215
in outline, order of, WP 133
placeholder, WP 170, WP 172
pull quote, WP 220
ragged along right margin, WP 63,
  WP 226
replacing, WP 98–100
restoring, WP 53–54
scrolling through, WP 27–29
selecting, *see* selecting text
shape of, in TextArt, WP 208–209
space between lines of, in
  newsletter, WP 206,
  WP 210–212
table, WP 141
TextArt image, WP 207–208
underlining, WP 80
vertically centering, WP 107–108
word wrap and, WP 26–27
TextArt
  creating title using, WP 206–209
  editing, WP 209–210
  newsletter and, WP 205, WP 206
TextArt 7 dialog box, WP 207–208
TextArt command (Graphics menu),
  WP 107
Text Box command (Graphics
  menu), WP 220
text boxes
  in data file, entering data in,
    WP 176–179
  for pull quote, WP 219–221
Text color button (TextArt 7 dialog
  box), WP 208
text file, WP 171
  creating, WP 175–176
text input mode, WP 10
text shape, changing in TextArt
  image, WP 208–209
Thesaurus, WP 103–104
Thesaurus command (Tools menu),
  WP 103
tiling windows, WP 150
time, status bar display and, WP 10
Times New Roman font, WP 9,
  WP 17
title
  chart, WP 252
  newsletter, creating using
    TextArt, WP 206–209
  outline, WP 133
title bar, WP 8
Title command (Chart menu),
  WP 252
title page, report, WP 107–108
today's date, inserting in document,
  WP 11–13, WP 112
toggle switch, WP 79
Toolbar (WordPerfect), WP 8, WP 9
  displaying, WP 10, WP 16
  opening document from, WP 34,
    WP 46
Toolbars dialog box, WP 10, WP 14
Toolbars/Ruler command (View
  menu)
  displaying Ruler and, WP 14,
    WP 16
  displaying Toolbar and, WP 10,
    WP 16
Tools menu
  Generate, Table of Contents com-
    mand, WP 160, WP 161
  Grammatik command, WP 105
  Merge command, creating data
    file and, WP 174
  Merge command, creating form
    file and, WP 180, WP 181
  Outline command, WP 133,
    WP 134
  QuickCorrect command, WP 20
  Sort command, WP 143
  Spell Check command, WP 101
  Thesaurus command, WP 103

top margin
  changing, WP 61
  format code, WP 83
  guideline, WP 8
trademark symbol (™), WP 222,
  WP 223–224
transferring data between documents, WP 148–152
TROUBLE? paragraph, WP 4
tutorials, using, WP 4
Two Page view, WP 16, WP 110–111
Typeover mode, WP 37
Typesetting command (Format menu
  Advance option, WP 211
  Word/Letter Spacing command,
    WP 211
typographic characters and symbols,
  desktop publishing and, WP 205,
  WP 206, WP 222–225

U

Undelete dialog box, WP 54
Underline button, new text and,
  WP 80
underlining text, WP 80
Undo button, WP 53
Undo command, WP 53
undoing edit, WP 53–54
updating link, WP 255, WP 259–260
Use file in active window button
  (Merge dialog box), WP 174,
  WP 180, WP 181
user styles, WP 116

V

value, format codes and, WP 83
Value/Adjust Numbering dialog box,
  page numbers and, WP 111
verb, agreement with subject, WP 106
vertical columns, aligning, WP 68–69
vertical line, inserting between
  newsletter columns, WP 230
vertically centering page,
  WP 107–108
vertical rule, newsletter and, WP 206
vertical scroll bar, WP 9
vertical space, before and after
  heading in newsletter, WP 211
very large font size, WP 116
view(s)
  Draft, WP 16
  Full Page, *see* Full Page view
  Page, *see* Page view
  Two Page, *see* Two Page view
viewing two document windows,
  WP 150–151
View menu
  Datasheet command, WP 253
  Draft command, WP 16
  Guidelines command, WP 11
  Page command, WP 16
  Reveal Codes command, WP 82
  Show command, paragraph sym-
    bol and, WP 18
  Toolbars/Ruler command, WP 10,
    WP 14, WP 16
  Two Page command, WP 110–111
voice, active versus passive, WP 106

W

What Is? command, WP 39
white space, WP 6
widow, WP 72–73
Widow/Orphan check box (Keep
  Text Together dialog box), WP 73,
  WP 120
width
  graphic image, WP 217
  newspaper-style columns, WP 215
  table column, WP 153
window(s)
  application, WP 8
  document, *see* document window
  Help Topics, WP 39–40
  Reference, WP 4
  Reveal Codes, WP 82–84

WordPerfect, WP 8
Window menu
  switching between open docu-
    ments using, WP 86
  transferring data between docu-
    ments and, WP 149
  viewing two documents and,
    WP 150
Windows 95
  common features, WP 8–9
  desktop, WP 7
  starting WordPerfect from, WP 7
  taskbar, WP 7, WP 9
Wingdings, WP 223
word(s)
  deleting, WP 36–37, WP 51
  duplicated, WP 101
  hyphenating, WP 226–228
  misspelled, WP 19–20
  finding, WP 96
  moving insertion point one at a
    time, WP 49
  number of in document, WP 85
  related, WP 103
  replacing, WP 98–100
  selecting, WP 50, WP 51
  spell checking, WP 19–20,
    WP 101–103
  symbol marking space between,
    WP 18
  synonyms for, WP 103–104
Word document, importing into
  WordPerfect, WP 242–247
Word/Letter Spacing command,
  WP 211
Word/Letter Spacing dialog box,
  WP 211–212
WordPerfect
  closing, WP 32
  default settings, WP 15, WP 61
  exiting, WP 32
  integrating with other Windows
    programs, WP 237–262
  producing documents with,
    WP 5–6, WP 15–32
  starting, WP 7–8
WordPerfect Characters dialog box,
  WP 223, WP 224
WordPerfect clipart, inserting into
  newsletter, WP 215–218
WordPerfect graphics, WP 216
WordPerfect icon, WP 7
WordPerfect screen
  components of, WP 8–9
  maximizing, WP 7
WordPerfect Toolbar, *see* Toolbar
  (WordPerfect)
WordPerfect window, WP 8
word wrap, WP 26–27
workspace, *see* document window
wpd filename extension, WP 25
wpg (WordPerfect graphics) filename extension, WP 216
wrapping text, WP 26–27
writing style, Grammatik and,
  WP 104–106

Z

ZIP code, sorting records by,
  WP 186–188

Corel WordPerfect 7 Task Reference

TASK	PAGE #	RECOMMENDED METHOD
Border, draw around page	WP 229	Click Format, point to Border/Fill, click Page, select border type, select border style, click OK button
Border, draw around paragraph	WP 155	Click Format, point to Border/Fill, click Paragraph, select border style, click OK button
Bullets, add to paragraphs	WP 76	Select paragraphs, click Insert, click Bullets & Numbers, select bullet style, click OK button
Character (symbol), insert	WP 222	Click Insert, click Character, select desired character set, click character, click Insert or Insert and Close button
Clipart, insert	WP 215	Click [icon], change to directory with clip-art files, click image filename, click Insert button
Columns, format text in	WP 214	Click Format, point to Columns, click Define, select Number of columns and column type, click OK button
Date, insert	WP 11	Click Insert, point to Date, click Date Text or Date Code
Document, open	WP 33	Click [icon], if necessary change drive and folder, click the filename, click OK button
Document, print	WP 30	Click [icon], click Print button
Document, print multiple copies	WP 87	Click [icon], change Number of Copies, click Print button
Document, save	WP 24	Click [icon]
Document, save using new filename	WP 38	Click File, click Save As, select new drive and folder, change filename, click Save button
Document information (statistics), get	WP 85	Click File, point to Document, click Properties, click Information tab
Document window, close	WP 21	Click document [icon]
Document windows, switching between	WP 86	Click Window, click name of document window
Document windows, viewing two	WP 150	Click Window, click Tile Top to Bottom or Tile Side by Side
Draft view, change to	WP 16	Click View, click Draft
Drop cap, insert	WP 218	Move insertion point anywhere in paragraph, click Format, click Drop Cap, select desired features, click Close button on Drop Cap feature bar
Embedded object (file), modify	WP 253	Double-click linked object, use commands from source application to modify object, click anywhere outside of object
Endnote, add	WP 113	Click Insert, point to Endnote, click Create button, type text, click Close button on feature bar

Corel WordPerfect 7 Task Reference

TASK	PAGE #	RECOMMENDED METHOD
Envelope, print	WP 31	Click Format, click Envelope, change settings in dialog box as desired, click Print Envelope button
File, import	WP 242	Click Insert, click File, select filename, click Insert button
Font, change	WP 17, WP 74	Click Font button on Power Bar, click a font name
Font appearance, change	WP 79	Select text, click **b**, *i*, or u
Font size, change	WP 12	Click Font size button on Power Bar, click a font size
Footer, insert	WP 109	Click Format, point to Header/Footer, click a Footer radio button, click Create button, type text, click Close button on feature bar
Footnote, add	WP 113	Click Insert, point to Footnote, click Create button, type text, click Close button on feature bar
Full Page view, change to	WP 29	Click [icon]
Grammar, check	WP 105	Click Tools, click Grammatik
Graph or chart, creating with Presentations 7 Chart	WP 251	Click Insert, click Object, click Create New radio button, select Presentations 7 Chart in Object Type list, click OK, modify information in datasheet, click in document window (outside of chart)
Graphic, resize	WP 217	Click graphic, drag resize handle
Header, insert	WP 109	Click Format, click Header/Footer, click a Header radio button, click Create button, type text, click Close button on feature bar
Help, get	WP 38	Click Help, click Help Topics, click Index tab, type an index word or phrase, click a topic, click Display button
Hyphenation, turn on	WP 226	Click Format, point to Line, click Hyphenation, click Hyphenation on check box, click OK button
Insertion point, move left or right one word	WP 49	Press Ctrl + ← or Ctrl + →
Insertion point, move to beginning of next or previous page	WP 49	Press Alt + PageDown or Alt + PageUp
Insertion point, move to beginning or end of document	WP 49	Press Ctrl + Home or Ctrl + End
Insertion point, move to beginning or end of line	WP 49	Press Home key or End key
Insertion point, move up or down one paragraph	WP 49	Press Ctrl + ↑ or Ctrl + ↓
Insertion point, move up or down one screen	WP 49	Press PageUp key or PageDown key

Corel WordPerfect 7 Task Reference

TASK	PAGE #	RECOMMENDED METHOD
Labels, mailing, create	WP 192	Click Format, click Labels, click label form name, click Select button, make document window a form file, associate a data source, insert appropriate merge codes, merge labels form file with data source
Line of text, center	WP 65	Move insertion point to beginning of line, press Shift + F7
Line spacing, set	WP 210	Click Line Spacing button on Power Bar, click desired spacing
Lines, keep together on same page	WP 71	Move insertion point to first line to keep together, click Format, point to Page, click Keep Text Together, click Conditional End of Page check box and set number of lines, click OK button
Linked object (file), modify	WP 261	Double-click linked object, use source application to modify file, save linked file, exit source application
Linked object (file), update	WP 259	Click Edit, click Links, select filename, click Update Now button, click Close button
Margins, change	WP 61	Click Format, click Margins, change margin values, click OK button
Merge, create data file for	WP 174	Click Tools, click Merge, click Data File button, add field names, click OK button, type information into records, click Close button
Merge, create form file for	WP 180	Click Tools, click Merge, click Form, select data file, click OK button, type text of main document, add merge codes
Merge code, insert	WP 182	Click Merge Code button on feature bar, click name of code, click Insert
Merge operation, perform	WP 185	Open form file, click Merge button on feature bar, click Merge button on dialog box
Merge record, sort in data file	WP 187	Open data file, click Operation button on feature bar, click Sort, click select a defined sort (or create a new one), click Sort button
Merge records, select	WP 189	Open main document, click Merge button on feature bar, click Select Records button, set conditions, click OK button, click Merge button
New document, start	WP 22	Click [icon]
Nonprinting symbols, view	WP 18	Click View, click Show ¶
Numbers, add to paragraphs	WP 76	Select paragraphs, click Bullets & Numbers, select style of numbers, click OK button
Object, embed	WP 248	Click Insert, click Object, click Create from file radio button, select filename, click OK button
Object, link	WP 255	Click Insert, click Object, click Create from file radio button, select filename, click Link check box, click OK button
Outline, create or edit	WP 133	Click Tools, click Outline, change outline definition to Outline, enter new paragraph text or edit existing paragraphs
Outline paragraph, move up or down	WP 137	Place insertion point in paragraph, click [icon] or [icon]

Corel WordPerfect 7 Task Reference

TASK	PAGE #	RECOMMENDED METHOD
Outline paragraph, promote or demote	WP 135	Place insertion point in paragraph, click ⬆ or ⬇
Page break, insert	WP 108	Press Ctrl + Enter
Page number, change	WP 111	Click Format, point to Page Numbering, click Value/Adjust, set the new page number, click OK button
Page number, insert into header/footer	WP 109	Click Number button on Header/Footer feature bar, click Page Number
Page view, change to	WP 16	Click View, click Page
Paragraph, hanging indent	WP 66	Select paragraph(s), click Format, point to Paragraph, click Hanging Indent
Paragraph, indent all lines from left margin	WP 66	Move insertion point to beginning of paragraph, press F7 key
Paragraph, indent from left and right margins	WP 66	Move insertion point to beginning of paragraph, click Format, point to Paragraph, click Double Indent
Picture, import	WP 245	Click 💎, change to directory with picture files, click picture filename, click Insert button
QuickFormat, format paragraphs with	WP 81	Select paragraph with desired format, click 🖌, click anywhere in target paragraph(s), click 🖌 again
Records, adding new to merge data file	WP 178	Open data file, click Quick Entry button, click New Record, add information, click Close button
Reveal Codes, display	WP 82	Click View, click Reveal Codes
Rule (horizontal or vertical line), insert	WP 212, WP 230	Click Graphics, click Horizontal Line or Vertical Line
Shading (fill), insert	WP 155	Click Format, point to Border/Fill, click paragraph, page or column, click Fill tab, select fill style, click OK button
Spelling, correct	WP 19	Right-click misspelled word, click correctly spelled word
Style, apply	WP 116	Click Style button on Power Bar, click style name
Style, create	WP 121	Click Format, click Styles, click Create button, type new style name, press Tab key, type description, select style type, insert format codes into Contents box, click OK button
Style, edit	WP 119	Click Format, click Styles, click style name, click Edit button, insert or delete format codes in Contents box, click OK button
Tab stops, move	WP 70	Display Ruler, drag tab stop markers to new locations
Table, automatically format	WP 157	Click Table, click SpeedFormat, select a predefined table format, click Apply button
Table, center	WP 158	Click ⌨, click Table tab, set Table position to Center, click OK button

Corel WordPerfect 7 Task Reference

TASK	PAGE #	RECOMMENDED METHOD
Table, create	WP 139, WP 148	Click Tables button on Power Bar, drag pointer to select table size
Table, sort	WP 143	Click Tools, click Sort, click New button, click Table row radio button, select Key definitions, click OK button, click Sort button
Table calculation, perform	WP 146	Move insertion point to desired cell, click Table, click Formula Bar, click Functions, select functions, click Insert, complete formula, click Close button
Table column width, change	WP 153	Drag vertical guideline in table
Table of contents, generate	WP 160	Apply Heading styles to headings, move insertion point where you want table, click Tools, point to Generate, click Table of Contents, click Define button on feature bar, select number of levels and numbering format, click OK button, click Generate button, click Close button
Table row or column, delete	WP 145	Select row(s) or column(s) to delete, click Table, click Delete, click Rows or Columns radio button, click OK button
Table row or column, insert within table	WP 145	Click Table, click Insert, click Rows or Columns radio button, select number, click OK button
Table row, insert at end of table	WP 145	Move insertion point to lower-right cell at end of table, press Tab key
Text, center justify	WP 63	Click Text Align button on Power Bar, click Center
Text, copy by copy and paste	WP 58	Select text, click [icon], move to target location, click [icon]
Text, copy by drag and drop	WP 55	Select text, press Ctrl key, drag selected text to target location, release Ctrl key
Text, delete	WP 36	Press Backspace key to delete character to left of insertion point; press the Delete key to delete character to right; press Ctrl + Backspace to delete word
Text, find	WP 96	Click Edit, click Find and Replace, type search string, click Find Next button
Text, find and replace	WP 98	Click Edit, click Find and Replace, type search string, type replacement string, click Find Next, Replace, or Replace All button
Text, full justify	WP 63	Click Text Align button on Power Bar, click Full
Text, left justify	WP 63	Click Text Align button on Power Bar, click Left
Text, move by cut and paste	WP 56	Select text, click [icon], move to target location, click [icon]
Text, move by drag and drop	WP 55	Select text, drag selected text to target location
Text, right justify	WP 63	Click Text Align button on Power Bar, click Right
Text, select a block of	WP 51	Click at beginning of block, press Shift key, click at end of block
Text, select a paragraph of	WP 51	Double-click in left margin
Text, select a sentence of	WP 51	Double-click within sentence

Corel WordPerfect 7 Task Reference

TASK	PAGE #	RECOMMENDED METHOD
Text, select a word of	WP 51	Double-click word
TextArt box, change size of	WP 217	Click TextArt box, drag resize handle
TextArt, create special effects using	WP 206	Click Graphics, click TextArt, type the text, format the text and select desired options, click Close button
TextArt, edit	WP 209	Double-click TextArt box
Thesaurus, use	WP 103	Click Tools, click Thesaurus, click desired replacement word, click Replace button
Two Page view, change to		Click View, click Two Page
Widow/Orphan, apply protection	WP 72	Click Format, point to Page, click Keep Text Together, click Widow/Orphan check box, click OK button
WordPerfect, exit	WP 32	Click File, click Exit
WordPerfect, start	WP 7	Click WordPerfect icon on DAD or click Start on Windows 95 taskbar, point to Corel WordPerfect Suite 7, click Corel WordPerfect